125 YEARS
1889 - 2014

SOMETHING TO SHOUT ABOUT

The History of Forest Green Rovers

Tim Barnard

Statistics by Heather Cook

The History Press

All Royalties from the sale of this book
are donated to Forest Green Rovers Football Club.

First published 2006, this edition 2014

The History Press
The Mill, Brimscombe Port
Stroud, Gloucestershire, GL5 2QG
www.thehistorypress.co.uk

British Library Cataloguing in Publication Data.
A catalogue record for this book is available from the British Library.

ISBN 978 0 7509 6090 8

Typesetting and origination by The History Press
Printed in Great Britain

CONTENTS

Introduction

This is the story of the 'Friendly Club on the Hill', Forest Green Rovers, founded in 1889. The history of other local clubs, including Shortwood FC, Stroud Rugby Club, Stroud AFC and Nailsworth AFC are also touched on in this book.

From the first reported match, the club has risen through the ranks to reach the pinnacle of non-league football. Forest Green Rovers were founder members of the Mid-Gloucestershire League in 1894, the first football league in Gloucestershire outside Bristol and, since that date, have always been forward-looking. Their rise has not always been smooth, but the ambition of those involved with the club has always seen it through.

A major step forward was taken in 1936 when the football club attended an auction, bid for and secured a ground of its own. The club will be forever indebted to Mr Owen Davis, a successful Nailsworth businessman and nineteenth-century player, who loaned the club the money to pay for the ground.

The dedicated band of officials and supporters, who have invested considerable amounts of their own time, money and energy in The Lawn, have been repaid as their club has continuously risen through the ranks. The result has been the creation of a football club with first-class facilities, admired throughout Gloucestershire and beyond.

The club moved forward after the Second World War under the chairmanship of first Peter Vick and then John Duff, winning the FA Vase in 1982 and gaining promotion to the Southern League. Following a disastrous name change to Stroud FC in 1989, the club reverted to the name of Forest Green Rovers in 1992 and entered a new phase in its history under the guidance of Trevor Horsley, another ambitious and forward-looking chairman.

Trevor Horsley oversaw the relocation of FGR to its new stadium in 2006 before handing over the reins to Dale Vince in 2010, with the club now looking to progress once again on and off the pitch. This second edition of the book has been published to coincide with the 125th anniversary of the football club.

Acknowledgements

My wife Sue and my kids, Catherine and Isabelle. All those who have helped behind the scenes including Richard Grant, Tom Vick, the late Roy Close, Colin Timbrell and Heather Cook. Bruce Fenn, Shane Healey and *The Citizen* for the photographs. All of those who have contributed their stories, and, of course, Trevor Horsley and Colin Peake for getting the club to a position that required its history to be told. And to Dale Vince for stepping in and taking over Forest Green Rovers again.

Part I
1889-1919

BIRMINGHAM

Forest of Dean

GLOUCESTER

Forest Green

BRISTOL

Forest Gate

LONDON

Forest Green
(Surrey)

Forest Row

1

Where is Forest Green?

Forest Green is a long-established community situated on the hill above Nailsworth, near Stroud in Gloucestershire. It is not in the Forest of Dean and nowhere near Forest Row, Forest Gate or any other forest. It isn't in Surrey, as the Worksop Town Supporters' Club found out when they arrived at Forest Green near Gatwick Airport a few years ago for an FA Trophy tie against Rovers. It isn't on many maps either.

The Origins of Forest Green

Back in the 1500s, the Nailsworth Valley and the surrounding hills were covered with woodland, with the odd mill in the valley bottoms below and no appreciable settlement. In 1598 (and again in 1685) the persecution of the Huguenots in France caused a large number to flee to England with many settling in the Stroud Valleys, where their skills in the manufacture of cloth were put to good use. Names such as Marmont, Malpas, Clutterbuck and Freem can all be traced directly to these settlers.

The history of Forest Green really starts in 1662, when around 2,000 clergymen refused to sign an act of religious conformity and were ejected from the Church. Many carried on their ministry as Nonconformists, wherever they could find a safe place. A place was found in a clearing at Colliers Wood in Forest Green and the Nonconformists worshipped here from the 1660s until the first chapel was built at Forest Green in 1687. The Act of Uniformity was repealed in 1689. Forest Green was the earliest dissenting chapel to be set up in the area, and it was registered in 1690. It is from Forest Green and Shortwood that nearby Nailsworth's development as a town can be traced.

The area known today as Nailsworth consisted of the outer reaches of three different parishes. Forest Green itself was in the parish of Avening, neighbouring Shortwood was in Horsley Parish, and Watledge in the parish of Minchinhampton. A Baptist chapel was eventually built in Shortwood in 1837 and, by 1840, the congregation numbered nearly 700, including most of the principal mill owners in the area.

The first school open to the public in the area was started in Forest Green chapel in 1773, two years before a similar school was founded in Gloucester, with a further Baptist school in Shortwood by 1785. New mills were built from around 1780 in the valley bottom served by the new Turnpike Road, which ran along the line of the current A46 from Nailsworth to Stroud. With time, the two communities of Shortwood and Forest Green expanded down the hill and into the valley. Shortwood Baptist church was physically moved down into Nailsworth in 1881 and is now known

Forest Green.

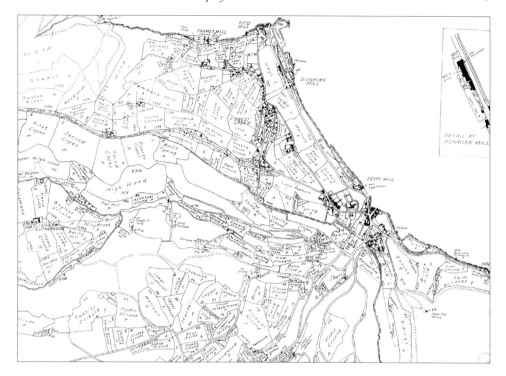

Tithe maps of Forest Green and Shortwood, 1840. Field reference 1260, called Two Acres, was the site of The Lawn, until 2006. Hurdle Ground, 973, and Tanners Piece, 822, were both owned by Forest Green Congregational church, just about the right sizes for a football pitch. The parish boundary between Avening and Horsley ran at the back of Two Acre Field. Forest Green and lower Nailsworth were in the parish of Avening. Shortwood was in the parish of Horsley.

Ordinance Survey map, 1902. Not as built up as it is today. Field 358 was the site of The Lawn until 2006.

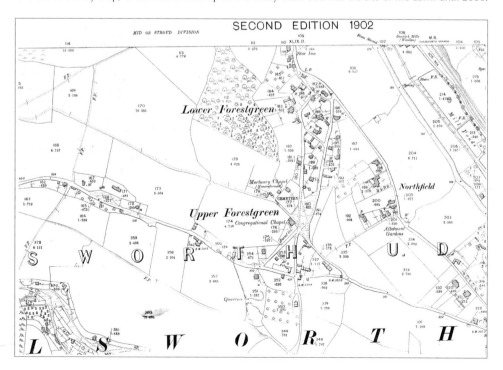

as Christchurch. By the late 1800s the town of Nailsworth, into which Shortwood and Forest Green had expanded, replaced Minchinhampton as the chief town in the area. It had a thriving brewery from 1820, famous for a strong stout, with pubs including the Foston's Ash at Birdlip, among many others.

The railway arrived in the town in 1867. The Church of England made Nailsworth a parish in its own right in 1892 and it became an urban district authority in 1894, both after the formation of Forest Green Rovers FC. Today, half of the 6,000 population of Nailsworth now lives up on the hill in Forest Green, a vast increase from the 300 or so people living there in 1861.

2

'Rugby' Rules and 'Association' Rules

In the early 1800s in Britain, football as an organised sport was a public-school affair. In the absence of any official rules of the game, two styles of play emerged: football (where the ball could only be kicked and dribbled) and rugby football (where the ball could be handled and carried). Rugby football is said to have originated at Rugby School in Warwickshire in 1923, when a pupil named William Webb Ellis picked up the ball during a game of football and ran with it. Soon after, in August 1845, pupils from the school wrote up the first set of official rules of the game, which boosted the sport's popularity. Three years later, Cambridge University compiled a new set of rules known as the 'Cambridge Rules', which stressed kicking over carrying, but were not widely adopted. Football's popularity gradually grew, and in 1855 the first non-school football club, Sheffield FC, came into existence. Notts County, the earliest surviving professional football club, was formed in 1862, and by 1863 a sufficient number of organisations were playing some form of football. The rise of the sport's popularity meant that the lack of nationally recognised rules was becoming a problem.

Influenced by the Cambridge Rules, the Football Association was formed at a meeting in October of 1863 by Forest (soon to change their name to Wanderers), NN (No Names) Kilburn, Barnes, War Office, Crusaders, Percival House, Blackheath, Crystal Palace, Kensington School, Surbiton and Blackheath School, and the first priority was to establish and finalise the rules of football for all members to abide by. Below is printed the original set of rules:

First 'Football Association' Laws, 1863

1. *The maximum length of the ground shall be 200 yards, the maximum breadth shall be 100 yards, the length and breadth shall be marked off with flags; and the goal shall be defined by two upright posts, 8 yards apart, without any tape or bar across them.*
2. *A toss for goals shall take place, and the game shall be commenced by a place kick from the centre of the ground by the side losing the toss for goals; the other side shall not approach within 10 yards of the ball until it is kicked off.*
3. *After a goal is won, the losing side shall be entitled to kick off, and the two sides shall change goals after each goal is won.*
4. *A goal shall be won when the ball passes between the goalposts or over the space between the goalposts (at whatever height), not being thrown, knocked on or carried.*
5. *When the ball is in touch, the first player who touches it shall throw it from the point on the boundary line where it left the ground in the direction at right angles with the boundary line, and the ball shall not be in play until it has touched the ground.*

6. *When a player has kicked the ball, any one of the same side who is nearer to the opponent's goal-line is out of play and may not touch the ball itself, nor in any way what ever prevent any other player from doing so, until he is in play; but no player is out of play when the ball is kicked off from behind the goal-line.*

7. *In case the ball goes behind the goal line, if a player on the side to whom the goal belongs first touches the ball, one of his side shall be entitled to a free kick from the goal-line at the point opposite the place where the ball shall be touched. If a player of the opposite side first touches the ball, one of his side shall be entitled to a free kick at goal only from 15 yards outside the goal-line, opposite the place where the ball is touched, the opposing side standing within their goal-line until he has had his kick.*

8. *If a player makes a fair catch, he shall be entitled to a free kick; providing he claims it by making a mark with his heel at once; and in order to take such a kick he may go back as far as he pleases, and no player on the opposite side shall advance beyond his mark until he has kicked.*

9. *No player shall run with the ball.*

10. *Neither tripping nor hacking shall be allowed, and no player shall use his hands to hold or push his adversary.*

11. *A player shall not be allowed to throw the ball or pass it to another with his hands.*

12. *No player shall be allowed to take the ball from the ground with his hands under any pretext whatever while it is in play.*

13. *No player shall be allowed to wear projecting nails, iron plates, gutta-percha on the soles or heels of his boots.*

The rules made it clear that the ball was not to be handled, and that 'hacking' was forbidden, and this led to many clubs refusing the join the FA, instead leaving to form the Rugby Football Union. 'Association Football' was born, but the game in the 1860s was still a far cry from soccer today, and would have appeared more akin to rugby football.

Forest Green in 1861

In 1861 the total population of the hamlets of Upper Forest Green, Lower Forest Green, Dunkirk, Inchbrook and Northfields numbered 580. The community had, for many years, if not centuries, been held together by their religious beliefs and their involvement in the local wool industry. Of the 580 people recorded in the 1861 census, nearly 200 people were actively employed as clothiers, weavers, shoddy manufacturers, dyers, wool-spinners and the like. The dyers would hang their cloth out on 'tenterhooks' to dry in the sun on the valley sides, making life a colourful experience. Around 100 people worked at home, as they had done for centuries before, while others were employed in the local wool and flock mills in the valley below.

Forty-two people were involved with agriculture and forty-five worked as servants. The residents included eighty-one-year-old army pensioner John Guy, three Almsmen and an Almswoman, a turnpike gatekeeper and two people of independent money. One hundred and twelve of the 580 people recorded were scholars, a tribute to the Non-Conformist tradition of education of the youth. Five people in the census are listed as schoolmistresses. The oldest working woman at that time was Ann Vizard who, at seventy-eight years old, was still employed as a woollen spinner.

The population would never be thirsty: there were six beer houses for the population of less than 600 in the hamlets, including the New Inn, which was one of thirty pubs owned by the Minchinhampton Forewood Brewery. The pub was soon to be renamed the Jovial Forester and is the only one of the original six pubs to survive today.

Pointing to the industrial times ahead, twelve people in 1861 were working in the local pin and zinc factory run by Mr Marmont. Names that crop up in the history of Forest Green Rovers also show up in the May 1861 census, including Furley, Evans, Tanner, Gardner, Teakle, Brinkworth, Marmont, Horwood, Iles, Dyer, Smith, Bruton, Walkley, Donohue, Harrison, Herbert, Burford, Clift, Mills, Close, Fletcher, Marks, Hill and many others.

An early photograph of the Jovial Forester pub. The date is not known but it was probably around the turn of the century. Joe and Gary Brown, stalwarts of the Forest Green team from 1911 onwards, lived in the cottages which were demolished to form the modern-day car park for the pub.

The Development of the Association Rules National Game

Away from Gloucestershire, the national Association Rules Football scene was developing rapidly. The Football Association had been formed in 1863 and received a major boost when the Sheffield Association clubs joined in 1870. Until that time, they had played to their own 'Sheffield' rules, as was the case with many other areas which played under their own local rules.

Early Association Rules Football favoured a playing formation of a goalkeeper, full-back, half-back and eight forwards. The full-back kicked the ball quickly up the field where the forwards would then play in a close pack, backing up the man on the ball, who could then dribble the ball at his discretion. Heading and short passing were introduced by the Northern Associations. The FA Cup was first played for in 1871 with few clubs competing. It was not unusual at this time for two semi-finals to be played simultaneously on adjacent pitches. However, by 1878, the game's popularity within the working classes meant a vast increase in spectators, and sparked the formation of many new clubs in large and small towns across the country. Growing demand for the game as a form of entertainment led to organisers being able to charge the public for entry. This in turn raised funds for the larger clubs, who were encouraged to seek out 'professors' of the game. These players were often imported from other regions, primarily Scotland. Until this time, the game had been almost completely amateur, played by people from each club's own locality.

By 1883, Preston North End was known to be paying some of their players up to £1,200 per year, a fortune at the time. This led to outcry from other clubs and supporters who condemned the teams with paid players. The Football Association could no longer ignore the situation and, at the end of 1884, matters were brought to a head when a group of the Northern Clubs threatened to break away from the FA and form a British National Football Association if professionalism within football was not legalised. In July 1885, in order to avoid the breakaway, the FA accepted professionalism. All matches were termed either cup matches, where teams would either play in the FA Cup or in the County Cups, or ordinary matches where a fixture list would be prepared for a series of friendly games between chosen teams. There were still no leagues but the fixture list was becoming more and more complicated to organise, which prompted a meeting to be held in Manchester on 17 April 1888, and from this the Football League came into being.

Further skills that started to emerge in the game at this time included the use of wingers to 'middle' the ball into the goal area. A new team formation had also emerged, consisting of a goalkeeper, two full-backs, three half-backs and five forwards.

Sport in Gloucestershire

In 1862, Dr H.M. Grace urged the establishment of a county cricket club in Gloucestershire and, in 1868, a first-class game was played against the MCC at Lord's, ending in a fine victory for Gloucestershire by 134 runs. Gloucestershire County Cricket Club was formally founded in 1870 with Dr H.M. Grace as treasurer. Gloucestershire's opening first-class county match was against Surrey, who they beat by 51 runs with a team that included E.M. Grace, W.G. Grace and G.F. Grace, all sons of Dr H.M. Grace. It was very much a family affair.

By 1870, the game of Rugby Rules football was also very popular in Gloucestershire. Painswick Rugby Club is the oldest village rugby club in England, a fact commemorated in the Museum of Rugby at Twickenham. Gloucester Rugby Club was started in 1873, although the first season when records were kept was 1879–80, and Stroud Rugby Club was also formed in 1873.

The first recorded Association Rules football match in Gloucestershire took place in 1882 between two Bristol clubs, St George and Warmley, and in March 1883 Warmley also met Wotton-under-Edge, soon to be one of Forest Green's regular opponents. Later in 1883, two further clubs were formed in the Bristol area, the Black Arabs and Clifton.

The Gloucestershire Football Association was formed in September 1886 by Clifton, Warmley, St George and Eastville Rovers (the Black Arabs changed their name to Eastville Rovers, and then Bristol Rovers in 1898). The first County Cup competition was held in 1887 and 2,000 spectators watched the final on the Downs, the match being drawn. Mr W.G. Grace was one of the two umpires assisting the referee. Clifton won after a replay.

It was into this footballing environment that the minister of Forest Green Congregationalist church launched his football team late in 1889.

3

'Socker' Comes to Forest Green: 1889–1894

'Association Rules Football' was a bit of a mouthful for journalists, and a shortened version 'Assoc Rules' soon appeared, which was then shortened to 'socker' and then to today's 'soccer'.

First Signs of the Forest Green Rovers: 1889

Despite still being officially made up from the back end of the parishes of Horsley, Avening and Minchinhampton, Nailsworth was feeling optimistic in 1889 and looking forward to recognition as a parish and a district council. In its 'Notes from Nailsworth' section, on 25 October 1889, the *Stroud News* reported the following:

> *Nailsworth is looking up. This phrase has been applied to Nailsworth so many times that to use it once more would certainly not be out of place. The young men especially seem to be well catered for. Here within the last week or two the Reverend E.J.H. Peach of Forest Green has started a night school for their special benefit, and with a staff of energetic assistants has created no small amount of interest among the large number of his younger Congregational friends.*
>
> *The same gentleman has also started a football club. Several years have elapsed since there was a club of this description in the neighbourhood, which perhaps accounts for the enthusiasm with which the game has been taken up. This, unlike the lads' reading room just started by the Nailsworth incumbent, and held every Monday and Friday in the parish room, is not restricted to sex, and there is but little doubt if any of the feminine gender evinced a desire to join, neither the members nor the captain would raise an objection – the other way round, perhaps.*

This is the first reference to a football team at Forest Green that has been found to date. It says that 'it is some years since a club of the same description existed in the neighbourhood'. If one did exist, it would most likely have been a Rugby Rules football club rather than an Association Rules club. The search goes on for earlier references and for whether any ladies did play the game back in 1889.

The 1 November 1889 issue of the same newspaper states:

Nailsworth has started a club

and on 8 November 1889 'Half-back' records:

So Nailsworth have forsaken their first love, and taken on with the non-handling code.

It is not surprising that the Football Club was set up by the local church. In Victorian times, the changes brought about by the onset of the Industrial Revolution and the phenomenal number of pubs in the area, meant that the Church was very keen to ensure that young men did not err from a righteous path. More than half of the teams now playing football in the Premiership were also started by local ministers and churches across the country. Football was seen as a way to keep young men occupied and to provide an entertaining outlet for both players and spectators alike.

The findings of the 1891 census for Forest Green are very different from those thirty years before, in every way except the population count, which was 590 in 1861 and 589 in 1891. Outwardly, little had changed, but the occupations of those living in Forest Green were now very different. Only seventeen of the 589 inhabitants were recorded as cloth workers, wool sorters, weavers and the like. New occupations included stick makers (at the local umbrella factory), tinplate workers, timber cutters, carpenters, a bookmaker, photographer and a travelling hawker. Three people were employed on the railway, with many other occupations similar to those found today, too numerous to mention. The revolution had hit Forest Green and Nailsworth below, where many new industries had sprung up in the old wool mills, now put to different uses. The old clothiers' and weavers' way of life, hard but simple, were almost gone forever, but the number of scholars and schoolmistresses was still very similar to that from 1861.

The Jovial Forester, which was to become the home of Forest Green Rovers for more than seventy-five years, was recorded as the New Inn in 1861, but had been renamed by 1871. The landlord and landlady were George and Kozia Brinkworth, the pub continuing with Kozia as landlady into the late 1880s. It may not be a coincidence that the Brinkworth family ran the pub for around thirty years just prior to the formation of the club and that the first recorded team in 1893 had three members of the extended Brinkworth family playing for it.

'Socker' Rules

By 1889, the Football Association's rules had changed slightly. Some are more recognisable as rules used today, whereas others still sound more like the Rugby Rules game:

A goal shall be won when the ball has passed between the goalposts under the bar, not being thrown, knocked on, or carried by any one of the attacking side.

No player shall carry, knock on, or handle the ball and any pretence whatever, except in the case of the goalkeeper, who within his own half of the ground, shall be allowed to use his hands in defence of his goal, either by knocking on or throwing, but not carrying the ball. The goalkeeper may be changed during the game, but not more than one player shall act as goalkeeper at the same time.

In no case shall the goal be scored from any free kick.

No player shall wear any nails, excepting such as have their heads driven in flush with the leather, or iron plates, or gutta-percha on the soles or heels of his boots or in his shin guards.

Each of the competing clubs shall be entitled to appoint an umpire, whose duty it shall be to decide all disputed points when appealed to; and by mutual arrangement a referee may be chosen to decide in all cases of difference between the umpires.

In 1889, in the Football League, Preston North End became the first league champions and won the FA Cup, becoming the first team to do the double. Other clubs formed in 1889 included Sheffield United, Brentford and Wimbledon FC.

The State of the Local 'Football' Game in 1889

On 8 November 1889, the *Stroud Journal* reported Rugby Rules football matches between Farmhill and Dursley, Lydney and Stroud and Painswick and Cheltenham Town (this was definitely a Rugby Rules fixture). Both the *Stroud News* and also the *Stroud Journal* included the following identical reports and letters on a match between Farmhill and Dursley:

The match resulted in a draw, each side scoring a try and a minor. Play was very even, Dursley scoring a try towards the latter end of the first half. In the second-half Farmhill was awarded a free-kick in front of the goal, when the greater part of the Dursley men unaccountably left the field, still wanting five minutes to time. By the direction of the umpires and the referee, the kick was made, and resulted in a try.

Simple. A drawn match. But on 15 November 1889, the following letter was published:

Sir, the account in your last week's paper re the football match, Farmhill v. Dursley, is very imperfect and needs correction … At the commencement of the game I compared my watch with the Referee's but when time should have been called, the referee insisted on playing another five minutes. The Referee granted a 'free kick' for 'handball' to the home team, but this was a wrong decision, and a 'scrum' ought to have been formed, as only in the case of the 'lineout' is the 'free' taken for 'handball'.

   Owing to the eccentric and partial habits of the Referee, the visitors lost many points, but succeeded in fairly defeating their opponents by one try and one minor to nil.
Kindly publish above in your next issue and oblige,
Yours obediently, W. E. Loxton, Junr. The Dursley Umpire.

Shortwood in the 1890s, looking across to Forest Green. The above photograph is taken from below the current Shortwood United ground and looks across the Newmarket Valley with Forest Green at the top of the hill in the background.

Everybody knew the rules better than the referee, even in 1889! The argument continued on 22 November 1889:

> *Sir, Mr Loxton, the Dursley umpire impunes the correctness of the reporting of your valuable paper, and accuses me of partiality in the game. He says that a free kick was granted for handball; in this he is incorrect: the kick was awarded not for handball, but for offside.*
>
> *I would remind Mr Loxton that the club he had the honour of representing has already obtained a considerable notoriety with local teams on account of the entirely new meaning they ascribe to certain rules when the game is going against them. Indeed, it is a common bye-word among footballers in this neighbourhood that it is not' Rugby' but 'Dursley' rules when playing this particular club. Trusting you will do me the favour to insert this, I remain yours truly, Frederick Elliott, Referee FFC*

Was the referee right or wrong? Most likely, it depends on whether you supported Dursley or Farmhill. Whatever the case, it is clear that football was as hotly debated a subject then as it is now.

The First County Matches in Gloucestershire – W.G. Grace and Football

The first president of the Gloucestershire Football Association in 1886 was Mr W.G. Grace and Gloucestershire's second ever Association rules county match was reported in the *Stroud News* on 8 November 1889, against Wiltshire:

> *The match ended as disastrously as the first one this season, only the beating was a trifle more severe. In being able to draw nearly the whole of their team from the Swindon Town club, the Wiltshire authorities are extremely lucky and the easy victory of their eleven on Saturday was due to this fact …*

Swindon Town were a well-established club by that time, having been formed in 1881 when the Reverend W. Pitt formed a club for the town's railway workers. They were still an amateur team, not turning professional until they became founder members of the Southern League in 1894. They then played continuously in the Southern League until it was absorbed as the Football League Third Division (South) in 1920.

On the cricket scene, Dr W.G. Grace was still going strong, having been a founder member of Gloucestershire County Cricket club some twenty years previously. In October 1891 the *Stroud News* stated:

> *Dr W. G. Grace has replied as follows to a correspondent who inquired whether there was any foundation for the report that he did not intend to take any active part in first-class cricket in England:- 'I have no more intention of giving up cricket than I had 20 years ago.'*

And so on he batted and in 1896, as usual, cricket was the game of choice in the summer, with Gloucestershire playing on the County Ground against Sussex and winning by an innings and 123 runs. W.G. Grace was out for 301 while W.G. Grace Junior, was out for 1. At that time W.G. Grace's innings was only the sixth of over 300 that had ever been made in first-class cricket, the highest being 424 while other innings of 344 and 318 were both from his bat in 1876, twenty years previously. The following rhyme was published in his honour in the local papers:

> *Not for strength alone, provide power to 'place'*
> *Thy stalwart form, by quick resource, O 'Grace'*
> *A nation agreed to be with its tribute praise,*
> *And crowns the champion with Olympic Bays*
> *Not for thine heart at 'point' thy subtle skill*
> *To vary the pace and pitch and twist at will*
> *Not for thy giant drives and sure defence*

Though all accord thee proud pre-eminence
Not for thy scores; though this our century dies
Envious at thy long role of 'centuries'
Oh high acclaim bids praise spontaneous wing
O Peerless amid 'Lords' O Cricket King !
Tis thine endurance and the power 'to stay'
Keeps green as Gloucester's sward thy fame for aye.

Oh for a nation with thy courage, will,
Thy heart undaunted and thy ready skill!
The boldness that would ever first confront,
And at the dangerous onset bear the brunt
The thews of steel, the grip, the Lion heart,
A leader still, e'en in subordinate part,
The eye to mark with eagle glance and swift
The vulnerable points, the armour's rift!
Oh for a manhood that like thine conserves
Its lusty health, its fire, its iron nerves!
The temperate habits and the vigorous health
A State's reliance and an empire's wealth.

By the beginning of the 1890s, plans were well advanced with regard to the creation of the civil parish of Nailsworth. Almost no local Association Rules football was being reported early in the year although problems with the local trains were a popular subject, just as they are today:

Stroud Journal, *Friday 11 April 1890*
It is rapidly becoming a proverb with Stroud and Nailsworth passengers travelling by a Midland train that it is more wearisome and unpleasant to get the last 4 miles of the return journey than it was, perhaps, to travel the whole portion of the trip besides. Yesterday, for example, myself and about a hundred other passengers were kept waiting a full hour on the platform at Stonehouse Station, on a cold, windy night, and were tantalised by seeing our train standing on a siding nearby, with steam up, ready to start, but didn't …

I trust, sir, this letter will meet the eye of whoever is responsible for this mismanagement, and that in the future these wearisome delays will be avoided, but if there is no alteration for the better, and if the company persist in neglecting our fair requests to be brought home with reasonable punctuality, then I would recommend my fellow tradesmen to follow my example in the future, and when tempted to go by a Midland excursion remember the hour's delay at night at Stonehouse and don't!

I am, serve, yours faithfully EXCURSIONIST

A very early photograph of Nailsworth during the construction of the parish church. A temporary church was erected, which can be seen in the foreground. Forest Green rises to the right of the photograph with Shortwood in the background.

'Association Rules' Rears its Head

At the end of March 1891, the Chalford Association football team was reported in a match against Swindon GWR Painters as winning 4–1. The match was not reported in any sports section but under a heading entitled 'Chalford' in the 'District News' section. A further Chalford win was reported in mid-April against Swindon Temperance, 'bringing Chalford's first season to a close' having played a total of 6 matches, 3 against Swindon teams easily accessible by train. Towards the end of 1891 the *Stroud News* started to publish a column called 'Football Gossip (By Olympian)'. On Friday 20 November 1891 the following Football League report was given:

> *In League matches the greatest surprise of the week was the defeat of Everton by Darwen 3-1. This is a result that requires some explanation other than the vagaries of football form. It is true that the Everton team, who won the league championship last season, are only the shadow of their former selves… the Everton sharp shooters are a long way from their best. The Darwen team thoroughly deserved their victory, which was the result of superior football. In Alexander, Darwen have a first-class centre forward, who can keep his team together as well as score goals.*

On the local front, a Forest Green fixture was reported against Brimscombe, Forest Green losing 3–1 on 13 November 1891. On the Rugby Rules front, in late November 1891, Gloucester played Newport, a fixture that had not occurred for three years. A special train was laid on for Newport spectators to travel to Gloucester, resulting in a crowd in excess of 4,000 for the match, which Newport won by a single try having beaten Cardiff the previous week. On the same day, Chalford beat Stroud Casuals 4–1, while in the Football League the *Stroud Journal* reported:

> *Notts County defeated Accrington by no fewer than nine goals to nothing but in the previous week Accrington, at home, defeated Notts by two goals to none. There is no accounting for such a variation of form, excepting that most clubs are only seen at their best when cheered on by the encouraging cries of their enthusiastic supporters. To the visiting team, again, this must have a correspondingly depressing effect – which soon tells up on their play, for football, I am convinced, is made up of three-fourths pluck and one fourth skill.*

The vocal spectator was having an effect well over 100 years ago!

In December 1891, Stroud Football Club (i.e. rugby club) opened its own clubhouse and also opened up two sides of the ground to spectators, charging 6d and 3d for admission. Off the pitch not much love was lost between the Rugby rules and Association rules fraternities:

> Stroud News, *Friday 18 December 1891*
> *Now, Mr Editor, I am on the warpath. A few fighting lines. At a public dinner in Stroud last Thursday week a well-known supporter of athletics in this district… went so far out of his way as to make a violent attack on Rugby football … but when he brings forward that silly well-worn ancient joke of the umpire (or his remains) being carried off the field in a bag, let me tell him that incident referred to a game under his pet 'Association' rules. As to his general sweeping comments on bad language, rough play etc etc coolly ascribing all these to the Rugby game, nobody who knows anything of football will hesitate to say that rough play, broken bones, referee baiting, fighting, gambling etc in connection with the 'Association' game far exceeds the records of the 'Rugby' code. He made some remark as to putting his views before the public. Let him do so, and if you can find room for the controversy I shall be pleased to take up the cudgels on behalf of our beloved amateur game under Rugby rules. The following referring to Association appeared on the contents bills of a Nottingham evening paper of Saturday last: Extraordinary scenes at League matches. Stand up fight between Oswald and Drummond. Notts finished with five men. Similar scenes at Burnley.*

The First Leagues in Gloucestershire: 1892–1893

The first Association Football League in Gloucestershire came into being in 1892/93, starting life as the Bristol & District League, with nine members, and then changing name to the Western League after three years (it is still in existence today). The South Bristol & District League came into being for the season 1893/94, its first champions being Bristol South, whose imminent collapse would lead to the formation of Bristol South End, later to be renamed Bristol City.

Forest Green Fixtures Come Thick and Fast: 1893–1894

It is clear from the way matches were reported in the early papers that it was the responsibility of the team to provide the report to the paper, rather than the paper sending a reporter. The first descriptive report of a match involving Forest Green, against Chalford, printed in the *Stroud Journal* on Friday 3 February 1893, proves that match reporting was not at the top of Forest Green's list of priorities:

> Stroud News, *Friday 3 February 1893, Forest Green v. Chalford*
> *The return match between these teams took place at Nailsworth on Saturday last. Forest Green kicked off against the wind, when the visitors at once commenced to press, and during the first half scored four goals. They succeeded in adding two more in the second half, thus winning a rather easy game by six goals to nil. The passing among the visiting forwards was the chief feature of the game. The following are the teams.*
> *Chalford: C. Pearce, goal; F. Whiting, E. Kilminster, backs; S. Smith, W. Staddon, J. Ollerenshaw, half-backs; G. Jeffries, C. Liddiatt, C. Bowen, T.H. Workman, H. Whiting, forwards.*
> *Forest Green: F. Brinkworth, goal; E. Allsopp, G. Holt, backs; Mr Harvey, A. Hallem, L. Williams, half-backs; E. Lock, W. Brinkworth, J. Birch, H. Place, W. Browning, forwards.*

In early 1893 all matches outside Bristol were still classed as 'ordinary' matches because no league existed yet for the teams to compete in. Association matches briefly reported one week earlier in the year included Stroud (Thursday) *v.* Stonehouse, Stroud Excelsior *v.* Thrupp, and Chalford *v.* Stroud Alliance. The Thursday team related to the early closing, or half day given to most trades on a Thursday, similar to the Wednesday given in Sheffield.

The 3 March 1893 paper includes a very long report of Stroud Rugby Club *v.* Cheltenham, and results of Association matches between Wycliffe College and Marling School Boys' teams, Wycliffe *v.* Crypt School Gloucester and Wycliffe Second XI *v.* Wotton Grammar School. It also includes the following report of the game between Forest Green and Marling School:

> Stroud News, *3 March 1893, Association Football, Marling School v. Forest Green*
> *This match was played on Saturday last on the school ground. In the first half the game was fairly even, but shortly before change of ends Mr Richards scored for the school. Playing up the hill, after half-time, the school immediately attacked, and Mr Greenstreet added a second point. Unfortunately, however, he was hurt soon after, and compelled to leave the field. With 10 men only the school held their own, and Mr Bruce scored again with a long shot.*
> *The school thus won by three goals to nil; the following played for the school:*
> *Goal, Davies; backs, Rowlands, Samuel; halves, Hagger, Mr Bruce, Mr Thomas; forwards, Thomas, Ward, Mr Richards, Stone, and Mr Greenstreet.*

Marling School opened in 1892 and played Association Rules rather than Rugby Rules for many years in common with many other schools, and included masters as well as pupils in its team. The team in the photograph on the following page were early opponents of Forest Green and Mr Greenstreet, the school's first headmaster, can be seen second from right, on the back row.

The 7 April 1893 edition of the *Stroud Journal* includes reports of Stroud Rugby Club's matches against both Chepstow and Pillgwennly, together with a single Association Rules report of the match between Chalford and Forest Green. Chalford won 3-0. No further Association matches of note can be found until 27 October 1893 where a brief report is given of Forest Green *v.* Brimscombe:

Marling School Association
Football team, 1892/93.

Stroud Journal, *27 October 1893*

The above teams met on the ground of the former on Saturday. The visitors won the toss and elected to kick with the wind behind them. The home team started the ball when some very fast play ensued, but 40 minutes passed before either side scored, when Brinkworth put the ball between the uprights from a good shot for the home team. After half-time Brimscombe restarted and soon became dangerous and but for the good play of Hallam at the back would have scored. After this the ball was chiefly confined to the visitors' end, the ball on several occasions just narrowly escaping the goal. At the call of time, nothing further having been scored, the home team were the victors by 1 goal to nil.

On 10 November 1893 a very short report is given of Forest Green's home game *v.* Gloucester Reserves, with Forest Green winning 3-2, the club's first recorded victory over a Gloucester team.

The previous two meetings were wins for Forest Green. The team was improving all the time and reported fixtures were becoming a regular event.

Gloucester Association Football Club

Gloucester AFC were formed in 1883 with a first reported match on 2 January 1886 losing 1-0 to Eastville Rovers (soon to be renamed Bristol Rovers). W.G. Grace was the referee.

Gloucester joined the Bristol & District League for the 1893/94 season and stayed in the league for three seasons. All of the other teams in the league were from the Bristol area or further south and it is likely that the financial burden of playing in the league led them to leave and move to leagues closer to home. Travel was very difficult in the 1890s. They became founder members of the Gloucester & District League in September 1897. The Gloucester & District League started initially in an attempt to create a county league open to all clubs in Gloucestershire. It shrank to its final title probably as a result of the same travel difficulties that caused Gloucester's withdrawal from the Western League. They also ran a reserve team who played regular fixtures against Forest Green at this time.

Gloucester foundered before the First World War and finally went out of existence when the players defected to the Gloucester YMCA Club, which was renamed Gloucester City in the 1920s.

The 'Rovers' Appear

The Forest Green 'Rovers' name is first reported in 1893 and, on 15 December 1893, Forest Green Rovers drew 1-1 with Wotton-under-Edge. A week later Forest Green 'Rovers' beat Dursley St James 2-0 at Dursley. The following week's paper contained a report of Stroud Rugby club's game against Cardiff reserves in front of a record gate, Stroud going down, with no disgrace, to the reserves 'by the kick'. Forest Green again beat Dursley St James in January 1894 and, in the same paper, Forest Green Rovers seconds beat Woodchester Athletic 3-1. This is the first reported match of a Forest Green reserve team and gives an idea of how strong the team was becoming. The *Stroud Journal* on Friday 26 January 1894 gives a report of the Gloucester Reserves *v*. Forest Green Rovers return match as follows:

> *The return match between the above teams was played on Budding's Field (Gloucester) on Saturday. The reserves had got together a strong team with the intention of reversing the defeat sustained at the hands of the Rovers earlier in the season. Edwards won the toss, and elected to play with the wind. Brinkworth kicked off, and the Rovers were soon attacking, till Alsopp secured a pass from Gardiner and landed a neat goal. The Rovers still held the upper hand, but had not scored when the whistle sounded half-time. On changing ends Gloucester played with great determination, and from a scrum in front of goal the home team equalised. The game was now taken from one end of the field to the other, but neither side had scored when the whistle sounded no side, leaving a fast, pleasant and well contested game in a draw of one goal each.*
>
> *The following played for the Rovers: goal, H. French; backs; A. Hallam, W. Brinkworth; halfbacks; L. Williams, E. Gardiner, and R. Blake; forwards, E. Alsopp, A.J. Marmont, T. Brinkworth, and J. Birch.*

The National Game

On 27 January 1894, in the *Dursley Gazette*, there is an interesting sports report covering 'The League, Midland League, The Amateur Cup, Middlesex Senior Cup, Lancashire Cup, Scottish Cup, Scottish League, London Senior Cup and Ordinary Fixtures.' Association football had definitely arrived.

In the Football League, Aston Villa and Blackburn Rovers were first and second respectively while Newton Heath and Darwen were bottom and second from bottom. In the Midland League, Leicester Fosse beat Doncaster Rovers 2-1. In the Amateur Cup, Sheppey United beat Folkestone. In the Middlesex Senior Cup, the 3rd Grenadiers beat Tottenham Hotspur 2-1. In the Lancashire Cup, Burnley beat West Manchester 2-1, Blackburn Rovers beat Liverpool 4-3, Bolton Wanderers vanquished Preston North End 4-1, Blackpool beat Fleetwood Rangers 4-1, Darwen beat Heywood Central 2-1 and Bury beat Accrington 6-0. Rossendale beat Ardwick 4-2 and Everton beat Newton Heath 7-1 at Everton. What a difference between the Lancashire Cup and the Gloucestershire Cup at that time!

In the London Senior Cup, Millwall Athletic withdrew, enabling Chiswick Park to pass to the second round. London Caledonians lost to Crouch End, the Casuals beat the City Ramblers, Old Westminsters beat Old St Marks 18-0, Crusaders beat Old Harrovians 4-1 at Harrow. Wimbledon Polytechnic beat Royal Ordinance Factories 2-1, Old Foresters ousted Ilford 2-1 and Old Carthusians drew with Clapton. There were certainly a lot of 'Old Boys' teams around in London at that time.

Ordinary matches played that week included Corinthians defeating Aston Villa 3-2, Woolwich Arsenal beating Chatham 4-0, Millwall Athletic vanquishing Reading 4-1, Luton Town beating West Herts 3-2 at Watford and Swindon defeated 2nd Scots Guards at Swindon 5-1.

There was certainly no shortage of reporting of national football by 1894.

Modern Reporting Techniques

In 1894, the *Stroud Journal* hit on the novel idea of reporting Association rules matches involving Stroud AFC as if the reporter was the match ball. On Friday 2 February 1894, a match between Stroud and Forest Green Rovers, at Forest Green, was reported as follows:

Saturday was about the worst kind of day possible for playing Association. The wind was very high, and the rain came down in sheets, at every gust of wind. The match was played nevertheless at Forest Green, right on top of the hill. Forest Green men were evidently bent on winning, and seemed to think Stroud would fall an easy prey to their good play. Captain Payne won the toss, and chose to play with the wind. Forest Green kicked off and I was soon down their end. The wind was blowing very strongly from corner to corner of the field, and Stroud had their work cut out to get me up to the top of the field from which place was the only chance of getting in a shot.

They came very near getting a goal several times, but did not quite manage it. The game continued for the most part in the Forest Green 25, till half-time; and when the whistle blew nobody had scored.

This looked rather blue for Stroud, and after I had been kicked off, I immediately went down into their quarters. The Rovers got very near scoring several times, but Fawkes defended smartly, and once when he missed me and Forest Green were coming down upon him, he got in a very neat kick, saving a goal but not himself. Stroud were not confined so much to their 25, for they made several very good rushes, which came near scoring once or twice.

I noticed that the Stroud men played a wise game in the second half, for whenever they could they would put me into touch, thus wasting time and giving the Rovers less chance.

The match ended in a draw ...

'The Ball'

At the end of February, Forest Green Rovers beat Chalford 3-2 and by early March the Rovers' forthcoming game against Dursley was anticipated as an easy win:

It is hardly expected that Dursley will come out winners against such a good team.

In fact, Dursley St James' won 3-2. It just goes to show that nothing is certain in football.

By the end of the 1894 season Forest Green Rovers had begun to establish a reputation for themselves and had managed to run the whole season at home undefeated but for the last reported game against Dursley St James.

Formation of the Mid-Gloucestershire League

The success of the National Association game, together with the formation of the Bristol and District League two years before, started people thinking about a league for other teams in Gloucestershire. The following letter appeared in the *Dursley Gazette* on 21 April 1894:

Dear Sir, Seeing the great amount of interest taken at the present time in football in this district, where there are now so many clubs, I think the game would be made more popular still if a league was formed, similar to the Bristol & District League. That league is, I believe, open only to those within a certain radius of Bristol, and therefore clubs outside that radius are debarred from joining, when but for the obstacle named they would do so. Could not therefore a league be formed somewhere in the centre of Gloucestershire, and thus give a number of unattached clubs an opportunity which I venture to think they would be only too glad to avail themselves of. If the matter was taken up by one or two of the secretaries of the leading clubs here about, and the proposition brought to the notice of other secretaries and a meeting called, I feel sure that a league for Mid-Gloucestershire would rise and be not only a success in itself, but a good thing for clubs and members generally.

Thanking you in anticipation for the publication of this letter in your paper, I am, dear sir,
Yours faithfully, ONE INTERESTED IN FOOTBALL.
Wickwar, 18 April, 1894

The Mid-Gloucestershire League came into being that summer in anticipation of the 1894/95 season with Forest Green Rovers as founder members.

4

The Mid-Gloucestershire League: 1894–1899

1894/95

The Mid-Gloucestershire League began on Saturday 29 September 1894 with a match between Brimscombe and Stroud. Rovers played their first ever league match at home against Brimscombe on 6 October resulting in a 1-1 draw. Wickwar were beaten at home on 13 October 1894 1-0 and on 20 October Chalford were beaten 4-0 at Forest Green, the scorers being Marmont, Timms, Birch and Caldicott. Not a bad start to league football for the Rovers. And then Forest Green played Stroud, and the dramatic style of reporting as 'The Ball' returned, a shortened version of which follows:

Stroud Journal, *2 November 1894*
WHAT IS GOING TO HAPPEN?
    This is the question, Mr Editor, which is raging in many of the Stroud men's minds just at present. Are the Stroud men going to appeal, or are they not? And if they do appeal, what will come of it? But I am premature in asking questions before anyone knows what they are all about. After a very hard-fought game, which I will describe further down, a 'hands' was given to Stroud on the very brink, so to speak, of their opponent's goal. Of course they took me, put me down, rolled me over, and kicked me through before anyone had time to look around, including the umpire, who was trying to get the Forest Green men on to the goal line. A very laudable occupation, no doubt, and the right thing to do, but I can't agree with him as to his next step. Considering he had been keeping Forest Green talking, and had not given them a fair chance, he blew the whistle and had me brought back. The Stroud men were dumbfounded and I am sorry to say commenced wrangling; but Mr Umpire was firm, and there I am with him, for I think that if an umpire decides a point to his satisfaction he should stick to it at thick and thin.
    He awarded Stroud another kick, but it was not successful, and Stroud were left at the end of the game losers by one goal to nil.
    Now I will give my promised description of the game itself. The wind was blowing down the field when the captains tossed up and Forest Green, winning the toss, chose to play with the wind. That made a considerable difference, for they began to press at once, and but for the admirable defence of S. Hooper and the backs, Payne and Coucher, I should have been often forced through these goals. Timms put me through once. He seems to kick most of the goals for his side. Stroud played up gallantly, nevertheless, and managed to keep their opponents out till the whistle declared half of the game over. Meanwhile Forest Green had been playing a fast game, doing their best to make the most of the wind. Nothing more than one goal came of it although Birch, otherwise 'Jimmy', and Marmont ought to have scored.
    Both teams took their places on the field after the usual five minutes, looking like giants refreshed, and both determined to do or die. Now came Stroud's turn at the fun, and they commenced at once, making desperate rushes down the field with the evident intention of scoring, but were again and again repulsed. Stroud worked

like galley slaves, but could not get me through in a more satisfactory manner, until the eventful free-kick that I have described.

The difference between the Forest Green team of today and that of last year is wonderful. Of course, they have got valuable additions in Timms and Rev. Cruickshank, but the general play is vastly improved. The Stroud forwards might take an object lesson from Timms in passing.

Stroud did lodge an appeal and lost, but their deposit money was returned to them.

Reporting on football leagues was a new business and there weren't any local precedents for journalists to follow when compiling league tables. In November, the *Stroud Journal* attempted its first ever table:

Stroud Journal, 16 November 1894
The following is a form showing at a glance how the different clubs in the Mid-Gloucestershire League are progressing. It will be seen that 2 points register a win, and 1 point to each of the combating teams registers a draw. The totals will be added up across the columns, so that if a 2 is seen opposite Stroud and under Brimscombe, it will show that Stroud beat Brimscombe:

LEAGUE SCORES UP TO DATE

	Brimscombe	Chalford	Forest Green	Gloucester Res	Stroud	Wickwar	Wotton	Total
Brimscombe	–	–	1	2	–	–	–	–
Chalford	2	–	–	–	2	2	–	–
Forest Green	1	2	–	–	–	2	–	–
Gloucester Res	–	–	–	–	–	2	1	–
Stroud	2	–	–	–	–	2	–	–
Wickwar	–	–	–	–	–	–	–	–
Wotton	–	–	–	–	–	–	–	–

The teams were listed in alphabetical order making it difficult to establish who was actually top and bottom of the league and the points total was not given. The points don't add up either; three teams have 1 point.

On the same weekend is a report of a match between Woodchester Association FC and Forest Green Congregational FC, with the Congregational side being beaten 4-0. It was now five years since the first report in the papers of the commencement of the team at Forest Green by the Congregational minister. It is assumed that the team he created became Forest Green Rovers. By 1894, it is possible that his team had moved into the world of competitive sport, playing games to win at all costs rather than as a pastime. Perhaps the minister, buoyed by the success of football in Forest Green, decided to recreate a church team or maybe the report in 1889 purely relates to the church team and the Forest Green Rovers team sprang up separately. This would appear unlikely, given the small size and extremely close nature of the community and the nominal population to choose from.

By December, Forest Green had 7 points to be joint top of the table with Wotton and Brimscombe, although Wotton were bottom of the table in alphabetical order.

In the same paper a match was reported between Marling School and Forest Green Congregational FC, with the school losing 4-2. In Friday 21 December 1894's *Stroud Journal*, a report is given of the match between Stroud and Cheltenham, the result being 2-2.

Another report by 'The Ball' of the game between Stroud and Forest Green was given in the *Stroud Journal* on 25 January 1895:

25 January 1895, Association Football Mid-Gloucester League, Stroud v. Forest Green
Defeated again! What is Stroud coming to?
This makes two league matches lost straight off the reel. The visions of the cup are fading away. Stroud men

must wake up or I shall never have the chance of making my notes immortal by writing such a poem as the Chalford bard did two weeks ago. By all appearances I shall never be able to say as he did 'Bravo, Stroud you are wreathed in glory, someone's felt your sting again.'

Once Montgomery sent me in at a fearful pace, but unfortunately I hit against the post, and brought down the cross-bar, but did not go through. The goal Forest Green got was also a very lucky one. I was quite by myself, and the Stroud goalkeeper rushed at me, but thinking Payne was going to do the kicking stopped. Payne also thought Turner was going to do it and so he left me to him, and tried to stop the man. The man, however, got by, and scored an easy goal. Now, in my opinion the goalkeeper ought never to hesitate. He ought to make up his mind to do what he thinks the best thing, and do it regardless of other players.

The only other report found in the *Stroud Journal* for this season was given on Friday 22 March 1895 for the game away to Chalford, the game ending in a 2-2 draw.

The league table was given on 12 April 1895, although some teams had yet to complete their fixture list. The table had now been changed from alphabetical order to points scored and takes the form of the modern-day format. Forest Green came third, not bad for their first competitive league season.

1894/95 season	Played	Won	Lost	Drawn	Points
Gloucester Reserves	11	9	1	1	19
Wotton	11	7	2	2	16
Forest Green	12	4	4	4	12
Brimscombe	12	4	5	3	11
Chalford	11	4	5	2	10
Stroud	10	3	6	1	7
Wickwar	11	1	9	1	3

It was time to look to the future and to consolidate. The league brought financial pressures involved with travelling to matches, league subscriptions and perhaps funding some of the expenses of players. No records exist to indicate whether or not players were paid any form of expense at this time.

Football as a Marketing Opportunity

By 1895, other commercial possibilities were being exploited in relation to football. Many different health products started to appear on the market with advertisements in various papers, including Elliman's Embrocation, fully endorsed by Forfar Athletic Football Club, in the *Dursley Gazette*. No doubt all of the footballers in the area rushed out to buy the embrocation before their next fixture.

Another interesting health product was advertised in the *Stroud News* in October 1896. I wonder who rushed out to buy it?

HEALING PROPERTIES OF PURIFIED PETROLEUM
Everyone knows of the healing effect of petroleum (Vaseline, petroleum jellies, etc) when applied locally to the skin for inflammation, bruises etc. Very few, however, stop to think that it can have an equally healing effect when taken internally upon inflammations of the mucus membrane (the internal skin, so to speak) lining the throat, lungs, stomach and intestines. Such, however, is the case, and when properly purified for internal use it exerts not only a soothing and healing effect, but an antiseptic or anti-fermentative action as well, preventing fermentation and aiding digestion and assimilation, while at the same time it possesses a food value equal to that of cod liver oil. Moreover, it acts directly through the blood, and being antiseptic tends to destroy the germs of disease. Angier's Petroleum Emulsion consists of a highly purified tasteless petroleum oil combined with hypophosphites. It is pleasant to take, and agrees with the most delicate stomach. It will cure the worst cough, heal any inflammation of throat, lungs, stomach, and intestines, and do more to prevent and cure consumption

MARCH 21, 1896.

An advert from the 21 March 1896 *Gazette*. Forfar Athletic used Elliman's Embrocation so it must have been good!

than any other remedy. It is a food as well as a medicine, and aids digestion, increases weight and strength, and builds up the system generally. It is far superior to cod liver oil in the treatment of all chest affections and wasting diseases. Prescribed by the medical profession, and sold by all leading chemists, 2s 9d and 4s 6d. A sample bottle sent free on receipt of 3d to cover postage.

Descriptive pamphlets post free.

Angier Chemical Company, 32, Snow Hill, London, EC

1895/96

The club had been attempting to raise funds in Nailsworth during their first season. Nailsworth had become an urban district council the year before and the town wanted a football team. Looking at the success and publicity that Association Football brought to those involved with the game, it would be a great addition to Nailsworth.

Stroud Journal, *30 August 1895, 'Nailsworth' Football Club meeting*
On Wednesday evening a meeting was held in the Nailsworth Subscription Rooms, for the purpose of furthering the promotion of a Football Club for Nailsworth. Mr A.P. Playne JP presided and others present included Mr A. Cakebread, Mr J. Walker, Mr T. Harris, Mr E. Benjamin, Mr W. Bruton, Mr John Morris, Mr H.M. Newman, Mr H. Horwood, Mr T.H. Hatton, Mr A.C. Marmont, Mr F. Grist, Mr F. Davis, Mr C.E. Hole, Mr Blake and others.

The chairman expressed his pleasure at being asked to take the chair at the meeting, the object of which was to start a football club for Nailsworth. There had been a football club at Forest Green, but it seemed to him that, as Forest Green was a part of Nailsworth, it would be better to start a club which should be called Nailsworth Football Club. He thought if this was done they would have a more successful club, and that the Nailsworth Traders would come forward and give them their share of support, which would be a very important point. They all knew that no club could flourish without plenty of funds to keep it going. He should be pleased to do all in his power to help forward the club, and thought there were those who, although too old to engage in manly sports, would be pleased to help support it. He asked Mr Cakebread, as a member of the Forest Green Club, to address the meeting. Mr Cakebread said that the members of the old club were most anxious the club should be started and he thought there was plenty of scope for a club there.

The Forest Green club had met with a great measure of success in the league competition. There was one point, however, upon which they did not get on quite so well; they did not get the support from Nailsworth people. When they broached the subject of funds, they found that they would support a Nailsworth club if one was started, whereas under the old name they did not get their sympathy. Therefore, rather than the club should fall through, they had taken it upon themselves the responsibility to call this meeting to see what could be done in Nailsworth. Fixtures had also been arranged in connection with the Mid-Gloucestershire Football League Cup competition. At present they had no money in hand, and they would have to rely on their sympathy and generosity.

Mr H.M. Newman proposed that all the work and recommendations done by Mr Cakebread in forming the Nailsworth Football Club be endorsed by this meeting. Mr Cakebread having responded, the election of offices was next proceeded with as follows: President , Mr Arthur T. Playne; Secretary, Mr S. Allsopp; Treasurer, Mr Joseph Walker; Captain, Mr Blake; Vice Captain, Mr H. Horwood; together with a committee of nine.

It was agreed that the entrance fee be two and six, and that the same field at Forest Green be used for playing.

The change of identity wasn't accepted by all. The initial Forest Green team became fragmented with some of the players leaving to make way for the Nailsworth lads. J. Blake, an old Forest Green player, became the Nailsworth team captain. 'The Ball' then reported on a forthcoming friendly between Stroud and Nailsworth, extracts from which follow:

Stroud Journal, *27 September 1895*
On my list of fixtures given last week, the first match was given for Saturday week, and now here we are with a match for tomorrow. Against Nailsworth too, a league team, with whom we have already two fixtures.

I wonder how many of the old Forest Green men, those mighty heroes of last season, will be playing? Who, I wonder, have joined the Woodchester Priory and who other clubs? And some of the games I have no doubt we shall find old friends on the football field pitted against each other, and playing on that account for all they are worth. It is a matter of some speculation, too, how the spectators at Nailsworth will welcome an old member of the Forest Green team who turns out to play for the opponents. Let us hope it will be with due respect and proper feeling.

The old field up at the top of the hill where the FG's of the last year won and lost many a glorious game, is appropriated by the new Nailsworth team, and that is where the two teams will meet tomorrow.

Signed: The Ball

So Nailsworth, playing in Forest Green on Forest Green's field, played Stroud in the league at the end of September and lost 3-0; only three of the previous season's Forest Green team were playing. Timms and Marmont, both old Forest Green names, were playing for Stroud.

In the meantime a match was reported in the *Stroud Journal* between Forest Green Third XI and Amberley School, the first match for the Forest Green youngsters, which they won 6-0. Forest Green Third XI was a youth team, keeping the 'Forest Green' name alive.

On the rugby front, Stroud Rugby Club were still making a name for themselves and not just locally, beating Bath by 2 tries and 2 goals to 1 goal in February 1896.

On 20 March 1896 in the *Stroud News* there is a short report of Stroud AFC *v.* Cheltenham Town (not a league match), resulting in a fine 3-1 win for Stroud.

No reports of the Nailsworth team have been found between January and March 1896. The final table was published on 28 March 1896 in the *Dursley Gazette* as follows:

The following is believed to be a correct statement of the result of this competition:

1895/96 season	Played	Won	Lost	Drawn	For	Against	Points
Wotton-under-Edge	10	9	1	0	48	8	18
Chalford	10	7	2	1	19	12	15
Stroud	9	5	4	0	19	18	11
Dursley St James	9	1	5	2	13	28	6
Nailsworth AFC	8	1	5	2	9	18	5
Gloucester Reserves	8	0	6	3	9	33	5

Nailsworth gave two points to Dursley by not playing the return match, and in the Stroud v. Gloucester, and Nailsworth v. Gloucester matches which were not played owing to the smallpox scare, the committee decided to give each side one point, the result being as stated above.

The Smallpox Epidemic in Gloucester

An outbreak of smallpox at Gloucester in 1895 assumed grave proportions in February 1896 when the disease spread among schoolchildren and then to many households in the south of the city. Children were moved from the union workhouse to Tuffley. The city was virtually in quarantine. A spectator from Dursley visited Stroud to witness the Stroud *v.* Gloucester rugby game with the following report in the 13 March 1896 *Stroud News*:

I am not at all surprised to hear that it is almost certain that this single case of smallpox at Dursley can be traced to the visit of the victim to Stroud to witness the football match, Stroud v. Gloucester, last Saturday week. It is quite clear he did not contract the disease from Stroud residents, as happily all are free from it; but he was rubbing shoulders with visitors from an infected area, from the time he entered the town during that time he was on the football field, and until his departure home of course. Rather than run the awful risk, I am certain that the local authorities, and every respectable resident and shopkeeper, would have gladly subscribed to any deficit, or have got up some big gathering to swell their funds, had the football club listened to reason and common sense and postponed or cancelled the match. As it is, I fear, they have lost caste in many quarters. I emphasise this the more, not only on the ground of the risk incurred, but also because of the inadvisability of bringing together such a rowdy lot of Gloucester fellows as were seen parading our streets and intimidating passers-by, and the shopkeepers who exhibited the bills in their windows. For hours the town was entirely at the mercy of about 1,500 immigrants from a city where smallpox is rampant, and where hundreds of cases are under treatment. Tradesmen were ordered to take the bills out of their windows or their shop fronts were to be smashed in. And yet the committee of our otherwise excellent football club seek to justify themselves in bringing such noxious visitors into the town!

While Stroud was very much a rugby town, the rugby club had overstepped the mark by continuing with their fixture against Gloucester, a town in the middle of a smallpox epidemic. The outbreak finally abated in July 1896. Of the 434 people who died since the outbreak at the end of 1895, 280 were children under ten years old. The city council was severely criticised for its handling of the epidemic and its initial decision not to enforce the vaccination of the population.

1896/97

The *Dursley Gazette* on 26 September 1896 lists the fixtures for Dursley St James AFC, including Nailsworth away on 31 October and Nailsworth home on 13 February, both matches being listed as Mid-Gloucestershire League matches. Also listed are League matches against 'Cheltenham' who joined the league for the 1896/97 season. At the end of September, the Nailsworth team travelled to Stroud to play a friendly match at Stratford Court. The following report is taken from the 2 October 1896 *Stroud Journal*:

I cannot assign a good excuse for Nailsworth turning out at Stratford Court, on Saturday last, at something after half past three, with only eight men, two or three of whom, I believe, arrived after the game had commenced … I suppose I ought to make a little allowance, this being the commencement of the season; but I must say I was really surprised in the way in which the players of either team had forgotten one another's game. Nailsworth was certainly much handicapped by having a very mixed lot, as they had to make up their compliment from the Stroud ranks; and I should judge, from last year's team, that they were not well

*represented by the eight men who did turn up ... Blake, Nailsworth's captain of last season, was playing in
the ranks of the Stroud boys ... He distinguished himself on Saturday by shooting several of the Stroud goals,
one of which at least was a smart one; H.E. Coley worked energetically on the behalf of the visitors, as did
E. Locke, who was apparently the life of the team. The man in goal for Nailsworth evidently did his best, but
the work was hard and constant, as the Stroud shooters were pressing throughout the game, which eventually
closed leaving Stroud winners by six goals to one.*

*The latest thing out in Stroud Association football is that the club is going to pay members' expenses.
Of course it is a good thing from the club to be in position to do this.*

We don't know how many other teams in the area were paying players' expenses, but Stroud,
in their attempt to become the dominant Association team in the area, obviously had high
ambition and reasonable funds. While Nailsworth, playing at Forest Green, were struggling,
Stroud were picking up all the best players by paying them expenses. Perhaps the Stroud
Association men were keen to emulate their Rugby rules counterparts' success on the field.

The Introduction of Goal Nets

In the 10 October 1896 edition of the *Dursley Gazette* there is an interesting
observation regarding the goals:

*The first thing that attracted my attention on visiting the Dursley St James (Association) enclosure last
Saturday was an appliance that, I think, has long been needed to add to the completeness of the ground,
viz, nets affixed to the goalposts. Hitherto a couple of uprights with simply the crossbar, has done duty,
without anything, as used by most other high-class clubs, to catch the ball or man – whichever the case might
be – when they are sent behind the posts. There have been cases when not only the spectators, but the referee
himself, has been baffled by the ball just going outside the uprights and, through being so far away, has been
unable to discern clearly whether it went inside or outside the posts. Under the new order of things, however,
this cannot be, as the ball is caught in the net as it passes through the posts, et al, thereby facilitating the
not too easy task of the referee, and also making it better for the spectators, who, under the old system, have
been repeatedly disappointed to hear the referee shout 'goal kick'.*

The 30 October 1896 *Stroud News* included a report of Stroud thrashing Gloucester 4–0 and
noted that Stroud were missing Blake (the old Forest Green player) in their forward line.
On 31 October 1896 the *Dursley Gazette* reported:

*Today St James's first XI (owing to Nailsworth having withdrawn from the Mid-Gloster league) will have
a holiday, but the second XI will meet Kingswood on the Dursley ground, when a good game is anticipated.*

No other reports have been found regarding the withdrawal; they would have been heavily
fined for leaving the league and it is equally likely that no one would have immediately stepped
forward to pay the fines. Opportunities for a replacement team to appear without paying off
the debt would have been very limited. The name change experiment to Nailsworth had failed
and left Forest Green without a league club.

The remaining teams competing in the Mid-Gloucestershire League for 1896/97 were
Cheltenham Town, Chalford, Dursley, Wickwar, Brimscombe, Wotton-under-Edge and
Kingswood AFC and Woodchester United.

Stroud AFC, expenses and all, did not feature in the league but, in the 20 November 1896
Stroud News, a report is included of the Stroud Rugby Club game against London Welsh,
resulting in a win for Stroud by 6 points to 3. Fixtures for the first XV this season included
Crumlin, Gloucester, Clifton, Bristol, Bath, London Welsh, Reading, Weston-super-Mare,

Canton, Cheltenham, Maindee, Cardiff Reserves, Newport A, Cardiff Harlequins, Cinderford, Civil Service and Manchester. On Friday 1 January 1897 there is a report of Stroud Rugby Club's victory over Cardiff Reserves.

The National Game

In the same copy of the *Stroud Journal*, the following report relates to matches in the Football League Second Division, involving teams that would go on to dominate Premiership Football a century later:

> *I would not, however, include Gainsborough Trinity (at home) 4, and Woolwich Arsenal 1, among the 'freaks', for we have all come to despair of the Arsenal ever playing up to true form away from home. At Plumstead previously the Trinity were defeated by 6 to 1! Newton Heath appear to be reviving into gallant form again. At home to Blackpool they scored 2 goals to 0. Their rivals, Grimsby Town, also did finely by defeating Newcastle United at Grimsby by 3 to 2.*

How times have changed!

Stroud Rugby Club was continuing a good season, beating Bath again by one try to nil in February. Stroud AFC were competing in many games against teams such as Cheltenham Town, Cirencester, and school teams such as Sir Thomas Rich's and Marling, but were not competing in any league. For the 1896/97 season they played a total of 16 games, which included victories against Gloucester. It is hard to try and gauge what kind of standard of football was being played in these early days. Stroud were attempting to become a premier team in the area but were not playing league football, preferring 'ordinary' matches and offering to pay players' expenses, and in at least two cases enticing old Nailsworth (Forest Green) players into their ranks.

The Bristol Clubs

In Bristol, professionalism came to local football in 1897. The first paid player, at least officially, in Bristol was George Kinsey, a half-back who joined Bristol Eastville Rovers from Derby County, and he saw his new club reach the final qualifying round of the FA Cup. South End changed their name to Bristol City at the start of the 1897 season to mark their arrival as a professional club, a move taken at the same time by Warmley and St George. Bedminster joined the professional ranks the following year while Clifton remained amateur.

National sports writers were forecasting problems in Bristol, pointing out that London and Bristol were the only cities supporting more than two professional clubs, and Bristol's population was a lot less than that of the capital. Of the five professional clubs in Bristol in 1898, only Bristol City and Bristol Rovers remained in existence by 1903.

By the end of 1899 Warmley hadn't had a single victory and was losing over £20 a week at a time when a weekly wage of £2 would have been considered above average. The club went bankrupt early in 1900. St George also went out of existence when the 1899 season closed, after financial calamity.

The FA Cup was important financially even at that time and St George's downfall was reported to be due to a 1-0 defeat by Bristol City as they became the first Bristol club to reach the first round proper of the FA Cup. City's reward was a home tie with Sunderland and, while they lost the match, the financial rewards were considerable. Who knows, if St George had won the game and gained financial security, maybe it would be Bristol St George rather than Bristol City in the Football League this century?

Bedminster agreed to amalgamate with Bristol City in 1900. City kept the name and colours but moved to Ashton Gate, Bedminster's ground.

The third Mid-Gloucestershire League table, 1896/97:

1896/97 season	Played	Won	Lost	Drawn	For	Against	Points
Cheltenham Town	10	8	2	0	32	10	16
Wotton-under-Edge	12	8	2	2	32	10	14
Dursley	12	6	5	1	20	17	13
Wickwar	12	5	6	1	22	22	11
Chalford	11	4	5	2	15	18	10
Brimscombe	10	3	5	2	16	23	8
Woodchester	11	0	9	2	2	39	2

Wotton, the cup holders from the previous season, had had 4 points deducted earlier in the season for playing unregistered men and lost their chance to retain the cup.

1897/98

Having been almost invisible for the previous season, on 29 October 1897, the *Stroud Journal* reported a match between Nailsworth Thursday AFC and Cirencester Thursday at Cirencester. The short report says that the Nailsworth team were defeated 2-1, although an improvement was shown in the combination of the visitors suggesting they were playing before this date.

On the same day, Woodchester entertained Cheltenham Town in the Mid-Gloucestershire League, the Woodchester line-up including old Forest Green players E. Locke and Timms. Woodchester lost 2-0. Stroud, again, did not enter the Mid-Gloucestershire League this season although Ebley AFC, which had started the year before, now entered. Stroud had quite a team and played Gloucester in early November, losing 3-2. Blake, the old Forest Green player, was still a lynchpin in the Stroud team.

Wycliffe College were also one of the leading teams in the area, regularly beating league teams, including Ebley in November 1897 3-1, the *Stroud Journal* describing the passing of the Wycliffe team as 'perfect'. They also beat Stroud 6-1 in the same month; and in December Marling School drew with Wycliffe 0-0, showing that 'school' football was still a force to contend with in the area.

Thomas and William Brinkworth, who both hailed from and played for Forest Green in their first league season, had played for the Chalford team the year before and were now named in the Brimscombe line-up. Further signs of football life in Nailsworth and Forest Green appeared in the *Stroud Journal* on Friday 17 September 1897 when Nailsworth were named in a fixture list for the Stroud Thursday team, the match to be played on 18 November.

By the turn of the year, the Ebley team was beating everything in its path, including Cheltenham Town, while in the 28 January 1898 *Stroud Journal*, there is a short report of the match between Gloucester Thursday and Nailsworth Thursday at Gloucester, Nailsworth losing 8-0. In February Nailsworth AFC met St Loes School 'on the common', quite a comedown from being founder members of the Mid-Gloucestershire League.

No Love Lost Between Dursley and Woodchester: the J.H. Blake Affair

A little bit too much force had been used in a Mid-Gloucestershire League game against Dursley in February, leading to a Woodchester player being taken to court for assault in March 1898. The Dursley spectators invaded the pitch and the visiting Woodchester players then declined to continue the match.

Stroud Journal, *18 March 1898*

At the Dursley Petty Sessions, before Captain Graham (chairman), Col Browne, Mr W. Phelps and Mr R.A. Lister, John H. Blake, a player in the Woodchester Association football team, was summoned by Mr J.F. Chambers, a player in the Dursley Association eleven and headmaster of the local grammar school, for an assault. On 5 February the teams were engaged in a Mid-Gloucestershire League contest at Dursley. Defendant was playing forward for Woodchester, and complainant was a full-back for Dursley. Towards the close of the game Blake was dribbling the ball down the field, when Chambers charged him and secured possession. This, it was alleged, caused defendant to lose his temper and to deliberately kick complainant severely between the legs from behind, when the ball was yards away. For the defence it was urged that the kick was intended for the ball and not for complainant, but after hearing the evidence on the bench decided that the assault had been proved, and fined Blake £2 plus costs.

One week later, the monthly general meeting of the Mid-Gloucestershire League was reported in the same paper and a completely different picture of events was portrayed as follows:

The monthly general meeting was held at Stonehouse on Monday ... Mr A. Cakebread of Stroud was elected to the chair ... The result of this protest was that the committee ordered the match between Dursley and Woodchester to be replayed and on account of the action of the Dursley spectators; the Dursley Club were ordered to distribute bills, warning the spectators as to their future conduct; and W. Short, one of the Dursley players, for deliberately striking two of his opponents in the face, and also having been adversely reported upon by various referees in other matches, was suspended for the remainder of the season.

The secretary of the league reported the fact that Dursley had persisted, notwithstanding the objection of the various captains and referees, in playing Short, and also that the required notices had not been distributed. After a short discussion, it was unanimously decided that Dursley's reasons for not carrying out the league's decision were frivolous. Thereupon it was proposed, seconded and carried unanimously that Dursley be expelled from the league. Upon this decision, the chairman requested the Dursley representatives to leave the committee room, which they did amid more applause.

J.H. Blake, having been found guilty by the Dursley magistrates of assaulting a schoolmaster, was viewed in a very different light in Stonehouse:

It was resolved that the Mid-Gloster League committee beg to tender Mr J.H. Blake their apologies for the indignity done him at their previous meeting in suspending him; that this suspension was caused by a garbled report that reached them from Dursley – but having made the strongest inquiries, the committee have no alternative than as above; also to record their emphatic protest against the monstrous injustice done him by the Dursley JPs, and more so against the action of the man who prosecuted him, and against the Dursley committee for the support accorded the plaintiff in his contemptible action.

Mr Cakebread was a member of the Forest Green club back in 1894 and a Mr Blake was a player for Forest Green in their first season. There was definitely no love lost between Dursley and the Mid-Gloucestershire League, in fact even the justice of the Dursley JPs and the word of a school headmaster had been brought into question. Dursley and the surrounding district exhibited the same rivalry seen in the newspaper reports back in 1889 when the referee's word had been the cause of the dispute.

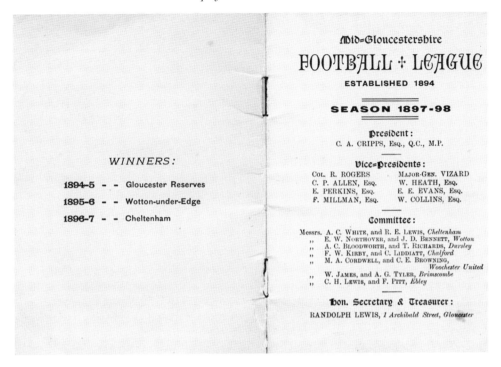

Mid-Gloucestershire

FOOTBALL ✝ LEAGUE

ESTABLISHED 1894

SEASON 1897-98

President:
C. A. CRIPPS, Esq., Q.C., M.P.

WINNERS:

1894–5 - - Gloucester Reserves

1895–6 - - Wotton-under-Edge

1896–7 - - Cheltenham

Vice-Presidents:

COL. R. ROGERS	MAJOR-GEN. VIZARD
C. P. ALLEN, ESQ.	W. HEATH, ESQ.
E. PERKINS, ESQ.	E. E. EVANS, ESQ.
F. MILLMAN, ESQ.	W. COLLINS, ESQ.

Committee:

Messrs. A. C. WHITE, and R. E. LEWIS, *Cheltenham*
  „ E. W. NORTHOVER, and J. D. BENNETT, *Wotton*
  „ A. C. BLOODWORTH, and T. RICHARDS, *Dursley*
  „ F. W. KIRBY, and C. LIDDIATT, *Chalford*
  „ M. A. CORDWELL, and C. E. BROWNING, *Woodchester United*
  „ W. JAMES, and A. G. TYLER, *Brimscombe*
  „ C. H. LEWIS, and F. PITT, *Ebley*

Hon. Secretary & Treasurer:

RANDOLPH LEWIS, *1 Archibald Street, Gloucester*

Mid-Gloucestershire League Handbook 1897/98. Seven teams competed in the league this season.

Mid-Gloucestershire League, 1897/98:

1897/98 season	Played	Won	Lost	Drawn	For	Against	Points
Ebley	12	10	1	1	31	5	21
Cheltenham Town	12	6	3	3	20	11	15
Wotton-under-Edge	12	5	4	3	29	16	13
Brimscombe	12	6	5	1	29	19	13
Dursley	12	4	5	3	18	23	11
Woodchester	12	2	7	3	9	24	7
Chalford	12	1	8	3	11	45	5

The Ebley team ended their second season very successfully, partly owing to the Stroud team having decided to give up early in the season so that Ebley were able to obtain the services of some of their best men.

1898/99

This season saw the inception of the Dursley & District League (DDL), probably formed as a result of the J.H. Blake affair. The Dursley League Cup was competed for by Brimscombe, Dursley, Uley, Stonehouse, Ebley and Chalford, the teams finishing in that order at the end of its first season.

The Mid-Gloustershire League started with only five teams for this season with Ebley, Wotton, Gloucester, Brimscombe and Chalford competing for the League Cup. It seems the other clubs voted with their feet and moved to the Dursley League. Wotton then withdrew in late 1898, leaving only four clubs at the end of the season.

The Gloucester & District League included Ross Kyrle, Gloucester, Ross, Ledbury Victoria, Tewkesbury Abbey, Ebley and Cheltenham Town, the teams finishing in that order.

Stroud, meanwhile, had restarted their Association club and had arranged fixtures against teams such as Gloucester and also Gloucester YMCA, Wycliffe College and Marling School.

Forest Green Formally Reappears

A report appeared in the 9 September 1898 *Stroud Journal* as follows under the 'Nailsworth Jottings' section:

> *The supporters of the Association football opened their season here on Saturday, on their ground at Forest Green, when the newly formed Forest Green Association and Nailsworth Saturday met. Notwithstanding the extreme heat, the game was fast. After an enjoyable game, victory rested with Forest Green by three to two, the winning point being gained through one of the Nailsworth backs kicking the ball through his own goal. E. Locke and S. Brinkworth notched goals for the home team, H. Locke registering two goals for Nailsworth.*

On Friday 23 September 1898 the *Stroud Journal* reported a meeting at which the amalgamation of the Nailsworth Thursday and Forest Green Rovers Association Clubs was approved, and the former handed over to the Rev. G.M. Scott, treasurer of the Forest Green Organisation, a balance of £1 1s 8d. The secretary, Mr Iles of Inchbrook, invited fixtures with other Thursday clubs, and stated there were a few open dates for the Saturday team. A long report then appeared in the *Stroud Journal* on Friday 7 October 1898 of the game between Chalford and Forest Green at Chalford, which Forest Green won 4-0. Thomas and William Brinkworth had both returned to the Forest Green team after two years away, being reported in the *Stroud Journal* as 'old Chalford men'. The two Marmont brothers, S. and C., were also reported to have had a good game.

E. Locke, having played for Woodchester the year before, now turned out again for Forest Green reserves in the return match against Chalford on the same day (which was drawn 2-2), scoring both Forest Green goals. The 'old' experienced players were all returning to the club. A return game was played against Chalford, reported in the Friday 2 December 1898 *Stroud Journal* that Rovers won 2-0; they were reported to be undoubtedly the better team. C. Marmont got both goals. Rovers continued with reported games, winning 7-0 against Stroud Juniors with both S. Marmont and C. Marmont scoring.

Meanwhile, Stroud Rugby Club were going from strength to strength and in the Friday 30 December 1898 *Stroud Journal*, a report is given of Stroud's victory over London Saracens by 1 goal and 1 try to 0.

Forest Green continued in their winning ways, beating Uley home and away, Craigmore College again (a return match), Sinwell Star and Wycliffe College. A long report is given in the *Stroud News* on 24 February 1899 of a match between Forest Green Rovers II and Woodchester juniors, which Rovers won 2-1. The team had become sufficiently established again to be running a reserve team.

In the first season of the DDL, all teams played 10 fixtures, the League being won by Brimscombe.

Forest Green Rovers had successfully re-established themselves in the local football world, becoming members of the Gloucestershire FA and the DDL for the following season, 1899/1900.

Forest Green Rovers AFC 1898/99. The names of most the players are currently unknown. A young Walter Brown is bottom right.

5

A New Century with the Red and Whites: 1899–1905

1899/1900

The club joined the Gloucestershire FA for the 1899/1900 season, the club being listed by the GFA as being formed the year before.

Date of formation: 1898
Secretary: T. Brinkworth, Forest Green
Colours: Red and white
Ground: Forest Green
Nearest railway station: Nailsworth
HQ: Jovial Forester, Inchbrook

This is the first official listing or documentation relating to the club. Rovers joined both the DDL and the Mid-Gloucestershire League for the forthcoming season. The *Dursley Gazette* recorded that Forest Green 'have not before been connected with any league, having been a well-known team for years'. The Rovers had actually been founder members of the Mid-Gloucestershire League five years before. They played their first home DDL match against Dursley on 4 November 1899, losing 3-2, the report noting that 'the Forest Green ground occupies a lofty position overlooking Nailsworth'.

The Mid-Gloucestershire League now included two divisions, with Division One being contested by Ebley, Gloucester, Brimscombe, Chalford, Forest Green Rovers and Stonehouse. Forest Green Rovers Reserves were playing in Division Two with eight other teams.

On 6 January 1900 Forest Green Rovers were due to play Dursley in the DDL at the same time that the England rugby team would play Wales at Gloucester. Rovers then lost 10-0 to Gloucester in the Mid-Gloucestershire League on 13 January 1900 having already lost 6-1 against Gloucester at home.

Rovers secured their first win in the DDL on 18 November 1899 away to Uley, winning 3-0, which was also the day of the fourth qualifying round of the English FA Cup. Among the matches, which were played in geographic divisions, Bristol Rovers drew 1-1 with Portsmouth, and Bedminster beat Bristol East 4-1, both in Division Ten of the cup. Rovers then played Chalford in a goal-less draw at Forest Green on 25 November 1899, followed by victory away, at Stonehouse, the following week 2-0. All the proceeds of the latter match were given to the Transvaal War funds of the Soldiers and Sailors Families' Association. 'Something over £4' was raised. The country was now at war against the Boers.

A draw with Brimscombe, the cup holders and current league leaders, was followed by a win against Uley with Forest Green finishing the century with 8 points and a mid-table position in the DDL, and 4 games played in the MGL, gaining 3 points to be second bottom of Division One. At the same time, Bristol City had managed to make it to the first round of the English FA Cup where they were to play Stalybridge Rovers in January 1900, the first-named club to have choice of ground.

Forest Green continued to do well in the DDL although they managed to lose 8-0 away to Ebley at the end of February 1900. No final league table has been found for either the Mid-Gloucestershire or the Dursley Leagues for the season.

Shortwood AFC Appears

Stroud Journal, *Friday 17 November 1899, 'A win for Shortwood Rovers'*
On Saturday last a capital Association match was played at Shortwood between Mr H. Gardiner's team and the Shortwood Rovers, captained by Mr R.W. Grant. Victory rested with Shortwood Rovers by one goal to nil.

This appears to be the first reported match of the Shortwood Club, who would become local rivals to Forest Green for the next century. The *Stroud Journal* of Friday 8 December 1899 contained a very brief report of the return match of H. Gardiner's XI against Shortwood Wanderers:

A pleasant return match was played last Saturday afternoon between Mr H. Gardiner's XI and the Shortwood Wanderers, resulting in another win for the Shortwood Wanderers by three goals to two.

The Boer War

In the latter part of 1899, Britain was at war in South Africa against the Boers. Many weekly war reports appeared next to Forest Green Rovers' match reports. The Anglo-Boer War finally ended in 1902 with the loss of over 11,000 young men, many of whom came from Gloucestershire.

1900/01

The local school teams were still very much a force in football and at the start of the 1900/01 season Wycliffe College were invited to join the Mid-Gloucestershire League. The school, however, declined to join. Forest Green again entered teams in the DDL and the Mid-Gloucestershire League Divisions One and Two. Shortwood had also joined Division Two of the Mid-Gloucestershire League, resulting in the first league derby matches between Shortwood and Forest Green Rovers reserves.

In the run up to Christmas, Forest Green may well have been accused of gamesmanship in the Mid-Gloucestershire League, trying to use the rules to their advantage. The rules applying to members with a first team and reserve team quite strictly required that players who turned out regularly for the first team could not play in the reserve team above a certain number of times. Forest Green hit on the idea of not arranging any Division One matches for the first half of the season so that they could play a stronger team in Division Two as Forest Green Rovers Reserves. The result was that the Reserves were lying second in Division Two in December 1900, whereas the first team were bottom of Division One having played no games. Forest Green finally played Gloucester in mid-December at Forest Green, losing 4–1, still a big improvement on the previous season.

In the DDL, Rovers were top of the league at Christmas with 12 points from 9 games. They had played 2 or 3 games more than any other team, probably because of their 'lack' of first-team fixtures in the Mid-Gloucestershire League. On Boxing Day the club held a fancy-dress match in the morning among themselves and entertained 'Swindon Wanderers' in the afternoon, acquitting themselves well and winning 8–0. With the turn of the year, all was well at the top of the hill.

Swindon Wanderers used to be a force in West Country football. They had entered the Bristol & District League for the 1894/95 season but withdrew without playing a game after most of their players jumped ship and joined Swindon Town because they didn't fancy playing Bristol & District League football. The Wanderers were deep in debt and finally had to give up their County Ground to Swindon Town (where they still play). They were rescued and entered the Bristol & District League for two years from 1894, seeing the league name change to the Western League in 1895. By the turn of the century Swindon Wanderers were again an amateur team.

By 1899, the Western League had a professional section but only Bristol Rovers, Bedminster, Swindon Town and Bristol City competed. Things were much brighter for the 1900/01 season and a much stronger professional league was formed by Portsmouth, Millwall, Tottenham Hotspur, Queens Park Rangers, Bristol City, Reading, Southampton, Bristol Rovers and Swindon Town. The Western League had a roll call of familiar big league names including the likes of Fulham, West Ham United, Southampton, Brentford, Plymouth Argyle, Brighton & Hove Albion and Chelsea. All of the big professional teams resigned at the end of the 1909 season to concentrate on their main competition, the Southern League, which had been extended, leaving no time for Western League fixtures any more. The Football League was also actively pursuing a policy to absorb Southern League teams into the Football League and the clubs did not want to be side tracked by the Western League. Many other professional provincial leagues still existed before the First World War, including the Birmingham League in which Bristol Rovers competed.

Forest Green, meanwhile, beat Stonehouse 3–1 to take a 4-point lead at the top of the DDL, while Chalford 'had a walk over Berkeley' on that Saturday, beating them 4–0. The Rovers still could not beat Gloucester in the Mid-Gloucestershire League, losing 5–0 in Gloucester at the end of April 1901.

Unfortunately, no final league table has been found for either the Mid-Gloucestershire or the Dursley Leagues for this season.

Forest Green at the turn of the century. Various postcards were published by local photographers and there was a keen market selling souvenirs to both locals and residents, including views of Forest Green. The following postcard was published just after the turn of the century and clearly shows the Jovial Forester and the goalposts of the pitch at upper Forest Green.

A close-up of the top left of the picture above, in which the goalposts can be seen (top left, to the right of the stone house), in the same position as The Lawn until 2006.

The Jovial Forester (centre left) from the same postcard, where the club's headquarters in the back garden can clearly be seen. The white-painted pub is from the same era as the picture of the Jovial Forester later in this chapter.

1901/02: The Makings of a Strong Team

The Mid-Gloucestershire League had ceased to exist at the end of the previous season, leaving Forest Green to compete only in the DDL. The reserve team arranged a card of 'ordinary' matches, mainly against those who had competed in Division Two of the MGL the previous year, as did Shortwood. The Dursley League descended into fiasco at the end of the season after a series of decisions by the committee, reported as follows in the *Stroud News* on 4 April 1902:

Stroud News & Gloucester County Advertiser, *Friday 4 April 1902*
The Brimscombe fiasco
  The committee of the DDL assembled at the Crown and Anchor hotel, Stonehouse, on Tuesday evening for their usual meeting …

The chairman said that the chief business of the meeting was to decide what the result of the Stonehouse v. Brimscombe match played last Saturday, should be. Mr Robins (Berkeley) proposed that the referee's report should be produced. The secretary said the game went well until within seven minutes of time, and then Price (Stonehouse) violently charged Webb (Brimscombe) and the referee at once gave a foul against Price, but Webb jumped up and kicked Price and he ordered Webb off the field. The crowd came on to the playing space, and the Brimscombe captain asked the referee to order Price off the field, which he refused to do; then the Brimscombe captain said he would not allow his team to play on …

Eventually Mr Robins, of Berkeley, proposed that the two points be awarded to Stonehouse. The proposition was carried by eight votes to three. The Brimscombe representatives then informed the committee that they had been instructed to tell them that they had done with cup and league competition altogether.

With regard to the match played between Stonehouse and Dursley under an unqualified referee, the Dursley representative said he had been instructed to say that they could not raise a team, and would forfeit the points, and the league committee decided to award Stonehouse a further two points.

Thus Stonehouse and Brimscombe were a tie as regards points, and the chairman asked those present where the match should be played. The Brimscombe representatives said there would be no match, because the Brimscombe team would not be there …

No final was played, with Brimscombe publicly declaring that the league was fixed. They then severed all ties with the DDL. The cup was presented to 'the Chocolate and Blues' and Stonehouse returned from Dursley in brakes to be met at 9 p.m. by the Stonehouse Band and a large crowd of people.

Forest Green's season was summed up in the *Stroud News* of 18 April 1902 as follows:

The Forest Green Club has just concluded their season. The club has had the misfortune to lose several players and, having no reserves, this was awkward. They have played 25 matches, won 11, drawn 7 and lost 7, and have scored 50 goals against their opponents' 32. The teams defeated were: Uley, Woodchester and Amberley (twice each), Berkeley, Wycliffe College, Dursley, Cirencester Victoria, Chalford, Kingswood and Ebley. Losses: Stonehouse (2), Brimscombe, Chalford, Berkeley, Dursley and Minchinhampton. Drawn games: Wickwar (2), Brimscombe, Kingswood, Wycliffe College, Ebley and St Michael's.

Forest Green Rovers 1901/02. The makings of a strong team. Walter Brown is again front right and Blake is the goalkeeper. The identity of the other players is currently unknown.

1902/03

The laws of the game had changed since 1889, when the club was first formed, including a rule limiting the number of players in a team to eleven. The setting out of the pitch followed almost exactly the modern-day layout and the game duration had been set at 90 minutes unless otherwise agreed on, with a maximum 5 minutes' break at half-time. The knock-on rule still applied and the goalkeeper could still roam anywhere in his own half and handle the ball. The two umpires had now been replaced by a referee accompanied by two linesmen.

The season saw the DDL going from strength to strength but this year without Brimscombe. It also saw the start of the Stroud League, in which Brimscombe competed. Nailsworth relaunched a football team, who played their first match against Dursley seconds in Nailsworth on 20 September 1902, winning 7-3. They had arranged a schedule of 'ordinary' matches against a mixture of reserve teams and non-league teams. Shortwood continued a schedule of 'ordinary' matches in the absence of a Second Division to either of the two local leagues.

At the beginning of the season almost half a page of the *Stroud News* was taken up with fixtures of various clubs, including Nailsworth AFC, but with no mention at all of any fixture list for Forest Green. Publicity was just not a priority for the club. By March 1903, Stonehouse were 4 points clear of Forest Green at the top of the DDL, with Forest Green lying second to Brimscombe in the Stroud & District League. Then, at the end of the season, Forest Green's fortunes took a turn for the better both on and off the pitch, emphasising again that nothing should ever be taken for granted in football. Stonehouse needed a point to secure the cup but lost 1-0 to Dursley, while Rovers beat Sharpness 3-2. With Stonehouse having blown it, and following on from the controversy last season, Rovers were about to challenge Stonehouse for the cup with a little help from the league committee.

Stroud News, *10 April 1903, Dursley & District Association League meeting*
A meeting of the Dursley and District Association Football League was held on Tuesday evening at the Bell and Castle Hotel, Dursley... With reference to the Forest Green v. Chalford match, which was to have been played on 28 March, when Chalford refused to play under the referee (Mr A. Baglin) it was decided to award the points to Forest Green, and also to report the Chalford club to the Gloucestershire Association. Kingswood were also reported by the Forest Green club for not putting in an appearance on the 26th instant (Thursday), a date that had been agreed upon by both clubs. The Kingswood representatives said they were quite willing to play the match on Good Friday, but the league rules state that all matches must be finished before 31 March, and it was resolved again to award Forest Green the points. This decision made Stonehouse (champions) and Forest Green equal in points, and it was necessary to play a final match to decide the championship.

The final was reported in the *Stroud News* on 17 April 1903 as follows:

The important contest had absorbed the interest of all football enthusiasts in the district, and in consequence a crowd of over 1,000 persons assembled to witness the match.
The teams faced each other as follows:
Stonehouse – H. Harrison, goal; A. Anderson and Sam Price (captain), backs; W. Box, C. Remes, and S. Perkins, half-backs; Sid Price, H. Anderson, Joe Price, C. Hall and H. Davis, forwards.
Forest Green – Blake, goal; Gardiner and W. Brinkworth, backs; Hill, Davis, and Taylor, half-backs; Grant, Marmont, Drysdale, Brown, and Brown, forwards.
Referee, Mr G. Bennett, (Fishponds); linesmen – Messrs F. Bright (Sharpness) and W.J. Pepworth (Dursley).
A strong wind was blowing from one side of the field to the other, Stonehouse winning the toss, gave Forest Green first advantage of the same. Stonehouse, however, were first to attack, and Hall several times beat the foremost line of the Forest Green defence, but was not supported as he should have been. Forest Green then returned the assault, and shortly got home, but the goal was disallowed on the ground that Harrison had been impeded. At half-time the scoresheet remained blank, there also being little to choose between either team. The second half too, was finely contested. Once Blake saved smartly from Sid Price, and Harrison brought off a similar feat at the other end. However, Forest Green were the first to score; Marmont, after beating Sam Price

Above left: Forest Green Rovers 1902/03, the first cup-winning team. From left to right, back row: G. Smith (linesman), W. Luker, O. Davis, A. Taylor, W. Brinkworth, H. Close, T. Brinkworth. Middle row: W. Hill, S. Marmont, H. Blake, G. Drysdale, W. Brown. Front row: F. Grant, A. Porter, F. Gardiner, W. Brown.

William and Thomas Brinkworth were members of the first reported Forest Green Rovers team in 1892. Owen Davis would go on in later life to be one of the most significant members of the club, enabling Forest Green to buy their own ground in 1936. Walter Brown was from one of two separate Brown families from Forest Green, whose members would have a connection with the club until the current day.

in fine style, netting very cleverly. Stonehouse on the restart, returned to their opponents' half, and Hall, with an exceedingly pretty piece of play, centring, Sid Price equalised for Stonehouse. The score remained that until the end, when it was decided to play another fifteen minutes each way. Directly after the changeover, Marmont put in a shot from some distance, which Harrison allowed to wander between his legs and into the net. After that, the Rovers had the best of the game, but no further goal was scored.

At the conclusion, amid loud cheering, the cup was awarded to the victors by Dr Campbell, the chairman of the league. There can be no doubt that Forest Green were the smarter team and that they lasted better. Marmont, for Forest Green, was the pick of the forwards. At Stonehouse (M.R.) Station, on the return of the team, the remark 'no conquerin' hero, no nuthin' was heard. Despite the importance of the game, and what the issue meant to either team, the contest was most friendly, and not once did unpleasantness arise.

The fifth league table for the DDL, 1902/03 was as follows:

	P	W	L	D	For	Against	Pts
Forest Green	12	8	2	2	30	17	18
Stonehouse	12	8	2	2	24	10	18
Wickwar	12	7	3	2	36	13	16
Sharpness	12	6	4	2	22	21	14
Dursley	12	5	6	1	24	23	11
Chalford	12	2	9	1	10	30	5
Kingswood	12	1	11	0	9	41	2

Right: Front of medal. The first silverware. A solid silver medal, measuring approximately 28mm across.

Far right: Back of medal.

Stroud & District League, 1902/03, the first season:

	P	W	L	D	For	Against	Pts
Brimscombe	12	8	1	3	48	14	19
Forest Green	12	8	3	1	25	19	17
Woodchester & Amberley	12	6	2	4	25	10	16
Cirencester Victoria	12	4	6	2	22	30	10
Minchinhampton	12	3	7	2	17	33	8
Ebley	12	3	7	2	17	27	8
Chalford	12	2	8	2	21	43	6

The winners of the leagues were awarded silver and sometimes gold medals as a token for their efforts for the season. The medal pictured above was won by Walter Brown, and passed through his family to his grandson Ray Brown, who sadly passed away in 2005. Both Ray and his father followed in Walter's footsteps, both playing for and winning medals for the Rovers.

This had been Forest Green's most successful season to date, but still no report of a club meeting, or a list of fixtures were published in the Stroud papers, while virtually every other local club had fixtures published in the football section of the paper.

Pubs in Nailsworth in 1903

A long report of the Nailsworth Licensing Session throws light on the local evening environment.

Stroud News & Gloucester County Advertiser, *Friday 13 February 1903*
Gentlemen,

I beg to state the number of licensed houses in this Petty Sessional Division of Nailsworth, Horsley, Avening, Minchinhampton and Woodchester is as follows: alehouses, 39; beerhouses (on), 19; beerhouses (off), 4; refreshment houses, with wine and grocers, 5; total, 67. The population of your Petty Sessional Division is 9,546 as presented in 1901, as against 9,916 in 1891, which gives an average of one licensed house to every 153 persons.

The bench then went on to consider the superintendent's report commenting as follows:
In Nailsworth there was an average of 1 public house to 100 persons. Within a distance of 300 yards, from the Crown to the Britannia, there were 6 public houses and 1 off-licence. The average for England was 1 to 326 ... Something should be done by way of restriction. At the same time they were disposed to do nothing arbitrarily, but they were anxious the brewers take the matter into their own hands and endeavour to make their own decisions as to the state of things before the next meeting. The figures were very striking indeed. They knew Nailsworth was a market town and was visited by many people at certain times but something should be done as regards the six licences within 300 yards ... The figures he had given were by no means satisfactory.

The Jovial Forester after a new lick of paint, and a new landlady, thought to be Mrs Smith. The landlord is still given as her husband, Sidney.

Nailsworth AFC

Nailsworth were first listed by Gloucestershire FA for the 1903/04 season, their date of formation given as 1901, with the following details:

Date of formation: 1901
Secretary: R.F. Bruton, Cossack Square
Colours: Blue and white
Ground: Tanners
Nearest Railway Station: Nailsworth
HQ: Subscription Rooms

Nailsworth continued to be listed as a playing team until the 1910/11 season, the ground moving from Tanners Piece in 1906 to Claycombe Field and then Malthouse Lane in 1907. J.W.D. Vick from Watledge was secretary in 1904, to be followed by J.B. Till until 1907 and then Mr A. Dee followed by Mr E. Dee in 1910. The Nailsworth Club were quite a nomadic side, their HQ moving year by year from the Coffee Tavern to Fountain Street, to the Temperance Hotel and finally to the Clothiers Arms in 1910.

1903/04

Forest Green kicked off their first season as champions with a match away to Stonehouse on 24 October 1903. They got their revenge, beating Rovers 7-2, with, 'Rovers seeming to go to pieces at the crossover'.

In mid-November, Sharpness, who were on a good run, were fully expected to send the cup-holders back to Forest Green minus a point. Rovers finished 3-0 winners, just going to show why football can be such an entertaining, unpredictable spectacle. Brimscombe visited Gloucester City in early January, losing 7-1. Gloucester was a strong team compared to those teams in the Dursley and Stroud Leagues.

Nailsworth AFC, thought to date from around 1903. Randy Bruton is at the left of the middle row and Fred Vick (Peter Vick's father) is second from the right of the front row. The parson on the left is probably the Rev. T.W. Metcalfe. Billy Hill, in the centre of the back row, was a bit of a character on a Saturday night after a few pints, always up for an argument.

By early March, Rovers were in second place to Dursley in the DDL and were holding third place in the Stroud League below Woodchester and M&SWJR. The latter team, Midland & South West Junction Railway, were based at Cirencester.

A short note summing up Forest Green's season is to be found in the *Stroud Journal*, 29 April edition under the title 'Nailsworth Jottings':

The Forest Green Association Football Club finished their season on Saturday by drawing with Cirencester Victoria, each side scoring two goals. The club started the season badly, but picked up at the end of October, and from then until 9 January did not sustain defeat. One of the team's best achievements was the defeat of Brimscombe in December at Forest Green. Matches played totalled 28 – won 13, drawn 5, and lost 10; goals for, 59; against, 62. Last season 28 matches were played – 16 won, 8 lost and 1 drawn, the scoring being 61 goals for and 45 against. W. Niblett has proved of great service to the club. A capital shot, he has placed 18 goals to his credit, and other scorers are E. Cridland 10, Dowdeswell 9, Marmont 6, Drysdale 5, C. Marmont and Grant 3 each, Taylor 2, Davis, Hartt and Kimmins 1 each.

The season was definitely not a disaster and, since their admission to the DDL in 1899, the club had become quite a force, albeit in local league football.

Stroud & District Association Football League 1903/04, no Dursley League table has been found:

	P	W	D	L	For	Against	Pts
M&SWJ Railway	14	11	1	2	60	20	23
Brimscombe	13	9	1	3	43	19	19
Woodchester & Amberley	14	9	0	5	35	25	18
Forest Green Rovers	11	5	2	4	28	25	14*
Ebley	12	4	1	7	17	28	9
Cirencester Victoria	13	3	3	7	23	33	9
Chalford	12	2	3	7	17	44	8
Minchinhampton	13	3	1	9	19	48	7

* 2 points awarded for non-appearance of Cirencester Victoria.

1904/05

Forest Green again competed in both the DDL and the Stroud League while Nailsworth continued, also in the Stroud League Division One. Nailsworth's season did not get off to a good start, losing 7-0 to Ebley in early September and then to Ebley Victoria 4-1 towards the end of September, and in October losing to Thornbury 4-1 while Nailsworth Reserves met Kingswood in Division Two of the DDL and were defeated 7-0.

Forest Green Rovers kicked off their DDL season late in September against Thornbury. The following report confirms that Forest Green wore red and white:

Stroud Journal, *23 September 1904*
Forest Green commenced their season on Saturday with a visit from the Thornbury team, which is a new one to the Dursley League. The match was played before a good crowd who were anxious to see the popular 'Red and Whites', and the new men included in this match, Reynolds, Evans and Bloodworth. The first named player is a capital player, hailing from Plymouth, a centre forward and a good shot. Evans is a recruit from the Woodchester second team and plays right half, while Bloodworth is last season's Nailsworth left-back.

The red-and-whites of Forest Green went on to lose the match 3-2, while the committee wrote to the league refusing to play again under the referee, Mr G. Bloodworth from Dursley. Rovers then played Nailsworth in a Stroud & District League match, winning 5-1, and by November were lying in fourth place in a league of nine teams, also beating Ebley Victoria 4-0.

Forest Green travelled to Wickwar by train for a DDL match on 10 December 1904. The report says that it is a curious fact that a strong team has never visited Wickwar from Forest Green. Half the team had been unable to leave work in time to catch the train to Wickwar in time for the match. It sounds as though the railway timetabling was having a detrimental effect on Forest Green's results at Wickwar.

Nailsworth played Forest Green at the top of the hill in the DDL towards the end of the season, the match resulting in a 1-1 draw, and then again played in the DDL, this time at Nailsworth when Forest Green won 2-1. Late in April, Forest Green beat Midlands & South West Junction Railway 3-1 before a record attendance at Forest Green. Sharpness went on to win Division One of the DDL with Forest Green third with 11 points, 6 points behind Sharpness.

Stroud & District League, 1904/05:

	P	W	D	L	For	Against	Pts
M&SWJ Railway	17	12	2	3	60	15	28
Brimscombe	18	12	3	3	62	20	27
St Michael's Gloucester	18	9	5	4	60	30	23
Woodchester & Amberley	17	9	4	4	33	20	22
Chalford	18	10	2	6	38	40	22
Ebley	16	5	2	9	23	31	12
Cirencester Victoria	18	4	3	11	27	46	11
Forest Green Rovers	13	4	1	8	26	43	9
Nailsworth	16	4	2	10	28	43	8
Ebley Victoria	16	2	0	14	16	64	4

Table is based on available results, and includes points deducted, awarded by the League.

6

Not so Hot on the Football Front: 1905–1911

1905/06

In September 1905, Forest Green decided to abandon their reserve team for the time being and entered both the Stroud League Division One and the DDL Division One. By October, after 5 games, Forest Green were second from bottom. In November, things picked up with Forest Green beating Ebley 4-0, but this didn't last and in March no games were won, leaving the club second from bottom of the Stroud League.

Stroud & District League, 1905/06, no Dursley League table has been found:

	P	W	D	L	For	Against	Pts
Woodchester	18	14	2	2	35	13	30
Brimscombe	17	14	0	3	66	12	30
Stonehouse	18	9	4	5	32	26	22
Stroud	17	7	4	6	25	22	20
M&SWJ Railway	16	9	1	6	36	28	15
Chalford	18	6	3	9	33	34	15
Nailsworth	17	4	4	9	13	40	14
Cirencester Victoria	16	3	3	10	17	29	9
Forest Green Rovers	17	5	1	11	22	39	9
Ebley	18	4	0	14	14	52	8

Includes points awarded and deducted by League.

1906/07

Forest Green, as usual, entered both the Stroud League and the Dursley League.

The season opened with the local derby against Nailsworth in the Stroud League, at the end of September 1906. Forest Green were defeated 5-0, their first defeat at the hands of Nailsworth. The defeat was a sign of things to come, and was followed by an 8-0 loss to Wickwar in early October and a 10-0 defeat to Sharpness at the end of the month.

By November, things were no better in either Division One or Division Two of the Stroud League and, at the end of November, R. Locke was suspended for fourteen days for an offence on the field of play. Forest Green were ordered to exhibit bills around their ground warning their spectators of penalties attending disorderly conduct. It would seem that the spectators were not particularly happy with the performance of their club this season.

The year 1907 continued in the same vein as the previous one. Forest Green did manage to beat Nailsworth in February in the Stroud League, but it was their only win that season. In the Stroud & District League, Rovers finished bottom with 0 points, having had 2 points taken away by the league committee for playing an ineligible player.

	P	W	D	L	For	Against	Pts
Brimscombe	16	13	1	2	54	15	27
Woodchester	16	12	1	3	45	12	25
M&SWJ Railway	16	10	2	4	28	12	22
Nailsworth	16	7	3	6	23	27	17
Chalford	16	7	1	8	30	35	15
Stonehouse	15	6	3	6	29	26	15
Minchinhampton	15	5	2	8	19	30	12
Amberley	16	3	1	12	24	30	7
Forest Green Rovers	16	1	0	15	10	69	0

No Dursley League table has been found.

1907/08

At the start of the season, in mid-September, Forest Green Rovers Reserves played a friendly against Shortwood, resulting in a 3-3 draw. Forest Green then lost to Stonehouse 4-1 in the DDL. Forest Green Rovers Reserves then beat Shortwood 1-0 in Division Two.

Stroud FC re-formed this season, playing in the newly formed North Gloucestershire League, but were strangely absent from the Stroud League. The Stroud papers were dominated by reports of the new Stroud team from the end of February until the end of the season. And so ended another mediocre season for Forest Green, a far cry from the early years of the century when the team would be expected to be competing at the top of the leagues.

Stroud & District League 1907/08, again the Dursley League table hasn't yet been found:

	P	W	D	L	For	Against	Pts
Brimscombe	14	10	3	1	49	20	23
Minchinhampton	13	8	1	4	34	26	17
Chalford	13	5	5	3	24	14	15
Forest Green Rovers	13	7	1	5	27	35	15
Woodchester	13	6	1	6	26	24	13
Nailsworth	13	3	3	7	13	29	9
Stonehouse	11	2	1	8	20	33	5

1908/09

In 1908, Forest Green competed in the Stroud League Division One and also entered a reserve team in Division Two, although they appear to have withdrawn from the Dursley League. The first game of the season was the local derby between Forest Green and Nailsworth at Nailsworth, which was played in front of a large number of spectators. The first half was very even, but Forest Green were unlucky in having a goal scored against them by one of their own players, Holmes having the misfortune to miskick and watch the ball rolling into his own net. The second half saw Forest Green having the best of the game, but luck was again against them and they were unable to score. Nailsworth got away and scored through Hill, winning the game 2-0.

In the meantime Stroud Football Club had entered their reserve team into Division One of the Stroud League, their first team playing in the North Gloucestershire League. Stroud Reserves beat Forest Green at Downfield 5-3 in September 1908.

Forest Green United Appears

A new team was reported this season at Forest Green with Forest Green United playing Chalford Thistle at Forest Green. Wilmot and Gardiner scored for United while C. Griffin scored the winner for Chalford with the result Chalford Thistle 3 Forest Green United 2. They were then again reported a week later playing against Nailsworth Church Lads' Brigade and also Spring Hill Rangers, winning the second game 16-0. E. Brown, C. Brinkworth, T. Holmes, E. Guy, G. Bathe and C. Stevens were the scorers. E. Brown (Gary) was to go on and be a lynchpin in the Forest Green team throughout the next twenty years. In October 1908 he was eleven years old! Forest Green United were a youth team.

Forest Green Rovers got their first points of the season at the end of November in a 2-2 draw against Chalford, with Stevens and Lusty scoring for the Rovers, and early in December Forest Green finally won a match against Minchinhampton 2-1, Teakle and Lusty scoring for the Rovers.

By March 1909, Forest Green applied to withdraw their reserves from Division Two as they could no longer raise a team. By the end of the season, Forest Green ended up seventh of nine and Woodchester became champions of the Stroud League Division One:

	P	W	D	L	For	Against	Pts
Woodchester	16	11	1	4	56	21	23
Stonehouse	16	10	1	5	44	22	21
Brimscombe	16	10	1	5	39	24	21
Nailsworth	16	8	3	5	29	25	19
Amberley	16	7	4	5	35	25	18
Chalford	16	6	3	7	23	31	15
Forest Green Rovers	16	5	1	10	19	44	11
Minchinhampton	15	3	2	10	18	43	6
Stroud (reserves)	15	2	2	11	16	45	6

Includes points deducted by League.

1909/10: Forest Green Enters the County Cup

Rovers again entered both Divisions One and Two of the Stroud League for the season, clearly feeling that they could raise a reserve team again, having disbanded it the season before.

Forest Green United were in action against a Nailsworth district team in early October, with the match ending in a goal-less draw. United were the smaller side, but had the better of things.

This year, Stroud entered their first team in Division One and their reserve team in Division Two of the Stroud League. A match between Stroud Reserves and Forest Green Reserves was reported in October 1909 as follows:

Stroud reserves journeyed to Forest Green with a fairly good team but unfortunately they had to meet a Foresters first XI. I am given to understand they played a plucky game although they were defeated by six goals to one. Up to the present Forest Green first XI have not yet played a game in the First Division and consequently nearly every match the reserves have fielded practically a first XI. Now this is very hard lines on the opponents they have met. The rules state that any player can play in a Second Division match providing he has not taken part in half or more of the First Division matches in the same season. It would seem that Rovers are perfectly in order but all the same I do not believe an eleven that consists of the first team should be put out in this way.

Forest Green were pulling the same trick they had used in the last century in the Mid-Gloucestershire League when no first-team games were played up until Christmas. Perhaps Forest Green were worried about their reserve team's strength, particularly after withdrawing the reserve team midway through the previous season.

Forest Green Rovers played Brimscombe away in the second round of the Gloucestershire Junior Cup at the beginning of November 1909, winning the tie 2-1. This is the first report found of Forest Green Rovers entering the County Cup competition. Although it was called the Junior competition, this was actually the main cup for all local amateur teams, the Senior Cup being for professional teams in Gloucestershire. For many years to come the Senior Cup was generally played for by Bristol City and Bristol Rovers. Forest Green went on to knock out Chalford in the next round of the cup.

In December, Forest Green Rovers played their first game in Division One, losing to Minchinhampton, and then beat Brimscombe in early January 1910. United, meanwhile, met Nailsworth Juniors in March 1910 and lost 4-0.

Rovers ended the season second from bottom with 11 points, with Woodchester again being champions. Stroud withdrew from the league after playing and losing 7 games.

Stroud & District League, 1909/10:

	P	W	D	L	For	Against	Pts
Woodchester	16	13	1	2	47	13	27
Chalford	16	12	1	3	49	22	25
Brimscombe	15	9	1	5	38	24	19
Amberley	15	7	2	6	31	24	16
Nailsworth	16	6	3	7	35	26	15
Stonehouse	15	5	2	8	39	22	12
Minchinhampton	16	4	4	8	18	36	12
Forest Green Rovers	15	4	1	10	22	27	11
Oakridge	16	2	1	13	8	81	5

Includes points deducted and awarded by League.

1910/11

The first win of the season arrived at the end of November 1910 in an away match with Nailsworth, which ended 3-1. Rovers again entered the Gloucestershire Junior Cup in October but this time lost 5-0 to Chalford in the first round.

In the meantime Forest Green United continued in their third season in October 1910, beating Tetbury Athletic 7-0, reported as a very good game, and then played Belmont, resulting in a 2-2 draw. By the end of the season, Forest Green Rovers finished seventh of eight in Division One with 10 points from 13 games, and the Reserves finished eighth of ten with 9 points from 15 games. The following intriguing report appeared in the *Stroud Journal* towards the end of the season:

> Stroud Journal, *14 April 1910*
> *In our last report of the Forest Green v. Sharpness game we were in error over the story that Mr Apperley the referee was bundled into the net and pelted with tufts of grass, this caused amusement among those present.*
> *Our information came from what we thought was a reliable source. A committee will sit on Saturday into the conduct of the Foresters' spectators who obviously didn't like a penalty being given against their team.*

Something had obviously happened the week before but whether the referee was actually thrown into the goal is in doubt. The supporters were not a happy bunch. The highs of Forest Green's early days were now long forgotten.

Stroud & District League, 1910/11:

	P	W	D	L	For	Against	Pts
Cirencester Town	14	9	3	2	44	22	21
Brimscombe	14	8	4	2	52	15	20
Woodchester	14	7	2	5	48	21	16
Chalford	14	6	4	4	32	17	16
Amberley	14	5	3	6	16	39	13
Stonehouse	14	3	6	5	20	25	12
Forest Green Rovers	13	3	4	6	14	29	10
M&SWJ Railway	13	1	0	12	8	62	2

Minchinhampton and Nailsworth AFC withdrew during the season.

7

Nailsworth and Forest Green United: 1911–1914

By the 1911/12 season, for a second time in their history, Forest Green Rovers were no more. The Nailsworth team had withdrawn from the league the season before and amalgamated with Forest Green Rovers. It is likely that there were simply not enough players to go around.

Further changes to the rules of the game included restricting the goalkeeper's use of his hands to the penalty area. Any player could still stand within six yards of a free-kick, the distance not being changed to ten yards until 1913.

Nailsworth wanted to amalgamate with Forest Green Rovers and maintain the Nailsworth name. Forest Green may not have objected – they were not strong themselves, and a separate set up in Nailsworth would only weaken them in the long run. No doubt the 1895 amalgamation of Forest Green Rovers to create a Nailsworth team had been long forgotten.

The team were listed by the Gloucestershire Football Association as follows:

Date of formation: 1911
Secretary: E. Dee, Nailsworth
Colours: Blue and white
Ground: Forest Green
Nearest Railway Station: Nailsworth
HQ: Jovial Foresters

The season started towards the end of September, with the newly formed 'Nailsworth and Forest Green United' winning 2-1 against Wickwar in the first round of the Junior Cup. In November 1911, Ramsay, the Nailsworth goalkeeper, was selected by the Gloucestershire FA to represent Gloucestershire against Bristol City reserves on Boxing Day. He was the first known player to be selected for the honour, which should not be underestimated even in today's climate.

By this time, three local leagues were well established in the Stroud area, including the recently formed North Gloucestershire League. Cheltenham Town played in the latter league and the Cheltenham & District League. By mid-March, United had a 4-point lead at the top of the Stroud League to second-place Brimscombe.

Ordinary matches were still commonplace and on 15 March the *Stroud Journal* reported a game between Wycliffe College, who beat Cinderford 2-1. In April 1912, Forest Green won their second cup.

Stroud Journal, *19 April 1912*
The interesting struggle for honours in connection with the First Division of the Stroud & District League eventuated on Saturday in Nailsworth and Forest Green United capturing the cup for the first time, and they are to be heartily congratulated on their fine achievement.

Their most formidable opponents were Brimscombe, who had a tough job on hand at Stonehouse, where they evidently suffered from the effects of the strenuous season, and lost by the odd goal in three. On the other hand Nailsworth were better situated being 'at home' to Chalford, and playing before one's home crowd is an advantage.

Nailsworth made arrangements for news of the progress of events at Stonehouse to be transmitted to them while their own match was being fought, and when it transpired that Brimscombe were down at the interval, Chalford's form fell off, and the rest of the journey was comparatively easy for Nailsworth, for whom Beale (2) and Blick scored. Shelford got one goal.

Brimscombe made a big effort to pull the match out of the fire in the second half at Stonehouse, and they were a bit unfortunate.

In the same paper, and next to the report of Nailsworth & Forest Green United's triumph, was a report of the loss of the *Titanic* with nearly 1,500 lives after a collision with an iceberg.

Stroud Journal, *3 May 1912*
Stroud & District Association Football League, Presentation of Cup at Nailsworth
Last Saturday a large crowd gathered on the Nailsworth and Forest Green United football field to witness the match Champions v. Rest of League. In the first half, with the wind in their favour, the champions were far the better side, and but for the fine defence of the league they should have been two or three goals to the good. The Nailsworth forwards were in fine form, and kept up a repeated attack. Cox on the right wing gave one of his best displays, his centres being splendid. In the second half the game was more even, and the league came within an ace of scoring once or twice. Ramsay dealt with one or two nasty shots being his usual good style. Towards the end Forest Green made desperate efforts to get the lead, Blick especially being prominent. The game eventually ended in a draw, there being no score.

But for the fine display given by the league goalkeeper Nailsworth would have won easily. They were the better team, each man being at his best. The league put up a good fight all through, but could not seem to settle down to each other's play.

Stonehouse AFC, 1911/12. They beat Brimscombe to hand the championship to Nailsworth and Forest Green United.

Nailsworth and Forest Green United, 1911/12. A young team, not all players are identified.

From left to right, back row: E. Dee (hon sec), W. Robinson, W. Brown, H. Harrison, W. Stephens, G. Brown (joint hon sec), E. Locke (linesman). Middle row: H. Cox, E. Blick, B. Ramsay, P. Rudge, W. Beale. Front row: J. Crease, G. Cowley, J. Brown.

At the close of the match the crowd gathered round a platform erected on the field. The secretary of the league, after announcing that Nailsworth & Forest Green United had been declared the champions in 1911/12, called upon the Rev. F.T. Smythe to present the cup.

The Reverend Gentleman was loudly cheered, and said he considered his a very great honour and privilege to have been asked to present the trophy. He assured the crowd that in inviting him to be there they had selected one who claimed to be second to none in the interest he took in football and all other forms of manly sport (applause). He remembered years ago when he lived at Bolton the inauguration of the Bolton Wanderers club, and since that time he had always evinced the greatest possible interest in association football (Hear, hear). Proceeding, the Reverend Gentleman said he believed that was the first occasion upon which Nailsworth had won the cup, though nine years ago Forest Green captured the Dursley League Cup (applause). He was very pleased to notice at the commencement of the season that the Nailsworth club and Forest Green had decided to join forces, and they could see what the result of this amalgamation had been. Through this they had won that handsome cup. It was far better to have one good club than half a dozen poor ones. He heartily congratulated the club upon the success they had achieved, and in respect of that afternoon's match he could not refrain from commenting in eulogistic terms upon the really fine display that Davis in goal had treated them to (Loud applause).

Bob Ramsay, the popular captain, received a great reception on stepping forward to receive the cup. He briefly returned thanks, remarking that in his opinion the club had well earned the cup, and he hopes the other teams in the league would agree that Nailsworth deserved it (Loud applause).

The blue-and-whites entered the record books as the second Forest Green team to win a football league trophy.

Stroud & District League, 1911/12:

	P	W	D	L	For	Against	Pts
Nailsworth & Forest Green United	10	7	2	1	21	11	16
Brimscombe	10	6	2	2	35	21	12
Cirencester Town	10	4	2	4	15	17	10
Chalford	10	2	4	4	13	15	8
Dyehouse & Woodchester United	10	2	2	6	19	26	6
Stonehouse	10	2	2	6	16	31	6

Amberley withdrew after 4 games, Brimscombe had 2 points deducted.

The second piece of silverware won by the club. This medal was won by Walter Brown, the only member of the team to have played in Forest Green's first cup-winning side in 1903. The medal measures 28mm in width.

1912/1913

The newly established Nailsworth & Forest Green United hoped to capitalise on their first season's exploits, entering the Dursley & District League Division One and the Stroud & District League Divisions One and Two for the second consecutive year but, by the turn of the year, all was not well in N & FGU camp.

Stroud News, *10 January 1913, Football, weekly summary*
Readers from my last week's notes will not be surprised to learn that the Nailsworth & Forest Green Club is no more. I cannot quite understand why a club of Nailsworth's standing should be allowed to go to the wall.

It will be remembered that two or three seasons ago they were compelled to drop their club. In the following it was decided to amalgamate with Forest Green and the club became known as Nailsworth & Forest Green United.

Matters however were not all rosy and there were a certain section of both Clubs' supporters who seemed to try and upset matters right from the time it was decided to amalgamate. Now, perhaps they are satisfied; they have brought out the crisis but with what result?

The committee have dealt with the matter according to the rules of the league. For scratching the match with Dursley they were fined 5s, also for scratching to Woodchester (third offence) they were fined another 7s 6d. Their application was refused until all fines concerned with the league are paid. When withdrawal is granted they are asked to pay another 10s and all their players will be banned from taking part in any Stroud League matches until all fines are paid. There is no doubt that several of the Nailsworth players are anxious to be transferred to another club but the committee will not grant this unless the above ruling is carried out.

For a second time in less than twenty-five years, an amalgamation, or annexe, involving the Nailsworth club had resulted in the collapse of Forest Green. This time we know that the financial penalties were quite severe and, with all players banned until all fines were paid, things did not look good for the future.

Stroud & District League, 1912/13:

	P	W	D	L	For	Against	Pts
Brimscombe	12	11	1	0	29	20	23
Dursley	12	7	1	4	30	20	15
Cirencester Town	12	5	4	3	15	13	14
Stonehouse	12	5	0	7	32	32	10
Chalford	12	3	3	6	18	24	9
Woodchester	11	3	1	7	22	27	7
Stonehouse Brush Works	11	1	4	6	15	43	6

Nailsworth & Forest Green United withdrew after playing 4 games, winning 2. Two of those points were deducted for playing an ineligible player.

1913/1914

No reports have been found of any activity in Forest Green for this season. It is not clear whether the fines levied by the Stroud League had been cleared to allow the formation of a new team or the registration of the old players. Probably not – who would clear them?

This would have prevented either a Forest Green or a Nailsworth team from re-forming for this season.

Stroud & District League, 1913/14:

	P	W	D	L	For	Against	Pts
Cirencester Town	12	8	2	2	21	15	18
Brimscombe	12	6	2	4	30	15	14
Stonehouse	12	6	2	4	25	16	14
Woodchester	12	6	2	4	21	22	14
Chalford	12	4	1	7	21	28	9
King's Stanley	12	3	2	7	17	31	8
Amberley	12	2	3	7	14	22	7

Stroud Rovers withdrew from the League after 10 games.

By 1914, the world had other things to think of.

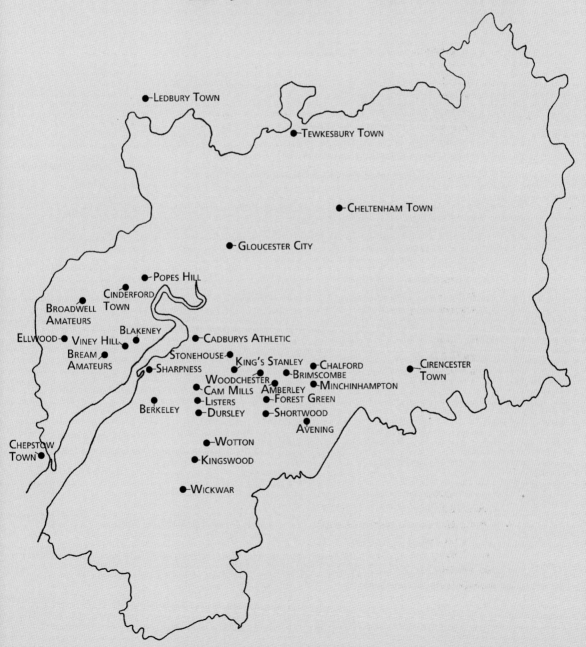

Part II
1919–1945

- Ledbury Town
- Tewkesbury Town
- Cheltenham Town
- Gloucester City
- Popes Hill
- Cinderford Town
- Broadwell Amateurs
- Blakeney
- Ellwood
- Viney Hill
- Cadburys Athletic
- Bream Amateurs
- Stonehouse
- King's Stanley
- Chalford
- Sharpness
- Brimscombe
- Cirencester Town
- Woodchester
- Amberley
- Minchinhampton
- Cam Mills
- Listers
- Forest Green
- Berkeley
- Dursley
- Shortwood
- Avening
- Chepstow Town
- Wotton
- Kingswood
- Wickwar

8

A New Beginning for Forest Green Rovers: 1919–1922

1919/20

Of the 231 young men from Nailsworth who joined up to serve in the First World War, forty-three are named on the memorial in Nailsworth, having never returned home. Names on the Roll of Honour at the cross in Nailsworth include those of E. Beale, W. Brinkworth and S. Marmont, names from a bygone Forest Green era.

> Stroud Journal, September 1919,
> Stroud & District Football Association Notes
> When war broke out in August 1914 the above league had made every effort for a record season. Then came the call to arms and by the beginning of September so many of these players had joined the colours that it was impossible for the clubs to carry out their programs. Many of the boys who at that time were looking forward to their favourite pastime have fallen on the different battlefields but their names will always live in the memory of those interested in the Stroud & District League.

Rovers got off to a fine start and by November 1919, King's Stanley were reported to have done very well against Forest Green Rovers, only losing 3-0, with the Stroud Journal noting that Forest Green were 'ranking among the premier clubs of the area'.

In December, Forest Green had a match with Chalford postponed because of a scheduled County Cup match with Cheltenham Town, which they lost 4-2. At the turn of the year, both Forest Green teams were at the top of their respective leagues, with Forest Green Congregational winning the local derby against Shortwood 3-1 on Boxing Day at the end of 1919 'on their own field'. By March, at the top of the league, it was becoming clear that Chalford, Forest Green Rovers and Stonehouse would fight it out for the championship and at the end of the season Rovers were tied on 21 points from 14 games with Stonehouse and Chalford, after Chalford had beaten Stonehouse in the final match 2-1 before a crowd in excess of 2,000. The second team were top of Division Three with Forest Green Congregational finishing runners-up in the same league.

A special meeting of the three clubs tied for first place was arranged and they were told that the league had obtained special permission from the GFA to extend the season until 8 May because of the triple tie. Under the English cup rules the teams were numbered 1, 2 and 3 and three balls with these numbers on were drawn out with Stonehouse and Forest Green contesting a semi-final on 1 May, the winners to meet Chalford on 8 May, both matches to be played at Fromehall Park.

> Stroud Journal, 23 April 1920,
> Forest Green v. Stonehouse, Stroud League semi-final
> All roads led to Fromehall Park on Saturday last, and an hour before the time to the kick-off there was quite a crowd clamouring for admission. It was not long before the ropes at either side with thickly lined with the large crowd. Colours of the rival teams were freely worn, and Forest Green had a mascot, one of their player's children dressed as a Pierrott. Several Stonehouse supporters, too, held mascots representing golliwogs; and rattles and megaphones were also in evidence.

The newly formed Nailsworth Brass Band was in attendance and played selections before the match and at half-time, and they are to be complimented upon the headway they have made in such a short time. With a little more practice they should prove one of the best bands in the district.

Both teams entered the field at about 3.15 and received a rousing reception from their supporters. Stonehouse won the toss, and decided to kick up the slope, defending the railway end. Brown was injured, but soon recovered. After even play Stonehouse came again to the attack, and their forwards, with pretty combination, got close in, and Smith beat Ramsay with a beauty. A fine bit of passing found the Rovers defence beaten, and Ramsay was again defeated with a shot in which he stood no earthly. Stonehouse supporters were naturally in high glee at the early success of the Magpies, but Forest Green stuck to their work manfully, the Forest Green halves and backs had to be smart in stopping their movements. Ramsay was again tested with a beauty, which he tipped over the bar in a masterly manner.

Half-time: Stonehouse 2 Forest Green Rovers 0

Rain began to fall heavily and playing uphill, and against the wind, Rovers put up a magnificent show. Stonehouse found it difficult to get past the halfway line, whereas Forest Green were constantly in the picture. Time after time Stonehouse repulsed the Rovers attacks. Back came the Foresters, and they forced a corner. This was beautifully placed, and appeared to be swerving into the net. Loud cheers from the Rovers supporters greeted the success and the game became very exciting. Cowley, the Rovers centre half, was playing a magnificent game, and time after time was loudly cheered for smart work. Beautiful centres from the right went begging, and from two of these Beale should have scored easily. For a few minutes Stonehouse kept up high pressure, and from fine passing Ramsay had to admit himself beaten by three goals to one, and about ten minutes to go. But right from the kick-off the Foresters went to the Stonehouse goal, and in less than a minute again reduced the lead. A daisy cutter, straight for the mark, was sent in. It was anyone's game now, and both sides were called upon by their supporters to score. Forest Green missed another glorious chance in the last few minutes.

Final score: Stonehouse 3 Forest Green Rovers 2

With a bit of luck the Rovers would have been on top. They had three or four fine opportunities in the second half. Whether it was open goals that seemed to mesmerise 'Paper' Beale it is hard to say, but usually such a fine shot, he was all at sea on Saturday. All the players of both sides did their best, but Scrubb Cowley was the best man on the field.

Forest Green had a settled team with a backbone of Bob Ramsay, the giant county goalkeeper, the brothers Brown in front of him and 'Paper' Beale tucking away the goals. 'Paper' Beale was interviewed in 1963 about his playing career, which makes interesting reading forty years on:

Stroud News & Journal, *25 January 1963,*

'Paper' Beale reminisces

Seventy-two-year-old Mr Walter Beale, or 'Paper' as he is much better known to his many friends, gave up active participation in the game of soccer before the Second World War, but the memories of over thirty years on the field are still as vivid to him now as they ever were.

How did he get the nickname, 'Paper'? 'Whenever anybody said something to me I used to reply 'on paper' and the nickname stuck,' he told us. 'Paper' played his first league match for Forest Green Reserves at Avening in 1904 when still at Nailsworth British School, occupying the inside-left berth – a position which he was to hold through the years that lay ahead.

He can tell how during the First World War he served with the 11th Gloucester's. He took part in local matches to raise money to buy cigarettes for his mates in the forces. His ability was recognised by the county selectors and he was chosen for the Gloucestershire team to meet Worcestershire at Fromehall Park, the game ending in a 2-2 draw.

Of course in 'Paper's' days, transport to away matches was by horse and brake, with the players also having to do some walking when they returned home from Wotton. The horse and brake went to the top of Wotton Hill, and waited for the players to make their own way up. And it was usually late at night when this happened. 'The public houses stopped open until 11 o'clock and it was always the next morning before we got back,' says 'Paper'.

One of 'Paper's' brothers, Harry Beale, played for Forest Green, while Harry's son 'Nip' Beale is the Rovers' first-team linesman. Who does he particularly recall in his own Forest Green side? Bob Ramsay in goal – 'one of the best sportsman who ever played football' – 'Scrubby' Cowley, Cecil Turner, and Ernie Brinkworth – 'the best partner I ever played with.'

Forest Green Rovers could once again hold their heads high, competing at the top of the League and finishing in a very creditable third place. Rovers were back.

The national rules of the game were now those familiar to us in the twenty-first century and at the same time, in May 1920, a Third Division was added to the Football League, embracing twenty-one members of the Southern League First Division. The Third Division (North) was added a year later in May 1921.

1920/21

Forest Green Rovers were officially listed by the Stroud League as follows:

Secretary: G. Brown, Northfields, Woodchester, Stroud
Colours: Black and white stripes
Ground: Forest Green
Headquarters: Jovial Foresters
Representatives: G.H. Brown and E. White

Forest Green Congregational were also listed as follows:

Secretary: L. Birt, Watledge, Nailsworth
Colours: All white
Ground: Nailsworth Cricket Field
Headquarters: Forest Green School
Representative: L. Birt

As well as the Stroud League, Forest Green also competed this year in the North Gloucestershire League against Cheltenham Town, the first league meeting taking place on 16 October 1920 at Forest Green. Gloucester YMCA were playing in the Thursday League at that time.

In September and early October 1920, Forest Green Rovers were unstoppable in both leagues. All games were won in both the First Divisions and the Third Divisions of both leagues. 'Paper' Beale was knocking goals in for fun for the first team. In the meantime Forest Green Congregational competed in Stroud League Division Four without success.

Rovers' blistering form continued in November, culminating in a 7-0 win against Brimscombe at the end of the month. By March 1921 Rovers were in contention for both leagues and it was reported that well over 1,000 spectators turned up to watch Rovers play Stonehouse in the North Gloucestershire League championship decider. 'Paper' Beale scored a last-minute goal to give Forest Green victory by the single goal. Forest Green then took on Stonehouse again, this time in the Stroud League.

> Stroud Journal, *15 April 1921*
> *Stroud League notes*
>   *By making a draw against Stonehouse last Thursday evening Forest Green made sure of the Division One championship by 1 point, it has been a fine struggle for them and we congratulate the champions on their success. Evidently the Rovers first eleven are going to win three more cups this season, they have already lifted two and look easy winners of the North Gloucestershire League, this is a record to be proud of.*

Forest Green Rovers won both the Stroud and North Gloucestershire Leagues, beating off Cheltenham Town in the first season that the two clubs had competed together in the same league. They had missed each other in the last century in the Mid-Gloucestershire League by

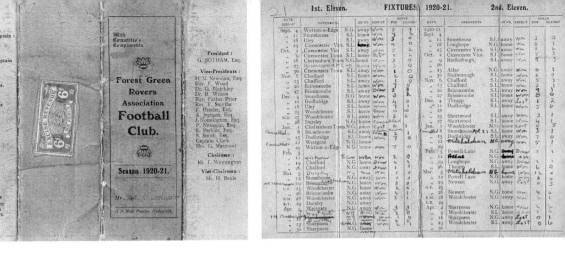

Above left and right: Fixture card for the 1920/21 season.

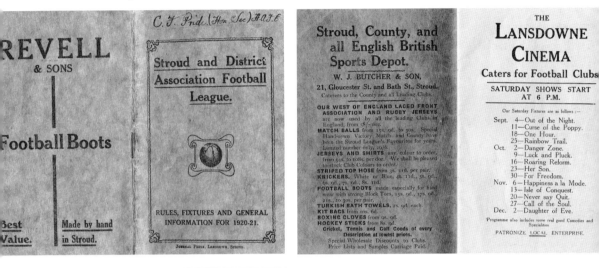

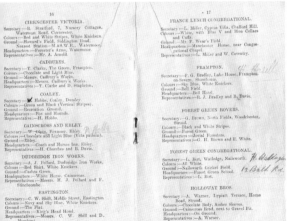

The Stroud League Handbook lists all clubs competing in the league, gives the details for Forest Green Rovers, and confirms Forest Green's change of strip to black and white stripes.

one season, Cheltenham joining the league the season that the Nailsworth club left it. They also won the Northern Junior Cup, which was competed for by all the amateur sides, the Senior Cup being played for by the professional sides. As was usual, Forest Green faced a final game of the season against a 'Rest of League' side but, having won two leagues, they played a representative team formed from both leagues.

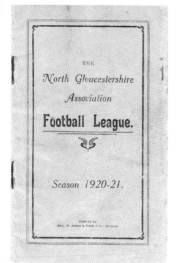

THE

North Gloucestershire

Association

Football League.

Season 1920-21.

PRINTED BY
GEO. H. JAMES & SONS LTD., STROUD.

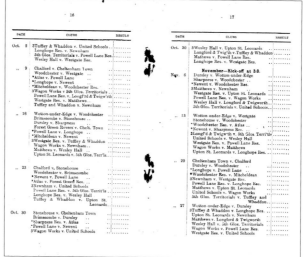

DATE	CLUBS	RESULT	DATE	CLUBS	RESULT
Oct. 2	3Tuffley & Whaddon v. United Schools		Oct. 30	3Wesley Hall v. Upton St. Leonards	
	Longhope Res. v. Newnham			Longford & Twig'th v.Tuffley & Whaddon	
	5th Glos. Territorial v. Powell Lane Res.			Mathews v. Powell Lane Res.	
	Wesley Hall v. Westgate Res.			Longhope Res. v. Westgate Res.	
,, 9	Chalford v. Cheltenham Town			**November—Kick-off at 3.0.**	
	Woodchester v. Westgate		Nov. 6	Dursley v. Wotton-under-Edge	
	*Atlas v. Powell Lane			Sharpness v. Woolchester	
	Longhope v. Newent			3Newent v. Woodchester Res.	
	*Mitcheldean v. Woodchester Res.			3Matthews v. Newnham	
	3Wagon Works v 5th Glos. Territorials			Westgate Res. v. Upton St. Leonards	
	Powell Lane Res. v. Longf'rd & Twig'r'th			Powell Lane Res. v. Wagon Works	
	Westgate Res. v. Matthews			Wesley Hall v. Longford & Twigworth	
	Tuffley and Whaddon v. Newnham			5th Glos. Territorials v. United Schools	
,, 16	Wotton-under-Edge v. Woodchester		,, 13	Wotton under-Edge v. Westgate	
	Brimscombe v. Stonehouse			Stonehouse v. Woodchester	
	Dursley v. Sharpness			*Woodchester Res. v. Atlas	
	Forest Green Rovers v. Chelt. Town			*Newent v. Sharpness	
	*Powell Lane v. Longhope			3Longf'd & Twig'w'th v. 5th Glos. Terri'ls	
	*Mitcheldean v. Newent			United Schools v. Wesley Hall	
	3Westgate Res. v. Tuffley & Whaddon			Westgate Res. v. Powell Lane Res.	
	Matthews v. Wesley Hall			Wagon Works v. Matthews	
	Upton St. Leonards v. 5th Glos. Terr'ls.			Upton St. Leonards v. Longhope Res.	
,, 23	Chalford v. Stonehouse		,, 20	Cheltenham Town v. Chalford	
	Woodchester v. Brimscombe			Dursley v. Woodchester	
	*Newent v. Powell Lane			*Longhope v. Powell Lane	
	*Atlas v. Forest Green Res.			*Woodchester Res. v. Mitcheldean	
	3Newnham v. United Schools			3Newnham v. Westgate Res.	
	Powell Lane Res. v. 5th Glos. Territ'ls			Powell Lane Res. v. Longhope Res.	
	Longhope Res. v. Wesley Hall			Matthews v. Upton St. Leonards	
	Tuffley & Whaddon v. Upton St. Leonards			United Schools v. Wagon Works	
				5th Glos. Territorials v. Tuffley and Whaddon	
Oct. 30	Stonehouse v. Cheltenham Town		,, 27	Wotton-under-Edge v. Dursley	
	Brimscombe v. Dursley			3Tuffley & Whaddon v. Longhope Res.	
	*Sharpness Res. v. Atlas			Upton St. Leonards v. Newnham	
	*Powell Lane v. Newent			Matthews v. Longford & Twigworth	
	3Wagon Works v. United Schools			Wesley Hall v. 5th Glos. Territorials	
				Wagon Works v. Powell Lane Res.	
				Westgate Res. v. United Schools	

LEAGUE CLUBS—GENERAL INFORMATION

Name of Club.	Secretary's Name and Address.	Captain	Colours	Ground	Headquarters	Telegrams or Telephone
Atlas, Div. II.	G. A. Vincent, Atlas Works, Glo'ster		Black Shirts, White Facings	Hempstead	Atlas Works' Ambulance Room	Tel. Vincent, Atlas, Glo'ster 'Phone 86, Glo'ster
Brimscombe, Div. I.	C. Adams, York Villas, Thrupp, Stroud	S. Evans	All White	The Meadow	The Polytechnic	Tel. Latham, Brimscombe
Chalford, Div. I.	W. Pritchard, Oaklands, Chalford Hill	O. Griffin	Red Jerseys, White Collar and Cuffs	The Sycamores	Duke of York Chalford Hill	Tel. Pritchard, Oaklands, Chalford
Cheltenham Town Div. I.	A. J. Parr, 5, Marlborough Place, Cheltenham.	E. J. Chard	Red Jerseys, White Knickers	Whaddon Lane	Imperial Hotel High Street	Tel. Parr, Marlboro' Place, Cheltenham
Dursley, Div. I.	H. E. Hewish, 19, Rosebery Terr., Dursley	W. Hewish	Scarlet Jerseys	Town Recreation Field	King's Head Inn	Tel. Hewish, 19, Rosebery Terr., 'Phone 41, Dursley
Forest Green Rovers, Div. I. & II.	G. H. Brown, Northfields, Woodchester	G. Cowley, 1st XI. W. Freeman, 2nd XI.	Black and White Stripes	Headquarters	Jovial Foresters	Tel. Brown, Northfields, Woodchester
5th Glos Territorials, Div. III.	F. L. Speck, Drill Hall, Glo'ster	F. G. Speck	Red & White or Red & Blue	Hempstead	Drill Hall, Brunswick Road	Tel. Speck, Drill Hall, Glo'ster 'Phone 998
Longford and Twigworth Div. III.	W. Cronoh, Longford, Glos	O. Hayward	Dark Blue, White Yoke	Longford	Club House	Tel. Cronoh, Longford, Glos.
Longhope, Div. II. & III.	O. C. Bradley, Sunnyside, Longhope	O. Sterry, 1st XI. P. Williams, 2nd XI.	Royal Blue, White Star. White 2nd XI.	Near Latchen Room	Latchen Room	Tel. Bradley, Sunnyside, Longhope
Matthews A.F.C. Div. III.	H. W. Baylis, Matthews Docks, Glo'ster	W. E. Leppington	Royal Blue, White Knickers	Hempstead	Nelson Inn, Southgate Street	Tel. Baylis, Matthews Works, Glo'ster

North Gloucestershire League Handbook, 1920/21 season.

Stroud Journal, *22 April 1921*

Saturday's match and presentation of Cups

Forest Green Rovers v. Pick of Leagues

The Rovers defended the Rodborough end, and consequently had the slope in their favour. Play opened very even, but the Leagues were the first to become really dangerous. Then the Rovers pressed, and from good work Blackwell was tested and saved a shot, but the greasy condition of the leather caused him to drop the ball and Rovers were one up, Alway being the scorer. The Leagues attacked and Ramsay, sidestepping to avoid one opponent, put in a kick which was taken off his boot by Elmer through good following up and the ball was in the net.

In the second half play travelled from one end of the field to the other and many good attempts were made by each side. Towards the end of the game the Foresters were a better side and had hard lines in not getting the lead. The defence on both sides held out, and the game ended Forest Green 1, League 1.

In handing the North Gloucester Trophy to Mr Cowley, Mr C. Lee Williams congratulated the Rovers upon their success. The occasion reminded him of the 1912/13 season, and he thought they ought to remember those who played the game that season but who had been called upon to make a great sacrifice during the years of war. They had played the game on the playing fields at home and on the battlefields, and he firmly believed they were still playing the game. Mr Dan Rowles then spoke on behalf of the Stroud League.

Captain Cowley, who was greeted with loud cheers, returned thanks, and said that he thought the Rovers deserved the rest, as they had been cup fighting ever since Christmas. He considered the success of the Rovers was due to the fact that they had been a united family on both the playing fields and in the committee room. He was very proud of his team's success.

Later, both teams, together with the league officials, sat down to an excellent tea at the Premier Cafe, Stroud. After tea the players made a move for the top of Rowcroft, where two brakes, decorated with club colours were in readiness to take them back to Nailsworth. Two cups were allocated to each conveyance.

At Inchbrook there was a large crowd waiting and, after the cups had been christened, the Nailsworth town band headed a procession and played popular marches. There was great excitement, and cannon firing was going on in the district. The team made a triumphant entry into Nailsworth, the streets being crowded with spectators who gave the Rovers a hearty reception. After a brief rest, the procession was re-formed and, after parading the town, a move was made to the club's headquarters, the Jovial Foresters, Forest Green. Here much enthusiasm was displayed and the festivities were kept up until a late hour.

We question whether such a large crowd has ever been seen before in the streets of Nailsworth.

Reminiscences by Lilian Northwood, resident of Forest Green, taken from the book entitled *Forest Green Lily* and published in 1997

Lily was born in Forest Green in 1909 and grew up in a cottage close to the Jovial Forester.

Forest Green was one of the best sides when I was a girl. The club had two mascots and one of them was my cousin Ernie Beale. Everyone knew Ernie's father, Walter 'Paper' Beale. He was a regular player for several years. My Dad, George Hart, played for the team for about two years from 1904.

After the Great War, Forest Green won lots of cups. One fine summer's evening most of the villagers celebrated that marvellous achievement by marching behind the Nailsworth town's silver band and the victorious side to the club's headquarters at the pub. The Rovers' black-and-white flag fluttered proudly in the breeze. After the refreshments and celebrations, we all gathered outside where the band provided music for dancing in the road. It certainly woke up Forest Green.

The Rovers supporters used to sing:

We are the Forest Green Rovers
Our forwards are hot on the ball
Our half-backs and full-backs want beating
And the goalie they can't beat at all

Chorus

Where will they be when the Rovers take the running?
Where will they be when the've done their level best?
Where will they be with all their strength and cunning?
Ten to one on the Rovers and nothing on the rest

Forest Green Rovers 1920/21, the full squad. Winners of Northern Junior Cup, North Gloucestershire League Div 1, Stroud & District League Div 1 & 3, Challenge Cups. S. Dangerfield, H. Harrison (joint hon sec), W. Curtis, W. Harrison, E. White, W. Turner, C. Gardner, W. Brown, E. Brown, E. King, R. Ramsay, H. Smith, J.V. Brown (hon. treas), A. Gardner, A. Lusty, G.H. Brown (sec), B. Turner, H. Evans, G. Cowley (capt), W. Freeman, C. Blick, A. Dangerfield, C. Turner, G. Iles, W. Leonard, H. Beale, P. Rudge, J. Smith, F. Turner, A. Cleveland, D. Vines, A. Bingle, S. Haines, W. Beale, E. Brinkworth, H. Always, O. Harrison (linesman), S. Dee (linesman), T. Heeley (mascot), E. Beale (mascot), P. Wilmot, R. Creed. Mr H. Beale was club chairman.

Forest Green Rovers first team, 1920/21. Winners of the Northern Junior Cup, North Gloucestershire League, Division One Stroud & District League, Division One Challenge Cups. From left to right, back row: G.H. Brown (hon sec), E. Brown, R. Ramsay, J.V. Brown (hon treas), W. Turner, S. Dee (linesman). Middle row: P. Wilmot, B. Turner, G. Cowley (capt), C. Turner, P. Rudge, H. Harrison (joint hon sec) H. Beale (chairman), J. Smith, F. Turner, H. Alway, A. Cleveland, W. Beale, E. Brinkworth. Front row: T. Heeley (mascot), E. Beale (mascot).

1921/22

The previous season was going to be a hard act to follow. Forest Green entered both leagues again and kicked off in September with a 0-0 draw away to Chalford. In October 1921, a report of the game between Brimscombe and Forest Green stated, 'So long as soccer games in the Stroud district keep up the high standard of the match on Saturday last between Brimscombe and Forest Green, so long will the soccer game remain supreme around us. It was a topping game to watch from start to finish and both teams might well be proud of such an an exhibition.' Rovers lost the game.

Stroud Journal, *27 January 1922*

Cheltenham Town v. Forest Green Rovers (North Gloucestershire League)

Town's Ground-Record Broken

The return match between the above teams was played at Whaddon Lane on Saturday afternoon, with their ground in a similar condition as it was when the Foresters visited the town last year and lost by the only goal scored. Earlier in the season Cheltenham had visited their opponents, but lost by the odd goal in five. Both clubs lined out their strongest teams, as under, Cheltenham with a determined intention to preserve their ground record.

Cheltenham Town

Abbotts; Simmonds (capt), Preece; James, Buckland, Young; Tovey, Woodrow, J.R. Surman, Langford, Marquis

Forest Green Rovers

Ramsay; J.V. Brown (capt), E. Brown; C. Turner, G. Cowley, F. Turner; A. Smith, W. Beale, A. Cleveland, J. Smith, J. Whitfield

Cheltenham went great guns for the first quarter of an hour, the ball hovering about in the visitors' goal in the most dangerous manner ... At the end of fifteen minutes the visiting halves, especially C. Turner, commenced to feed the forwards, who soon showed their superiority in combination. The centre forward made no hesitation in letting the ball go, and for the next ten minutes Forest Green had all the game ... Whitfield put in a long first-time grounder, which forced its way through Abbott's hands into the net. Beale pegging away, the Foresters forwards came again and, following a fine piece of combination, the ball was sent in to Cleveland, who put in a grand lightning shot, a foot from the ground into the corner of the net.

Half-time; Forest Green Rovers 2, Cheltenham Town 0.

The Town went off again on the restart and Buckland had very hard lines with a fine dipping shot that Ramsay just tipped over the bar. Cleveland led the Forest forwards away again for another five-minute spell but with Young defending well they failed to score, as did Cheltenham who took the next turn and attacked strongly, but found the defence sound. Thus the game continued for a long time, each side taking periodical spells but, twelve minutes from time, when Cheltenham were attacking, the referee took the unusual but perfectly legitimate policy of enforcing the rule preventing shouting at the man to put him off his shot, and ordered a free for Cheltenham. Buckland dropped the ball right at the goalkeeper's feet, Simmonds shot against his legs, the ball glancing off across the goalmouth, so that Surman had only to tap it into the net. Immediately on the kick-off Cleveland again led the Forest forwards in fine style, passed to J. Smith and he across to Beale

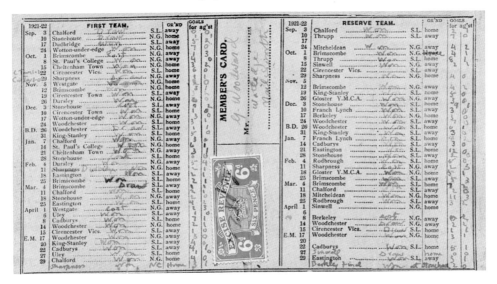

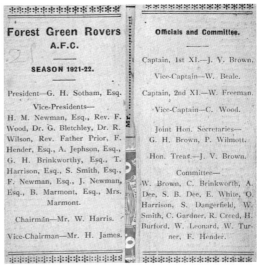

Forest Green Rovers fixture card 1921/22. The fixture list shows fixtures for both the Stroud League and the North Gloucestershire League, bringing Forest Green Rovers' second season of competitive matches against Cheltenham Town in the North Gloucestershire League Division One. Forest Green Rovers won both matches.

Gloucester YMCA (soon to become Gloucester City) were competing in Division Two of the North Gloucestershire League against Forest Green Rovers Reserves.

at inside left then dribbled to within a yard of goal and then beat Abbotts easily thus making sure of breaking the Town's ground record which had lasted since Boxing Day 1920. Forest Green fully deserved their victory, for their forwards were far and away the superior line.

Final score; Forest Green Rovers 3, Cheltenham Town 1.

By the end of the season Forest Green had emulated the champions of the year before and won another four cups, including the First Divisions of both leagues. Despite doubts that the 1922 season could live up to the year before, it had proved a roaring success.

Stroud Journal, *5 May 1922*

Forest Green win four cups, a grand record

Last season Forest Green created a record by lifting four cups, there were many of us who were of opinion that such a fine achievement would not be recorded in the Stroud district for many years. The Rovers, however, have again surprised everyone by again carrying off four trophies. They lost the Northern Cup, but their reserves on Saturday captured the Second Division North Gloucestershire League in a final with Berkeley played at Stonehouse. Naturally the Rovers and their supporters are again jubilant, and there was great

Forest Green Rovers 1921/22 the full squad. Winners of North Gloucestershire League Divisions One and Two and Stroud and District League Divisions One and Three. Challenge Cups season 1921/22.
C. Brinkworth, R. Creed, E. White, W. Turner, A. Whiley, S. Dangerfield, P. Wilmot, (joint Hon. Sec.).
W.H. James, H. Burford, E. Evans, R. Beale, H. Brown, R. Ramsay, A. Porter, J.V. Brown (Capt. 1st XI, Hon. Treas.), G. Iles, W.J. Harris (Chairman), G.H. Brown (Hon. Sec.). H. Watts, P. Rudge, C. Turner,
W. Seymour, J. Smith, D. Vines, A. Cleveland, W. Beale, E. Brinkworth, A. Stephens, A. Bingle, T. Haines.
S. Dee (linesman), C. Blick, G. Cowley, B. Turner, E. Beale (mascot), T. Heeley (mascots), F. Turner,
W. Freeman (Capt 2nd XI), A. Dangerfield, O. Harrison (linesman).

excitement in Nailsworth on Saturday evening, when a triumphal march was carried out through the town with band playing and cups held aloft. Cheers were given for the champions, and a procession was formed and a triumphal march made to Headquarters, to the strains of See the Conquering Heroes Come.

After the players had changed into mufti both teams assembled in the clubroom at the Foresters Arms. Here a substantial tea with everything of the best had been provided by Mrs Smith the landlady. Three of the cups were on the tables and were much admired. Mrs Smith, with a willing band of lady helpers, was soon busy seeing to the wants of the players. The Forest Green Club were fortunate in having such headquarters and fine accommodation. He had heard nothing but praise from visiting clubs and also referees as to the manner in which Mrs Smith provided for their comfort week after week.

The Rovers Reserves then arrived in high in glee with the cup they had captured that day against Berkeley, and needless to say they were heartily congratulated. Mrs Smith again showed her kindness by also providing tea from this contingent and also the band. Later, a procession was formed and the Nailsworth streets paraded by large crowds. Later on, the officials and players with supporters wended their way back to headquarters, where the grand wind up to 1921/22 was brought to an end.

9

A Countywide Competition: 1922–1926

1922/23

The 1922 season brought about a major change to local amateur football in Gloucestershire. Until this time clubs competed in a multitude of leagues, mostly with divisions of ten or fewer teams. The Gloucestershire FA was keen to resolve the situation and were in favour of the creation of a single senior league for Gloucestershire, which would give the clubs the opportunity to improve the standard of their football.

In an attempt to overcome travelling difficulties to and from Bristol, a Northern Council of the Gloucestershire Football Association was formed in 1919. This had the effect of splitting the county in two. As years went by the north became detached from the Gloucestershire County FA, which became an almost exclusively Bristol-orientated organisation.

The Gloucestershire Northern Senior League came into existence in June 1922 with the full backing of the local leagues, who effectively became feeders to the Senior League. Forest Green Rovers were invited to become founder members along with Cheltenham Town, Gloucester YMCA, Stonehouse, Chalford, Brimscombe, Cinderford, Sharpness, Wickwar, Woodchester, Kingswood, Wotton, Dursley Town, Dursley Rovers, King's Stanley and Broadwell Amateurs.

For the first time a league existed with a sufficient number of teams to fulfil a fixture list for a season. The reserve teams carried a rule that 'Any player who has taken part in half or more than half of any club's matches in the Gloucestershire Northern Senior League, shall be ineligible to play for the reserve side.'

Forest Green found that the better standard of opposition brought about a more testing time. There were no weak links. By the end of 1922 the first team was competing well, beating the likes of Sharpness, Woodchester and Wotton quite comfortably while losing to the new opposition from the Forest of Dean such as Broadwell Amateurs.

The Stroud Hospital Cup was founded on 4 July 1922, at the AGM of the Stroud League. The competition followed on from Forest Green's play-off at the end of the 1919/20 season where all proceeds from the play-off game against Stonehouse, and the final decider, went to the hospital, the games raising over £60, quite a sum in 1920. The formation of the Hospital Cup was an attempt to ensure a regular donation from the league to the hospital and it attracted twenty-six entries in its first season.

In the Hospital Cup the reserve team had been playing in the early rounds, and then Forest Green Rovers fielded their first team in February against Tetbury in the semi-final. Forest Green won 3-1, leaving them to face Avening in the final. Tetbury lodged a protest, claiming that the cup competition was for teams competing in the Stroud League but the protest was not upheld, with the Cup Committee pointing out that the competition was for clubs and not teams. Forest Green had done nothing wrong but in following years the Hospital Cup was split into a senior and a junior section.

Forest Green played 4 games in the Senior League over the Easter break, beating Gloucester YMCA 4-1 in the last of 4 Easter matches.

Stroud Journal, *12 May 1923*
Stroud Hospital Cup Final, Forest Green defeat Avening
   Both teams were anxious to win the trophy and thus have the honour of being the first winners of such a popular competition cup. In spite of the somewhat inclement weather, a large crowd assembled and both sides were well represented. Prior to the commencement of the match the Nailsworth town silver band played selections and they also played the champions off the field at the close.
   The game commenced at a fast pace, both teams appearing to be evenly matched, Stratford then headed in well out of the goalie's reach; the scoring opened with first blood to Avening. Forest Green attacked vigorously, but Vines was unfortunate in a subsequent attempt. The same player put another shot in later, but the goalie managed to clear. Shortly afterwards Furley transferred to Brinkworth on the left wing and that player scored with a shot from a somewhat oblique angle. Even play followed and half-time arrived with the score: Avening 1; Forest Green 1.
   On the resumption, play favoured Forest Green who pressed stoutly but the Avening backs were sound, and scored another goal. W. Seymour scored one for Forest Green. The score was unchanged when the final whistle went, each side having scored two goals. It was therefore decided to play extra time, during which a corner was forced by Forest Green and a good goal scored by Furley. Forest Green thus ran out winners by 3 goals to 2.

Forest Green finished their first season, winning the inaugural Hospital Cup and finishing fourth in the Northern Senior League having won 18 of their 30 matches. E. Brinkworth of Forest Green played in the Rest of League team against champions Brimscombe in the final game of the season. King's Stanley finished bottom and, after the test match system playing against other teams wishing to join the league, lost out to Tewkesbury Town, who entered for the first time.

1923/24

The second season in the Northern Senior League again saw Forest Green having to work hard, losing at home in September to Cheltenham Town 3-2, and Broadwell Amateurs from the Forest of Dean. Their form picked up with a 3-3 draw against Brimscombe in October, followed by an 8-1 thrashing of Kingswood, their first win of the season.

The behaviour of some of the Forest Green supporters merited coverage in the *Stroud Journal* for all the wrong reasons at the beginning of April when Mr C. Tanner, a Forest Green spectator, struck Mr A. Wingfield, the Stonehouse linesman, in the face. Tanner in his defence said that the linesman had threatened him and lifted his hands whereupon he, thinking that he was about to be struck, hit out in self-defence. The council recorded the institution of police court proceedings against Tanner, who would be suspended *sine die*.

The cost of running a team in the Northern Senior League was certainly considerable compared to the Stroud League. It is unlikely that the move to the Senior League was accompanied by increased admission charges or even an increase in the crowd and financial pressures on the Little Club on the Hill were probably building. Forest Green Rovers withdrew from the league at the end of the season.

Sharpness won the league, with Forest Green Rovers finishing in sixth place with 35 points from 30 games. E. (Gary) Brown was selected at right-back for the Rest of League team to play Sharpness. After three very successful years, Forest Green Rovers finished with no silverware but had shown that they were more than capable of competing with the best amateur teams. The committee were not prepared to allow the club to run itself into financial trouble.

Forest Green Move to Nailsworth

Until this time, it is certain that Forest Green had played on a field at the top of the hill, a ground that is clearly visible in a photograph taken around the turn of the century. But the club did not own the ground. For some reason the club left Forest Green for the 1924/25 season, probably through necessity. It moved down into Nailsworth for two seasons and then moved back to The Lawn, its newly improved field for the 1926/27 season.

A report appears in the *Stroud Journal* on 12 September 1924 of a match between Forest Green Rovers and Brimscombe Thistle, stating that the match 'was played on the Rovers' new ground', Forest Green winning the Second Division match 8-2. Ray Davis, son of Owen Davis who played around the turn of the century, lived in a house near the present day site of Hayes Road, close to the Jovial Foresters. He clearly remembers watching Forest Green play near Hayes Road as well as in Nailsworth.

Having spoken to many people while researching the history, we have heard talk from those connected with the club at this time, but now sadly no longer with us, of Forest Green matches played in Nailsworth at Tanner's

RAY DAVIS

We used to live up near where Hayes Road is now and I remember as a kid they used to play there. When mother lived next door to the field as you might say, we could watch them out through the bedroom windows. That would have been when I was very young, in the 1920s.

Piece (now located in the middle of Park Road), Enoch's Field (now King George V Playing Fields) and at Hayes Road close to the Jovial Foresters.

Forest Green Congregational also played football in the Stroud League, with their headquarters in Nailsworth, playing on the Nailsworth Cricket Field, according to the 1920 *Stroud League Handbook*. The Congregational team may well have played its football from 1919 in Nailsworth and also have played at Hayes Road where a 'football pitch' size field was recorded in the early tithe maps as being owned by Forest Green Congregational church.

1924/25

Forest Green returned to the Stroud League with the first team in Division One and the second team in Division Two. There would have been a shortage of fixtures for the coming season. Back in the Northern Senior League, Gloucester YMCA formally changed its name to Gloucester City, the team that still exists today.

The first team won their first game in September 1924 against Whiteshill 12-0, followed by wins against Stonehouse, Chalford and Woodchester. All the latter teams were still playing in the Northern Senior League, leaving Forest Green to compete against their Reserves, all a bit of a comedown from the previous seasons.

The first team were having a good run in the Senior Amateur Cup, reaching the second round in February in a match played at their new home:

Stroud Journal, *6 February 1925*
Northern Senior Amateur Cup second round
Forest Green Rovers v. Aylburton Institute
*   The game at the Enoch's, Nailsworth, on Saturday between Forest Green and Aylburton, a Forest team, proved very exciting despite the wretched weather conditions, and the homesters, proving themselves the superior side, ran out winners by no fewer than six goals to two.*

In February 1925, the *Stroud Journal*, which had been doing a series of articles on local footballers published a small biography of Cecil Turner, the Forest Green player:

Stroud Journal, *20 February 1925*
*   Who's who in football, local biographies*
*   Cecil Turner*
*   Cecil belongs to a family well known in local football circles and he is one of the quartet of brothers who are among the best-known players in the county. He is undoubtedly a tower of strength to his team of Forest Green Rovers. He started playing about 1907, appearing first for the Nailsworth Reserves, and later he joined the now-defunct club Dyehouse Rangers. The following season, however, Dyehouse amalgamated with Woodchester, but this arrangement was short lived, the Rangers soon resuming their former Constitution. Cecil continued to play for the Rangers until the war.*
*   He was a member of the Forest Green club in 1920-21 when the Rovers made a collection of four cups, viz; the Stroud & District and North Gloucestershire League Championships, the Northern Junior Cup and the Third Division Stroud League Cup.*
*   In 1921 he was selected as first reserve to the county in a match against Worcestershire at Stroud, and on that occasion there were included in the team no fewer than four local representatives that is, Otto Griffin (the captain), Stan Evans, Lindsey Farmiloe and 'Paper' Beale.*
*   His usual position is left half, but he is at home practically anywhere in the team, and can be depended upon to give a good account of himself under any circumstance. Whether playing in the defence or forward he plays with a will and he is clever alike in clearing under pressure or in making an opening when opportunities offer. At the present time he is the only representative of the family playing for the Rovers, but his brothers are still very much in the game, Oliver and Francis belonging to the Woodchester Club, while Bert is a member of the Box team.*

Forest Green continued in the Senior Amateur Cup, beating Woodchester in a replay in Nailsworth 3-0, and then went on to beat Fairford Town, again at home in Nailsworth 4-0, the scorers being W. Brown, Hall, Watts and Bingle. A semi-final against Broadwell Amateurs, their old foes from the Northern Senior League, awaited them in April 1925, Rovers losing 1-0, leaving Broadwell to meet Sharpness in the final.

Dudley Vines, who had returned to Forest Green, had a great day out in May against Cirencester, scoring 7 goals in a 9-1 victory with W. Furley and R. Dickman also scoring. The season ended in May 1925 with defeat in the Stroud Hospital Cup final to Rodborough Old Boys in front of an estimated 3,000 spectators at Brimscombe's ground, The Meadow. The Old Boys had also won Division One of the Stroud League with Forest Green finishing runners-up. No silverware this season, then.

1925/26

Forest Green again entered Divisions One and Two of the Stroud League, not feeling able to apply for membership of the Northern Senior League, even though life in the Stroud League was relatively easy.

In October 1925, Frank Butt, the Forest Green goalkeeper, was reported to be receiving trials at Bristol Rovers for the reserve team. Frank may not have been the first Forest Green player to get a trial for a Football League club.

In November 1925 Forest Green Rovers entertained Cirencester Town at Enoch's Ground in Nailsworth in the Stroud Hospital Cup, winning 3-1 and, moving into 1926, Forest Green Rovers were finally checked by Avening in Division One, Rovers going home with a 0-0 draw. Controversy fell on Forest Green Reserves after a further match against Avening, with a report in the *Stroud Journal* on 8 January 1926.

Stroud Journal, 8 January 1926
Stroud League meeting
   The next business was the regrettable incident that occurred in a match between Avening and Forest Green, in which, after Avening had scored a goal which gave them the lead, but which was disputed by the Rovers, who alleged that the ball was tipped back into play by a spectator from the line, three Forest Green players left the field and the game later had to be abandoned seven minutes from time owing to bad light. The whistle was several times sounded for the resumption, but as soon as the ball was centred it was, on several occasions, deliberately kicked away. When play was eventually resumed one of the players was injured, thus causing a further delay and the referee had to order the game to be stopped owing to bad light. The referee also wrote an explanation and added that when he asked the Rovers captain for the names of the players who had left the field he could not see who they were as it was so dark. Some of the Forest Green supporters swarmed on to the ground.

Alan Beale

My father, 'Nip' Beale was Forest Green Rovers through and through. His older brother, Alf Beale, played in goal from Avening but when they played against Forest Green Rovers, after the First World War, his father Henry forbade him to play against Forest Green because of the rivalry between the teams and because the game usually ended in a punch-up.

Adrian Brown

My father told me a story that my Uncle Bill, the eldest one, came home one night when they all were living at home. Well, he came home one day and said he wasn't going to sign on for Forest Green next year. 'Oh, where you going?' 'I'm going with my mates to Avening.'
   'I see.' So when he come to start playing football that season my grandfather, Walter Brown, said to him, 'You don't bring any football kit in here, your mother will not be washing your kit, you get your Avening cronies to wash it for you.'

And our Uncle Bill stayed for a season then in Avening, and my Dad told me that our grandfather wouldn't allow him to bring any of his kit, even his boots; and when he signed back on for Forest Green, well no problem, bring it all back; that's how it was back then.

Not to be outdone by the high-scoring first team, Rovers reserves secured what is thought to be a record when they beat Brimscombe reserves 15-1 on 26 March 1926.

The Northern Senior Amateur Cup

Since winning the Northern Junior Cup in 1921, there were now separate junior and senior amateur cups to give the smaller clubs a chance of winning. Rovers reached the final of the Senior Amateur Cup for the first time against Broadwell Amateurs on 10 April 1926, the game being played at Lydney Rugby ground. Rovers were the first team from outside the Northern Senior League to reach the final.

The Forest Green team that day consisted of A. Porter; E. (Gary) Brown (capt), J. Brown; W. Brown, P. Haines, C. Turner; W. Furley, W. Seymour, D. Vines, W. Beale, L. Holborough. They had beaten Chalford, Cirencester Town, Cam Mills and then Tewkesbury in the semi-final, while Broadwell had beaten Cheltenham Town, Sharpness and Stonehouse. Albert Porter was the father of John Porter, who would play for the club in the 1960s. A very close game followed with the score at half-time being 0-0. Broadwell Amateurs went on to win the game 1-0, scoring in the last 5 minutes of the very closely fought game.

Following on from the cup defeat, Forest Green then played King's Stanley at Enoch's Field in Nailsworth in the championship decider for the Stroud League.

Stroud Journal, 7 May 1926
Stroud & District League, Forest Green v. King's Stanley
The match between Forest Green and King's Stanley at Enoch's on Thursday evening last week, and which determined whether or not there would have to be a final for the championship of the Stroud & District League, attracted a large crowd of football enthusiasts from all parts of the district. The ground, which had been played on several nights previously, was in a very poor condition and consequently hampered the game considerably. The teams were very evenly matched, although at certain phases of the game the Foresters showed signs of fatigue which was undoubtedly caused by their three previous matches that week, and King's Stanley thus secured the cup by a 1-0 victory.

And so, for a second season on the trot, Rovers finished runners-up in the Stroud League, and runners-up in a cup competition; this time the Northern Senior Amateur Cup.

Their frustrating season hadn't ended yet, however, losing the Stroud Hospital Cup final again to King's Stanley, 1-0 after extra time in May 1926. The Reserves faired better in Stroud League Division Three, winning the title. Having come so close to some silverware, there was no doubt both the players and the committee were well motivated for the forthcoming season.

10

County Cup Success: 1926–1936

1926/27

Rovers returned to the Northern Senior League, winning their first game against Dursley 4-0 in September. Albert Porter, who had played in the cup final the year before, broke his leg badly and retired from football.

This season also saw two revolutionary developments off the pitch. For the first time, clubs were reported to use the telephone to confirm postponement of matches, and permit players (ex-professionals who had returned to the amateur game) were accepted by the league. W. A. Buckland of Cheltenham Town became the first permit player in the Northern Senior League.

Forest Green finally beat Broadwell Amateurs for the first time, 3-1 on 8 October 1926. We can also be sure that Forest Green Rovers returned to their much-improved old home on top of the hill. While Rovers didn't yet own their own ground, they felt sufficiently secure to invest in the facilities having played down in Nailsworth for the two previous years.

> Stroud Journal, 15 October 1926
>
> *Praise is due to members of the Forest Green Committee and others for the excellent appearance of the new football field (The Lawn). New doors bearing the club's name have been erected in place of the old gate, wire netting placed above the wall around the field, the grass is cut short and a strong wire being held by good posts has been fixed around the playing pitch so that in future all spectators will get an uninterrupted view of the game. A 40-foot flagpole flying the club's colours has also been fixed up.*

At the same time, Forest Green were top of the Northern Senior League, and went on to beat Wotton 8-2 at the end of October, with 'Paper' Beale scoring 5 goals.

JOHN 'WACKER' PORTER

My dad played in goal for Forest Green but he broke his leg; see that gash there on mine? He had one like that, and they had to bathe that for years and years and years because, his went down and in, almost like the bone had been taken away, but he always had this gash, and he used to have to bandage it up, bathe it, for years and years. Now I would ask 'why can't somebody do something about that?' But that was that back in them days if you had that sort of accident, that finished dad as far as football was concerned. But he always said that he enjoyed himself, his football up at Forest Green.

> Stroud Journal, 29 October 1926
>
> *Northern Senior League, Forest Green v. Cam Mills*
>
> *Just before the commencement of the game the ground was officially declared open by the president of the club, Mr T. Harris. He said that the field was not brought to its present greatly improved condition without much hard work and he was pleased to present Mr W. Harrison on behalf of the committee, with a case of pipes and tobacco, to show the club's appreciation of the hard and difficult work he had put in. Among the others he would like to thank T. Beale, D. Blake, F. Burford and W. Brown for their help. In reply the president and Mr G.H. Brinkworth were both thanked for their help that they had given the club in obtaining the ground and helping to improve it. The game was played before a very large crowd and proved to be fast*

Forest Green defend a Cadburys attack.

The 'chocolate boys' fall to the brothers Brown again.

Some of the spectators at 'Brimscombe Meadow', come to witness the semi-final win for Rovers.

and interesting. W. Fletcher opened the scoring after fifteen minutes' play for the Rovers but Cam quickly equalised and then took the lead. This reverse made Rovers buck up and W. Beale brought the scores level at two goals each just before half-time. After the changeover Rovers were much the better side, scoring two more goals through G. Govier and W. Beale, thus gaining two more useful points. Tomorrow Rovers travel to Sharpness by train where they expect stiff opposition and will be at full strength.

In fact Forest Green lost to Sharpness 2-1. The Senior League was hotting up into a three-way contest between Forest Green Rovers, Sharpness and Cheltenham Town for the title, while Gloucester City languished at the bottom of the table with only 5 points from 16 games. In late January, Forest Green played Viney Hill, the runaway leaders of the Forest of Dean League, in the Senior Amateur Cup third round, winning 5-2.

Who knows, maybe a touch of complacency entered the heads of the Forest Green Rovers players when they entertained bottom club Gloucester City on 5 February 1927 and lost 7-1. Continuing the busy season of fixtures, Forest Green Rovers met Cadburys Athletic at Brimscombe's Meadow the following week in the semi-final of the Northern Senior Cup.

The team that won through to the final. Back row: Bill Burford, Cecil Turner, Zachy Haines, Joe Brown, Gary Brown, Fletcher, Frank Butt. Front row: Bill Seymour, Gilly Govier, Jim Humphries, 'Paper' Beale, Charlie Holbrow.

Stroud News & Gloucester County Advertiser, *Friday 25 February 1927*
Northern Senior Cup semi final, keen semi-final tussle at Brimscombe

The Rovers commenced a vigorous attack, but were unable to break through a fine defence, and after a hard struggle Cadburys got right down the field, and for a few minutes the struggle round the Forester's goal was intense, the fine work of the brothers Brown eventually saving the situation. Getting away again the Rovers attained a corner, but were unable to turn it to good account. However, they kept up a good attack, but their efforts were unrewarded. In retaliating the chocolate makers made a great attempt to score, but a fine shot was cleverly saved by Butt, the Rovers' goalie. Keeping up the attack Cadburys were eventually rewarded after a fine passing movement, Lawrence, their centre forward scoring with a fine shot. They kept up terrific pressure and the two Browns again had their work cut out to get the ball clear. After a desperate struggle, however, Beale took the ball down the field but he was unable to score. Cadburys were now proving themselves the slightly better team, and Butt was continually called upon to save. The Rovers, however, became a little more aggressive and got right up the field, and during a melee were awarded a penalty, which Seymour turned to good account. The Foresters held their own until half-time which arrived with both teams equal.

After the interval the Rovers opened up with a vigorous attack and Fletcher obtained a somewhat easy goal. The Athletic were not to be daunted, and forcing their way through the Rovers defence 'Doss' Long equalised with a beautiful shot. Play remained for some time around the Rovers goal and Cadburys eventually took the lead from a penalty taken by Lawrence. The 'Chocolate Makers' kept up great pressure and a beautiful shot from their left wing was cleverly intercepted with a beautiful header by J. Brown. Cadburys were now decidedly superior in attack and combination, and it looked as if they would obtain their position in the final. The Foresters defended well, however, and play gradually became more even, and setting up a fine passing movement the Rovers got right through the Cadburys defence and obtained a corner. This was successfully cleared, but the ball was quickly sent back again, and during a great struggle round the Cadburys goal one of the backs, in trying to clear, sent the ball into his own net much to the delight of the Forester's supporters. Play now became extremely exciting, both sides going all out to score, but both defences held out, and the game concluded with both teams equal with three goals each

Forest Green Rovers won the replay 2-0 the following week, with goals by Turner and Fletcher, setting up a final against Sharpness to be played at Dursley's ground on 9 April 1927. Sharpness had now sneaked ahead by 1 point at the head of the table with a game in hand over Rovers. At the end of March, Sharpness beat Cheltenham Town 2-0 to move 5 points ahead of Cheltenham with a game in hand at the top of the table, with Forest Green Rovers hanging on to Sharpness's shirt tails with a 4-0 win over Gloucester City at Gloucester.

The team for the final of the Senior Amateur Cup was selected as follows: F. Butt; J. Brown (capt), E. Brown; C. Turner, J. Humphries, T. Haines; M. Holbrow, W. Beale, W. Fletcher, W .Seymour and G. Govier.

Stroud News & Gloucester County Advertiser, *Friday 15 April 1927*
Another Stroud success, Forest Green win Senior Cup, A Splendid Contest

The gate at Dursley, estimated as 4,000, included over 400 making the journey by the LMS excursion from Nailsworth, while scores of cyclists and numerous motorcyclists travelled by road. Spectators of both sides were optimistic and either team was accorded a veritable roar of welcome on entering the enclosure.

Above: A large crowd gathered ready for the final.

Right: The crowd get excited in anticipation.

Above: Forest Green attack the Sharpness goal.

Right: Sharpness work the ball towards the halfway line.

Above left: The officials gather for a photo, with the drummer in the background.

Above right: Forest Green race on to a loose through ball watched by the grandstand crowd.

The game itself started sensationally, with Sharpness getting a goal in the very first minute, this following some splendid combination forward play. After this reverse the Rovers became aggressive, but on the whole were not quite so convincing as their opponents, who were slightly quicker on the ball and who brought much havoc with their long swinging but marvellously accurate passes. However, the Rovers gradually settled down and soon the Sharpness goal was in difficulties, Holbrow putting in a splendid drive that forced Thomas, the goalie, to concede a corner. The Rovers, however, forced several more corners, and eventually, when the game was half an hour old, equalised after a corner, the ball passing over the line from a melee, Seymour being credited with the goal.

On the whole things did not look too bright for Rovers at half-time, for there was every indication that the Sharks, with the slight slope favouring them, would be veritable demons. However, after the breather, Gary Brown (who during the interval had been presented with a horseshoe decorated in the Rovers colours) and his men played altogether a better game. Right from the outset they took to aggressive and subsequently interesting end-to-end play, with the Stroud team now holding a perceptible advantage. Several times the Sharks' goal was in grave danger, and eventually, amid scenes of wild enthusiasm, Beale netted after fine work by the brothers Brown.

With the all-important goal in their possession the Rovers proved excellent spoilers, and it was rarely that the Sharks could get really dangerous. They did once, however, and with Butt out of reach, Long had a splendid chance, but shot over the top from five yards out, and soon the final whistle announced that the senior trophy was destined to spend twelve months in the Stroud area. The Cup was presented by Mr W.J. Pepworth, the Rovers leaving the field to the strains of Where Will They Be *and it is stated that the haste of the team to get back to Forest Green to celebrate the victory caused not a few amusing incidents.*

The Forest Green Song: 'Where Will They Be'

At the end of the game, the crowd sang the song 'Where Will They Be?' first mentioned by Lilian Northwood in the previous chapter. The Forest Green song was apparently very popular and was sung regularly at cup-winning celebrations and annual dinners. Peter Vick, who played for the club from 1936, remembers the song well and gave a vocal recitation in 2005.

By the end of April, the season was drawing to a close with Rovers runners-up by 4 points to Sharpness, beating Cheltenham Town into third place. It wasn't quite over yet as Rovers beat Brimscombe 2-0 to make it to the Hospital Cup final on 13 May at Brimscombe. Rovers were reported as 'obviously a tired team'.

The cup-winning heroes.

A goalmouth scramble.

The Hospital Cup final took place on a perfect spring day.

A large crowd gathers for the Hospital Cup Final.

The ball comes down the wing.

The second cup of the season in Rovers' hands.

Stroud News & Gloucester County Advertiser, *Friday 13 May 1927*
Stroud Hospital Cup, Senior Section

It will be remembered that Forest Green were winners of the Senior Amateur Cup and runners-up of the Northern Senior League, and King's Stanley last year's holders of the Hospital Cup, the champions of the North Gloucester League and runners-up of the Stroud League, and, bearing in mind the Bluebells' fine display against Chalford in the semi-final round, it was generally expected that the contest would be a tight one. The Brimscombe meadow, with its natural grandstand, it is doubtful if a more fitting venue for the match could possibly have been arranged, and to the great delights of the organisers a splendid gate was declared to be a record for the ground.

Giving a pretty display of the combination for which they hold an enviable reputation, Stanley got smoothly off the mark and the first thrill was served up by a first timer from Roy Malpas, which, however, failed to reach the net. The Rovers retaliated, but Everard Malpas, cleared finely, and once again the Stanley front rank took matters in hand and Butt did well to save from a dropping and deceitful shot that he might well have been excused for missing. In the subsequent play Joe Blanche was often in the picture with clever feeding of his forwards, and eventually before the Rovers had had a real look in came a true 'Malpas' effort. Rory passing out to Melvin for the latter to force a corner and place this beautifully for Bob to send in a shot that easily outwitted Butt. Stanley continued to be the aggressors, but eventually Gary Brown cleared in his usual hefty manner, and in so doing placed the ball nicely for Fletcher to indulge in one of the brilliant solo runs of the afternoon and score a beauty, half-time arriving with the honours even.

In the second half, the Rovers were an unquenchable element and not many minutes had passed before they forced a corner, which, well placed by Holbrow, was capably converted by Harris. Stanley retaliated, but were repulsed, their shooting being erratic, and, breaking away after a period of quiet play, the Rovers further improved their position through Beale. Two goals down, Stanley tried all they knew to put things on a more even footing, and Melvin Malpas, securing on the right, ran through and forced a corner. His kick looked a likely one, but the Rovers, as ever, were capable spoilers, and, at the other end Fletcher, fed by the right wing, made no mistake with a shot that resulted in the fourth goal.

This effort put the issue beyond all doubt, but the Rovers were now in a thoroughly aggressive mood and soon Govier netted what appeared to be number five. And this was apparently allowed until one of the linesmen conferred with the referee with the result that a goal kick was ordered. Stanley fought valiantly, but were unable to entirely raise the siege, and the match ended in victory to the Rovers by 4 goals to 1.

The cup final brought the 1926/27 season to a close. Forest Green had moved back to the top of the hill, to their improved ground, The Lawn, complete with boundary wall, entrance gates and a forty-foot-high flagpole!

Forest Green's early loss to Gloucester City also made it into the annual meeting minutes of the Senior League as the most sensational result of the season. Gloucester City finished fourth from bottom. Forest Green's success coincided with the first and only time that the FA Cup was taken out of the country, when Cardiff City defeated Arsenal and also won the Welsh Cup. Another Welsh team, Aberdare Athletic, left the Football League, never to return. This season also included the first ever live radio broadcast of a match between Arsenal and Sheffield United at Highbury.

Right: Rovers swoop in on the King's Stanley goal.

Right and below: Brimscombe meadow was a natural stadium with a perfect grandstand bank.

Forest Green Rovers AFC 1926/27,
back home outside 'the Jovials'.
Winners Northern Senior Amateur
Cup, Stroud Hospital Cup, runners
up in the Gloucestershire Northern
Senior League. H. Holbrow,
H. Knee, H. Burford, L. Bennett,
R. Creed, A. Horwood, D. Close.
W. Harvey, F. Turner, E.M. Brown,
F. Butt, J.V. Brown, (capt),
J. Lloyd, G. Vaughan, W. Gardner,
A. Dickman. C. Brown, R. Dickman,
G. Govier, W. Brown, W. Fletcher,
L. Holbrow, G. Furley, W. Seymour
(vice capt). J. White, W. Furley,
T. Haines, W. Beale, C. Brown,
A. Totterdale (hon sec).

At the end of the season, the foul and abusive language rule was introduced for the first time. The year before, in 1926, the international board had also decided that a player could not be offside if two (instead of three) opponents were nearer their own goal-line.

1927/28

The Stroud Premier League

Off the field, the Stroud & District League, having seen the continued success of the Gloucestershire Northern Senior League, decided to pursue a senior league of its own, and most of the old Stroud League teams rejoined to play in a new Stroud Senior League. However, the GFA refused to sanction another senior league in the county, stating quite categorically that such a new league was 'not wanted'.

> Stroud News & Gloucester County Advertiser, *Friday 9 September 1927*
> *Senior League application refused*
> *It has been proved that teams drawn from the villages around Stroud, while quite able to equal, and in not a few cases surpass, the quality of football served up by teams from far larger areas, are unable to afford the very considerable expenditure entailed in operating in the present senior league. Six teams lost on football over £100 between them last season … It has been pointed out time and again that the Stroud Clubs cannot afford – not cannot compete with – Northern senior football, and so far as we can judge, the GFA are quite content for them to be relegated back to junior footer. But perhaps the question is not finally settled yet. Who knows?*

Forest Green Rovers ended the season in fourth place to Stonehouse, King's Stanley and Chalford in a league of eleven teams.

The English FA Amateur Cup

For some years, many local teams had been entering the FA Amateur Cup preliminary rounds, but not Forest Green. Perhaps the reason was the additional expense of having to travel far afield. In the previous year Chalford had beaten Cheltenham Town and Cadburys had defeated Bristol Union Jack in the preliminary rounds before being knocked out.

For the 1927 season, Stonehouse drew Swindon Victoria, Cadburys drew Hanham Athletic and Brimscombe drew St Anne's (Oldland's) away. Only Brimscombe progressed to the later qualifying round, where they lost to Kingswood in a replayed match. Chalford, in the meantime, having beaten Sharpness, were drawn at home to Hanham Athletic for a match which it was hoped would attract a record gate. Gloucestershire teams had never really done very well in the FA Amateur Cup and very few teams had made it past the preliminary rounds over the years.

The first Gloucestershire team to make it into the first round proper of the FAAC was Cheltenham Town in 1919 when they lost 2-0 to Clandown. Bristol St George then made it through to the first round against Bournemouth Gasworks Athletic in 1923 before Kingswood from Bristol (not the Kingswood near Wotton-under-Edge that Forest Green played regularly at the time) made it through the first round beating Uxbridge 1-0 in 1926. They then lost to Welton Rovers in the second round.

The only other teams to progress to the first round up to the Second World War were Kingswood, again in 1929, when they lost 4-1 again to Welton Rovers, and then Gloucester City in 1934, who lost 3-0 to Frome Town in the first round.

1928/29

Having effectively returned to local football the year before, Rovers rejoined a Gloucestershire Northern Senior League of thirteen teams and also kept their first team in the Stroud Premier League, to ensure a full season's fixtures, and no doubt quite a lot of fixture congestion.

In November 1928, R. Peachey and R.F. Clift transferred to Forest Green Rovers from Brimscombe and Woodchester respectively. Both players would play key roles in future successes of Forest Green Rovers, who beat Gloucester City 1-0 at the beginning of the month.

Forest Green's secretary, Mr Totterdale, had upset both the GFA and the Gloucestershire Northern Senior league. He was suspended because he had been mis-recording names of the Forest Green Team, submitting the team 'as selected' rather than the 'team played'. It was the end of his career as secretary and Lionel Bennett of Forest Green became the new club secretary and representative at senior league meetings.

Rovers made it through to the semi-final of the Senior Amateur Cup, losing to Broadwell 3-2 in March. Rovers had drawn with Cheltenham Town 1-1 in January but it wasn't enough to stop Cheltenham winning the Northern Senior League for the first time with Viney Hill as runners-up, while Sharpness won the Senior Amateur Cup with Broadwell the beaten finalists. The Rest of League team selected to play the champions included Mr J.V. Brown at left-back and Mr S.G. Harrison on the left wing, with Mr A.J. Lampard as first reserve for goalkeeper. 'Snowy' Harrison also played in the game, which was drawn 2-2.

Forest Green Rovers finished eighth of thirteen in the Senior League and sixth of ten in the Stroud Premier League, a step down compared to the battle that they had at the top of the Senior League when they were last there.

1929/30

Rovers were again in danger of overstretching themselves, entering the Northern Senior League and Stroud Premier League with the reserves entering the Dursley and Stroud Leagues.

In November it was reported that Forest Green's young goalkeeper, A.J. Lampard, had joined Bournemouth & Boscombe and was doing very well in his new sphere of action in the Football League. Rovers were reported to be bringing through a young team alongside veteran players like Gary Brown.

The season also brought the first competitive league fixtures between Shortwood and Forest Green's first team in the Stroud Premier League, Shortwood having been promoted the previous season. Rovers won 3-0 in March, and by April they were playing 2 games a day in a desperate bid to complete their fixtures, Stonehouse in the morning and Cadburys in the afternoon, taking 1 point from the later game. In the Stroud Hospital Cup, Rovers won the senior final 1-0, beating King's Stanley. The reserves finished runners-up to Tuffley YMCA.

At the end of the season, Viney Hill won the Senior League with Cheltenham Town as runners–up, a reverse of the position last year, with Snowy Harrison of Forest Green again playing for the Rest of League against the champions, the Rest beating Viney Hill 3-0.

Forest Green Rovers finished seventh of twelve in the Senior League and sixth of eleven in the Premier League, a season that included heavy defeats to Cheltenham Town, Listers and Sharpness, although the Rovers did manage to beat Cheltenham Town 5-3 at home.

1930/31

Rovers only played in the Northern Senior League this year, finally accepting that they had been overstretching themselves, but the reserves entered the Stroud League Division Two and the Dursley League Division One.

Rovers beat Cinderford in the Senior Amateur Cup at the end of January but went out to King's Stanley in the semi-final; they also lost 4-2 to Shortwood in the Hospital Cup senior section.

Forest Green's run of poor form continued into the new decade, the Roaring Twenties now a distant memory. By the end of the season, Forest Green Rovers had slipped to tenth in a Senior League of twelve teams, with Brimscombe champions and Cheltenham Town runners-up. Both Broadwell and Sharpness left the league at the end of the season. Snowy Harrison again made the Rest of the League team to play against Brimscombe, where he was joined by S.H. Jones, the new Forest Green Rovers goalkeeper.

PETER VICK

Well, I was born in April 1921 and watched Rovers from about the age of nine or ten. I wasn't a Forest Green boy, I was born at Newmarket down over the hill. Newmarket boys and Forest Green boys were rivals, like Shortwood.

I used to watch the famous Joe and Gary Brown and 'Scrubby' Cowley who played centre half. Then there was Dudley Vines, a local coal merchant, who played centre forward. He had quite a reputation for being a bit robust, if you know what I mean. He was a big, raw-boned man, and a real rough diamond – all arms and legs. And yet he was an excellent ballroom dancer!

Football was much more robust in those days, a lot of things were allowed and you were a local character if you made your presence felt. In those days, you could charge a goalkeeper into the net to score. That's one thing about football that has improved nowadays, except that in the old days the fouls were straightforward. There was nothing sneaky.

I can remember there being the odd spar on the pitch between players – and between supporters, come to think of it.

1931/32

Rovers again entered the Northern Senior League while the Reserves entered the Dursley League Division One and Stroud League Division Two and the Severn Vale League.

By the turn of the year, in a report of a 9-1 win over Cam Mills in the Northern Senior League, it was noted that, 'Forest Green were a very young team and at the beginning of the season the inexperience and lack of good combination play saw them in difficulties that they had now surmounted successfully, giving them a style of football that when fully developed will bring back the success that the club needs.'

In February, Rovers played Brimscombe in the Northern Senior League, where it was reported that their plans 'went all awry... they also had a Dursley League match on the same day and sent their strongest team down to play Dursley, where they were high up in the League. The second string did beat Brimscombe 2-1, with the Rovers' reserve left-back, Haines, evidently under the impression that a prize was offered to the player who could kick the ball into the adjoining field the greatest number of times.'

By March, Forest Green were playing their first team in the Dursley League, leaving the reserves to play in the Senior League, and won the Dursley League Division One, with Dursley runners up. Rovers' policy in the Northern Senior League was reflected in their position at the end of the season, finishing ninth of twelve, losing 9-1 against Cheltenham Town, 9-0 against Chalford, 11-0 against Chepstow and 8-0 against Gloucester, among other defeats! No doubt Haines had a torrid time against the first teams of Cheltenham Town and Gloucester City.

The reserves carried off the Severn Vale League Championship whilst in the Stroud Hospital Cup, Forest Green Rovers finished runners-up to Chalford after a replay.

1932/33

Forest Green Rovers again kicked off in the Northern Senior League, along with Cheltenham Town. In actual fact, the Cheltenham team entered in the Senior League was now a reserve XI, the Cheltenham committee having decided that their first team should join the Birmingham Combination and move to semi-professional status.

The Birmingham Combination was the junior feeder to the Birmingham League. Cheltenham played there from 1932 until 1935, when they moved across to the Southern League to join the Western Section (one of three sections: the Western, Eastern and Central). They remained in the Southern League until their recent history saw them rise through the football ranks. Cheltenham became the first reserve side in the Northern Senior League, although they have never been referred to as Cheltenham Town Reserves in any table or fixture list. Cheltenham Town (Reserves) comfortably won this season's Northern Senior League, winning all their home games.

Forest Green's form in the Senior League had greatly improved on previous years, ending the season in fifth place behind Cheltenham Town (Reserves), Gloucester City, Chepstow Town and Cinderford Town respectively. Rovers managed to beat Gloucester City 3-2 at home, with a 1-1 draw away. Other notable results included an 8-1 win at home against Brimscombe and a 6-2 win against Chepstow Town, although Rovers lost away from home 7-0 to Blakeney, 6-0 to Cheltenham Town and 6-1 at Listers.

In the Dursley & Wotton League, formed that season, Rovers faced Listers at home and Wickwar away in mid-October, fielding two half-and-half teams, taking only 1 point against Listers. It was reported to be 'their custom' to field their first team in the Dursley & Wotton League by this time, having won it the year before. They played 2 games a day throughout most of April to complete their fixture list.

Forest Green Rovers won the Stroud Senior Hospital Cup for the fourth time, beating Chalford 2-1.

Nailsworth British School football team 1932/33. More than half the team would play for Forest Green after they returned from the Second World War. Back row: M. Wallace, S. Fream, Jack Day. Middle row: W. Gardiner, G.Cole, H. Heaven, C. Brown, L. Dangerfield. Front row: H. Freeman, Johnny Ranger, R. Tanner, H. Harrison, unknown.

1933/34

DENNIS DANGERFIELD

I remember going up to the club. When we were very young we used to go up there and help, you know, before the war, keep the ground up together, cutting the ground and we used to help Fred Porter do the balls. My father used to do the balls. Then I took it over and Les, my brother, took it over for a bit. Fred Porter used to live up on Bunting Hill. He used to have enough balls to do, because all the hedge round the ground was blinkin' thorns, years ago, and they all had to be taken out.

Rovers again entered the Dursley & Wotton League Division One and the Northern Senior League, and effectively rotated their first team and reserve teams between the two leagues, depending on who they were playing. They lost 10-0 to Cam Mills in the Dursley & Wotton League with a reserve side, and drew 3-3 with Cheltenham Town in the Senior League. At other times the teams were reversed, the first team beating Sinwell 11-1 in November. They definitely played their first team against Chepstow in December in the Senior Amateur Cup at The Lawn, winning 7-5 with goals from Herbert, Peachey, N. Vick, Webb (2) and Marks (2).

Gloucester City won the Northern Senior League for the first time, and the players were awarded miniature silver cups rather than the medals that had been the norm until this time.

Forest Green Rovers finished eleventh of fourteen in the Northern Senior League and finished twelfth of fourteen in the Dursley & Wotton League, with Woodchester champions and Sharpness runners-up. They were playing 52 league games in addition to cup games. It was simply too much football if they hoped to win anything.

Rovers again gave notice through Lionel Bennett that they intended to withdraw from the Northern Senior League for the forthcoming season, citing financial problems associated with the expense of staying in the league. Forest Green were not alone and, at a meeting of the Senior League in May 1934, a motion was put forward to split the league into two geographical sections with a 'view to saving travelling expenses'. The motion was voted down by twenty-two votes to two.

Forest Green Rovers AFC 1934/35. Winners of the Dursley and Wotton League Division One and Stroud and District Premier League. Back row: F. Porter, T. Donohue, E. Brinkworth (chairman), A. Dickinson, L. Bennet (hon sec), R. Peachey, B. Weager, N. Newport, J. Brock, D. Herbert, W. Brown, S. Lunberg, T. Wallace, A. Miles, G. Cowley. Middle row: B. Fletcher, E. Morse, F. Grant, W. Shipway, V. Cowley, H. Fletcher, W. Beard, A. Mills, L. Blick, L. Burge. Front row: R. Gannaway, A. Grant, A. Wykes, H. Webb, T. Newport, D. Marks (capt), S. Harrison, R. Humphries, G. Mills, L. Johnson.

1934/35

Stonehouse won the Gloucestershire Northern Senior League for the first time by a single point from Gloucester City, while Forest Green stayed local and won the Dursley & Wotton League Division One and also headed the Stroud League Premier Division, with King's Stanley the runners–up after a play-off. Both leagues were won at a canter.

1935/36

At the 1935 AGM it had been decided that goal average should be used for the first time to decide the championship if the top two clubs were level on points. Prior to this, a play-off had always been required. Cheltenham Town Reserves moved from the Northern Senior League into the Birmingham Combination following the Cheltenham first team's move into the Southern League. Gloucester City left their reserves in the Northern Senior League, moving their first team into the Birmingham Combination until they joined the Southern League in 1939. Chepstow Town finally left the league due to never-ending travelling difficulties and Tewkesbury Town left for financial reasons. Stonehouse won the Northern Senior League for a second consecutive year unbeaten at

MARSHALL WOODWARD

In the 1930s, before the war, when I was a boy there used to be quite a few who'd go up and watch.

Mr Lunberg was a supporter and he had a Rovers suit. You know where the café is now, down by the copper kettle? Mr Lunberg lived in there, he had a lot of kids. He was a shoe snobber, fitting men's shoes; and for some sort of games he used to black himself all over. He had a bit of a pair of long johns over the top and he had a spear and he'd frighten all of those kids of his! He used to put the teams up in a little box outside his shop to advertise the game; first team and second team.

I always remember him, he was very closely connected with Forest Green and you could always hear him. He had a deep gruff voice. He used to say 'COME ON ROVERS! JUST ONE MORE BEFORE I GO!' and you could hear that all over the ground. And he used to have contests with the bloke up at the Newmarket end named Charlie Tiffin. Any time anybody kicked the ball over the touchline out of play he would say 'WINDYYYYYY!' in great loud booming voice. Then Mr Lunberg would start shouting and he was always saying 'JUST ONE MORE BEFORE I GO!' They'd be winning about 10-1 or something!

He used to frighten all the kids – he had a shield and a spear. I can see him now, I can picture him going up Spring Hill now; and he used to wear a black-and-white-striped top hat and matching trousers for the finals and semi-finals.

home with Cinderford Town as runners–up. Forest Green again won the Dursley & Wotton League Division One and the Stroud Premier League, and followed up at the end of the season by winning the Stroud Senior Hospital Cup for the fifth time, beating Brimscombe 2-1.

Forest Green Rovers AFC season 1935/36. The photo was taken below the Jovial Forester with Dunkirk Mill in the background. Winners Stroud and District League Division One. Dursley and Wotton League Division One. Stroud Hospital Cup competition (senior section). Back row: T. Donohue, T.H. Wallis, T. Newport, G. Peachey, J. Brock, S. Freem, N. Vick, W. Beard, J. Humphries, R. Humphries. Middle row: F. Porter, A. Miles, S. Lunberg, A. Fletcher, V. Cowley, R. Peachey, L. Bennett, G. Cowley, G. Clift. Front row: D. Brown, R. Clift, R. Lyford, D. Herbert (Capt.), D. Marks, S. Harrison (Vice Capt.), B. Weager (Vice Chairman). T. Wallis was Chairman.

11

A Great Leap Forward: 1936–1939

Many people have wondered what enabled Forest Green's rise from the ranks of local village football into a force to be reckoned with. The biggest leap in the first half of its history was the decision by the club committee to take a risk and buy their existing ground at auction without having the funds at hand to pay for it. 1936 is the first year for which the club minute books have been found. The minutes give an extraordinarily detailed account of the club's affairs and illustrate just how seriously the running of the club was taken.

The Structure of the Club: 1936, From the Minutes

All players were required to pay a 1*s* fee for the privilege of playing for Rovers for the season and had to pay a travelling fee to away matches. Joe Brown, a player from 1910 until the late 1920s, was the club treasurer. At the AGM on 22 June 1936, he reported that the club had a credit balance of £18 16*s* 1*d*. The committee decided to compete in the Dursley & Wotton, and Stroud & District Leagues while the reserves were entered in Division Three of the Stroud & District League. The Northern Senior and Minor Cups and the senior and junior sections of the Stroud Hospital Cup were also entered. One of the previous season's committee members, Rev. Jeffrey Lynch, resigned from the committee, stating that he intended to play again. Charlie Mortimer, the local Nailsworth taxi driver, was chosen more often than not to provide the transport.

PETER VICK

We had a reverend playing for us before the war from the Catholic church, a good player too. He was what they call a novice at the Catholic church in Woodchester. Well, he was learning the job, let's put it that way. He was like a trainee; good player.

Buying 'The Lawn'

The ground had been purchased at auction in June for £120, Mr Donoghue having paid a deposit of £12 at the sale for which he was reimbursed immediately. Mr Percy Smith of A.E. Smith & Sons, Solicitors, undertook all of the legal work free of charge. The purchase had to be completed by 29 September.

Owen Davis agreed to lend any money to the club that they could not raise by the due date. A hearty vote of thanks was given to both Owen Davis and Percy Smith for their backing. The local printers also agreed to provide subscription lists free of charge, which were distributed by the committee members among local businesses and supporters. In mid-September Owen Davis stepped forward to loan the club £70 to see them through, the legal side being wrapped up by 26 October, when Percy Smith confirmed that he would waive the £7 13s 4d charge.

1936/37

The season kicked off in late August for the first team with a 6-1 win against Woodchester. A very strong team included John 'Jack' Brock in goal. Swindon Town called Jack Brock over for a trial in October along with Norman Vick. Ben Weager visited Swindon Town later in October to resolve the situation with the Forest Green players. It appears that Swindon offered financial compensation for their services, forwarding a cheque for one guinea to the club at the beginning of November as a small donation towards the ground purchase fund. Jack Brock went on to play for the first team at Swindon Town for the 1936 season, making many appearances. In February, Forest Green had received no further payment and wrote to the club. Swindon replied that, owing to Swindon's financial position, they would be unable to give a further subscription. Swindon Town secured their new first-team goalkeeper for the sum of one guinea.

Fifteen-year-old Peter Vick made his debut for the reserve team on 26 October, at home to Slimbridge, on the left wing.

It is let with Windsoredge Farm to Mr John King on an annual Michaelmas tenancy the rent apportioned to this lot being £7 a year.

It is subject to tithe rent charge amounting to £1 2s. 7d. a year.

LOT 25

MOUNT PLEASANT HOUSE

A Detached Dwelling-house

situate at Forest Green and occupying a pleasant position on high ground close to Nailsworth.

It is constructed of brick with tiled and slated roofs and contains two living-rooms, kitchen, scullery and three bedrooms.

Water is laid on.

The house is let to Mr John King at a rent of £25 a year and is sublet to Mr W. H. Chandler.

The property is subject to a land tax of 3s. a year.

LOT 26

A Valuable

ACCOMMODATION PASTURE FIELD

with frontage to the road at Upper Forestgreen.

It is numbered 358 on the Ordnance Survey Map of the Parish of Nailsworth and contains an area of

2a.   0r.   33p.

It is let to Mr John King on an annual Michaelmas tenancy with other lots the rent apportioned to this lot being £5 a year.

It is subject to a tithe rent charge amounting to 9s. 11d. a year.

36

FORM OF AGREEMENT

An Agreement made the 19ᵗ day of June 1936 between ARTHUR LESLIE LONG of Nailsworth in the County of Gloucester Manufacturer and BASIL ALFRED PLAYNE of "Stramore" Marine Parade Lee-on-Solent in the County of Hants, Group Captain in Royal Air Force (hereinafter called the Vendors) of the one part and Richard Harriott Donohue of Forest Green Nailsworth. Gus Builder. (hereinafter called the Purchasers) of the other part WHEREBY IT IS AGREED that the Vendors shall sell and the Purchasers shall purchase (the property) (Lot) 26 described in the above Particulars at the price of One hundred and twenty pounds subject to the foregoing Special Conditions of Sale and The Law Society's Conditions of Sale (1934 Edition).

As Witness the hands of the parties hereto or their agents.

Purchase Money	£120 : :	
Less Deposit	£12 : :	
Balance	£108 : :	6d. Stamp
Valuation Money (if any)	£ : :	
Total	£108 : :	

Agent
As Vendors we hereby acknowledge the receipt of the above-mentioned deposit this 19ᵗ day of June 1936.

Abstract of Title to be sent to —

A.E. Smith & Son
Nailsworth -

Top: Lot 26, described as an 'accomodation pasture field', otherwise known as a football pitch.

Above: The agreement to purchase, signed by Richard Donohue at the auction, from this sprang security and a springboard for future custodians of the club.

To The Personal Representatives of W. H. Playne deceased.

I Richard Vincent Donohue of Forest Green Nailsworth
Builder hereby request that the property purchased by
me from you on the 19th June 1936 (being lot 26 at the
Longfords Estate Sale) be conveyed to myself and my Co-
trustees in accordance with the draft Conveyance drawn
by my Solicitors. Messrs A.E. Smith & Son.

Dated this 21 day of September 1936.

(sgd) R.V. Donohue.

Appointment of the first trustees, July 1936.

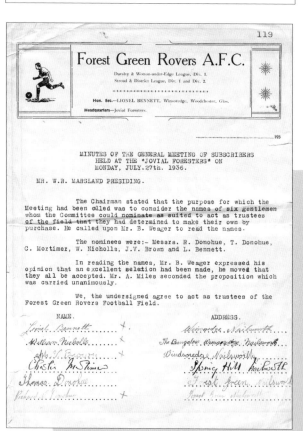

119

Forest Green Rovers A.F.C.

Dursley & Wotton-under-Edge League, Div. 1.
Stroud & District League, Div. 1 and Div. 2.

Hon. Sec.—LIONEL BENNETT, Winsoredge, Woodchester, Glos.

Headquarters—Jovial Foresters.

....193

MINUTES OF THE GENERAL MEETING OF SUBSCRIBERS
HELD AT THE "JOVIAL FORESTERS" ON
MONDAY, JULY.27th. 1936.

MR. W.R. MARSLAND PRESIDING.

       The Chairman stated that the purpose for which the
Meeting had been called was to consider the names of six gentlemen
whom the Committee could nominate as suited to act as trustees
of the field that they had determined to make their own by
purchase. He called upon Mr. B. Weager to read the names.

       The nominees were:- Messrs. R. Donohue, T. Donohue,
C. Mortimer, W. Nicholls, J.V. Brown and L. Bennett.

       In reading the names, Mr. B. Weager expressed his
opinion that an excellent seletion had been made, he moved that
they all be accepted. Mr. A. Miles seconded the proposition which
was carried unanimously.

       We, the undersigned agree to act as trustees of the
Forest Green Rovers Football Field.

NAME.	ADDRESS.
Lionel Bennett	Winsoredge Nailsworth
William Nicholls	The Bungalow Winsoredge Nailsworth
John V. Brown	Windsoredge Nailsworth
Charlie Mortimer	Spring Hill Nailsworth
Thomas Donohue	Forest Green Nailsworth
Richard V. Donohue	Forest Green Nailsworth

PETER VICK

When I first started playing I was working as an apprentice, earning 8s 6d a week for the first year, and I had to pay 2s 6d every away game to help cover expenses. In those days you had to provide all the kit yourself. You could wear whatever shorts and socks and boots you liked, and you had to wear the black-and-white striped shirt, the same as today. My parents provided the kit and I expect it was a job as mine brought up seven children, including two sets of twins, and three of the four boys were playing for Forest Green. The club couldn't help players buy any kit because they didn't have any money either.

I used to score a few. I'd go up and get the odd goal with my head and things like that. You could always expect a rough, tough game down in the Forest; a lot of fouls. There weren't many big arguments or anything back in those days. I mean, they're just petulant schoolboys today aren't they, all these professionals? They're like a lot of big kids. It was hard in our day, it was football, you could imagine going down to the Forest of Dean. You had hard men down there, but we really didn't fear anybody if we could help it.

We had some good strong players in my day, Bob Peachy and Scrubby Cowley, good hard tacklers and good players. Before me there was the Brown brothers. That's Doug's father Joe Brown, and his brother Gary, they were the two full-backs before my time. Ben Weager was the 'bag man'. He carried the first aid kit and attended the injuries. He was a local school attendance officer, so he used to chase you up if you played truant. He came from the Forest of Dean originally, and he played full-back for the club at one time.

We'd always get big crowds for the local derbies. If you played Woodchester, Brimscombe, Chalford or Stonehouse you'd always get 5, 6 or 700 people. But other games there would sometimes be just be a smattering of people who were interested in the club and players. A lot of the young lads used to creep in through the hedge to watch. I was one of them originally!

The first team played what was apparently an annual fixture against Shortwood on Boxing Day, winning 7-0 without Jack Brock. Having made his debut earlier in the season, Peter Vick travelled with the seconds to Frampton Mansell on 30 January 1937 for their away game in the Stroud League.

The first team won the Stroud League, heading the table of seven teams and dropping only 1 point, and won the Dursley & Wotton League, both for the third consecutive year, heading a league of fifteen teams including Shortwood, dropping only 5 points all season.

The Stroud Senior Hospital Cup was also secured for the sixth time against old rivals King's Stanley 4-1. The fact that two Forest Green players had trials for Swindon, and that one stayed for virtually the whole of the season playing for the first team, must give a reasonable idea of the strength of the Rovers at the time. Jack Brock and Norman Vick weren't the first players to be called up to trials at Football League teams either, and they weren't to be the last.

1937/38

Forest Green re-entered the Northern Senior League for the fourth time with a very strong and confident team. At the beginning of January 1938 Forest Green Rovers beat Brimscombe 3-1 to progress into the third round of the Senior Amateur Cup. A week later, Rovers beat Chalford away 5-4 to remain top of the Senior League, 5 points ahead of Cinderford Town. Forest Green were now unbeaten after 15 games, having only drawn 2 matches.

Rovers beat Gloucester City in the Senior Amateur Cup 3-1 in February, and kept up their good league form with a 1-1 draw against Stonehouse, in third place in the league, equalising in the last minute of the game. Forest Green suffered their first defeat of the season on 12 February 1938, losing to Charlton Kings 3-0 in the semi-final of the Senior Amateur Cup, played at Gloucester. By April 1938, Forest Green and Cinderford had pulled 8 points clear of the chasing pack, with Cinderford top by 2 points while Forest Green had 2 games in hand.

The Easter programme of matches would go a long way to deciding the destiny of the league for the season. On Easter Saturday, 16 April, Forest Green visited Longlevens and defeated Gloucester City 2-1 in a very fast game. Clift shaved the bar with a hard drive and Harrison hit the upright before Gloucester City went ahead. Bob Peachey levelled the scores and Scrubby Cowley headed in a grand centre to give Rovers 'a well earned victory'.

The league decider would be at King's Stanley at the end of April.

Stroud News & Gloucester County Advertiser, *Friday 22 April 1938*
Association Football, King's Stanley draw with Forest Green

Well over 1,000 spectators witnessed a keen struggle between Forest Green and King's Stanley on the latter's ground on Tuesday evening. The match had aroused such interest by the fact that the visitors – potential winners of the league – had yet to be beaten by a league side, and also that they needed the points to make their chances safe. The game, however, ended in a goal-less draw, and it is probable that Forest Green have not been so near to defeat this season when they so much required victory.

With no score in the first half it appeared that the remaining forty-five minutes would produce the thrills. And so it was. The visitors strained all their efforts to secure the all-important goal, but score they could not. On the other hand the homesters, backed up by the display of their defence, made spirited attempts on the Rovers goal and Clutterbuck and Gale came near to scoring. With only five minutes till time excitement became more marked around the line and on the pitch and mouths were open when Marks hit the crossbar with a powerful drive and McTiffin cleared with a remarkable kick from off the goal line. With only two minutes to go the referee became involved in a mix-up of players and ball with a result that he had to receive attention. The game ended with Forest Green still attacking.

Stroud News & Gloucester County Advertiser, *Friday 29 April 1938*
Forest Green deservedly Champions

Forest Green achieved a jewel performance when they beat Ellwood at The Lawn on Saturday; with an unbeaten record – one of the finest ever, if not the finest of the Northern Senior League – Forest Green Rovers are deservedly champions. They have held the lead throughout the season and only one team, Cinderford, have offered any serious challenge, although it must not be forgotten that King's Stanley also robbed the Rovers of 2 points by forcing a draw both at home and away.

The final of the Stroud Hospital Cup took place on 7 May, with Forest Green defeating Woodchester 2-1. In the words of the Forest Green captain, Bob Peachey, 'Woodchester had given Forest Green one of their hardest games of the season.'

Forest Green Rovers captain Bob Peachey being presented with the Northern Senior League Cup 1937/38.

Forest Green Rovers AFC 1937/38. Winners Gloucestershire Northern Senior League, Stroud and District Senior Hospital Cup competition. Runners up Cirencester Senior Hospital Cup competition. Back row: F. Porter, A. Bathe, P. Vick, E.G. Smith. Middle top row: W.J. Webb, N. Vick, L. Dangerfield, G. Peachey, B. Ford, D. Herbert (Vice Capt.), H. Weaving, L. Bennett (Hon. Sec.), E. Farmiloe. Middle bottom row: R. Clift, S. Harrison, R. Peachey (Capt.), D. Marks, H. Webb. Front row: H. Vick, V. Cowley, E. Peachey,

MARSHALL WOODWARD

You see George Peachey there, in that photo of the 1937 team; he scored 55 that season but there was a chap named Lyford who also played before the war. I used to go up and watch him with me father, you know, as a boy, and he was still playing for the seconds then, he scored something like 109 goals in one season. Oh I must have been about ten or something like that when I saw him before the war.

One of the most successful seasons on record for Forest Green Rovers was rounded off at the annual dinner at the George Hotel in Nailsworth, with a full report of the season and the dinner appearing in the *Stroud News* on 3 June 1938.

1938/39

The committee's primary concern this season was the erection of the new 40-foot-long grandstand to improve the ground, for which Donahue Brothers had provided a quotation of £60. A subscription book was opened to help cover the costs for 200 subscriptions of 5s each. The order was placed with Donahue Brothers in the sum of £50. The committee drove a hard bargain.

RAY BINGLE

I must have been about eight or nine when I started watching. And I can always remember watching Brimscombe; there was a lot of rivalry with Forest Green and Brimscombe, more so than Forest Green and Chalford, say. I don't know why, but that's how things go. We used to cycle over the Common to watch them.

I can remember Harold and Norman Vick. They were good players. Norman used to take the penalties, and it used to be always about a foot inside the post, but I can never remember him missing. And Ronnie Clift, he was a good player. He was killed in Crete I think.

The price of admission to watch a game was set at 4*d* to the field with 2*d* extra to the stand, and it was agreed to abolish any charge for children under fourteen years of age. Previously they had been charged 1*d* for entry. Fifty season tickets for the grandstand were printed at 2*s* 6*d* for first-team games only.

The first team opened its fixture list in the Senior League against Stonehouse away on 3 September, drawing 1-1, followed by the first home game of the season on 10 September with an 11-1 thrashing of Listers. B.H. Ford played in goal in place of Jack Brock, who wasn't with the club this season.

The stand was officially opened by Owen Davis prior to the home match against Dursley at the end of September, which was drawn 2-2

Basil Newport joined the club for the 1938 season and played his first match for the second team at Forest Green against Coaley on 1 October, winning 6-1. In October, Forest Green Rovers suffered their first defeat in two seasons, losing 4-1 to Cinderford, leaving them lying fifth in the league after 5 games with 6 points. The club chartered a red-and-white coach to take the players, officials and supporters down into the Forest for the match.

The following week, Forest Green beat Chalford 4–1 away on 8 October. In the meantime Chalford had continued in their attempts to make headway in the FA Amateur Cup, but were beaten 5–3 by Wells City of the Western League at the end of October. Forest Green still showed no interest in the national cup, content to continue playing within Gloucestershire. On the same day that Chalford lost in the FA Amateur Cup, Forest Green beat old rivals Sharpness 8–1 in the league to move into second place, with 12 points from 8 games. By this time, the club was also running a fund-raising football competition, with a prize payout to the winner at each game. We don't know the details of the competition format, though we do know that due to an oversight eight winners were paid out on 15 October, with a substantial loss on the game!

Basil Newport was picked to play for the first team and made his debut in the match away to Dursley on Saturday 31 December 1938.

BASIL NEWPORT

Saturday 31 December 1938.
Dursley 1 Forest Green Rovers 2
The goals were coming for me in the seconds, one of those times when you couldn't do anything but score. I played for the seconds when I was sixteen or seventeen. I came up one night and went across to the players like and they said, 'Basil you've got a bloody job.' I said 'Come off it!' He said 'You have! You're in the bloody firsts!' Honestly, I got in there and then was never out.

I remember my first game was against Dursley Town. They picked me up at Horsley. Since then I went from strength to strength you know. We had some good games against them. You got to know one another like. You knew who you was going to come up against, they was more or less the same team. I got quite friendly with one of the full-backs down at Dursley. He was a good chap to play against.

And then there were the referees, There was a chap named Hawker. When there was a bad match, like a wet rainy pudding, he'd find one dry spot and there he'd ref the match. He was a bloody character mind. I expect Peter Vick will tell you about him. I've had no trouble between me and the refs.

I went into a good team and decided to stay. Mind, you go into a good team and you can generally play well in it.

By December Rovers had progressed in the Senior Amateur Cup and were still lying in second place in the League to Stonehouse, who had played 3 games more. Forest Green's exploits in the Senior Amateur Cup appeared to have been brought to a halt for the second time by Charlton Kings in the third round at the end of January 1939, as they lost a tight game 1–0. But the following week it was reported that the club had reason to believe that some members of the Charlton team were not registered, and a protest was lodged. The game was then replayed on 20 February, this time with Forest Green winning 3–2. The semi-final was to take place at Gloucester City's ground on 11 March and the committee were not sure whether Ronnie Clift would be cup-tied, as he had already played for Bristol Rovers reserves that season in the Southern Section Cup. He did play in the semi-final, which is recalled by Basil Newport below.

BASIL NEWPORT

One of the best games I had was at Gloucester City against Cinderford in the semi-final in 1939. I was brilliant that day, even if I say it meself. We won 2–1, I think. I used to like the wet. We played at Longlevens then and I really enjoyed that match. As I said, sometimes they go for you, but I can't make men out when they play with a ball week in, month in, year in, and they say he got it on the wrong foot. I can never make that out when they say he's on the wrong foot. They shouldn't have a wrong foot, should they?

I remember our Alan, my son, saying that when he went down to Bristol City from Forest Green, he did play with his arms tied behind his back. I think that's wrong. I think that's his natural way.

We had a brilliant captain in Bob Peachey. He was honest. If the side weren't going how he thought they should then he'd cuff us all about you know. And Dougie Marks. They were a good bunch of lads, you know, from the goalkeeper down. Ronny Clift, he stood out. He was an 'ard no messin' centre half with Scrubby Cowley. You've got to have a couple like that out there, haven't you?

Towards the end of the season in March, Forest Green marched through the early rounds of the Cirencester Hospital Cup with 9-0 and 16-0 victories before the day of the Senior Amateur Cup final arrived on Saturday 1 April.

MARSHALL WOODWARD

I remember cycling to Wotton to watch Forest Green in the 1938/39 Senior Amateur Cup final. I can remember the team; Brock, Peachy, Herbert, Bob Peachey, George Peachy, Ted Peachy. I was about eleven or twelve and Ray Bingle and me, we cycled over to Wotton. Forest Green drew one each. Albert scored the goal.

Forest Green had a penalty, and I'll always remember this. George Peachy was right back. He took the penalty. It used to be sawdust for the penalty spot in them days, and the touchlines. Anyway, he scuffed the penalty and he trickled along the ground and there was a great cloud of sawdust. Then the goalie said something. Anyway this chap here, Dennis Herbert, he said to him 'You shouldn't have mentioned that to him. That's like red rag to a bull.' There were a lot of people there, we used to get a quite a big crowd at that time.

BASIL NEWPORT

George Peachey missed a penalty. Oh God, poor George! In that first match at Wotton, we could do anything but score! Oh yes, Dursley had the luck, we were definitely the best team on that day.

Before that cup there, they come and interviewed me. If you had a good game on the Saturday, the *Stroud News* used to come down to the factory. And they'd ask if they could interview you, you know. I thought I was it!! They'd give you a write up, you know. They come and took my photograph. I was the youngest in the team. I was seventeen and playing down in the final at Wotton. Anyway, we lost the replay 3-1. There was another good crowd. They used to come out and watch all right.

We used to play a lot in the evenings then. Kick off was about quarter past or half past six and we'd be finished by about eight.

The cup final replay was followed by a home game against Gloucester City, which Rovers won 2-0 to bring some cheer back to the club, followed by a visit to Gloucester and another win, this time 2-1. Forest Green again had a good season in the Northern Senior League, finishing fourth to Cinderford Town, Stonehouse and Brimscombe. The reserves won the Severn Vale League and the Second Division of the Stroud League.

The cup run and bad weather earlier in the year had again led to serious fixture congestion and the first-team this year played on 1, 3, 4, 8, 10, 13, 15, 18, 21, 22, 24, 25, 27, 29 April and 1, 2, 4, May. The second team had a similar run in, bringing another successful season to an end.

SENIOR CUP FINAL

THE TEAMS ON VIEW AT WOTTON

TO-MORROW one can expect a real cup-tie tussle at Wotton when Forest Green and Dursley meet in the final of the Northern Senior Cup.

It seems only fitting that Dursley should have scored so much success during their jubilee. For many years they kept plugging steadily on, doing nothing outstanding, but nevertheless being one of the bulwarks of the local league. Then, in 1923, the Northern Amateur Cup came to Dursley—and they have not seen it since, although they have been successful in both junior and senior sections of the Berkeley Hospital Cup Competition. It is twelve years since Dursley competed in senior league football.

One can safely say that the Dursley club has seldom stood in a better position, both from the point of view of football and finance, than they are to-day. They have between forty and fifty playing members, and, presumably because of their advent into higher football circles, are receiving increasing support from the townspeople.

The average age of the Dursley team is just over 21 years; the majority of these players are surprisingly young to be in such a high class of football, but what they lack in experience they make up in spirit. It would seem that Dursley have many promising seasons in front of them if they can hold their personnel together.

Forest Green have earned a reputation for themselves by virtue of the high positions which they attained time after time. They have not held the senior cup, however, since 1926-7. During the past few years they seem to have been doing things in cycles of three years.

They have been in the senior league for the past three years; previous to that they were in the Dursley and Wotton league, and succeeded in winning the championship for three years in succession. They held the Stroud Premier cup for three years in succession, and for a similar period they were winners of the Stroud Hospital Cup.

Forest Green have a few experienced players in their team and they have a good influence on the younger players. Forest Green did not care to win their reputation as doughty cup finalists by taking things easily, but by

R. CLIFT (19), inside right (left); has been included in Forest Green team for three seasons; Bristol Rovers Reserves have played him four times this season. V. COWLEY, centre half (right); graduated to the Forest Green eleven from Shortwood; has been playing for the Green for three seasons.

H. FORD (22), goal-keeper (left); previously played for Woodchester; he has featured in the Forest Green eleven for a couple of seasons. S. HARRISON (29) outside left (right); veteran of the team has eight seasons' experience and many cups and medals; previously for Shortwood.

D. HERBERT, left back (left); played for Shortwood in his earlier days; joined Forest Green six seasons ago, and has been with them ever since. D. MARKS (26), inside left (right) has played six seasons for Forest Green.

B. NEWPORT (17), outside right (left); 'baby' of the team; commenced only this season with Forest Green; played in junior football last season. E. PEACHEY (22) centre forward (right); got into competitive local football by joining Minchinhampton; has been playing for Forest Green for three seasons.

G. PEACHEY (24), right back (left); also graduated from Minchinhampton; joined Forest Green three seasons ago and has featured regularly in their team ever since. R. PEACHEY (29), captain and left half (right) originally played for Brimscombe; has been with Forest Green for half a dozen seasons.

H. VICK, right half (left); started his football career with Uplands; is in his first season for Forest Green.

LIONEL BENNETT, (right); secretary of the club, has been in office for some twelve years. He is very popular among the members.

RAY BINGLE

We played Dursley in the final at Wotton; they drew one each. I shouldn't say it really, but George Peachey had missed a penalty. George was always a bit touchy about it.

Of course the players didn't go away in buses. They had Charlie Mortimer's taxis. I can always remember Charlie, he had a grey one and a black one; the old upright. I can remember because the team passed us when we were cycling to Wotton to see the final.

Medals and cups won by Dennis Herbert, pre-war captain while at Forest Green Rovers. Dennis was not to play for Forest Green Rovers after the war because of injury.

Dennis Herbert was an Avening man who came up to Forest Green in the early 1930s and then broke into the first team. He was captain for the 1935/36 season and played until the outbreak of war. He carried on playing for the RAF in the Second World War until he injured his knee and had to give up football. He then became very active in the Nailsworth Bowling Club.

12

The War Years: 1939–1945

1939/40

By August 1939 events on the world stage overshadowed everything, but the Stroud League still managed to kick off and the second team played against Brimscombe, winning 2-0 on 26 August. The return game against Brimscombe for 2 September was cancelled. Preparations went on at The Lawn with a load of sawdust delivered to mark out the pitch in October, but the committee reported that they were not sure whether they were playing home or away the

MARSHALL WOODWARD

During the Second World War, there was no league football, and Lord Lee from Avening, Lord Lee of Fareham, I think t'was; he put up a cup for Avening to win. There was Avening and Minchinhampton, Tetbury, and about five sides and Nailsworth. We were sat in my mother's doing some studying for our higher nationals. We lived at Forest Green and we had to give a name to this team and we discussed it; and along the road about a hundred yards lived a chap named Johnny Ranger, and we decided to call ourselves Nailsworth Rangers. He was in the area above us, you know. He was too old for us.

We used to play up in the Enoch's. We used to throw down these little white pebbles as markers. Now Enoch's Field is where King George V Playing Field is, with a slope down.

We played six-a-sides and all that. And Ray Bingle, who I played with at the time, he's on the photo. I've known him all me life. We played football together for Nailsworth Rangers. Anyway, we won the league and Lord Lee had to bring the cup in the box and the cup went down to the Britannia up on the shelf; and nobody ever knows where the cup then went to. I don't believe Lord Lee had it back. During the war we had to go somewhere, because there was no football around, so we used to go on our bicycles to play, up to Aston Down to play the RAF sides and all that.

We used to play cricket as well at Tanners Piece. We all watched the Nailsworth Rangers cricket team after the war. Now then, a local wrote in the *Nailsworth News* that Nailsworth Rangers was the cricket team and I was going put a letter in saying t'was a football team as well to start with. Arthur Humphries started running the cricket team, I'll bet you that was the birth of the boys' club, cause the cricket team amalgamated with Selsley and they called it Nailsworth & Selsley Rangers I think, and Arthur started the boys' club through being attached to the cricket.

These are photo's of Nailsworth Rangers during the Second World War.

following Saturday. Arrangements for matches were becoming difficult. In all, only 3 matches are noted in the minute books, with the last being a team to play Chalford at Chalford in the Northern Senior League on 21 October. The game didn't take place.

Chalford were finding it almost impossible to travel, being a team that relied heavily on the railway, and their match against Blakeney was cancelled, noting that all available transport in the Stroud area was being used to collect evacuees from Stroud Station as they arrived from London.

A committee meeting was arranged for April 1941 to endorse the loan of the pay huts to the Home Guard to the place at Lynch Knoll, with the expense of the dismantling, removal and redirection to be met by Mr J.B. King.

A whist drive was held in February 1942 to keep the club ticking over and, at the committee meeting in March, it was agreed to run further whist drives throughout the year with cigarettes as prizes. The money from the whist drives was used for maintenance at the ground. The first rules of the club were also drawn up at the committee meeting on 16 April 1942 as follows:

Nailsworth Rangers 6-a-side team.

1. *The club shall be called Forest Green Rovers AFC*
2. *Headquarters: Jovial Forester Inn*
3. *Ground: The Lawn*
4. *Colours: Black and white stripes*
5. *The club shall be directed and run by officials and committee duly elected at an Annual General Meeting called by the secretary, only previous season's club members being allowed to vote for the offices and committee for the ensuing season.*

Nailsworth Rangers 11-a-side team.

6. *All members must pay a subscription for the season, which shall be decided by the Annual General Meeting and must be paid by any date decided by the meeting. Any person not doing so shall not be considered a bona fide member of the club and it shall be left to the discretion of the committee to decide if any such person be allowed to take part in the management of the club or to play any games.*

7. *All playing members must in accordance with the GFA rules be proposed, seconded and voted as members by the committee.*

8. *The committee shall have the power to order the attendance of any player at a meeting on any matter concerning playing or club discipline.*

9. *Any five members shall have the right to ask for the calling of a General Meeting. Such request to be made in writing stating the reason and forwarded to the secretary.*

10. *These rules shall be read at the commencement of each Annual General Meeting and the signing of any league or competition playing form shall be considered as an agreement to observe and abide by these rules on the part of any person so signing.*

11. *Any person who accepts an official position consents to serve on the committee of the club and shall endeavour to enforce the observance of these rules.*

12. *Any proposed alteration to these rules must be made in writing to the secretary fourteen days before the date of the Annual General Meeting.*

Funds were running low again by the time of the next meeting in October 1943, and a target was set to raise £25 before the next annual meeting. A dance was arranged at the Comrades Hall for 1 January 1944, which raised a total profit of £13 7s 4d. A further dance was subsequently arranged for April and again profits were in excess of £14.

A good deal of discussion took place at the meeting in October 1943 regarding the state of the field, which had now been pasture for nearly four years. While Mr King had agreed to keep the turf in reasonable condition under his 'grass keep' agreement; this turn out not to be a practical option, with the field left to be grazed by pigs and sheep.

By August 1944 the field was in a terrible state and the committee hit upon the idea of writing to the ATC, suggesting that rather than playing football matches on the field they might like to help put it back to a playing state in lieu of paying rent. In the end the ATC boys made do with Nailsworth playing fields, the ATC reporting to the club secretary that 'The boys found the field in such a poor condition that it would be impossible for them to get it anything like fit for football before Christmas.' By the end of 1944, the only subject of the minutes was the state of the pitch with Mr King finally admitting his liability and promising to put the ground right. The committee took over to get the field ready to play on in August 1945, for what could potentially be the first new football season since 1939.

The chairman read correspondence from the Northern Senior League at the committee meeting on 28 May 1945, calling a meeting in Gloucester with a view to restarting the league. Marshall Woodward and Ray Bingle were also elected to the general committee as 'boys' representatives'. And with that, thoughts turned to the forthcoming football season and a welcome return to sporting pastimes after the past six years of war.

Nailsworth home guard assembled for a drill, including quite a few old Rovers footballers.

Part III
1945–1975

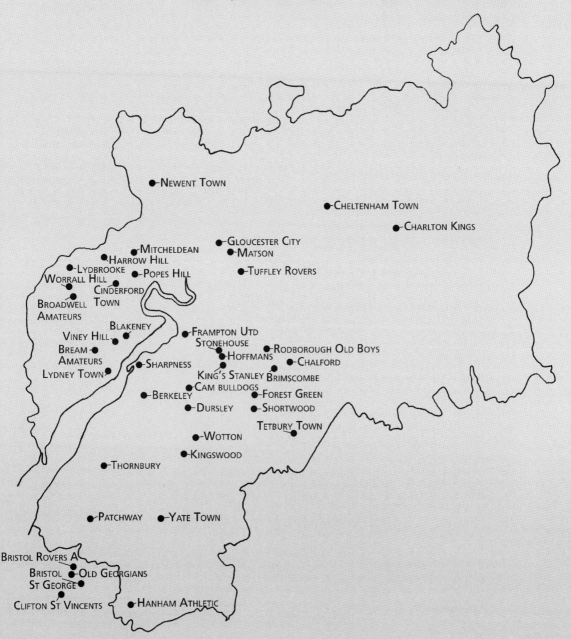

●–Newent Town

●–Cheltenham Town

●–Charlton Kings

●–Gloucester City
●–Matson
●–Mitcheldean
Harrow Hill●
●–Lydbrooke   ●–Popes Hill   ●–Tuffley Rovers
Worrall Hill●
Cinderford
Broadwell●   Town
Amateurs
Blakeney
Viney Hill●   ●–Frampton Utd
Bream●   Stonehouse
Amateurs   ●–Hoffmans   ●–Rodborough Old Boys
Lydney Town●   ●–Sharpness   ●–Chalford
                King's Stanley Brimscombe
                ●–Cam bulldogs
●–Berkeley   ●–Forest Green
          ●–Dursley   ●–Shortwood
                Tetbury Town●
          ●–Wotton
          ●–Kingswood
●–Thornbury

●–Patchway   ●–Yate Town

Bristol Rovers A●
Bristol● ●–Old Georgians
St George●
Clifton St Vincents●   ●–Hanham Athletic

13

Post-war Success: 1945–1950

1945/46

Not enough clubs were yet up and running to restart the Northern Senior League, but the Stroud League had enough and Rovers entered their first team for the season. It kicked off on 8 September with a home match against Brimscombe. Marshall Woodward and Ray Bingle went straight into the first team to play alongside Basil Newport, Bob Peachey and Peter Vick from the pre-war team. Ronnie Clift and Tom Harris lost their lives during the Second World War, leaving spaces to be filled in the team. Rovers had a very strong team, which only became stronger as old faces returned from the Second World War to take their place.

Nailsworth band were also back up and running and were hired to play at The Lawn for the Northern Senior Cup tie on 29 December, helping to bring a sense of normality back to Forest Green. Les 'Sailor' Dangerfield was still in uniform at the end of November and the club agreed to pay his travelling expenses back from Andover each Saturday to play whenever he was available. Enough players had returned by November for a second team and the reserves kicked off their season with a series of friendlies, including a young Jim Turk in the side.

Forest Green's 18-1 win over Dursley in March produced a gate of £11 6s 6d, which went to the Welcome Home fund. Off the field, it was very difficult to obtain supplies and a permit system was in operation, so that the club had to apply to the War Office for permits to buy footballs, kit and anything else for the club. Fundraising was still a major concern and, towards the end of the season, Forest Green arranged a friendly against RAF Southern Command, which attracted a very large crowd and a very good gate. A further friendly was arranged against Cinderford Town for Easter Monday.

Forest Green romped to victory in the Stroud League and also made it to the Northern Senior Amateur Cup final at Hoffmans, where they faced RAF Records from Quedgley. Four coaches were arranged to transport the supporters not making their own way to the game.

As well as the Stroud League and the Senior Amateur Cup, Forest Green also won the Stroud Hospital Cup, beating Rodborough Old Boys.

MARSHALL WOODWARD

The first game I played for Forest Green was in 1945. I was eighteen. T'was just the right age to start playing football. I played centre half for some unknown reason, just straight after the Second World War. It might have been John Pearson who got me up there, we had to put our name forward or something. He was our teacher before the war. We just turned up and they selected sides and that's how it went from there.

We had a bloody good team straight after the war and a good run in the cup. I can't remember much about the cup final, but I can remember something about the game against Dursley! I had seven shots and they all went in; that was the Stroud League. 18-1! And I reckon I remember the goalkeeper had a good game; as it went on he made a lot of good saves. It was bit embarrassing really. We couldn't understand what was wrong with the rest of the team.

Northern Senior Amateur Cup winners certificate, 1946.

GLOUCESTERSHIRE FOOTBALL
INCOR. ASSOCIATION 1886

This Certificate is awarded to

M.J. WOODWARD

Member of FOREST GREEN ROVERS

WINNERS of the NORTHERN SENIOR Cup

Season 1945-1946

A.C.Chappelle HON.TREASURER ... CHAIRMAN ... HON.SECRETARY.

PETER VICK

After the war the Stroud League started up again and we won the Senior Amateur Cup in 1946. We never got issued with a medal but we got a certificate instead, and that's the only one ever been produced. That season we got a beautiful colour certificate. That was THE cup in them days.

BASIL NEWPORT

There was a few killed in the war, Ronnie Clift was one of them. Some of 'em hung on to their place, like meself when I got back. That's when Marshall Woodward and others come in. We won nearly every game that season. We beat RAF Records in the Senior Amateur Cup final that year. Forest Green was always the big team.

Drainey Grant was playing for Forest Green then. They were good days mind. I got 16 goals that season – wasn't bad was it? When you're on a goal run they tend to come quite easy, you know. There was a big crowd again when we won the cup against RAF Records.

Another good side in them days was Broadwell. I'd been up at Forest Green when we played Broadwell. They was a brilliant side, honest they was, and they had some good players. We were up there playing them in the semi-final at home and the crowd was thick all the way round the ground. That's the thing, they soon gather for a winning team. They'd be out there tomorrow if Forest Green started winning again.

NORTHERN SENIOR AMATEUR CUP FINAL

Forest Green Rovers 4; R.A.F., Quedgeley 1

A light ball and a hard ground foiled many an attack by opposing forward lines in this final at the Hoffman's Sports Ground on Saturday, between Forest Green Rovers, champions of the Stroud & District League, and finalists with R.O.B. for the Stroud Hospital Cup, and R.A.F., Quedgeley, a team with an unbeaten record in the Gloucestershire Hurran League. Play started at a fast speed and it was soon evident that a keenly contested game was to be witnessed. It was pleasing to watch the brilliant passing movements and combination of the R.A.F. team, whilst the Rovers themselves proved no mean opponents. The first goal came through Woodward after some twenty-five minutes play, and shortly afterwards, the R.A.F. centre forward broke through, and after weaving in and out of the Rovers defence, successfully netted. Half-time score 1—1.

The second half brought a number of surprises. The R.A.F. showed signs of tiring, whilst the Rovers previous uneasiness was soon dispelled and they were a changed team. A second goal came from Peachey, and shortly afterwards the Rovers were awarded a free kick. Woodward sent in a really glorious shot right up under the cross-bar and completely beat the R.A.F. 'keeper. One R.A.F. forward was obliged to leave the field owing to injury, but returned some time later. A number of breakthroughs were made by the R.A.F., but these failed to be really dangerous, and the Rovers defence always made perfect clearances. Some minutes before the final whistle, Webb scored a fourth for the Rovers. Summing up,—two grand teams, who played first class football.

LEAGUE TABLES TO DATE

Division I.

	P.	W.	L.	D.	Goals F.	A.	Pts.
Forest Green	19	17	0	2	92	17	*34
Stonehouse	21	14	6	1	67	35	29
Brimscombe	20	12	6	2	77	41	26
King's Stanley	22	12	8	2	89	50	26
Chalford	22	10	7	5	71	45	25
R.O.B.	20	11	8	1	73	53	23
Aston Down	20	8	7	5	67	40	21
Min'hampton	23	8	15	0	52	71	16
Avening	21	6	13	2	47	83	14
Leonard Stanley	19	5	12	2	44	96	12
Dursley	20	5	15	0	40	110	10
Uley	19	2	15	2	33	125	6

*Two points deducted for playing an ineligible player.

Division II.

	P.	W.	L.	D.	Goals F.	A.	Pts.
Stonehouse	9	7	1	1	40	20	15
R.O.B.	10	7	2	1	40	18	15
Chalford	8	5	3	0	39	20	10
King's Stanley	9	3	4	2	25	35	8
Forest Green	6	3	3	0	20	16	6
Avening	10	3	7	0	26	46	6
Min'hampton	8	0	3	0	9	44	0

FOREST GREEN ROVERS, this season's Stroud Hospital Cup winners, with the Cup and Mascot, after their triumph on Saturday. Back row (left to right): B. Weager (trainer), B. Newport, J. Pearson, S. Harrison, H. Broadhead (Secretary), H. Vick, E. G. Smith (Chairman), R. Bingle, B. Ford, L. Ponter (Linesman); Front row: B. Peates, L. Dangerfield, R. Peachey (Captain), M. Woodward, H. Webb.

SEASON'S RECORD.

PLD.	W	L	D	F
37	34	0	3	173

Winners of

Stroud League Div. 1.

Stroud Hospital Cup.

Northern Senior Amateur Cup.

GOAL SCORERS.

R.Peachey (Capt.)	54	H.Thomas	2
H.Webb	36	B.Fletcher	1
M.Woodward	20	B.Fisher	1
B.Newport	16	A.Grant	1
L.Dangerfield	13	J.Pearson	1
B.Peates	10	H.Vick	1
R.Bingle	5	D.Brown	1
R.Lyeford	4		
D.Harvey	2		
D.Herbert	2		

2/3	S.L	Dursley	Home Win	18-1	Woodward 7
					Newport
					R. Peachey 5
					Webb 2
					Pearson. Vick.H.
					L.Dangerfield

Marshall Woodward also kept a complete record of his first season at Forest Green, including the scorers in the 18-1 defeat of Dursley.

1946/47

In September 1946 Stan White formed an official supporters' club which came about after the success of the Welcome Home Fund Committee. It immediately became the driving force behind Forest Green, making up any gate for first or second team games to £4 to assist with funds from the day they were formed.

A decision was made to travel to away matches by bus, sometimes two buses against teams like Cinderford. Supporters were charged 2s 6d to subsidise transport costs. Jack Brock returned to the district in November. Bert Ford dropped to the reserves and then transferred to Hoffmans to get first-team football. Nailsworth Rangers Cricket Club also agreed to use the football field for the forthcoming summer for a rent of £2, the same as Newmarket Cricket Club's rent before the war.

Forest Green finished eighth in a Senior League consisting of fifteen teams, finding the going a bit tougher than in the Stroud League the year before.

JOHN DUFF

When I was a boy I walked from Watledge with the crowds that were going up there on Saturdays, because there would only have been Saturday matches then. And there were some big crowds walking up there, particularly if they played somebody like Brimscombe, and they would have walked over the common from Brimscombe to Forest Green, or vice versa if the match was over there. The crowds would be three or four deep around the ground. The lads all went – not only the lads but lasses as well – to see Forest Green play, and they would turn up in their hundreds.

ASSOCIATION FOOTBALL

This week's Zenith Soccer team photo is of Forest Green, who shared points with Brimscombe in a N.S.L. duel at The Meadow.

The team that played Brimscombe on 26 October 1946.

MARSHALL WOODWARD

We played a lot of games down in the Forest of Dean. Some of them were a waste of time; they used to come out the pub drunk and just kick anything in sight.

Blakeney was the worst I ever went to; and they had a plank across a brook and when the referee wasn't going their way they would shake that plank and he would wobble; and sometimes their own players would end up in the brook. They used to come out the pub all drunk; waste of time going down there to play football. Viney Hill had tree stumps growing out in the field!

NORTHERN SENIOR LEAGUE				STROUD LEAGUE			
'46 Au. 31	Brimscombe	H 2 3		'46 Au. 31	Brimscombe	W	A 1 2
Sept. 7	Bream	A 1 0		Sept. 7	Tetbury	W	H 4 1
14	Chalford	H 0 1		14	Chalford	W	A 2 4
21	Sharpness	A 2 2		21	Whiteshill		A 6 0
28	Broadwell	H 1 1		28	Frampton		A 1 2
Oct. 5	Cinderford	A 2 5		Oct. 5	Woodchester	W	H 0 5
12	Maudsleys	A		12	Frampton		H 1 2
19	Blakeney	H 1 1		19	Woodchester		A 0 3
26	Brimscombe	A 2 2		26	Brimscombe		H 3 2
Nov. 2	King Stanley	A 4 4		Nov. 2	King Stanley		H 2 0
9	Hospital Cup			9	Hospital Cup		A 0 1
16	Stonehouse	A 3		16	Stonehouse		H 3 1
23	Junior Cup	W 4		30	Leonard Stanley		A 5 0
30	Senior Cup	L 4 5		Dec. 7	Avening		H
Dec. 14	Chalford	A 1 2		14	Chalford		H 2 3
21	Stonehouse	H		21	Stonehouse		A
B.D. 26	Rodborough O.B.	H 2 1		B.D. 26	Rodborough		A
28	Hoffmans	A 1 6					
'47 Jan. 4	Cup Round			'47 Jan. 4	Amberley		A
11	King Stanley	H 3 2		11	King Stanley		A 0 5
18	Popeshill	H		18	Tetbury		A
Feb. 1	Dursley	A		25	Amberley		H 1 2
8	Popeshill	A		Feb. 1	Leonard Stanley		H
15	Hoffmans	H		8	Minchinhampton		H
22	Rodborough O.B.	A		15	Avening		A
Mar. 1	Broadwell	H		22	Rodborough		H
8	Bream	H		Mar. 1			
15	Cinderford	H		8			
22	Sharpness	H		15	Minchinhampton		A
29	Ruardean	H		22			
Apr. 5	Dursley	H		29			
12	Ruardean	A		Apr. 5			
26	Blakeney	A		12			
E.M. 28	Maudsleys	H		19	Whiteshill		H

Forest Green Rovers fixture card, 1946/47.

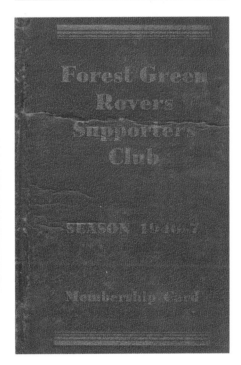

1947/48

A selection committee was created for the first time in the club's history to consist of five, plus two team captains (the captains themselves would still be chosen by the committee). The first selection committee consisted of Norman Vick, Bob Peachey, Joe Brown and Cecil Turner, all past players, and Ben Weager.

Off the field Mrs Smith, the landlady of the Jovial Foresters, was finally to retire. She had been there since before the First World War, almost as long as Forest Green had. The new landlord, Tom Stockwell, confirmed that everything could carry on as before.

Above: Brimscombe's 1946 programme. Brimscombe were as big a club as Forest Green and had started producing match day programmes.

Right: Brimscombe's programme from 1947 for the Senior League match. Forest Green lost 5-1.

Stonehouse turned semi-professional, joining the Western League, where they would compete for the next thirteen years as a professional club. They were replaced by Charlton Kings, who Forest Green knew well from the cup before the Second World War.

At Forest Green, tickets had been sold with a lucky number prize, and that proved to be a very successful money-raising scheme. Peter Vick started looking into the possibility of a match programme. He worked at Arthur's Press. A coupon system was still running, so that the club could not obtain new shorts without obtaining coupons from the FA to confirm that they were actually needed.

PETER VICK

I used to play in glasses after the war, that caused problems. It caused no problem football-wise but it caused problems to me because nearly every week I had a cut nose. The glasses were unbreakable but my nose wasn't. They were service glasses, provided for people with short sightedness to go inside gas masks, with steel frame and steel sides. I didn't injure any other players, more myself. I headed the bloody heavy ball and then it would cut me; cut me nose. That's alright, that didn't matter did it? T'was all in the spirit of the game, wasn't it?

Ben Weager, in the meantime, got himself into trouble after passing remarks at the end of a game in February and was interviewed by the committee to investigate the alleged misdemeanour. Negative thought was not acceptable!

Mr Purser was being paid 10s per month to turn up for the first team, hardly enough to break the budget. The supporters' club continued to make the weekly gate for both first and second team matches up to £4 and handed over a further sum of £17 for repairs to the ground.

Forest Green Rovers 1947/1948. Third in the Northern Senior League. Back row: Wilf Riley, Doug Brown, John Pearson, Jack Brock, Ray Bingle, Scrubby Cowley. Front row: Basil Newport, Cliff Purser, John Pettit, Marshall Woodward, Cecil Hudd.

MARSHALL WOODWARD

That's one of the best teams; John Pearson's. He was a teacher up at the school up Spring Hill. I went to school up there at a certain age and then I went off to Stroud Boys Central and he taught up there then. John Brock, he played in goal for Swindon Town. His father used to keep the George Hotel; he lived in a house along the road at Watledge. He was a class goalkeeper. The big bloke in the middle; that's John Pettit, who's I think was a schoolmaster, a friend of John Brock, and there is Purser, who's also a school master I believe. Was also a friend of his. And they didn't play for very long.

So that was Brock, Riley and Cowley. Scrubby Cowley, Doug Brown, John Pearson and Ray Bingle went to school with me. That's the forward line as it was. Basil Newport, then I can't remember his first name, Purser his name was. It's on one of them programmes. John Pettit – the crowd didn't like him; he scored a hat-trick in one game. He had a hell of a shot on him, he played centre forward. They didn't like him, the crowd got on to him and it upset him and he didn't play anymore. He went back to wherever he come from. And Cecil Hudd's down there on the right.

Ron Davis was elected club secretary at the AGM in May 1948, a position that he would hold for twenty years. In a short report, the previous secretary, Mr Broadhead, reported that the senior team had finished third in the Northern Senior League behind Sharpness and Brimscombe, and the junior team had finished sixth in the Stroud League.

Samples of programmes were presented to the committee in July, and the *Stroud Journal* were appointed to provide 7,000 programmes for £43 15s 0d. It was decided that a 5s voucher should be given each week to the holder of a lucky number and that the voucher would have to be spent with one of the advertisers in the programme.

1948/49

For the first time ever, programmes were produced for home matches and 250 programmes were ordered for the first game, on sale at the George Hotel in Nailsworth and the Jovial Forester from the Friday night before the match. They were all sold and for the next game 500 were printed, with minutes confirming that 414 were finally sold. The crowd would have been somewhere in excess of this. Between 450 and 500 programmes were then ordered for first-team games and fixtures against Shortwood, and around 250 were ordered for the reserve fixtures. Five hundred and fifty programmes were ordered for the home tie against newcomers Charlton Kings towards the end of the year. It was effectively a championship decider. By the end of the season 13,500 programmes had been bought, with 11,114 being sold, generating a profit of £71 15s 10d.

Left: Forest Green Rovers Reserves 1947/48. Back row: Don Gannaway, Stan Fream, Harold Vick, Norman Vick. Front row: Peter Larner, Des Dangerfield, Phil Sawyer, Peter Vick, Des Harvey, Harold Holloway, Bob Hanks, Harry Freeman.

Below: The last game of the season, Brimscombe away; this time in the semi-final replay of the Stroud Charity Cup. Forest Green lost 2-0, bringing their season to a close.

DATE	GROUND	NATURE OF GAME	FIXTURES	RESULT
23rd AUG. 1947.	HOME.	FRIENDLY.	FOREST GREEN ROVERS. 1. SMETHWICK UNITED. 2. — OWN GOAL. — H.T. (0-0).	LOST.
30th AUG. 1947.	AWAY.	G.N.S.L.	FOREST GREEN ROVERS. 5. DURSLEY TOWN. 0. — PEACHEY.E. 2. HUDD.2. PURSER. — H.T. (2-0).	WON.
6th SEPT. 1947.	HOME.	G.N.S.L.	FOREST GREEN ROVERS. 4. DURSLEY TOWN. 1. — HUDD.3. (1 PEN). WOODWARD. — H.T. (2-1).	WON.
13th SEPT. 1947.	AWAY.	G.N.S.L.	FOREST GREEN ROVERS. 2. POPESHILL. 0. — HOLLOWAY. PEACHEY.E. — H.T. (1-0).	WON.
16th SEPT. 1947.	HOME.	FRIENDLY.	FOREST GREEN ROVERS. 4. R.A.F. ASTON DOWN. 2. — PERIT. WOODWARD. — H.T. (3-0).	WON.
20th SEPT. 1947.	HOME.	G.N.S.L.	FOREST GREEN ROVERS. 6. VINEY HILL ST. SWITHENS. 0. — NEWPORT.3. DANGERFIELD.L. WOODWARD. PURSER. — H.T.(0-0).	WON.
27th SEPT. 1947.	AWAY.	G.N.S.L.	FOREST GREEN ROVERS. 3. RUARDEAN. 2. — HUDD. OWN GOAL. PERIT. — H.T. (1-1).	WON.
11th OCT. 1947.	AWAY.	G.N.S.L.	FOREST GREEN ROVERS. 4. CINDERFORD TOWN. 1. — WOODWARD. 2. HUDD. NEWPORT. — H.T. (1-1).	WON.
18th OCT. 1947.	HOME.	G.N.S.L.	FOREST GREEN ROVERS. 5. BERKELEY. 1. — HUDD. 3. PURSER. 2. — H.T. (1-0).	WON.
25th OCT. 1947.	AWAY.	G.N.S.L.	FOREST GREEN ROVERS. 1. BROADWELL AMATEURS. 3. — PERIT. — H.T. (1-2).	LOST.
1st NOV. 1947.	HOME.	G.N.S.L.	FOREST GREEN ROVERS. 6. KINGSTANLEY. 1. — NEWPORT. WOODWARD. PURSER. PERIT. 2. OWN GOAL. — H.T. (3-0).	WON.
15th NOV. 1947.	HOME.	FRIENDLY.	FOREST GREEN ROVERS. 1. BRISTOL ROVERS 'A'. 2. — HARVEY.D. — H.T. (0-1).	LOST.
22nd NOV. 1947.	AWAY.	G.N.S.L.	FOREST GREEN ROVERS. 1. BRIMSCOMBE. 5. — WOODWARD. — H.T. (0-3).	LOST.
6th DEC. 1947.	AWAY.	G.N.S.L.	FOREST GREEN ROVERS. 4. KINGSTANLEY. 5. — HUDD. 2. (PEN). HARVEY.D. WOODWARD. — H.T. (3-2).	LOST.
20th DEC. 1947.	HOME.	G.N.S.L.	FOREST GREEN ROVERS. 1. BRIMSCOMBE. 6. — RILEY. — H.T. (0-3).	LOST.
26th DEC. 1947.	HOME.	G.N.S.L.	FOREST GREEN ROVERS. 7. BREAM AMATEURS. 1. — HUDD. 3. NEWPORT. 2. DANGERFIELD.L. WOODWARD. — H.T. (3-0).	WON.
27th DEC. 1947.	AWAY.	G.N.S.L.	FOREST GREEN ROVERS. 2. CHALFORD. 3. — HUDD. OWN GOAL. — H.T. (1-2).	LOST.

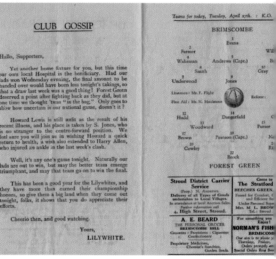

DATE	GROUND	NATURE OF GAME	FIXTURES	RESULT
14th APRIL. 1948.	HOME.	G.N.S.L.	FOREST GREEN ROVERS. 2. SHARPNESS. 1. — WOODWARD. (PEN). DANGERFIELD.L. — H.T. (1-0).	WON.
19th APRIL. 1948.	HOME.	G.N.S.L.	FOREST GREEN ROVERS. 2. CHALFORD. 2. — HOLLOWAY. WOODWARD. — H.T. (1-1).	DRAW.
21st APRIL. 1948.	HOME.	STROUD HOSPITAL CUP. SEMI-FINAL.	FOREST GREEN ROVERS. 3. BRIMSCOMBE. 3. — WOODWARD. (PEN). DANGERFIELD.L. HUDD. — H.T. (0-2).	DRAW.
24th APRIL. 1948.	AWAY.	G.N.S.L.	FOREST GREEN ROVERS. 3. BLAKENEY. 2. — HUDD. COWLEY.Y. STOKES. — H.T. (1-1).	WON.
27th APRIL. 1948.	AWAY.	STROUD HOSPITAL CUP. SEMI-FINAL. REPLAY.	FOREST GREEN ROVERS. 0. BRIMSCOMBE. 2. — H.T. (0-2).	LOST.

Marshall Woodward again recorded the 1947/48 season's exploits, which are shown here.

DATE	GROUND	NATURE OF GAME	FIXTURES	RESULT
3rd JAN. 1948.	HOME.	G.N.S.L.	FOREST GREEN ROVERS. 4. RODBOROUGH. O.B. 0. — HUDD. WOODWARD. SWIGGLE. — H.T. (0-0).	WON.
10th JAN. 1948.	HOME.	G.N.S AMATEUR CUP. 2ND ROUND.	FOREST GREEN ROVERS. 3. RODBOROUGH. O.B. 3. — HUDD. NEWPORT. — H.T.(1-2).	DRAW.
17th JAN. 1948.	AWAY.	G.N.S AMATEUR CUP. 2ND RD. REPLAY.	FOREST GREEN ROVERS. 5. RODBOROUGH.O.B. 3. — HUDD. 2. (PEN). FREEMAN. 3. — H.T. (1-2).	WON.
24th JAN. 1948.	AWAY.	G.N.S.L.	FOREST GREEN ROVERS. 1. RODBOROUGH.O.B. 3. — HUDD. — H.T. (1-2).	LOST.
31st JAN. 1948.	AWAY.	G.N.S.L.	FOREST GREEN ROVERS. 3. BERKELEY. 2. — HARVEY.D.2. NEWPORT. — H.T. (2-0).	WON.
7th FEB. 1948.	HOME.	G.N.S AMATEUR CUP. 3RD ROUND.	FOREST GREEN ROVERS. 0. CHARLTON KINGS. 4. — H.T. (0-3).	LOST.
14th FEB. 1948.	AWAY.	STROUD HOSPITAL CUP. 1ST ROUND.	FOREST GREEN ROVERS. 2. BERKELEY. 0. — NEWPORT. RILEY. (PEN). — H.T. (2-0).	WON.
28th FEB. 1948.	AWAY.	G.N.S.L.	FOREST GREEN ROVERS. 5. VINEY HILL ST. SWITHENS. 2. — WOODWARD. 3. NEWPORT. DANGERFIELD.L. — H.T. (4-0).	WON.
13th MAR. 1948.	AWAY.	G.N.S.L.	FOREST GREEN ROVERS. 2. SHARPNESS. 1. — DANGERFIELD.L. WOODWARD. — H.T. (2-0).	WON.
20th MAR. 1948.	HOME.	G.N.S.L.	FOREST GREEN ROVERS. 2. RUARDEAN. 0. — PURSER. WOODWARD. (PEN). — H.T. (2-0).	WON.
26th MAR. 1948.	HOME.	G.N.S.L.	FOREST GREEN ROVERS. 4. POPESHILL. 2. — HUDD. 2. GANNAWAY. D. PEACHEY. R. — H.T.(1-2).	WON.
27th MAR. 1948.	AWAY.	G.N.S.L.	FOREST GREEN ROVERS. 5. BREAM AMATEURS. 2. — PURSER. 2. NEWPORT. 2. DANGERFIELD. L. — H.T. (2-1).	WON.
25th MAR. 1948.	HOME.	G.N.S.L.	FOREST GREEN ROVERS. 2. CINDERFORD TOWN. 2. — NEWPORT. COWLEY.Y. — H.T. (0-2).	DRAW.
3rd APRIL. 1948.	HOME.	G.N.S.L.	FOREST GREEN ROVERS. 2. BLAKENEY. 0. — PURSER. HUDD. — H.T. (1-0).	WON.
7th APRIL. 1948.	AWAY.	STROUD HOSPITAL CUP. 2ND ROUND.	FOREST GREEN ROVERS. 3. CHALFORD. 1. — WOODWARD. DANGERFIELD.L. NEWPORT. — H.T. (3-1).	WON.
10th APRIL. 1948.	HOME.	G.N.S.L.	FOREST GREEN ROVERS. 2. BROADWELL AMATEURS. 3.	LOST.

On the footballing front, Charlton Kings, a Cheltenham team, became the season's biggest opponents. Forest Green failed to get the measure of them either in the league or in the cup during the first half of the season, although they managed a 3-3 draw in March.

An action shot from the home cup game against Charlton Kings.

ALL EYES are turned anxiously towards the Forest Green goal as a Charlton Kings player shoots during Saturday's N.S.A. cup

MARSHALL WOODWARD

I had a row with John Pearson once. He had trials with different clubs; he was a county player and was a great centre half. We used to say if a ball comes across in the goalmouth he didn't used to jump he was so blooming tall. You can see how tall he was; his head used to come out like on a stalk! Sailor Dangerfield was inside right, John would say 'Sailorrrrr' and you know he would come sailing straight towards yer; nobody could beat him in the air. And right at the end, just before he finished, a little tiny bloke beat him in the air and that was about when he packed up. Last time I saw him, I was outside Newman Henders one dinner time, he must have been on his way back to wherever he lived. He put his head out the window in a big bellowing voice and he shouted out at me. I thought 'What the hell was that?' 'Marshallllll!' 'Christ, that's John Pearson!' That's the last time I saw him. He was a brilliant centre half.

Anyway, t'was a match against Broadwell I was trying to remember. Pearson came along; we were losing 2-0 then down at Broadwell.

I used to like playing at Broadwell, they were a Forest team, and we was losing two nothing and Pearson wandered up at half-time, and Mrs Harvey. She came out the hut with oranges or lemons or something, handing 'em round. John Pearson came up and said 'What's going on? You ain't none of you even got a sweat on. You ain't done nothing.' He cussed and cussed and picked on me and I said 'Next week you can leave me out if you like.' He went on and cursed all half-time. Anyway, we was 2-0 down and then in the second half I remember Peter Larner. He hadn't played very well and he was outside right. He hit a cross and I was in the penalty area I suppose, and I just thought I'd lash it; and so I did and I didn't care where he goes, and he went straight in the blinkin' net, top right. Then I had a free kick, he would've been some way out on the left wing. I remember Sailor Dangerfield and the goalkeeper going up and Sailor goes around him and I hit that and that went in for two; and then I got one after that and we won 3-2.

And John Pearson, he never said a word after the game! And I remember thinking 'Bloody hell, I told him I would play for the seconds,' but nobody did nothin' terrible after us being 2-0 down. I had three down there and that was because I didn't care two hoots where the ball went. Just have a go and sometimes it goes in and sometimes it doesn't. You can get over elaborate sometimes, but as it happened that first 'un I smacked him and he went right, that was a low drive as well. I used to like them low. You see Hasselbaink do it, he's a great player.

Above: Forest Green Rovers' first-ever programme from the opening game of the 1948/49 season.

Left: Brimscombe away 1948, Forest Green won 3-1 (Mctiffen 2, Sailor Dangerfield).

Below and opposite above: Marshall Woodward's records of the season.

			SEASON 1948 - 1949		
DATE.	GROUND	NATURE OF GAME	FIXTURES		RESULT
4th SEPT. 1948.	HOME.	G.N.S.L.	FOREST GREEN ROVERS. 2. BRIMSCOMBE. 2.		DRAW.
			McTIFFIN. DANGERFIELD. L.	H.T. (2-1).	
11th SEPT. 1948.	AWAY.	G.N.S.L.	FOREST GREEN ROVERS. 3. VINEY HILL St SWITHENS. 2.		WON.
			WOODWARD. LARNER. HUDD.	H.T. (2-1).	
18th SEPT. 1948.	AWAY.	G.N.S.L.	FOREST GREEN ROVERS. 3. BROADWELL AMATEURS. 2.		WON.
			WOODWARD. 3.	H.T. (0-1).	
25th SEPT. 1948.	HOME.	G.N.S.L.	FOREST GREEN ROVERS. 4. CAM BULLDOGS. 1.		WON.
			WOODWARD. 2. HUDD. 2.	H.T. (2-1).	
2nd OCT. 1948.	AWAY.	G.N.S.L.	FOREST GREEN ROVERS. 0. CHARLTON KINGS. 3.		LOST.
				H.T. (0-2).	
9th OCT. 1948.	AWAY.	G.N.S.L.	FOREST GREEN ROVERS. 3. BRIMSCOMBE. 1.		WON.
			McTIFFIN. DANGERFIELD. L.	H.T. (1-1).	
16th OCT. 1948.	HOME.	FRIENDLY.	FOREST GREEN ROVERS. 6. CHIPPING SODBURY. 3.		WON.
			DANGERFIELD. GANNAWAY. H. TURK. 4.	H.T. (2-1).	
23rd OCT. 1948.	HOME.	FRIENDLY.	FOREST GREEN ROVERS. 4. LECKHAMPTON. 3.		WON.
			HARVEY. D. GANNAWAY. H. TURK. HUDD.	H.T. (2-1).	
30th OCT. 1948.	AWAY.	G.N.S.L.	FOREST GREEN ROVERS. 1. TETBURY TOWN. 0.		WON.
			TURK.	H.T. (1-0.)	
6th NOV. 1948.	HOME.	G.N.S.L.	FOREST GREEN ROVERS. 2. SHARPNESS. 1.		WON.
			COWLEY. V. (PEN.). BROWN. D.	H.T. (0-0).	
13th NOV. 1948.	HOME.	G.N.S.L.	FOREST GREEN ROVERS. 2. BERKELEY. 1.		WON.
			McTIFFIN. GANNAWAY. H.	H.T. (0-1).	
27th NOV. 1948.	AWAY.	G.N.S.L.	FOREST GREEN ROVERS. 3. DURSLEY TOWN. 1.		WON.
			McTIFFIN. HARVEY. G. 2.	H.T. (2-0).	
4th DEC. 1948.	HOME.	G.N.S.L.	FOREST GREEN ROVERS. 9. DURSLEY TOWN. 0.		WON.
			HARVEY. G. 5. TURK. 3. WOODWARD.	H.T. (4-0).	
11th DEC. 1948.	HOME.	G.N.S. AMATEUR CUP. 1st ROUND.	FOREST GREEN ROVERS. 4. BERKELEY. 0.		WON.
			TURK. DANGERFIELD. L. HARVEY. G. GANNAWAY. H.	H.T. (2-0).	

BASIL NEWPORT

Marshall Woodward was a pretty player you know, but he didn't like hard tackles. He had a beautiful touch, he did. I think he was in the best team we ever had. Raggy Bingle, Sailor Dangerfield, Jimmy Casey. I have honestly always said to my boys, I reckon that was the best side. That team had either Jack Brock or Ben Ford in goal, they were two big six-footers you know. They was good goalies.

Rovers finished runners-up to Charlton Kings and also reached the semi-final of the Junior Charity Cup. In all, the firsts played 36 games and the seconds 35 games. The top scorer for the firsts was J. Turk with 33 goals. M. Woodward scored 22 and J. McTiffin 17. R. Hanks scored 19 goals for the seconds.

Marshall again kept a record of the season's exploits. This was the last year that he did it. The club decided to keep an attendance register from the 1950 season onwards, recording all players and scorers for all matches associated with the club.

| 18th DEC. 1948. AWAY. | G.N.S.L. | FOREST GREEN ROVERS. | 2. | KINGSTANLEY. | 0. | WON. |

HARVEY. G. TURK. H.T. (1-0).

27th DEC. 1948. HOME. G.N.S.L. FOREST GREEN ROVERS. 6. BREAM AMATEURS. 0. WON.
TURK. WOODWARD. McTIFFIN. H.T. (4-0).

1st JAN. 1949. AWAY. G.N.S.L. FOREST GREEN ROVERS. 2. RODBOROUGH.O.B. 0. WON.
McTIFFIN. TURK. H.T. (0-0).

8th JAN. 1949. HOME. G.N.S. AMATEUR CUP. 2nd ROUND. FOREST GREEN ROVERS. 0. CHARLTON KINGS. 1. LOST.
H.T. (0-0).

15th JAN. 1949. HOME. G.N.S.L. FOREST GREEN ROVERS. 3. KINGSTANLEY. 1. WON.
HARVEY. G. WOODWARD. McTIFFIN. H.T. (1-0).

22nd JAN. 1949. HOME. G.N.S.L. FOREST GREEN ROVERS. 2. TETBURY TOWN. 0. WON.
TURK. WOODWARD. H.T. (1-0).

29th JAN. 1949. AWAY. G.N.S.L. FOREST GREEN ROVERS. 1. SHARPNESS. 3. LOST.
TURK. H.T. (0-1).

5th FEB. 1949. HOME. G.N.S.L. FOREST GREEN ROVERS. 5. BLAKENEY. 1. WON.
TURK. HARVEY. G. McTIFFIN. NEWPORT. BINGLE. H.T. (2-1).

19th FEB. 1949. HOME. G.N.S.L. FOREST GREEN ROVERS. 4. VINEY HILL ST. SWITHENS. 1. WON.
HARVEY. G. McTIFFIN. WOODWARD. H.T. (3-0).

26th FEB. 1949. AWAY. G.N.S.L. FOREST GREEN ROVERS. 1. BLAKENEY. 2. LOST.
WOODWARD. (PEN.) H.T. (0-1).

5th MAR. 1949. HOME. G.N.S.L. FOREST GREEN ROVERS. 3. CHARLTON KINGS. 3. DRAW.
McTIFFIN. WOODWARD. TURK. H.T. (2-0).

12th MAR. 1949. HOME. G.N.S.L. FOREST GREEN ROVERS. 4. RODBOROUGH.O.B. 0. WON.
McTIFFIN. BROWN. D. OWN GOAL. TURK. H.T. (1-0).

19th MAR. 1949. HOME. G.N.S.L. FOREST GREEN ROVERS. 9. BROADWELL AMATEURS. 2. WON.
BROWN. D. WOODWARD 2 (1 PEN). TURK. HARVEY. G. 2. McTIFFIN. 2. BROCK. (PEN). H.T. (4-2).

26th MAR. 1949. AWAY. G.N.S.L. FOREST GREEN ROVERS. 1. BERKELEY. 2. LOST.
McTIFFIN. H.T. (1-2).

2nd APRIL 1949. HOME. G.N.S.L. FOREST GREEN ROVERS. 3. CHALFORD. 0. WON.
OWN GOAL. WOODWARD. 2 (2 PENS). H.T. (0-0).

6th APRIL 1949. AWAY. G.N.S.L. FOREST GREEN ROVERS. 5. CHALFORD. 0. WON.
TURK. 3. GANNAWAY. H.

| DATE. | GROUND. | NATURE OF GAME. | FIXTURES. | | | RESULT. |

9th APRIL 1949. AWAY. G.N.S.L. FOREST GREEN ROVERS. 2. CINDERFORD TOWN. 3. LOST.
TURK. WOODWARD. (PEN). H.T. (2-3).

11th APRIL 1949. AWAY. STROUD HOSPITAL CUP 2nd ROUND. FOREST GREEN ROVERS. 1. HOFFMANS ATHLETIC. 3. LOST.
WOODWARD. H.T. (0-2).

18th APRIL 1949. HOME. G.N.S.L. FOREST GREEN ROVERS. 5. CINDERFORD TOWN. 2. WON.
WOODWARD 2. (1 PEN). TURK. STEVENS. McTIFFIN. H.T. (2-1).

21st APRIL 1949. AWAY. G.N.S.L. FOREST GREEN ROVERS. 2. CAM BULLDOGS. 1. WON.
TURK. 2. H.T. (1-0).

23rd APRIL 1949. AWAY. G.N.S.L. FOREST GREEN ROVERS. 4. BREAM AMATEURS. 1. WON.
STEVENS. TURK. BROWN. D. WOODWARD. H.T. (0-0).

30th APRIL 1949. HOME. FRIENDLY. FOREST GREEN ROVERS. 3. HAMBROOK.A. 1. WON.
McTIFFIN. TURK. STEVENS. H.T. (2-1).

2nd MAY 1949. AWAY. CHAMPIONS v RUNNERS-UP. FOREST GREEN ROVERS. 0. CHARLTON KINGS. 1. LOST.
H.T. (0-1).

Right: Charlton Kings' programme for the match against Forest Green for the Champions *v.* Runners-up match at the end of the season.

Left: Forest Green Rovers 1948/49, a successful season. Forest Green finished runners-up in the Northern Senior League to newcomers Charlton Kings. Back row: Peter Vick, Ray Bingle, Graham Harvey, Jack Brock, Les Dangerfield, Vic Cowley, Ron Davis. Front row: Harold Gannaway, Jim Turk, John Pearson, Marshall Woodward, Jack McTiffen. The picture is taken in the field below the Jovial Forester.

RAY BINGLE

Another team we used to play was Charlton Kings, Cheltenham. They had a good side. Greg Banks, I think he played amateur football for England; but Charlton Kings, they had a very good side. There was one or two of their players who played for Cheltenham Town as well I think. I forget the name of the policeman used to play centre half for them, he was an old-fashioned centre half player, and I can remember a bloke, Crisp, played for Charlton Kings. One or two of our players come off with rather bruised legs; but they were a good side.

I was a left half, a stopper. A lot of pre-war players used to be up there after the war – Cowley and Basil Newport, Peter Vick used to play, and John Pearson of course, he used to. But we used to always think we had to keep John in the middle because he was very good in the air. He wasn't particularly good at passing. We used to do his running, just to keep him in the middle.

MARSHALL WOODWARD

After a while I went to play for Stonehouse, because they were becoming a bigger team than Forest Green.

Stonehouse started off semi-professional. I went down there for a few seasons, and then they started bringing older professional players, like Forest Green are bringing in now, who had nearly finished their careers, from Bristol City and Bristol Rovers. Gradually the local players disappeared and I think it were a mistake really, bringing in new bigger players. Well, they done better because they had experience I suppose. If you had to miss work or something, then you could put in expenses or you had boot money or something.

I remember a bloke who used to play, who worked at Chamberlains. He was centre forward at Stonehouse. Every time they wanted him to have a game he used to say he was working so they used to say if you play for us we'll cover your money.

Forest Green's first game of the season against Viney Hill, a strong Forest of Dean team.

1949/50

Jack Brock moved to Chipping Sodbury and was ably replaced in goal by Alf 'Golfer' Francis.

In December 1949 Mr Twistleton, manager of Stonehouse, now a semi-professional club, and a Gloucester City representative both requested that Jim Turk travel to the clubs for trials, which the committee agreed to.

Gloucester City had joined the Southern League in 1939 and their reserves played in the Birmingham League. Alf Francis also had a trial and played for Gloucester City together with Jim Turk against Wolverhampton Wanderers A in the Birmingham League early in 1950.

Rovers released both Jim Turk and Alf Francis when requested by Gloucester City and both players played quite a number of games for the semi-professional club. Things had certainly turned a full circle since the early days of the Senior League in the 1920s when Forest Green regularly thumped Gloucester City. In the meantime, Marshall Woodward moved to Stonehouse after a fully legal approach by Mr Twistleton.

Forest Green Rovers 1949/50 early in the season before Jack Brock moved to Chipping Sodbury but after Marshall Woodward had gone to Stonehouse. Back row: Ben Weager, Reg Baker, Les Dangerfield, Vic Cowley, Jack Brock, Des Harvey, Ray Bingle, Ron Davis. Front row: Wesley Stokes, Jim Turk, John Pearson, Ray Anderton, Jack McTiffin, Bob Peachey.

TIM BARNARD

I remember one such soldier as Uncle Tom, who lived next to my uncle's farm at Twatley Cottage up above Shortwood. He had been Polish Army wrestling champion before the Second World War and then had fought through Italy with the Polish Free Forces. Valentin Tomczk was a very gregarious man and we would all go up to his house every Saturday afternoon in the late 1960s and 1970s for a tea of Polish pancakes and lemonade and watch the wrestling on ITV with such wrestlers as Mick McManus.

Valentin was a sergeant in the Polish Fourth Army, fighting his way through Italy and Monte Casino, and was married with a family before the outbreak of the Second World War. He didn't see his wife and children until the Soviet-controlled government gave his family permission to come to the UK for a weekend to see their father in the mid-1970s; a bittersweet joy. By then he and his wife had grown old and his children were all adults. They had their life in communist Poland and he had his in Shortwood. It was a very short and emotional reunion.

Babdown Camp

The reserves were playing in the Stroud League and came up against a team called Babdown for the first time this season. Babdown was a military airfield during the Second World War and was used as a hospital base by the US Air Force. As the war drew to an end, there were many Polish soldiers who had fought alongside British troops to liberate Europe from Nazi control. After the war, Poland became a Soviet-controlled country and the soldiers were not welcomed home and many settled in the district. Babdown became a camp for Polish soldiers unable to return to Soviet Poland for fear of persecution.

After the war, and the dispersal of all the soldiers, the camp became a civilian base, still for Polish refugees, and they set up a football team and were registered to play in the Stroud League from 1949 until 1954.

Seven hundred and fifty programmes were ordered for the Charlton Kings fixture and, for the return game on 3 April, three extra coaches were ordered to transport supporters to Cheltenham for the match. As the season progressed, so did the building of the changing rooms and, following the trials of the Forest Green players, Gloucester City agreed to send their first team for the match to open the changing rooms when they were completed.

Forest Green Rovers *v.* Babdown, 12 November 1949. Forest Green's first 'international match'. Programmes were produced for reserve team games as well.

Forest Green's Boxing Day game against Stonehouse Reserves, 26 December 1949, including Marshall Woodward who had moved to Stonehouse earlier in the season.

Ron Davis's report for the season read as follows:

> *Congratulations were given to both the senior and junior elevens and their captains on a very successful season. The senior team won the Gloucestershire Northern Senior League championship, only losing 1 game and creating a record for the League by scoring 55 points out of a possible 60. The junior team finished well up in the Stroud Premier League and were generally considered the best reserve side in the district.*
>
> *Top scorers were J. Turk with 63 goals (47 in the league and 16 in other games), W. Stokes with 18 in the league and 4 in other games, J. McTiffin with 15 in the Senior League, 5 in the Stroud League and 5 in other games; R. Hanks scored 7 in the Stroud League and 4 in friendlies. The secretary also congratulated J. Pearson, R. Baker, A. Francis and L. Dangerfield in being picked to represent the League.*
>
> *The Committee authorised that £2 be spent to fill the cup with port for players and supporters.*

RAY BINGLE

I can remember when they put the first changing room up. Going back to that time, there was a hell of a lot of people involved that used to go up and do things, and that's how the club developed. The ones that spring to mind are, of course, Stan White – he ran the supporters' club; Charlie Cuff, he built the first changing room and Ray Stevens. Charlie Cuff, I think he had something to do with the stand as well. He did a hell of a lot of work. Stan White, of course, apart from the work he did, he was also responsible for raising money, with Bert Russell. And there was people like Arthur Hannis, they used to always go up and do quite a bit of work. The players used to as well – under Cyril Bruton's supervision – they did a lot of the pipe things and plumbing work in the changing room. That's how the club was and that's how I like to remember it.

Forest Green Rovers 1949/50. Back row: Ben Weager, Ron Davis, Ray Bingle, Les Dangerfield, unknown, Alf Francis, Vic Cowley, unknown, Geoff Smith, Nip Beale. Front row: Wes Stokes, Jim Turk, John Pearson, unknown, Jack McTiffin.

14

The Start of the 1950s: 1950–1955

1950/51

Having won the Senior League for the first time since 1937, Hoffmans, who played football in the Western League, invited Forest Green over for a pre-season friendly.

Hoffmans

Following the game, Jack McTiffin left Forest Green Rovers in November to play for them. Gloucester City arrived with a full team for the official opening of the new changing rooms on 30 August 1950, for which 500 programmes were produced, the game ending 4-4.

The club installed a loudspeaker system and a radiogram to provide

MARSHALL WOODWARD

Hoffmans, they were in the Western League. The factory moved down from Chelmsford. They were down at Stonehouse. If you were any good at football and you wanted a job, they would give you a job and you played football.

One or two I know went there, and there was a chap down there named Joe Murray, who used to play for Millwall. Big bloke, he also played for Stonehouse firsts. He used to come up sometimes and take me off down there. I don't know whether we had to sign a form to play or what they were playing in, no idea. They had some super players down there.

So Hoffmans the company was paying. Not paying players to play, but giving them a job so they could come and play for Hoffmans. That would have been in the 1950s. They used to play the finals down there.

Medals and cups won by Ray 'Bomber' Brown, his father and his grandfather; the first being won in 1903.

entertainment before the match and at half-time. Fred Porter became the first stadium announcer. Walter Brown, who had played for the club before the turn of the century was made a life member. Another newcomer to the team, R.F. (Ray 'Bomber') Brown, Walter Brown's grandson, continued in the family tradition and played for Forest Green.

ADRIAN BROWN

Me and my cousin 'Bomber' were very close. He was Forest Green through and through, like my father and my grandfather Walter. He played in the first teams before the First World War. He played until he was forty. Our Bomber always said he wanted to emulate Grampy Brown, as we always called him. He wanted to play until he was forty. Our Bomber had to go to Avening to do that, and he did so.

There was Walter, then there was his eldest son, which was Uncle Bill, that would be another W. Brown. Then our 'Bomber's father, which I think was on one of the old photographs, C. Brown. And I think my dad, who was W. Brown, I think he only played for the seconds, but I haven't seen any photographs of him. And then there was a younger brother, Charlie Brown. He started his football at Shortwood, and I don't know what the story is behind it, but then I know in later years he came to Forest Green.

Forest Green faced new opposition in Lydbrook from the forest in the Senior Amateur Cup at the end of January. Five hundred programmes were printed. The match ended 1-1 and all copies of the programme were reported sold. A replay took place the following week, which again ended 1-1 and a second replay was necessary, for which 600 programmes were ordered and sold. The match was finally won by Forest Green 3-0, Jim Casey with 2 and Cecil Hudd being the scorers.

In February 1951, John Pearson won the honour of being named Player of the Year by the Gloucestershire Referees' Association, and also played for the county again.

First Attempts at a County League

Forest Green Rovers felt that their horizon was limited in footballing terms by the Northern Senior League. The club formally made an application to the Northern Section of the GFA to start a County League. The club also sent a circular letter to all clubs in Gloucestershire, including the Bristol clubs, Gloucester City and Cheltenham Town, asking them to send in letters of support to the GFA for a County League. By the end of the season, it became clear that there was near unanimous support from the Northern Section clubs and no support from the Bristol clubs for a County League. The committee resolved to continue their lobbying process for the forthcoming season.

The club progressed in the Senior Amateur Cup, beating Leckhampton 4-2 in the semi-final at Cirencester. Three double-decker buses were ordered to transport the supporters not making their own way there. By this time, J. Kalewski, who had been playing for the reserves, made it into the first-team, having moved from Babdown Dispersal Camp's Stroud League team the previous season.

The Senior League requested the use of The Lawn for the Interleague final against the North Gloucestershire League, with Alf Francis, Ray Bingle and Jim Turk all playing in the match.

ADRIAN BROWN

I used to watch as a kid, regular. John Pearson, Marshall, and there was a fellow named Reg Baker. I think he was from Stonehouse, and Alfie Francis. John Pearson was very good; he was a school teacher; he taught me when it was Nailsworth British School. I passed my eleven plus and went to Boys Tech; but Pearson, he always used to tell me at school that the penalty was one of the easiest things to take. If you ever watched him play, he would walk up, and it was a side-foot. He didn't belt it, the side of the foot placed it; it was all about placement.

Marshall was brilliant, a very clever dribbler. A lot of them went to Stonehouse – John Pearson didn't – with the money there was in the Western League. But Reg Baker and Raggie Bingle – they was good players. Wes Stokes was very, very good. In them days Wesley played for Gloucestershire; you had to be very good to get in, and he did. Scrubby Cowley, we loved Scrubby because when a winger was coming down, he'd just start sliding a few yards away. He'd get booked nowadays, but he never injured anybody. Well, he might have injured a few, but not malicious.

PC Hiron, Stan Hiron, I know we used to see him play for Forest Green and everybody as little kids would have a giggle, 'come on copper', that sort of thing. He was the Nailsworth copper, he lived at Park Road, and there was the playing fields in Forest Green. All us lads used to have a regular football match, and all of a sudden you'd see this copper stood on the line, and you heard a shout, 'Don't do it like that.' You'd look up and think, 'Oh we know who he is, he plays for Forest Green.' When you think about that, there was a bit of respect. I saw Jack Brock a few times but then Alfie Francis – 'Golfer' they called him – took over. Jack Brock was in goal, I always remember he used to have white tape round his boots, round the middle.

By the end of April, Forest Green had a chance of the league and cup double, reaching the final of the Senior Amateur Cup to take on Stonehouse Reserves, and lying top of the league. A fleet of coaches was ordered to transport supporters to Hoffmans in Stonehouse for the game. Stonehouse would play in blue-and-white shirts and they lent Forest Green white shirts for the final. In the league at the end of March, Forest Green met Viney Hill at The Lawn for what was effectively a championship decider. The behaviour of a section of the Viney Hill supporters at the game was noted to be deplorable and a letter was sent to the GFA regarding the matter.

MARSHALL WOODWARD

The crowd for the final, they was three or four deep all the way round the field, it must have been quite a crowd. That above is a photo of the first game against Forest Green; that's Sailor Dangerfield on the left. I was playing for Stonehouse then in blue and white; and that ball come across from the right and the goalie and Alf Francis went up for it. Somehow the ball came out and he was on his way out towards me. I got there before Sailor and passed him into t'other corner.

Then Forest Green equalised and then went into the lead. Then, about a quarter hour before time, it looked as though we were going to lose because Forest Green should have won. They had plenty chances but they didn't take 'em. Penny Lennard, who was right half for Stonehouse, he was in the Air Force, he hit a kick from way out and Ray Bingle was left half, and he was on the edge of the penalty area. He went up to head the ball. The ball flashed off his head and flew into the top corner, giving the goalie no chance; own goal, 2-2. We had to have a replay then, which we won 2-0.

Bob Peachey before the final in 1951 at Hoffmans. Come on Rovers!

RAY BINGLE

I can remember playing Lydbrook in the cup. I had a free-kick and I managed to get it in the right position for Jim Turk to score, and that put us through to the next round.

We played in the final down at Hoffmans. That's when I scored against Forest Green. I couldn't get out of the way of the ball, it come off my head and it went right up in the air. I can remember watching it, and I said, 'Oh well that's easy,' because Alfie was in goal. I thought he had no problem there, and he let it through. We drew that and then we lost in the replay. We had to come back from honeymoon to play in the finals that weekend. That's when we got married. Well I know we didn't get much of a honeymoon. But, oddly enough, that goal I scored against Forest Green in that final, that's the only one I've ever given away as a penalty or an own goal.

SECOND HALF MASTERY WON CUP

Fighting come-back by Stonehouse Res.

FIRST RESERVE SIDE TO WIN N.S.A. TROPHY

DUE to a fighting come-back in the second half during which they turned apparent defeat into victory Stonehouse Res. won the replay final of the Northern Senior Amateur Cup against Forest Green Rovers at Hoffmann's ground on Wednesday evening. Their 2—1 victory earned for them the honour of being the first Reserve side ever to have won the trophy.

Brian Colebourne, the Magpies' firework inside right, and only eligible player of the 1st XI to play in the Competition, scored the match-winning goals. His presence—Lennard was unfit— brought added zest and punch to the hard-hitting Stonehouse attack and he certainly deserved the "chairing" he had from the Stonehouse supporters immediately after the final whistle.

It was ironical that the moves that led to both Colebourne's goals came from the tactical play of Woodward who was playing against the club from which he joined the Magpies. His two through passes—the first one to Phillips on the wing which led to the equaliser and the second a perfect ground pass through the defence to Colebourne—were masterly blows at the Rovers' defence. It was only left to Colebourne to brilliantly head home Phillips' centre and, 21 minutes later, crash into the roof of the net the match-winner.

Battling against a strong wind the Rovers were deserving of their goal lead at half-time. In fact, they should have scored more than one— Casey being guilty of missing practically an open goal before he did eventually beat Hinder after 25 minutes' play with a ground shot. Honours, however, in this first half went to Forest Green.

Inspired Football

It was a new and refreshed Stonehouse that came out after the interval. At times they played inspired football and found that strong wind of little nuisance. Rather, it was to their advantage, for they played good, constructive football which brought the goals. The Rovers' defence was taxed from the onset and within three minutes the equaliser had flashed past the capable Francis from off Colebourne's head. The goal that counted came five minutes from the end. Chilled Stonehouse supporters roared as team-mates rushed to congratulate Colebourne and Woodward on the match-winner.

The remaining minutes quickly sped by and after 180 minutes of battle Stonehouse captain John Taylor was able to collect the Cup for his team-mates and settle the destiny of the Cup for the next 12 months. From the hands of Mr. W. J. Pepworth he received the trophy. His fellow players and members of the Rovers' side received medals from Mr. Pepworth's grand-daughter.

The Cup—last won locally by Forest Green—was back in the Stroud Valley. It had been a hard fight, but Stonehouse had won it due solely to a fine second half display.

THE CUP REMAINED UNPACKED

Rovers and Stonehouse Res. to fight again

WHEN, a few minutes before time, a Hoffmann club official carried with extreme care a large cardboard box along the touch-line at Saturday's final and jocu`arly remarked "here it is" he had been one of the very few of a crowd, numbering over 2,000, to have had a glimpse of the box's contents. It was th Northern Senior Amateur Cup.

His journey to the presentation table proved to be unnecessary for the Cup remained in the box, unpacked. All-Stroud finalists Forest Green Rovers and Stonehouse Res. had failed to reach a decisive result, and for possession of the Cup the teams will replay on the same ground on Wednesday, May 2nd. Saturday's tussle had ended in a 2—2 draw.

Steeped in cup fighting tradition Forest Green almost had the Cup within their grasp. Captain John Pearson saw a "lucky touch" of the Cup during the interval almost saw his wish come true when his side took the lead five minutes after the resumption. Then his wish was dashed to the ground as he stood, helplessly, and watched the ball deflected high into the Rovers' net some 25 minutes later. It was the Stonehouse equaliser and one which earned them the replay and the chance to become—as a Reserve side—first holders of the Cup.

The Rovers relied on their selected side but Stonehouse were presented with a last minute problem and had not manager Twiselton himself turned out to complete the side, the club would have had great difficulty in fielding a representative team owing to other possible players being cup-tied.

The teams were:

Forest Green: Francis; Cowley, Harvey; Dangerfield, Pearson, Bingle; Turk, Stokes, Casey, Baker and Hudd.

Stonehouse Res.: Hinder, Upton, Williams; Lennard, Taylor; O'Loughlin; Elliott, Herdman, Twiselton, Woodward and Phillips.

EARLY GOAL

With the advantage of a strong wind Stonehouse went all out for the early goal, and got it. After Woodward had missed an excellent chance to score against his old club—Francis just managed to clear off the goalline—a move which Bingle intended to start for his side ended with Stonehouse eventually scoring. His sl'ced pass went to a Stonehouse player and

---

RAY BINGLE, Forest Green half back, does not mean to miss the N.S.A. Cup Final replay. On Saturday, he is to be married and misses the Viney Hill game. After a three-day honeymoon he will be back in the Rovers' side for Wednesday's replay. The Rovers' hope to field the same XI.

goals had followed as the 'keepers lay sprawling on the ground.

Not until the interval had come and gone did another goal materialise. This struck a telling blow for Forest Green when five minutes after the resumption Casey raced through the middle unchallenged and with controllable ease placed the ball wide of Hinder's outstretched hands into the net.

THE EQUALISER

Strangely enough the equaliser came again in the 31st minute—when a terrific shot from Lennard was met by Bingle's head and the ball ricochetted high into the net, far and away from the unsighted Francis. It was a lucky goal, but proved to be the equaliser which earned the replay.

The Stonehouse half-back trio of Lennard, Taylor (who captained the side) and O'Loughlin, was a formidable trio who were their opposites in Bingle, Pearson and Dangerfield. Phillips, under sponge treatment after three of his lively bursts, was always a danger, but Twiselton, nursing two bad foot blisters, did not make such a capable leader as Casey. Baker, as expected, was as good as ever.

Gate receipts — £100/4/8.

The crowd came streaming away from the ground as undecided as the result.

At the end of the season, Ron Davis reported as follows:

The firsts were congratulated for winning the Gloucestershire Northern Senior League for the second year running and also for reaching the final of the Senior Amateur Cup. During the season the firsts had played a total of 42 games, winning 25 with 11 drawn and 6 lost; 116 goals for and 51 against. They only had 28 goals against them in 28 league games.

Leading goalscorers were J. Casey 52, J. Kalewski 33, D. Brown 24, J. Turk 15, C. Hudd 15, W. Stokes 11.

The committee started to think about the possibility of employing a trainer or a manager to further the ambitions of the club. Mr Hillman from King's Stanley was approached, but declined the offer of a position.

RAY BINGLE

We always had hard games down in the Forest, down at Blakeney and things like that. But Cinderford, I suppose, was one of the better sides down there. I think that's where Marshall injured his leg. I think somebody caught hold of his leg as he was about to shoot, and I think it twisted somehow or other. Viney Hill was always what was considered a difficult team for us. A rough team. But if you got caught in those days you didn't hang on the floor and wait for a free-kick and things like that. You just got up as quickly as you could and got on with the game. I think that's spoiling the game to be quite honest, because that's all they go down for is to get a free-kick.

When we used to play down in the Forest, we used to stay sometimes for a dance. They had an arrangement with Blakeney Football Club, they laid on teas and things like that. We went down there in the bus.

Above: Forest Green Rovers Reserves 1950/51. Back row: Cecil Brown, Ray Stevens, Graham Harvey, John Beckett, Les Smith, Harold Gannaway, Peter Vick, George Bathe, Norman Vick. Front row: Bob Tanner, Ray Brown, Doug Brown, Brian Peats, Des Dangerfield.

Opposite above: Forest Green Rovers 1950/1. The full squad and officials. Forest Green retained the Senior League title. Back row: R. Peachey, H. Jones, S. Harrison, W. Riley, A. Humphries, A. Woodward, W. Hill, R. Beard, B. Beale, F. Porter, C. Hughes. Second row: E. Robinson, J. Allen, G. Bathe, O. Davis, R. Baker, R. Bingle, J. Turk, A. Francis, R. Beard, H. Payne, D. Dangerfield, J. Beckett, G. Harvey, J. Lloyd, W. Brown, A. Fletcher, C. Brown, J. Lavis. Third row: G. Elton, C. Hudd, J. Casey, L. Dangerfield, W. Stokes, J. Pearson, H.J.H. King (President), D. Brown, P. Vick, S. Brown, D. Gannaway, H. Gannaway, G. Smith. Front row: R. Davis, D. Harvey, V. Cowley, J. Kalewski, R. Tanner, R. Brown, R. Stevens, B. Weager. The picture includes Walter Brown and Owen Davis who had played before the turn of the last century and had won the club's first ever silverware, the Dursley League Cup in 1903. The team also included Joe Kalewski who had joined the club from Babdown Camp.

1951/52

The club's league and cup success would prove a hard act to follow. The supporters' club continued to invest an immense amount of time and their own money in the improvement of the facilities and were still continuing to top-up gate money when required to ensure financial stability.

Lydbrook joined the Senior League this season, considerably strengthening the competition. Mr Twistleton from Stonehouse was again in the committee's bad books in August for an illegal approach to R. Tanner and was reported to the FA. Stonehouse were regularly trying to entice Rovers players away to the professional club. Gloucester City and Stonehouse met in the FA Cup second qualifying round at the beginning of the season and played out the match in front of a crowd of 5,500 proving the ongoing popularity of football in the area.

A Change of Club Colours

The club was also considering a change of colours from black-and-white stripes and seriously considered green-and-white vertical stripes for the 1951 season. After a lengthy debate, it was decided to stick to the black-and-white colours used since 1919.

Ray Anderton, who had made himself a fixture in the first team, broke his leg in early February and Ray Stevens, who had moved into the first team, went down to Broadwell on 23 February and broke his leg too. Without Ray Anderton, Ray Bingle and Ray Stevens in the first team, Bill Malpas moved up from the reserves, along with Ray 'Bomber' Brown. 'Raggy' Bingle left for East Africa in December 1951, playing his last game on 10 December against Tuffley.

John Duff also made his debut for the reserves in a Junior Charity Cup game against Randwick on 15 March 1952, and he made it into the first team as a cover player for the match against Dursley on 5 April to play alongside Scrubby Cowley in defence.

JOHN DUFF

I remember my first game for the first team was away at Dursley, where I was apprenticed at Listers. Alf Francis, our goalkeeper, was beaten by a high lob and I was on the line and could only punch the ball out. Penalty, but then Alf saved the spot kick. It would have been a straight red card today but all I got was a load of stick for the next week.

Another game that sticks in my mind was going to Lydbrook, who were the best team in the Northern Senior League for several seasons. Going down there I was seventeen years old and I came up against a guy on the left wing for Lydbrook, a guy called Gus Stow, who had played for Bristol City. He sorted me out; in fact he put me over the rail, or certainly under it. Scrubby Cowley, who was the left-back, quite an experienced hard man, said to me, 'John, just swap with me for a minute,' so I went to left back, he went to right back, Mr Stow came down the Lydbrook left wing and Scrubby put him over the fence. Scrubby said to me 'John, I don't think he'll be any trouble to you now, you can come back,' so we swapped again.

John Pearson was our schoolteacher and captain at thirty-eight years of age. I never really knew whether to call him 'John' or 'Sir', having just left school. I always played in defence; I am told I was one of the first overlapping full-backs in the country, but that was only because I was too slow to get back from anywhere else, you know.

By the end of the season, a proposal to enlarge the Senior League had been adopted, with Forest Green in Section A alongside Lydbrook, Cinderford, Charlton Kings and Swindon Town A. Lydbrook won the league at the first attempt, having drawn 5 of the last 6 matches, a league record for points conceded yet still winning it.

```
F O R E S T    G R E E N    R O V E R S

          A. F. C.

      SPECIAL BENEFIT MATCH

             for

        RAY ANDERTON

             and

        RAY STEVENS.


  ───────────────────────────────
   OFFICIAL PROGRAMME        Price 2d.

  ───────────────────────────────
   Refreshments, Teas, etc., will be on
            sale on ground.
                      . .

  ───────────────────────────────
  Hon. Sec: R.J. Davis, Spring Hill, Nailsworth.
```

Above and opposite above: Programme for the benefit match for the two Rays, each of whom had broken a leg that season.

RAY STEVENS

I was persuaded to sign for Forest Green by Don Gannaway the season before in 1947, when I was fifteen years old. I used to go up and watch games and then went up for training. We would walk up to The Lawn across Bunting Hill to a hut by the side of the pitch where the social club is now to change into our boots and shirts. After the match I used to go straight home.

I eventually claimed a place in the reserves under Bobby Hanks the captain, and then in the 1948/49 season I claimed a very occasional place in the first team and got myself a runners-up medal in the Gloucestershire Northern Senior League with the firsts. I remember the champions were Charlton Kings and we had to play them on their own ground in what was a good hard game. I was on the left wing and up against a full-back called Greatbanks, who was a county player, and he gave me a roasting that day.

I had a decent run in and out of the first team up until 1952 when I broke my leg playing against Broadwell. I was out for a season after that. I then went into the reserves and really enjoyed the rest of my days at Forest Green, becoming captain of the seconds and taking over from Doug Brown in 1956 until I hung up my boots in 1960.

Opposite below: Forest Green Rovers 1951/52. Back row: Ben Weager, Derek Sibley, Reg Baker, Alf Francis, Cecil Hudd, Les Dangerfield, John Duff, Ron Davis. Front row: Ray Brown, Wesley Stokes, John Pearson, Jim Turk, Ron Berry.

Ron Davis reported as follows:

On the playing programme, the club was to be congratulated on the season's performances, the Senior XI had finished fifth in the Senior League, had played 3 games in the Senior Amateur Cup and were most unfortunate to lose in the semi-final of the Senior Charity Cup. The Junior XI had finished higher in the league than any other local amateur reserve team. They had two Northern Junior Amateur Cup games and reached the semi-final of the Junior Charity Cup.

H.J.H. King died in August, having supported the club as president over their very successful previous period. He was followed by Lt-Col J.F. Evans.

1952/53

At the start of the season, the chairman welcomed Mr J. Morrison as coach, an ex-professional of Motherwell Football Club now working at Hoffmans. Unfortunately Mr Morrison was called away to Scotland shortly after training began.

Rovers played in Section A of the divided Northern Senior League, while the reserves entered the Stroud League as usual and also entered the Severn Vale League, which they hadn't played in since the 1930s. They resigned after just three matches because of fixture congestion.

Marshall Woodward returned to Forest Green from his spell at Stonehouse and played in the first team alongside John Duff and Jim Turk. Unfortunately for Forest Green, Cecil Hudd received a fractured fibula in a friendly

TO-DAY'S LINE-UP 23RD AUGUST. --- KICK-OFF 3.0 p.m.

FOREST GREEN.

Right.

Left.

1. FRANCIS A.
2. DUFF J.   3. COWLEY V.
4. STOKES W.   5. PEARSON J.   6. BROWN R.
7. SIBLEY D.   8. BAKER R.   9. DANGERFIELD L.   10. WOODWARD M.   11. HUDD C.

Referee   D.W. Smith.

11. TOWNSEND. 10. WATSON. 9. ROBBINS. 8. SMITH. 7. PERRITT.
6. ASHENFORD. 5. FARLEY. 4. EVANS.
3. DAY.   2. DAVIS.
1. WITHEY.

Left.   Right.

HOFFMANN'S ATHLETIC.

'NEXT HOME GAME - 26TH AUGUST.

1ST XI v SHORTWOOD (Friendly) Kick-off 6.30 p.m.

Good Afternoon Friends and Supporters,

This afternoon we welcome Hoffmann's Athletic to the "Lawn" for a benefit match for our two players, Ray Anderton and Ray Stevens, who fractured their legs last season. I am pleased to say they have now restarted their work and I am sure you will join me in wishing them a complete and speedy recovery and hope to see them again before long in a black and white shirt. We also wish to thank Hoffmann's for this grand opening fixture to the season.

Our referee to-day is Mr. D.W.Smith who so kindly offered to ref this match. You might remember Mr. Smith for his very efficient handling of the County Match between Glos. and B'ham here last season. He is most certainly in the top flight and we are indeed lucky to have his services this afternoon. Thank-you Mr. Smith.

To-day we have a "New Look" programme at the reduced price of 2d. We hope to improve the front cover as it is only a temporary lay-out until we can get some stencils cut. For our advertisers who have supported us in previous seasons we shall probably have some space for their adverts. Would you please apply to the Hon. Sec.? For the success of this venture we must have everyone's support; we on our part will supply the programme if you the public will support it.

Next week we have two friendlies with our neighbours, Shortwood. The Senior XI's play at the "Lawn" on Tuesday next, while the Reserve XI's play on Thursday at Shortwood. Kick-off for both games 6.30 p.m.

'TOUCHLINER'

match against Shortwood, the third first-team player within a year to break his leg. Forest Green again faced Shortwood, who included veteran Basil Newport in their team, in a Senior Charity Cup game in the October, winning 1-0.

Forest Green's progress in the County Cup was stopped in its tracks in the third round at home to Lydbrook in December, with a hard fought 3-2 loss. Lydbrook were definitely the team to beat and, when Forest Green visited for a league game soon after their cup defeat, two coaches were booked to leave at 1 p.m. to take the supporters down. On not such a good day, Rovers lost 5-1.

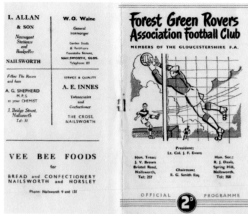

Above left: Forest Green Rovers Reserves, 1952/53. Back row: Cecil Brown, Peter Vick, Graham Harvey, Don Gannaway, Derek Smith, Stan Brown, Eric Whiting, George Bathe. Front row: Derek Sibley, Ray Brown, Doug Brown, Bill Malpas, Stan Turk.

Above right: The front cover of the new-look 'first edition' programme issued for the match against the Cheltenham based team, and old Forest Green foe, Charlton Kings, 22 November 1952.

JOHN DUFF

I remember supporters going to matches. Certainly not many people had cars in those days, but there would have been reasonable crowds who travelled to away games by coach or bus, or whatever they used. I do remember, however, going to a match that the reserve team played in. It was a cup final at Cirencester against Bibury; there must have been five coaches went, five old coaches. There was another one as well. We went to Wotton to play in a cup final, and took Nailsworth Silver Band to celebrate the victory, which we failed to achieve.

In February 1953, Forest Green went into the Forest of Dean to play Cinderford in the newly divided Senior League. Marshall Woodward came away with what turned out, a season-and-a-half later, to be a career-ending injury.

It was coronation year for Queen Elizabeth II and the obvious fixture to arrange for such an event was a game against Shortwood, which took place on Wednesday 20 May at Forest Green, 9d for adults, 3d for children. A second coronation game was arranged against Stroud Rugby Club, to be played under 'Association rules' and 500 programmes were printed for the game. The game itself was a complete success with a gate of over £23 being taken.

The end of the season was summarised as follows by Ron Davis:

> Our Club had finished as runners-up to Lydbrook in section A of the Northern Senior League and so would be members of a very strong Division One for the following season. New members who would be visiting The Lawn next season included Harrow Hill (winners of section B) Hawkesleys and Ross.
>
> Our efforts to obtain a genuine County Cup competition had been recognised inasmuch as that we were informed that recommendations would be made at the GFA annual meeting that the cup should be called the Gloucestershire County Cup, with the words Northern or Southern in brackets after the title. With reference to the partition of the county, this was still under consideration. We had sent a resolution to the GFA annual meeting proposing that alternate annual meetings should be held at Bristol and Gloucester. We were informed that this also was to be recommended by the Rules sub-committee.
>
> Both teams are to be congratulated on their performances during the past season. They set up another record by both reaching the finals of the Senior and Junior Charity Cups, and although the seniors were successful, the juniors must be considered most unfortunate to have failed. The juniors also finished third in the Premier Section of the Stroud League and reached the final of the Northern Junior Amateur Cup.
>
> Leading goalscorers were J. Turk 56, G. Hardy 30, H. Gannaway 22, D. Brown 16, E. Young 15, and W. Malpas 14.

Good Afternoon Everyone,

Our visitors to-day are Charlton Kings to play our Senior XI in a Northern Senior League game. As our team has not appeared on 'The Lawn' since October 4th, I will take this opportunity to congratulate them on still being undefeated in both League and Cup matches. Charlton Kings, as you all know, have been regular and most welcome visitors in past seasons, and I am sure we shall see the usual keen struggle this afternoon.

Although the Senior XI has been away, I am sure all will join with me in congratulating our Reserves for some sparkling games on 'The Lawn' recently. Last Saturday's match was certainly an eye-opener, especially for their opponents Charfield, who must still be wondering what happened. The lads are playing at Babdown to-day and we wish them the best of luck.

To-day we have our new-look programme on sale. No, the goal-keeper is not Alf Francis (he doesn't wear a cap!). We are also restarting our lucky number on the programme. Unfortunately we can only offer a 2/6 prize for a start as last year the programme was poorly supported. When it is possible this prize will be increased. Any comments or ideas for this programme will be warmly welcomed.

From half-time onwards (Not before) tickets will be on sale at the

---

TO-DAY'S LINE-UP 22ND NOVEMBER --- KICK-OFF 2.30. p.m.

FOREST GREEN.

Black and White Stripes.

Right.   Left.

1. A. FRANCIS.

2. J. DUFF.   3. V. COWLEY.

4. W.STOKES.   5. J. PEARSON.(Capt.) 6. R. BROWN.

7. J. TURK.   8. R. BAKER.   9. J. CASEY.   10. M. WOODWARD. 11. W. MALPASS.

Referee   ---   A.N. OTHER.

11. D. PERRY.   10. A. JOHNSON.   9. M. DUNN.   8. J. NORMAN.   7. G. WELLFAIR.
   (Capt.)
            6. V. HAWKINS.   5. M. SEABROOK.   4. L. COWLE.

         3. G. GREATBANKS.   2. D. CONSTANCE.

                  1. D. FLOOK.

Left.   Red with White Collars and Sleeves.   Right.
                     CHARLTON KINGS.

Above and left: The first new-look programme against Charlton Kings.

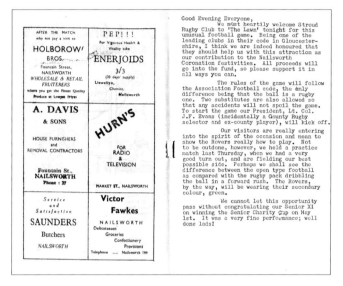

AFTER THE MATCH
why not pay a visit to

HOLBOROW
BROS.

Fountain Street,
NAILSWORTH
WHOLESALE & RETAIL
FRUITERERS
where you get the Finest Quality
Produce at Lowest Prices

PEP!!!

For Vigorous Health &
Vitality take

ENERJOIDS

3/3

(30 days' supply)

Llewellyn,
Chemist,
Nailsworth

A. DAVIS
& SONS

HOUSE FURNISHERS
and
REMOVAL CONTRACTORS

Fountain St.,
NAILSWORTH
Phone : 27

HURN'S

FOR
RADIO
&
TELEVISION

MARKET ST., NAILSWORTH

Service
and
Satisfaction

SAUNDERS

Butchers

NAILSWORTH

Victor
Fawkes

NAILSWORTH
Delicatessen
Groceries
Confectionery
Provisions
Telephone .... Nailsworth 199

Good Evening Everyone,

We most heartily welcome Stroud Rugby Club to 'The Lawn' tonight for this unusual football game. Being one of the leading clubs in their code in Gloucester-shire, I think we are indeed honoured that they should help us with this attraction as our contribution to the Nailsworth Coronation festivities. All proceeds will go into the fund, so please support it in all ways you can.

The rules of the game will follow the Association Football code, the only difference being that the ball is a rugby one. Two substitutes are also allowed so that any accidents will not spoil the game. To start the game our President, Lt. Col. J.F. Evans (incidentally a County Rugby selector and ex-county player), will kick off.

Our visitors are really entering into the spirit of the occasion and mean to show the Rovers really how to play. Not to be outdone, however, we held a practice match last Thursday, when we had a very good turn out, and are fielding our best possible side. Perhaps we shall see the difference between the open type football as compared with the rugby pack dribbling the ball in a forward rush. The Rovers, by the way, will be wearing their secondary colour, green.

We cannot let this opportunity pass without congratulating our Senior XI on winning the Senior Charity Cup on May 1st. It was a very fine performance; well done lads!

Above and below: The programme of the game between Stroud Rugby Club and Forest Green Rovers.

TO-NIGHT'S LINE UP WEDNESDAY 13TH MAY 1953.   KICK-OFF 7.0 p.m.

FOREST GREEN.

Right.   Left.

1 A. Francis.

2 J. Duff.   3 J. Pearson.

4 R. Brown.   5. W. Stokes.   6. D. Sibley.

7. L. Dangerfield. 8. H. Gannaway. 9. J. Turk. 10. D. Gannaway. 11. C. Hudd

---

11. M. Brookings. 9. B.W. Smith. 8. T.P. Shill. 7. A.J. Moore. 6. D. Flynn.

5. R. Kearse. 4. G. Cullimore. 3. G. Harrison.

2. J.T. Garner. 1. F.J. Marriott.

A. Curtis.

STROUD.

Left.   Right.

Forest Green Substitutes.   Stroud Substitutes.
D. Brightwell.   D. Haines.
D. Brown.   G. Guy.

For a Pleasant Evening in Good
Company come to the

JOVIAL
FORESTERS

Proprietor : T. STOCKWELL
Open all day for Cigarettes,
Cereals, Confectionery and
Household Sundries
The Rovers' "Home"
is your "Home"

Motor and Cycle Engineer

P. H. TAYLOR

Repairs Speedily Carried Out
All Cycle Accessories in Stock

Fountain St.,
NAILSWORTH

'Phone : 73

L. Taylor
& Sons

(BUTCHERS) LTD
for

PERSONAL
SATISFACTION

Telephone : 91

W. E. HART, Ltd.,

The Cross,
Nailsworth

Draper,
Milliner
and Ladies' Outfitter

For BOYS' and MEN'S
OUTFITTING & BOOTS

YARNOLD

& SON
NAILSWORTH
SANDOM COATS
IMPREGNABLE FOOTWEAR

W. BRUTON

General Ironmonger
&
Electrical Engineer

COSSACK SQ.,
NAILSWORTH

'Phone : 39

Something to Shout About

- HOW THE TEAMS FINISHED UP -

WESTERN LEAGUE

Division I

	P	W	D	L	F	A	Pts
BARNSTAPLE Tn.	32	18	8	6	77	37	44
Street	32	19	6	7	89	43	44
Trowbridge Town	32	17	7	8	76	48	41
Bideford	32	13	12	6	79	52	39
Chippenham Town	32	17	3	12	84	58	37
Weymouth	32	16	5	11	75	58	37
Chippenham Utd.	32	15	5	12	62	62	35
Salisbury	32	11	10	11	60	65	32
Glastonbury	32	15	1	16	61	49	31
Bath City	32	10	11	11	64	68	31
Stonehouse	32	11	8	13	57	58	30
Portland Utd.	32	11	8	13	66	77	30
Bridgwater Town	32	12	4	16	58	73	28
Wells City	32	9	6	17	53	71	24
Clandown	32	7	9	16	40	74	23
Dorchester Town	32	8	5	19	46	74	21
Paulton Rovers	32	8	5	21	42	125	17

Division II

	P	W	D	L	F	A	Pts
CHIPPENHAM Tn.	34	24	4	6	90	51	52
Ilfracombe Town	34	20	11	3	67	28	51
Poole Town	34	21	7	6	97	43	49
Peasedown M.W.	34	19	3	12	76	63	41
Minehead	34	15	8	11	81	55	38
Clevedon	34	17	3	14	82	82	37
Cinderford Town	34	15	6	13	77	50	36
Bristol City	34	14	6	14	75	56	34
Bristol Rovers	34	12	9	13	74	54	33
Frome Town	34	13	6	15	66	66	32
Yeovil Town	34	13	5	16	82	78	31
Gloucester City	34	11	6	17	81	97	28
Radstock Town	34	11	6	17	74	102	28
Trowbridge Tn. R.	34	4	19	70	89	26
Stonehouse Res.	34	11	6	18	53	107	26
Welton Rovers	34	10	5	18	58	96	26
Weston-S-Mare	34	10	4	20	66	113	24
Hoffmann Ath.	34	8	4	22	60	100	20

NORTHERN SENIOR LEAGUE

Section A

	P	W	D	L	F	A	Pts
LYDBROOK	26	20	2	4	147	45	42
Forest Green	26	19	2	5	85	42	40
Brimscombe	26	17	4	5	79	38	38
Charlton Kings	26	13	5	8	77	52	31
Broadwell	26	12	3	11	69	60	27
Tuffley Rovers	26	12	3	11	61	60	27
Cam Bulldogs	26	9	8	9	65	69	26
Stag Rovers	26	10	5	11	51	56	25
Frampton	26	8	7	11	56	58	23
Swindon Town A	26	7	5	14	61	81	19
Rodborough	26	6	6	15	41	76	16
Synwell Rovers	26	5	5	18	33	100	11
Lydney Town	26	3	2	22	39	142	6

Section B

	P	W	D	L	F	A	Pts
HARROW HILL	26	21	1	4	116	43	43
Wotton	26	14	6	6	81	53	34
Berkeley	26	13	7	6	85	51	33
Sharpness	26	14	3	9	101	47	31
Ross U.S.	26	13	5	8	75	76	31
Hawksbury	26	11	6	9	74	65	28
Chalford	26	11	6	9	66	71	26
Viney Hill	26	10	7	9	60	57	27
Dursley Town	26	11	4	11	92	79	26
Mitcheldean	26	8	4	14	65	93	20
King's Stanley	26	6	6	14	45	64	18
Tetbury Town	26	6	6	14	65	94	18
Shortwood	26	6	6	14	51	85	18
Minchinhampton	26	1	1	24	42	128	9

STROUD YOUTH LEAGUE

Division I

	P	W	D	L	F	A	Pts
TETBURY COLTS	16	14	1	1	112	27	29
Cashes Green	16	12	1	3	80	41	25
Cirencester	16	12	0	4	62	35	24
Hoffmann Colts	16	10	2	4	54	36	22
Dursley	16	7	0	9	67	59	14
Vindicatrix	16	5	1	10	44	73	11
Frampton	16	4	1	11	39	77	9
Nailsworth	16	2	3	11	29	82	7
Rodborough	16	1	1	14	28	81	3

Division II

	P	W	D	L	F	A	Pts
UPLANDS	12	11	0	1	133	12	22
Thrupp	12	9	0	3	122	23	18
Nailsworth	12	9	0	3	58	32	18
Cashes Green	12	6	1	5	64	35	13
Amberley	12	3	0	9	21	80	6
Beeches Green	12	1	1	10	16	94	3
Woodchester	11	1	0	10	8	145	2

STROUD LEAGUE

Premier Section

	P	W	D	L	F	A	Pts
EASTINGTON	26	20	2	4	115	42	42
Babdown	26	19	5	2	94	43	43
Forest Green	26	18	2	6	82	47	38
Hardwicke	26	15	3	8	95	44	37
Charfield	26	16	3	7	97	57	35
Frampton	26	13	1	10	75	68	31
Dursley	26	12	2	12	90	85	26
Uplands	26	9	5	12	68	74	23
*Chalford	25	10	2	13	64	68	20
Avening	26	6	6	14	51	73	18
Tetbury	26	7	3	16	58	88	17
Oley	26	8	2	16	61	105	14
Rodborough	26	4	5	19	47	129	11
Brimscombe	25	2	3	20	27	82	7

* Two points deducted for playing an ineligible player.

Division I

	P	W	D	L	F	A	Pts
FRAMILODE	24	19	3	2	82	40	41
Paganhill	24	19	2	3	93	35	40
Coaley	24	11	6	7	90	59	28
King's Stanley	24	11	5	8	71	43	27
Sharpness	24	13	1	9	80	51	27
Cam Bulldogs	24	11	5	8	59	50	27
Randwick	24	10	2	10	54	57	22
Tuffley	24	9	5	9	55	62	23
Thrupp	24	7	5	12	61	71	19
Shortwood	24	7	1	16	61	86	15
Bisley	24	6	2	14	47	78	14
Berkeley	24	3	6	15	41	94	12
Wotton	23	4	2	17	41	94	10

Division II

	P	W	D	L	F	A	Pts
SLIMBRIDGE	20	17	3	0	82	23	37
Minchinhampton	20	16	2	2	89	34	34
Eastcombe	20	12	2	6	80	39	26
Oakridge	20	11	3	6	65	40	25
Hardwicke	20	9	0	5	55	47	22
Leonard Stanley	20	7	3	10	51	71	19
North Nibley	20	7	1	12	46	57	15
Amberley	20	5	5	10	47	74	15
Woodchester	20	4	3	13	41	75	11
Nympsfield	20	4	1	15	33	89	9
Synwell	20	2	5	13	41	100	9

Division III

	P	W	D	L	F	A	Pts
CHARFIELD	23	20	1	2	114	29	41
Arlingham	24	18	3	3	106	24	39
Haresfield	24	14	5	5	88	49	33
Paganhill	24	13	4	9	82	63	28
Sapperton	24	13	3	9	85	77	26
*Dursley	23	13	2	8	78	71	24
Slimbridge	23	9	2	11	48	63	20
Stad	24	7	6	11	61	61	20
Whitminster	23	9	2	13	62	61	20
Randwick	23	5	2	13	63	73	18
Avening	24	6	4	13	55	92	16
Eastington	23	4	2	17	34	113	10
Framilode	23	2	2	20	27	96	5

* Four points deducted for playing an ineligible player in two matches.

Final League tables, 1952/53.

1953/54

Cecil Hudd made a comeback in the reserves, moving back to the firsts in January 1954. Marshall Woodward played almost a full season for the firsts, his last for the club.

Harrow Hill, another Forest team, proved to be stiff opposition in both the league and the Senior Amateur Cup, knocking Forest Green out at home 4-0; and winning 5-0 at Harrow Hill and 2-1 at The Lawn in the league. At the end of March, Forest Green played away to Charlton Kings under floodlights at Cheltenham Town's ground in midweek, winning 7-1, with Jim Turk netting 5 of the goals. The Cheltenham Town manager was so impressed that he offered Jim Turk the chance to play against High Wycombe in Cheltenham's next match, an offer that Jim couldn't possibly refuse. Having impressed in that game, Jim then stayed at Cheltenham for 2 seasons.

At the end of season AGM in May 1954, the secretary's report summarised the season as follows:

> As expected, Division One of the Senior League proved very strong and our Senior XI had to fight hard to finish ninth of fourteen. In the Senior Charity Cup we reached the final for the second year running. This time we lost 1-0 to Brimscombe during extra time.
>
> Our Junior XI achieved the distinction of being the first reserve side to win the championship of the Premier section of the Stroud League. In doing so it was necessary to call upon twenty-nine different players. In the Junior County Cup we won three games before falling to Popes Hill in the third round. Our passage in the Junior Charity Cup was a stiffer journey and we won three games before failing at Coaley in the semi-final.
>
> Forty-four players had signed on during the season and only six had not played in any games. Three players had transferred to other clubs. Players with most appearances were H. Gannaway, 38, J. Duff and P. Smith, 37, C. Hudd 36 and W. Stokes 35. Leading goalscorers were G. Harvey 40, J. Turk 30, H. Gannaway 27, G. Murdoch 18, D. Brown and E. Young 15 each.

1954/55

Peter Vick was still playing in the forthcoming season, having first played in 1936. The committee were still hell-bent on trying to promote a County League and the GFA commented in August that in the past thirty years no other club had sent in any resolutions to positively benefit the system. Forest Green submitted their familiar resolutions for the third year running for the consideration of the GFA.

Marshall Woodward appeared in the first game but retired injured and then made one further appearance for the reserves against Charfield before retiring from the game altogether.

MARSHALL WOODWARD

My injury started when I played with Stonehouse against Trowbridge. I went to hook the ball clear from the penalty area and somebody was coming in and he swept everything there and jarred my knee. That was the start of it. Later on at Forest Green we played Cinderford and it was there that it happened. Sailor Dangerfield, he was right half, he put this ball across, a real good cross to me at inside left. I was sort of going to run on to it and the goalkeeper started to advance and I got my right foot to the ball, as he dived at my feet and I flipped the thing, took him further that way; all I had to do was put my left foot forward.

I was swerving and he grabbed my foot and held it down on the ground. With my speed, he yanked it. I heard a crack and I went up in the air and I couldn't get up. And the ref didn't give a penalty. It should have been a penalty, it was a favourite trick with that particular goalie. There was a cartoon in the Pink 'Un a few weeks after, he was playing at Gloucester City for Cinderford and it said 'A lot of leg pulling by the Cinderford Town goalkeeper.' I wish I had kept that at the time, because that's what happened.

He didn't break my leg, he done something and something snapped. I got in the changing room and there was something wrong, you know, I couldn't walk. I had to have a lot of treatment in Stroud Hospital, kept going there and having springs on my leg, up and down, on and on and all this treatment. Then I had to go back and see the chap. He asked how it was. I said it seems perfectly normal now, seemed alright. So, he said he didn't know as I'd need to have an operation. All he said was don't play football again and I didn't play football for several months. Then I thought it was alright. I said to whoever it was up at Forest Green, probably John Pearson, I reckon I could try out and maybe have a game in the seconds or something and try him out.

At the end we had to go to Charfield. Every time I was on that leg it just capsized and I was on the floor, there was no way I could stop on me feet. So I tried to get up but it happened again about twenty times. I thought I couldn't go on like that every game. I kept coming off. I was about twenty-six or twenty-seven, something like that; so it cut me off a few seasons and so I started playing golf, which I've enjoyed ever since.

The first team now included a new keeper, Harold Smith. Several reserve team players moved up to fill vacancies following the loss of first-team players such as Marshall Woodward, Alf Francis and John Pearson. Jim Turk, Rovers' top scorer over the past few years, had also moved on to play professionally for Cheltenham. Peter Vick even made a comeback in the first team in the Charity Cup game against Chalford in September 1954.

The settled team of the previous decade was gone. By the time they played Swindon Town A at the County Ground in mid-October, they had lost their first 5 games and ended up losing to Swindon 4-2 as well. This was followed by a 6-1 loss to Sharpness who were back in the league with a vengeance before a 1-1 draw was achieved with Berkeley followed up by a 4-1 win against Wotton.

P. Smith made his debut in goal for the first team in November with Harold Smith demoted to the reserves. By the end of 1954, Rovers had lost 9 games, drawn 2, with a single win at Wotton and were bottom of the league, a position they had not been in since 1907 in the Stroud League. A wretched season continued, losing to Swindon Town A on Boxing Day 2-1 at the County Ground with Bill Malpas fracturing his leg so badly that silver plates had to be inserted. Noting that there might be a delay on the payout of insurance monies, the club forwarded him a sum of £12.

After Christmas, following 5 draws, 3 further wins and 5 losses, the season drew to an end with Forest Green third from bottom of the league and relegated for the first time in their history, along with Wotton who finished bottom and Ross United. Wesley Stokes, John Duff, Ray Brown and Cecil Hudd all missed only a single game in the season. Twenty-six different players were selected, which was no more than usual.

Left: Forest Green Rovers 1954/55. Peter Vick, Alf Francis, Harold Gannaway, Harold Smith, Bob Tanner, Graham Harvey, Ernie Young, Les Dangerfield, Wes Stokes, John Duff, Bill Malpas.

Opposite: Forest Green Rovers reserves 1955/56. Back row: Danny Harrison, John Walker, Keith Robbins, Alan Wright, Ray Stevens, Doug Brown, Derek Cowley, Peter Vick. Front row: George Perkins, Vic Cowley, Les Dangerfield, Malcolm Vick, J. Webb.

15

Under New Management: 1955–1968

1955/56

Having previously attempted to secure the services of a trainer in a half-hearted fashion, Bill Thomas, from Stonehouse Football Club, became the first paid manager of Forest Green, hoping to guide Rovers straight back from relegation.

On the playing front, 'Raggy' Bingle had returned from Africa keen to return to action for the first team. John Duff went in the other direction, moving off to do his National Service. By June 1955, the committee had invested in a complete range of training equipment. Their usual frugal attitude had been overruled by the need to obtain a winning team formula again.

Bill Malpas was reported to be making disappointing progress and would require further operations on his plated leg. The committee resolved to arrange a benefit match for him against Shortwood. Many clubs sent donations of several guineas towards the benefit game played on Boxing Day. Unfortunately (and ironically), the game, which had been arranged to provide funds for Bill Malpas's broken leg, resulted in Basil Newport, who was playing for Shortwood at the time, breaking his leg and effectively ending his football career.

Forest Green donated all the gate receipts from their league match against Shortwood to Basil Newport.

RAY BINGLE

I went off to East Africa to work after the Hoffmans final in 1951. When I got back, that was Bill Thomas's era then. I went up and started training a bit and he asked me if I wanted to play again, and I agreed. I used to like Bill, he worked at Redlers I think.

It made a big difference having a coach because he introduced training as well. He brought mobile floodlights up to The Lawn at that time and we started training, whereas before we didn't. It didn't affect us too much because we were young enough, but yes, we had fitness training, ran round the ground and all things like that. It was extended to Shortwood players as well. Quite a number of Shortwood players came up as well because at that time they didn't have their own facilities.

BASIL NEWPORT

I was playing in the charity match, for Bill Malpas and I broke me leg in a tackle! The wife and the two kids were up there. Poor old Mrs Bathe, she had a son playing and his name was Basil as well. You heard it go, you heard the bang right across the ground. They turned round to poor old Mrs Bathe who was working in the tea hut and said Basil's broken his leg. And she went out of there like lighting!

I should say when I broke me leg I heard it go. 'I think I broke me leg,' and at that point you know. Mine was a clean break. I broke it in three places. And that was the end of that. I was thirty-five.

Both my sons got into the schoolboy county team, and they both played for Forest Green. Neil also broke his leg playing for Forest Green when he was only twenty. He had an awful break. It was a compound one, the back of the leg was at the front.

Thirteen wins on the trot were achieved this season, including Gloucester City Reserves, Stonehouse and Shortwood who were beaten 4-1. Forest Green now carried a set of away strip shirts, all green, which were borrowed by Shortwood for their Northern Senior League game. Bill Thomas resigned in April but stuck around and arranged summer training, which was eagerly taken up by all of the players.

Ron Davis's report at the AGM in June 1956 was much more upbeat than the year before:

Reporting on the players, the secretary congratulated Wesley Stokes on being elected captain of the County XI. Leading goalscorers were John Smith with 48 goals, Alan Wright 44, Ray Brown 21. Before the season started the supporters' club erected floodlights to assist the players in training. Some players had taken advantage of this but the majority had failed to do so. It was disappointing to the club and also to the coach, Mr Bill Thomas, who had worked very hard and could claim most credit for a very successful season. It was to be hoped that training would be more serious next season when the opposition would be much tougher.

George Mills, a player in the 1930s and a very public figure in Nailsworth politics, became president of the club for the forthcoming season.

1956/57

Programmes were discontinued, although season tickets were still being issued and Mr Martin Middleditch, who was a very ardent supporter despite the fact that he had to attend in a wheelchair, was awarded a complimentary season ticket for the forthcoming season.

Forest Green Rovers 1955/56, winners of the Second Division of the Northern Senior League. Back row: Ben Weager, Bill Thomas, Ray Bingle, Ray Brinkworth, Les Dangerfield, Percy Smith, Ray Brown, unknown, Geoff Smith, Ron Crossland. Front row: Bert Beale, unknown, John Hatherall, Wesley Stokes, Jim Casey, John Hudd, Ron Davis.

Action photos of a game against Brimscombe at The Lawn before the pitch was levelled.

John Hudd had had a very successful trial for Bristol City. He played for Forest Green for most of the season but, in April, Bristol City requested his services full time. By October the club still hadn't traced a potential coach. Peter Vick took the training sessions, which were generally felt to be very productive.

Forest Green met Lydbrook in the league in January, losing away 5-1 and, in the Senior Amateur Cup third round, Forest Green met Lydbrook at home. The score was at 3-3 after 90 minutes but Rovers lost 6-3 after extra time. Perhaps the players weren't training quite as hard as the committee thought they were.

Ron Davis reported, as usual, at the annual general meeting in May 1957 as follows:

Both teams were to be congratulated for this season's performance. The Senior XI had found the opposition tough but had finished halfway up the Senior League Division One after making a bad start. They lost in the third round of the County Cup after giving Lydbrook, who eventually won the cup, quite a shock. The club lost to Stonehouse in the Senior Charity Cup after playing that club three times.

The Second XI finished fourth in the Stroud League Division One and could still claim to be the best amateur reserve side in the district.

The secretary congratulated John Hudd and John Llewelyn, both having played with Bristol City and Wolverhampton Wanderers respectively. Harold Smith and Ray Stevens were congratulated for 100 per cent league and cup appearances. Leading goalscorers were J. Smith 25, A. Wright 22, H. Mauler 16, L. Parker-Ashley 16.

Forest Green Rovers 1956/57. Back row: Ron Davis, Mike Stribbling, John Hatherall, John Llewellyn, Harold Smith, Ray Bingle, John Smith, Bert Beale (linesman). Front row: George Perkins, John Hudd, Ralf Webb, Derek Sibley, Cecil Hudd, Ben Weager. This photograph was taken in front of the grandstand first erected in 1938.

1957/58

Eddie Cowley, Cinderford Town's coach, joined for the forthcoming season. He got it right from the start, helped by the return of Jim Turk from Cheltenham Town as a permit player, (a paid professional allowed to play for an amateur team). The season kicked off against Charlton Kings with a 6-0 home win with Jim Turk, John Llewelyn and Eddie's brother, Don Cowley each scoring 2 goals. Rovers went 10 games unbeaten, drawing at home 1-1 with Lydbrook in early November. Jim Turk scored at least 1 goal in the first 6 matches of the season. The reserves also got off to a flying start. Peter Vick had semi-retired, playing only 1 game this season and a further game in the following season, no doubt playing when called upon because the team were short. In all, Peter's playing career for the club lasted twenty-three years, not a bad run at all.

But, by March, Eddie Cowley was finding the Selection Committee difficult to deal with. Eddie refused to stay, a decision the committee felt was undemocratic. Don Cowley stayed on, both as a player and to undertake basic skills training.

Rovers played a friendly against Southampton 'A' in March 1958 without the coach's input, losing 3-0.

AGM Season Summary
The secretary congratulated both elevens on a very successful season. The First XI had finished fourth in Division One of the Senior League and had won the Senior Charity Cup. The reserves had finished runners-up in the Stroud League Division One and had won the Junior Charity Cup. This was the first time any club had won both the charity cups in one season.

Leading goalscorers were A. Wright 45, M. Evans 42, D. Cowley and M. Vanstone 28, J. Turk 27, J. Llewellyn 18 and E. Hatherall 17. M. Vanstone was congratulated on scoring 7 goals in one game and John Llewellyn on being selected several times for the County Youth XI.

Forest Green
Rovers in action at
Brimscombe Meadow
in the late 1950s,
against Brimscombe.
Brimscombe's ground
had not changed in
appearance since the
1920s when Forest
Green beat King's Stanley
in the Stroud Hospital
Cup Final. It was still
much the same in 2006.

Forest Green Rovers reserves 1957/58. Back row: Harold Gannaway, Doug Brown, Harold King, Reg Baker, Ray Bingle, Peter Vick. Front row: Jock Patterson, Cecil Hudd, Les Dangerfield, Wesley Stokes, Jim Turk.

Left: A selection of the medals won by Vic Cowley and his father between 1912 and 1950. The medals with the Cross of St George are for the Stroud Hospital Cup.

Below: Miniature cups won by Vic Cowley and his father, the cups were given as an alternative to medals.

1958/59

Don Cowley stayed on as a player-coach, scoring 5 goals in the first 5 games, but only 1 for the rest of the season. Adrian Brown signed on for the team where his cousin, Ray 'Bomber' Brown, had now been playing for a number of years. Another veteran player, who started his playing career for Forest Green long before the Second World War, Vic 'Scrubby' Cowley, signed on again as a player for the twenty-seventh and last time!

In November, Mr Fred Ford, who was a Bristol Rovers coach, agreed to come up to Forest Green for a sum of 25s per visit to take further training sessions, and carried on doing so until Christmas. Ron Davis's annual secretary's report at the AGM in June 1959 was upbeat:

In presenting the report the secretary said, from a playing point of view, this was the most successful year in the eleven years that he had been secretary. The club had won five cups, including the last-minute surprise, the Linesman's Cup. For the second year running we had won both the Senior and Junior Charity Cups.

The First XI had finished seventh in the Senior League Division One and were the only team to beat Lydbrook all season. Besides winning the Junior Charity Cup, the Second XI had also won the Junior Amateur Cup, the first reserve side ever to do so, and the Stroud League Division One.

In congratulating both captains on the season's performances, the secretary said credit must also go to H. King, D. Cowley and F. Ford for some fine coaching and training. Mr Ford had been coming up from Bristol Rovers and the club were extremely fortunate in having the services of a man who also coached the England under-23 team.

Leading goalscorers were M. Evans 52 in 40 games, S. Stephens 29 in 25 games, R.F. Brown 31 in 38 games, J. Turk 27 in 29 games and M. Workman 23 in 30 games. S. Stephens with 41 games had played most games during the season. M. Stribbling and P. Price were the only players with 100 per cent league and cup appearances. The teams had scored 304 goals in 80 games, an average of 3.8 goals per game. A special word of thanks was due to Mr Ben Weager, who had been forced to retire after many years as First 11 bagman.

The treasurer reported that the running costs were rising every year and that it was only due to the supporters' club that the club existed at all at this level. The club had a balance at the end of the season of £32 and during the year the supporters' club had donated £243 to the club in addition to the £108 gate money collected. There were no other forms of sponsorship and no programmes to top-up funds and it was certainly no exaggeration when it was said that the supporters' club kept the club afloat.

ADRIAN BROWN

The most memorable game that I played was a charity cup final, down on Hoffmans' ground, and I can remember getting the ball in the second half just past the halfway line, on the right-hand side. I looked up to see our Bomber waving like this on the left. I put a pass to our Bomber who goes past this bloke. I ran in the middle, he put it over and I caught it on the volley with my left foot of all things, which I only stood on, bang in the back of the net. Must be the best goal I scored, and really I didn't know a lot about it. I can remember Mick Evans behind the goal saying, 'You didn't know a lot about that, did you Adie!?' That didn't count though, it was the goal that counted. That was probably my best playing-wise.

We came back to the Jovials and had quite a few beers as you do, and I can remember our Bomber and I walking up Star Hill and across the Green with our cups still with some beer in, singing, our arms round each other, singing our heart out.

Forest Green Rovers Reserves 1958/59. From left to right, back row: Vic Cowley, Mike Stribbling, Brian Woodward, Jim Turk, Harold Smith, Adrian Brown, Dave Gardiner, Peter Vick. Front row: Malcom Vick, Mike Evans, Ray Stevens, Wesley Stokes, Colin Gay.

ADRIAN BROWN

I had a lot of years with Jimmy Turk. He was everyone's hero. He had come back from Cheltenham Town. Well, when Jimmy and Wes Stokes got past their first-team appearances, they came down and played for the seconds to bring the youngsters on. Well Jimmy, he would give out the verbals – not nastily – and there was a lad named Mike Workman who played, and in the end Mike, after quite a few years, became captain of Stroud Rugby Club. I can remember Mike was centre forward and I was either inside right or right wing, that area, and Jimmy used to be on to us all the time. If the ball was going over the line for a goal kick he would be shouting 'Chase it Adie, chase it Mike!' Workie, I think he used to call Mike. You didn't answer back because you know full well he'd played at a higher level, and he'd done it a lot better than you ever would.

Above left: Forest Green Rovers reserves 1958/59. Back row: Vic Cowley, Dave Gardiner, Brian Woodward, Mike Workman, Les Smith, Malcolm Vick, Mike Evans, Peter Vick. Front row: Alan Wright, Harold Mauler, Ray Stevens, Adrian Brown, Dave Peterson, R. Davis. On the extreme left and right are the referee and two linesmen.

Above right: Ray Stevens with the Northern Junior Cup.

Left: At the annual dinner with the five cups for the season.

FOREST GREEN A.F.C. enjoyed a most successful season, and five trophies were displayed at the club supper at the Town Hall, Nailsworth, on Friday evening. Our photograph includes club officials, players and Supporters' Club officials. Seventh from the right in the back row is Mr. Peter Vick who was presented with the Stroud League Linesman's Cup during the dinner.

.... SO THE ROVERS HAD FIVE CUPS ON SHOW

HERE was a surprise for Forest Green footballers and officials, Mr. Peter Vick in particular, at club dinner at the Town Hall, lsworth, on Friday evening.

before the dinner began four cups n by the club during the past son were on display, but then ne the news that a fifth was to added to the number—the Linesn's Cup.

Donated by Mr. S. G. Finning for petition amongst the linesmen in oud League teams, it was won Mr. Peter Vick who was sented with it by Mr. Finning.

The Rovers second eleven earned points, Cope Chat and Slimbridge ning second with 81 points each, n Chalford Reserves third with 69.

Not surprising the five trophies upied pride of place at the dinner,

and references were made to the performance in winning the cups.

They were the Stroud Senior Charity Cup, won by the first eleven, the Northern Junior Cup, Stroud League First Division Cup and Stroud Junior Charity Cup, won by the second eleven and of course the Linesman's Cup.

The Loyal Toast was proposed by Mr. E. G. Smith the club chairman, and after the presentation of the Linesman's Cup, a toast to the various soccer Leagues, visitors and Press, was proposed by Mr. G. C. Mills, president of the club.

He noted the successes achieved and said that the fact that the second eleven had won the majority of the trophies, showed that there was a strong reserve strength available for the first eleven when it was needed.

It was particularly pleasing that the younger players had done so well, and he wished to pay a special tribute to Mr. John Pearson, the former Rovers player and captain, who was unable

to be present, for the way in which he had in past years coached the youngsters. "I think we owe John Pearson a debt of gratitude for what he has done for this club in past years," remarked Mr. Mills.

The club had been grateful to a number of the older players who had " hung up their boots " and then come back again to help out, the work of the committee and officials having also contributed much towards the success of the club as a whole.

MANY ATTRACTIONS

In these days there were so many attractions and interests and the running of amateur societies of all descriptions was becoming difficult, but at Forest Green the club carried on well and many gave of their time.

" I say as one who knows this district very well that you by your efforts and activities at Forest Green are making to the recreational and social life of this neighbourhood a far greater contribution than you might be aware," declared Mr. Mills.

He referred to the work of the G.F.A., Northern Senior League, and Stroud League, noting that the last named were doing a wonderfully good job in providing football for the smaller areas of population in the north of the county.

The Stroud Charity Cup Competition was also referred to, Mr. Mills, after welcoming all the visitors, thanking the Press.

A reply was made by Mr. D. Mason, Sports Editor of the Stroud News and Journal, who congratulated the club on their achievements.

The second eleven had, he said, set up a record by becoming the first club reserve side ever to win the Northern Junior Cup since it was started in 1913-4, while the first eleven also had the knowledge that they were the only side to beat the Northern Senior League Division One champions, Lynbrook, in the League.

He congratulated the Supporters Club on their work and wished the two teams every success in the future.

A dance followed the dinner.

Fame at last.

Peter Vick receives the Linesman's Cup.

JOHN PORTER

I started playing for Shortwood when I was seventeen, along with Rafe Webb. I was interested in Forest Green because they were a more senior side, and I had a chat with Pete Vick. I went up and signed for them. Forest Green was playing with better players and against better teams; Cinderford, Harrow Hill, Lydbrook and teams like that, which were obviously a better class. Lydbrook used to make it into the FA Amateur Cup, and that's the sort of thing you wanted to do, so that's why I signed for Forest Green.

The other thing about Forest Green is that they had a manager. Can't remember his name, but one thing I will always remember was going on the bus to Lydbrook and the manager talking about this Charlie Punter who played for Lydbrook, and he said that's going to be the chap that you're going to have to mark this afternoon. I'd never had anything like this before. At Shortwood they didn't have a manager. You just went out and played and did your best and came back off. I'd read in the *Stroud News & Journal* about Charlie Punter; and it was something almost foreign to me. I had never had a coach instructing me: 'Get your arse over here,' that sort of thing.

It was the first game of the season and I went out and we went 1-0 up and things were looking good. I thought this was easy, and then I think I just lost my nut a little bit. We was told off to a certain extent – not a real telling off – but we lost our shape, you know. You think, 'We got this one goal against the best team in the league, let's go for another.' We lost 8-1 in the end! That was my introduction to Charlie Punter, and I had two or three seasons after where we played against each other. I think Lydbrook, they always looked to me like they took to the game as though they were going to win and that was it.

But Charlie Punter, he was the Wayne Rooney of the Senior League, that's the only description I can give of the bloke. Everybody else, I think, that played against him or seen him would say that was the right description. He played with a lot of courage and used his weight. I was, I think, about ten-and-a-half stone so I was giving him about three or four stone I expect, plus six inches higher in bloody legs and arms, twice the size of me. He was tall, he really was, but I don't think I've ever seen anybody else better than him that I had to play against. Never. Lydbrook were the team to beat for years.

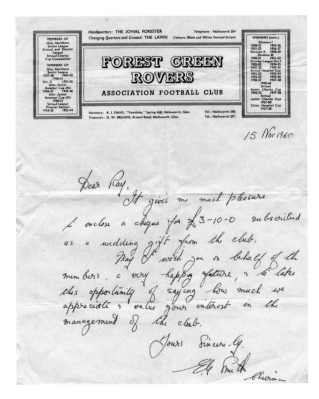

Letter from Forest Green to Ray Brown enclosing his wedding gift.

Lydbrook Athletic

In six seasons, starting in 1956/57, Lydbrook won five titles and were runners-up once. No club has dominated the league before or since. In 1957/58 they were champions again, only losing one game all season and that was to Forest Green. Two more championships followed and for the 1959/60 season, Lydbrook were chased to the title by Harrow Hill and Forest Green Rovers. Lydbrook were runners-up in 1960/61 and then returned as champions the following year. They, like Forest Green at the beginning of the 1950s, were frustrated by the lack of a County League for Gloucestershire and left to play in the Warwickshire Combination.

They also brought national recognition to Gloucestershire football in the 1961/62 season with their FA Amateur Cup exploits, managing to get to the second round, where their opponents were Bishop Auckland, who had won the trophy ten times previously. Lydbrook were in no way disgraced in losing 5-0 to the nationally known amateur club. The following season, Lydbrook drew Woking at home and played the game at Westbury, their pitch down by the river Wye not really fit for such a large match. They lost 1-0. In all of their ten seasons in the Senior League Lydbrook never won the Senior Amateur Cup. In 1959/60 Forest Green only lost 5 games all season, finishing with 46 points, 1 point behind Harrow Hill and 6 behind Lydbrook.

1959/60

The club always looked after its players and with Ray Brown's wedding approaching, the club wrote to him enclosing its gift as a wedding present.

Don Cowley continued as a coach in an unofficial capacity, but was paid travelling expenses in addition to a fee for training. The first game of the season was against Lydbrook, who were to go on and win the league for a fourth consecutive time since joining in 1952. John 'Wacker' Porter moved from Shortwood to Forest Green to follow in his father's footsteps.

JOHN PORTER

John Llewelyn, 'Lewie', played on the left and I was at right half, as it was then. I was expected to feed him and the inside right or maybe somewhere else, but these long cross balls then was never bloody used. The ball was too heavy. You couldn't hit the bloody thing like they can now. You see goalkeepers kick them from one goal and the other goalkeeper says, 'Thank you very much – now we'll start from this end.'

Because the ball was heavy with the old laces and all that, we used to dread it if it rained. The ball got sort of double the weight, and when somebody did kick it, it didn't get as far as the halfway line, if it got that far. And sometimes you'd look up and think, 'I've got to head this,' and it come down, and if you had a lace you could always guarantee that nearly every game you came off with a mark. I used to play centre half mainly, but even at right half you used to dread the ball coming out of the goalkeeper's kicking from the one half and trying to get it up the other half. But there was a big difference in the ball compared to now.

And the grounds! When you played anywhere like Harrow Hill, it was on a slope – well, Shortwood played on a slope as well – but Christ almighty it was like trying to play twenty-two instead of bloody eleven at Harrow Hill when you were going uphill and it was raining. I mean, I don't know when it don't rain down the Forest of Dean. It rained every day I went down there, I think. But you know, looking back I've got no regrets at all. Luckily I came out of it and I can still walk. I got no limps or lumps or nothing like that. I didn't break anything other than me ankle, but that's by the by.

You can't believe what they can do with the ball nowadays, but the bloody thing isn't laced up with lumps of leather and the place where they used to put the bloody inner tube in. All them laces round and all that sort of thing, and that coming down on your head, on a wet bloody Saturday …

Well, most of them would be claiming compensation these days every bloody game I should think if they had to head that thing. But I wouldn't change a thing. I know Webby and people like that, that I bump into, wouldn't either. We had a good time, and things got to move on.

1960/61

Don Cowley left to become player-manager of Cinderford Town, leaving Forest Green without a coach again. The committee couldn't even agree on members for a Selection Committee and decided that the full General Committee would pick the teams each Monday night. But by August, a Selection Committee was back, which included 'Nip' Beale.

One of the drawbacks of the existing playing surface at The Lawn was the slope. Mr Evans agreed to rent his field to Rovers for the season, and a contract was let for the ground levelling from April 1960. The field used as their temporary home is next to the New Stadium roundabout, opposite Carters Way.

Supporters club cards leading into the 1960s.

ADRIAN BROWN

I can always remember that while our Bomber was on National Service, I'd been dropped a couple of times and I wasn't happy about this. I can remember I saw someone from Shortwood, and I said 'Get me a signing on form, it's not getting me down.' I'll go and play for Shortwood, I'll go where I can.

Anyway I had a letter from Malaya from Bomber – 'Don't you dare sign for Shortwood – Browns play for Forest Green. I don't want to hear none of this rubbish, you write me a letter soon. I don't want to hear this silly talk, go and get your place back.' Someone had told him in a letter, perhaps our uncle, or his dad. I had a letter telling me off. And I can always remember seeing Jimmy Grant, who was secretary of Shortwood for years and years. Well, I seen him a week after and I said that I didn't get that form. He said, 'Well, I see you had your name in the paper in the game and I thought that there was no way you'd come to us.' And that was it; nothing funny. But I got back in from there.

By March the levelling work was completed back at The Lawn and all thoughts and labour turned to smartening up the ground in anticipation of a grand opening at the beginning of the next season. The season was summed up at the AGM in May 1961:

> The First XI had finished eighth in the Senior League Division One and had been knocked out of the Senior Amateur Cup and Senior Charity Cup, both in the second rounds. The Second XI had narrowly missed the runners-up position in the Stroud League Division One. They could still claim to be the best local reserve side. They had been knocked out of the Junior Amateur Cup and the Junior Charity Cup on both occasions by Chalford.
>
> Leading goalscorers were T. Edwards 34, J. Llewellyn 20, J. Hudd 20, R. Brown 18 and A. Brown 16.

Ray Bingle retired, having played for the club over a sixteen-year period.

RAY BINGLE

Forest Green – that's the only team I ever wanted to play for really. I played for the pick of the league a few times, but Rovers were the only team I ever wanted to play for.

Of course, the other thing is old Nip Beale was the linesman. I can't remember Forest Green without him. We didn't have officials. We provided our own linesmen, and Nip was ours before and after the Second World War for a long time, and I can't remember him missing a match. Very fair, he was an umpire at cricket.

ALAN BEALE

My father was Forest Green Rovers through and through. Bertram Edward Beale, 'Nip' to his friends.

Saturday evenings at home after a Forest Green Rovers game was not a pleasant one if they had lost. He wouldn't speak to anybody. It was off down the pub to mull over the result, and if they won it was off down the pub to celebrate!

I remember the team used to travel away in Ivory coaches, who were based at Tetbury, and, on the return journey, especially after a win, I will always remember the noisy singing that was the order of the day. Nip and his brother Alf were cousins to the prolific goalscorer from the earlier years 'Paper' Beale.

ADRIAN BROWN

My last game was against Sharpness. It was nearly the end of the season, and I can always remember this now because we used to have a little move. I was then playing right half as they called it, and our Bomber was left half. He had the throw in and I always used to hang right back and wait until the last minute, then dart across quietly to the left wing and he would flick the ball down there. That was him and I. This time he threw it a bit earlier and I was in the middle, and the bloke banged me, clobbered me. I don't think it was a foul, it was just a hard tackle and my leg went, and that was it. And that mucked me up completely because I can't move that knee properly even now. I didn't break the leg. The ligaments were ripped open, it severed the nerve, that was the problem. Of course, I couldn't play anymore.

1961/62

The entrance fee was doubled from 6*d* to 1*s* for Senior League games, old-age pensioners half price and children for 3*d*. The levelling works had been undertaken by a contractor and funds had to be raised to keep the finances in order. Bristol City arrived to play the inaugural match on the newly levelled ground on 19 August 1961.

On the pitch, new players were again brought in to try and improve results. Lawrence Duxbury had one season with Rovers before deciding that his future lay with Stroud Rugby Club. Adrian Brown sustained his career-ending injury at the age of twenty-two in April in a reserve match against Coaley.

The GFA arranged with the club to play the Senior Amateur Cup final at the new-look Lawn with everybody expressing satisfaction with the facilities. By the end of the season, the secretary summed the year's affairs up as follows:

The firsts had finished fifth in Division One of the Senior League and an outstanding feature of this programme was 12 drawn games out of the 30 played. The reserves had finished runners-up to Sharpness in Division One of the Stroud League, the first time for many years that we had been topped by another reserve side. The reserves had also reached the semi-final of the Junior Amateur Cup before being knocked out by Lechlade first XI.

Top scorers for the season were D. Weager 27, P. Raymond 19, H. Wilson and M. Evans 16 and T. Edwards 13.

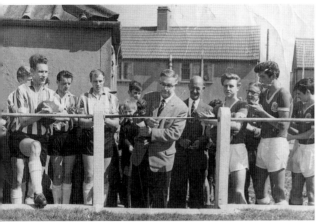 

Above left: The newly levelled pitch is officially opened by Stan White prior to the game with Bristol City, 19 August 1961. Rex Dyer is featured with the ball.

Above right: Forest Green Rovers first team photo 1961/62. Back row: Rex Dyer, Brian Vanstone, Trevor Wheeler, Rafe Webb, John Hudd, John Porter. Front row: David Clift, Lawrence Duxbury, Barry Sturgess, Malcolm Vanstone, David Weager.

The supporters' club had broken all records and raised over £293 for the club in the year. Jim Turk was still appearing from the reserves.

Bristol Rovers wrote to the club in March 1962 confirming that they would be willing to pay £100 to sign an amateur player with a further £100 if the player played in the first team, in the hope that this would encourage more players to attend trials when requested to do so.

JOHN PORTER

I look at other players that I was with, and I think Rafe Webb went down to Bristol Rovers. He didn't have a car – none of us had a car, we didn't even have a bloody push-bike I don't think, leave alone a car. He was going on the bus, leaving at somewhere around nine, ten o'clock in the morning and going down on the bus from Nailsworth to, I think it was Wotton-under-Edge – somewhere like that – and you had to change and go to Bristol, then change at Bristol, and then get a bus across to the Bristol Rovers. It was all travelling. He didn't have a car, he didn't have a motor-bike – nobody could afford that sort of thing.

Rafe was in the reserves at Bristol Rovers, but they were very, very disappointed when he left. They didn't say, 'We'll send a car to pick you up.' Cars wasn't around then, leave alone anything else. It was unfortunate really that he was in the wrong area, but he was a class act in every way. I've seen him, goalkeeper, ball and all in the back of the net. He'd just go in and if the ball bounced and the goalkeeper was up there getting it to his chest or something like that, you could bet your bottom dollar that Webby was on his way in there somewhere, and the ball and all would go in the back of the net fine. In them days it was fair.

1962/63

John Duff returned from South Africa and played for the reserves. Rovers entered the FA Amateur Cup for the first time and a forty-one-seater coach travelled to Moreton-in-the-Marsh on 29 September 1962. Everybody came home happy after a 3-2 win. The club then drew 2-2 with Paulton Rovers away, with Forest Green winning the replay 7-1 in October. They then lost 4-2 at Hoffmans, having already beaten Hoffmans 3-1 in the Northern Senior League.

In the Senior League, results were a little better than in past seasons and included the defeat of Lydbrook 2-1 and only one loss to Harrow Hill by the turn of the year. The main feature of January 1963 was extremely cold weather and snow, which turned out to be the beginning of the big freeze and a fixture backlog when the pitches became playable again in April. Ron Davis summed up the season as follows at the AGM on 10 June 1963:

> *The secretary opened his report by referring to our loss in the passing during the year of Mr Owen Davis, a life member and vice-president of the club, and Mr R. Donahue, a trustee and ex-vice president. Both would be sadly missed.*
>
> *The playing season would probably be remembered for the severe weather when we could not play a home game after Boxing Day until 9 March. We had a good run in the FA Amateur Cup, finally losing to Hoffmans away where, due to a transport fault we had to play a man short. We were able to gain our revenge over Hoffmans when we beat them in the final of the Senior Charity Cup. We also played the second half of this game with ten men when Brian Vanstone had to go to hospital with a badly cut eye. The First XI had finished third in Division One of the Senior League and the Second XI had also finished third in Division One of the Stroud League. A very satisfactory season. John Hudd could claim most appearances, 43 during the season with 100 per cent Senior League appearances.*
>
> *Jim Mail was top scorer with 38 goals. Tony Smith had 26, all scored in the Stroud League, David Weager 19, Phillip Price 18, Michael Evans 15 and Michael Stribbling 13.*
>
> *During the season Roger Vanstone had had a trial for Swindon Town and both Roger Vanstone and Tony Townsend had been watched by an Aston Villa scout. It was expected they would go to Villa Park for a trial in July and August. The secretary said the club were again indebted to the supporters' club's financial support and ground improvements, including the terracing and the new main gates.*

1963/64

The club entered the FA Amateur Cup, being drawn against Hanham Athletic away for 28 September, the fixture being taken very seriously with a trial game played between the probables and possibles. The team selected included the three Vanstone brothers. Unfortunately, the game was lost 2-1.

Shortwood were promoted to the Northern Senior League Division One, producing competitive league matches again between the two teams. Forest Green won 2-0 at home but lost to Shortwood 3-2 towards the end of the season. John Porter was now a stalwart of the Shortwood side. One of the great local rivalries was that between Forest Green Rovers and Shortwood United. For the majority of the time, Shortwood were in a lower league than Forest Green and the 1963/64 season brought them together for the third time in a league, as well as their regular cup games. Forest Green's green shirts proved again to be useful when they were lent to Rodborough.

Walter Brown, who, along with Owen Davis, had featured in the nineteenth-century Forest Green Rovers team and won league championship medals in 1904 and 1912, passed away as the last surviving member of that first cup-winning team. The family tradition of playing for Forest Green was being upheld by Ray 'Bomber' Brown, while Adrian remained a staunch committee man following his career-ending injury

The Vanstone brothers, Malcolm, Roger and Brian, 1963/64.

JOHN PORTER

I've got fond memories of both sides of the valley really. Pete Vick and all the people at Forest Green were always very good to me when I came over from Shortwood. There was never anything mentioned about Shortwood or anything, you know, you just went up – do your job as best you can, and enjoy yourself.

We had a good team up there at Forest Green. Because I came from Shortwood didn't make any difference really. It was a matter of everybody not treating you as a foreigner. You were accepted and it was said, 'Well if he's going to do a good job for us up here, then yes, thank you very much.'

But I said it was my Dad that said 'I would like to see you playing with your brother at Shortwood. I would like to see you playing in the same team.' He was goalkeeper at Forest Green himself in the 1920s mind.

Above left: Forest Green Rovers, before a game. M. Stribbling, P. Price, M. Evans, D. Weager, J. Llewellyn, M. Vanstone, R. Vanstone, J. Hudd, T. Townsend, B. Vanstone, J. Mail with ball.

Above right: Forest Green Rovers 1963/64. Back row: Ron Davis, Tony Townsend, John Llewellyn, Mike Stribbling, Roger Vanstone, Brian Vanstone, Ticker Newman, Peter Vick. Front row: Jim Mail, Phil Price, Tommy O'Loughlin, Trevor March, Derek Huxford.

the year before. By March, the new pitch had been laid for three years and the grass had fully matured, producing a 'carpet-like' playing surface much admired around the county.

The season was summarised as follows at the AGM by Ron Davis on 15 June 1964:

> We had a fair playing season, both elevens finishing third in the First Division Northern Senior League and First Division Stroud League. The First XI had a poor run in the cup competitions, being knocked out in the first game on three occasions. The Second XI did much better and reached the semi-final of the Junior Charity Cup. Leading goalscorers were Phillip Price 23, Michael Evans 22, Ryan Newman 20, Ray Brown 18, John Llewellyn 17 and David Weager 16.

ADRIAN BROWN

Well, I didn't do anything for a year after I got injured because I was a little bit evil. I went up to the first game when I could walk and walked in the dressing room. Our Bomber and I always used to change side by side, and to see him sat down and someone else there and not me, I thought 'I'm not having this.' Then Peter Vick come over to see me one day. He said that until I was fit we'd like you to come on the committee. I thought he was joking. I was twenty-two. You didn't talk to the committee in them days. It was full of old men, but I joined.

In them days for the teams you had to provide a linesman. Nip Beale was the first-team linesman, and the reserves had one too, that was me. I didn't like that at all. I could stand by the line and watch and you can tell that linesman exactly whose fault it is. But when you're doing it, I made one of the biggest cock-ups there was. I was up on the line on the stand end, facing the Newmarket end, and I was there dreaming away watching the game and somebody said, 'Offside Adie?' The bloke went through and scored. I said 'No, no, it wasn't.' I didn't want to do this again.

Forest Green Rovers reserves 1963/64. Back row: Adrian Brown, A. Cleaver, Tony Thorley, Trevor Wheeler, Ray Brown, Peter Nurding, John Llewellyn, Peter Vick. Front row: Ron Davis, Tony Smith, John Duff, John Creed, Tony Townsend, Mick Evans.

1964/65

Neil Newport, Basil Newport's son, registered to play for the team for the first time. For the third year running Forest Green entered the FA Amateur Cup, drawn away this time to Keynsham on 26 September, losing 3-0. In the 2 league games against Shortwood, Forest Green managed a draw at Shortwood but lost 3-1 at home at the end of the season.

By the end of the season, the secretary's report confirmed that, for the first time in very many years, both teams had finished in the lower half of their respective divisions, with the first team finishing ninth in Division One of the Senior League and the second team finishing tenth in Division One of the Stroud League. Both elevens had been knocked out of the cup competitions in their first games of every competition. Brian Newman was top scorer with 19 goals.

Shortwood finished five places above Rovers in the Senior League. The supporters' club in the meantime had presented the club with a very fine grandstand at the end of the season in addition to the usual substantial financial support in the sum of £294.

1965/66

With the grandstand finally completed, a match was arranged at the beginning of the season to mark the official opening. The game was played against Clifton St Vincent AFC from Bristol on 21 August and was officially opened by Mr Hook, the GFA president, with an entertaining 2-2 draw.

The opening of the new grandstand also got Rovers on to television for the first time when Peter Vick, Stan White and Ron Davis were all interviewed and shown on the BBC *Points West* programme after the opening. Any progress in the FA Amateur Cup was proving futile, Forest Green this year being drawn away to Hanham Athletic, losing 3-1. Neil Newport made progress, playing for the Gloucestershire FA against a Bristol City youth team in October, being a 'shining light' among the other players.

Having not published programmes on match days since the 1950s, the committee decided to produce a programme for the county FA game to be played in November 1965. The club was notified in February 1966 that the Northern Senior League was planning to introduce the idea of a substitute should a player become injured. The committee expressed its 'cautious interest' in the idea. The two Northern Senior League games against Shortwood were played very late in the season this year, the home game being lost 5-0 and a 2-2 draw being achieved at Shortwood in the last game of the season. At the end of the season, Shortwood finished six places above Rovers in fifth place. On a brighter note, David Dangerfield, Les 'Sailor' Dangerfield's son, played for England schoolboys in March 1966.

Opening of the new Stand and Terracing by H. Hook, Esq., President of the G.F.A., on the 21st August, 1965

Above: Mr Hook the GFA president opens the grandstand before a 2-2 draw against Clifton St Vincent.

Right: Forest Green Rovers Reserves, Junior Amateur Cup Winners 1965/66. Back row: Tony Herbert, Robert Vick, Trevor Wheeler, Jim Mail, H. Wardle, Dave Weager. Front row: K. Dryden, John Dangerfield, Tommy O'Loughlin, J. Hulme, Trevor March.

Below right: Forest Green Rovers 1965/66. Back row: Derek Huxford, John Llewellyn, R. Skone, unknown, Brian Newman, Trevor March. Front row: Bruce Russell, Roger Vanstone, Tommy O'Loughlin, Neil Newport, D. Coombes.

The season was summed up by Ron Davis at the AGM on 6 June 1966 as follows:

The season has been a series of ups and downs. Other events included a county game against Hampshire and the Senior Amateur North Cup final between Sharpness and Bishops Cleeve. This final produced a record gate for the competition. This was a very frustrating season for the Selection Committee. We had forty-seven signed on including two transfers from other clubs. In the Senior League with 30 games, twenty-seven different players were played and in the Stroud League with 32 games, forty-one different players took part. Out of 30 Senior League games, only 13 were played with the team as selected and in the Stroud League with 32 games only, 12 played as selected. Our First XI were knocked out of four cup competitions in the first round and only after a sprint at the end of the season managed to finish eleventh of sixteen in the Senior League.

It was left to the Second XI to rescue our good name: they finished third in the Stroud League Division One and reached the semi-final of the Junior Charity Cup, but the highlight was their winning the Junior Amateur Cup North for the second time.

Tony Herbert with 42 played most games for the club with Rod Gingell, Trevor March and Roger Vick 40 each. Chief scorers were B. Newman 23, A. Herbert and D. Weager 19, G. Collins and J. Mail 17 and B. Coates 16. Congratulations were extended to David Dangerfield, who had the great distinction of playing for England Schoolboys, Alan Matthews played for the county, Ryan Newman, North of County trial, and Neil Newport county youth trial. The committee had felt for some time that with coaching we could have a more successful side. The supporters' club were thanked for their financial support and practical help on the ground.

Above left: Presentation of the Junior Amateur Cup to Tommy O'Loughlin.

Above right: Forest Green Rovers 1966/67. Back row: Rodney Gingell, Trevor March, Brian Vanstone, Trevor Wheeler, David Lamb, Bob Vick, Jimmy Sewell. Front row: Adrian Brown, Brian 'Ticker' Newman, David Dangerfield, John Dangerfield, Bob Cowley, Clive Mutton.

1966/67

Jimmy Sewell was appointed as coach just in time to begin the new season. Rovers finally got through the first preliminary round of the FA Amateur Cup with a bye and then met Wells City at home, losing 3-0. By January 1967, David Dangerfield was picked for the county youth team following his England schoolboy cap. His brother John was now a regular fixture in the first team and by the end of the season he was also joined by David.

The committee agreed to award Mr Sewell a gratuity of £25 in appreciation of his efforts for the club as coach and told him that his services were no longer required. Alan Morris had applied for the position of coach. He was offered £104 a year as player-coach subject to review at the end of December. Shortwood finished above Forest Green for the third consecutive year, this time in fourth spot in the Senior League.

The season was summed up at the AGM in June 1967:

> *The playing season had been very mediocre and the First XI had quickly been eliminated from all the cup competitions. The Second XI had reached the semi-finals of the Berkeley Hospital Senior Cup and the Stroud Junior Charity Cup. Leading goalscorers were B. Coates and J. Dangerfield with 22 goals, G. Parsons 19, D. Dangerfield 15, B. Newman 14 and R. Cowley 13.*
>
> *Special congratulations were extended to David Dangerfield on his playing for England Schoolboys for the second successive season. Congratulations also to Brian Newman, playing for the county, Robert Vick substitute for the county and J. Dangerfield on his several trial games for Wolverhampton Wanderers. Sympathy was extended to Ian Brown who broke his leg in the last game of the season. We staged a county game and the Senior Amateur Cup final on our ground. In the latter game last year's record gate receipts were exceeded. Thanks were extended to the supporters' club for their financial and practical help. Due to their efforts it was hoped we should shortly have our own clubhouse on the ground.*

The treasurer, Doug Brown, reported that the club turnover had now reached nearly £800 for the year with the supporters' club again raising £286, with £111 being received from gate receipts.

1967/68

1967 was to be the last year that Rovers would play in the Northern Senior League and the last season when they would meet Shortwood competitively in league football, losing 1-0 at home and 4-1 away. Shortwood went on to be runners-up in the Senior League in the season during which David Dangerfield also moved on too. Alan Morris took up the post of coach. He insisted that the players play in socks of a colour chosen by the club as a mark of professionalism, the colour chosen was red.

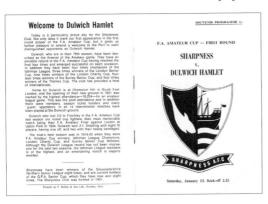
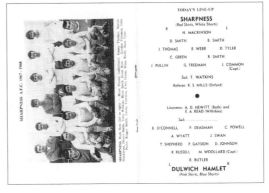

Sharpness play national opposition in the FAAC, January 1968.

Preparations to create a County League were well under way and some of the Bristol clubs who had been so set against the league over past years requested friendlies against Rovers, no doubt to sound out the opposition. Rovers visited Crusaders AFC, Ashton Gate Sports and Bristol St George in August. The new County League would appoint neutral linesman for every match. This would be Nip Beale's last season as the linesman for Forest Green Rovers, ending a tradition that stretched back into the Victorian era and the inception of the club.

Progress on the new social club was being made and by December the roof timbers were on. A very proud supporters' club commissioned A.E. Smith & Son to draw up a lease for the new 'Forest Green Rovers Sports and Social Club' for a term of ten years at an annual rent in the first five years of £100 and the second five years of £1,000, funds that had only been dreamt of before. The building of the clubhouse had been paid for by a £5,000 mortgage held by the supporters' club to avoid the football club having to carry the financial burden.

By Christmas, things were not looking good in the league, with Rovers having lost 8 games and won only 3, with a single draw. A players' meeting was held in April, confirming that there was a very good club spirit but there were grumbles about team selection and the methods of coaching. Alan Morris was sacked as coach at the end of April but still remained with the club. The season had been an almost complete failure on the football pitch, leaving Forest Green Rovers in a relegation position, only to be saved by their move into the County League.

Elsewhere in Gloucestershire, Sharpness were going from strength to strength and drew Dulwich Hamlet in the FA Amateur Cup in the first round proper, their sixth game in the competition, having seen off Rovers in the third qualifying round. The committee sent a telegram wishing them luck. Unfortunately, Sharpness progressed no further.

On a much brighter note, the AGM was held for the first time in the new social club in June 1968. John Dangerfield played most games with 42, followed by Tony Budden with 40 and C. Gardiner with 39. Trevor March and Brian Newman led the goalscorers with 25 goals each. Alan Newport had a trial with Bristol City and both John Dangerfield and Brian Newman were congratulated on being selected for the Senior League in the three counties inter-league competition. John Duff, having been a player in the 1950s and 1960s, was appointed chairman of the club for the forthcoming season.

JOHN DUFF

Well, I came back in 1962 and became players' representative on the main committee. In 1967 I went along as a players' representative and ended up coming away as chairman. Really, I didn't know what I'd let myself in for.

The social club was being built by the supporters' club, who leased it to the Sports and Social Club Committee, who ran it on their behalf. It was tremendously important in raising funds for the club.

It definitely led to Forest Green moving ahead of the local competition, because prior to that Forest Green was no more prominent than Stonehouse or Brimscombe. But then, income from the social club, and I think I can remember – because at that time we had no steward and all the bar work was done by volunteers, in fact my wife and I used to do Sunday evenings – taking over a hundred pounds on one night. One night! That was a lot of money at the end of the 1960s/early 1970s. And imagine that now. Some people go in there and buy a round and it would be half of that, I expect.

16

The County League: 1968–1975

1968/69

Forest Green kicked off against Hanham Athletic in August with a 1-1 draw. Alan Morris had been reappointed as trainer, only on the condition that he had 'the full backing of the committee when dealing with difficult players', suggesting that things were far from rosy between the coach and players.

An old foe was encountered. Stonehouse, who had taken the decision to go professional back in the 1940s with limited success in the Western League, had since moved into the Wiltshire Premier League before returning to the new County League.

Forest Green lost 4-0 to Lydbrook in the FA Amateur Cup and lost 1-0 to Bishops Cleeve in the Senior Amateur Cup. In September 1968, committee member Geoff Smith was approached by Peter Goring, the ex-Cheltenham Town and Arsenal player, who intimated that he was keen to join Forest Green, although in what capacity it wasn't clear. It was obvious from his remarks he would be a great asset to the club in working with Alan Morris on coaching and tactics. A strict disciplinary code was to be introduced.

Peter Goring was a local lad hailing from Cheltenham and had originally played for Cheltenham Town before being spotted and snapped up by Arsenal. He was top scorer for Cheltenham Town in the 1947/48 season when Cheltenham reached the FA Cup second round. He went on to have a prolific career at Arsenal, wearing the famous number 6 shirt, and won the FA Cup. He had retired from playing football and returned to run a butcher's shop in Cheltenham, but wanted to retain his contacts with football, much to Forest Green's benefit.

ADRIAN BROWN

Peter Goring arrived. I've always been an Arsenal follower, I can't say a fan. I can remember having a Stanley Matthews football album, and Arsenal had won the FA Cup, and in there it was in writing: young Peter Goring with the cup. I remember meeting him once, he was with Gloucester City running the line and I was running the line for Forest Green. I thought 'That's Peter Goring, what's he doing on the line?'

Anyway he offered his services to Forest Green. He asked me to become first aid man, and I did. He thought the club should have one.

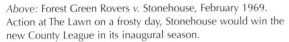

Above: Forest Green Rovers *v.* Stonehouse, February 1969. Action at The Lawn on a frosty day, Stonehouse would win the new County League in its inaugural season.

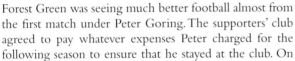

Right: Peter Goring with the FA Cup won while at Arsenal.

Forest Green was seeing much better football almost from the first match under Peter Goring. The supporters' club agreed to pay whatever expenses Peter charged for the following season to ensure that he stayed at the club. On the field, 9 games were lost in the first season in the County League with 13 wins and 8 draws. Stonehouse won the inaugural league, finishing 10 points clear of Bristol St George, Derroll Loveday being top scorer for Stonehouse with 37 goals. Forest Green finished a very creditable sixth in the league of sixteen teams, which also included Bristol Rovers A. At the end of the season, Bill Truman summarised events:

The secretary was especially pleased with the position of the First XI in the new County League, finishing sixth, a very sound position. Again, we disappointed in the cup competitions and should at least have been in two finals. Steve Gannaway played most games, 44 in the league and cup, with Chris Bird, Brian Coates and Clive Mutten all with 42 games. The leading scorer was Clive Mutten with 20 goals, Harold Morgan had 18 and Brian Coates 12.

1969/70

For the second time, a Forest Green player had made the step up to league football to play for Swindon Town, in the shape of David Dangerfield. Swindon had won the League Cup two seasons before, and they met Liverpool at the County ground in October 1970 in the third round. David Dangerfield started a move that led to Swindon's second goal in the sixty-eighth minute. He won the ball following a poor corner and carefully picked out Smith with a pass. The Town midfield general then fired a long ball down the centre. Rogers raced on to it, beating the converging figures of Alec Lindsay and Larry Lloyd and tucked the ball into an empty net. In the closing stages Dangerfield nearly made it 3 with a well-struck shot from twenty-five yards out but clipped the crossbar. He appeared to be a star of the future. Bill Shankly said 'It's a ludicrous result!' Swindon had just defeated Liverpool, playing their normal defence that had conceded only 5 goals against ten First Division teams prior to this match.

By July, Peter Goring got committee approval to sign David Walker for 35s per week, more than twice the cost of a season ticket. Derroll Loveday was also tempted to the club from Stonehouse who were reaching the end of their semi-professional heyday.

Forest Green Rovers 1969/70. Back row: Micky Francis, Jimmy Seal, Bernie Wardle, Jan Burridge, Seth Evans, Brian Coates, David Lamb. Front row: John Dangerfield, Dave Watkins, Tony Townsend, Dave Walker, Chris Bird.

DERROLL LOVEDAY

Stonehouse had won the Wiltshire Premier League the year before we moved into the County League. I'd had two seasons with them before the move and it seemed like quite a step down. Stonehouse kept on saying they would have this and they would have that and everything else, but it was the council who owned their field, not them, and so they couldn't really do anything about it. They never did anything that they said they would and I wanted to see how far I could go, and Forest Green were the team to go to for that.

Peter Goring was a really nice guy. We tried very hard to make him play for us but he didn't want to know. He said he was too old, but he still had a fantastic touch. I used to mess about in goal in the warm-ups before the matches and he would turn round about thirty yards out and just whack the ball into the top right-hand corner every time without fail.

The committee gave the go-ahead for the production of a programme for the forthcoming season. One hundred and fifty programmes were printed for the first game and by April this had risen to 200. The social club was proving to be a big hit, not just with local residents and club members but also with visiting teams often requesting if they could stay on for a social evening after the match.

The treasurer reported that the cost of running the football club on a week-by-week basis had risen to £35 a week, including all players' expenses. This sum vastly exceeded gate receipts, which averaged around £11 a week.

At the AGM in mid-June 1970, the season was summarised as follows:

BRIAN COATES

There was a noticeable difference when Peter Goring came, having a big name manager. It got more professional, and we had a proper first aid man, Adie Brown. There was money involved as the years went on. Some of the players started to get what we called expenses. They were getting like a small fee just for turning up really.

Cadburys, they were always a good side. Sharpness was always a hard side to beat. Cinderford Town. Bristol Rovers A was nearly always sixteen-year-olds – a very young side. We used to play them on the training ground. They never used to play on Bristol Rovers' pitch.

The playing season had been a great success, the First XI being third in the County League and winning both the Berkeley Hospital Cup and the Stroud Charity Cup. The Second XI were winners of Division Two of the Northern Senior League and also won the County Junior Cup. Derroll Loveday was top scorer with 49 goals, 20 in the League, Jan Burridge and Clive Mutton both had 34.

The treasurer reported that income was up to £2,981 from the season. The social club had led to a tripling of the club's income.

In the FA Amateur Cup, Forest Green lost to Mangotsfield in the first preliminary round 2-1, and lost in the third round of the Senior Amateur Cup to Shortwood 2-1.

FOREST GREEN
ROVERS A.F.C.

Members of:
GLOUCESTERSHIRE COUNTY LEAGUE
&
GLOS. NORTHERN SENIOR LEAGUE

Official Programme Price 6d

Saturday, 29th November 1969 Kick-off 2.30 p.m. versus

SHORTWOOD UNITED

IN THE

GLOS. SENIOR AMATEUR CUP (NORTH)

No. 1758

Top left: Forest Green Rovers v. Shortwood United, November 1969.

Top right: Forest Green Rovers v. Stonehouse, 30 March 1970. Brian Coates in action watched by Dave Watkins.

Middle right: Filling the cup, the team deserved a drink after their efforts against old foe at Chalford in the Charity Cup.

Above left: Trevor March (2nd XI Captain) and Graham Day (1st XI Captain) with the season's trophies: County Junior Cup (north), Northern Senior League Division Two Championship Cup, Stroud Charity Cup (senior), Berkeley Hospital Cup (premier).

Middle left and above: Programme against Shortwood in the Senior Amateur Cup.

1970/71

The club entered its third year in the County League and the third year under Peter Goring's reign. Neil Newport had broken his leg very badly and Bristol City and Swindon were approached to arrange a benefit match for him, the match finally being arranged for Sunday 8 August 1971, with 1,000 tickets being printed. The club had made extremely good progress on the pitch and now sat close to the top of the County League but, in the FA Amateur Cup, lost in the first qualifying round to Cadbury Heath. Towards the end of March 1971, Bill Truman presented a club badge, which was officially adopted.

Towards the end of March, the club was approached to accompany an official party from Stroud to travel to Duderstadt in Germany as part of the town-twinning celebrations. Stroud asked Forest Green Rovers to join their team on a tour.

DERROLL LOVEDAY

Stroud took a team to Germany but they weren't really good enough and, while we were playing and beating the local village side of Brochthausen 5-3, Stroud lost 9-1 to Lindau. The next day, Sunday, they were due to play against what was the county eleven and they asked us to take over the fixture late that Saturday night. We had all had a good drink by then and I remember our goalkeeper Seth Evans crawling out of bed at 6 a.m. wondering what the hell was going on.

Our pre-arranged game was third on the day. First was a local cup final, then Seulingen played Hertha Berlin, a Division One German side with World Cup stars playing. The crowd was well over 5,000 and stayed to watch us play. It was a close game and we ran out winners 1-0.

We all had a great time and thought it would be good to try and make it a regular tour. I think, in total while we were on tour, we played five games in six days. We all made many friends and I still visit.

Opposite above: Fund-raising was key to the everyday existence of Forest Green.

Opposite below: Forest Green Rovers *v.* Matson, 22 August 1970, with the new clubhouse in the background.

ANDY WHITING

The first time I ever went up to Forest Green was Easter Monday 1971 for a match against Stonehouse. I remember walking from Stroud and then paying to go in through the turnstiles at Forest Green, getting a programme, and then it was just an eye-opener for me as non-league football. There was a proper ground with stands and terracing. It was a proper stadium, so compact but incredibly tidy and a brilliant pitch. I used to then go up probably once or twice a season, but I was watching Swindon mainly at that time.

At the AGM in June 1971, the season was summarised as follows:

The First XI finished third in the County League as last season after holding top position for so long. For the second year running we again won the Berkeley Hospital Cup and the Stroud Charity Cup. The Second XI had held a respectable position in the First Division of the Senior League, their first season in that league. Also, for the second season running, they had reached the finals of the Junior Amateur Cup, a good achievement considering the team was pulled to pieces from the first round. They had also reached the final of the Stroud Charity Junior Cup.

The leading scorer was again Derroll Loveday with 38 goals, Jan Burridge had 30 and Dick De La Hay 25. The secretary congratulated Derroll Loveday, John Dangerfield and M. Francis on playing for the county on four occasions and gaining their County Caps.

The team had finished behind Sharpness and Cadbury Heath, who won the league. Three of the league's top ten scorers were from Rovers.

1971/72

Programme *v.* Stonehouse, 12 April 1971.

The club was moving in the right direction with Peter Goring at the helm, but ever-rising costs were worrying. Further ideas were explored to raise funds, including a '250 club' prize draw.

Forest Green finally progressed in the FA Amateur Cup, beating Frampton 5-1, followed by a 4-3 win over Coleford, a 3-1 win over Worrall Hill and a 1-0 win over Sharpness before finally being beaten at home by Wantage 3-0 in the last qualifying round. John Dangerfield, Derroll Loveday and Mike Francis all played for the county in November, Derroll scoring in a 3-1 defeat. In April, John Dangerfield wasn't selected for the first team and Chris Bird was dropped to substitute for the reserves. John had intimated that he wanted to leave the club and move on to a higher level. Peter Goring wanted a settled team.

SECOND MEETING WAS MORE PROFITABLE FOR THE ROVERS

But injury-hit Magpies staged great comeback

FOREST GREEN ... 4, STONEHOUSE ... 2

BEATEN 2—1 AT Oldends Lane on Good Friday, Forest Green gained revenge in their return County League meeting with Stonehouse at The Lawn on Monday, but they were certainly given some anxious moments before making sure of the spoils.

Leading 3—0 with the second half only just under way, the Rovers looked to be home and dry against a side who lost their goalkeeper Geoff Pellatt with the game six minutes old, but the Magpies came back to such purpose that they netted twice in four minutes and the outcome looked in some doubt.

However the Rovers notched a fourth goal to clinch matters.

The loss of Pellatt with concussion, after a collision with John Dangerfield was a sad blow for the visitors, although Andy Brookes, who donned the jersey did his best.

Whether it would have all worked out differently had Pellatt not been injured is a matter of conjecture. Suffice it to say that the Rovers, although taking the spoils, did not show the form of which they are capable — the form which has put them so high in the table.

There was too much indecision play on their part with no consistent build up. They could more than once have taken a leaf out of the Magpies' book in this respect.

No player did more in the excellent conditions than Alan Watts, who was constantly in the fore in breaking down efforts by the Rovers to penetrate. He had a particularly fine game.

The Rovers took the lead with a good goal.

Jan Burridge pushed the ball through and Graham Gay with some smart running off the ball was waiting on the by-line to book it back for John Dangerfield to drive it home from a not too easy angle.

The Rovers must have been rather disappointed not to have been able to build up a greater lead for the half way stage, yet they soon made their presence felt on the changeover.

In the first three minutes they had, as later events were to prove, won the game, by netting twice.

Jan Burridge drove the ball to Brookes' left for the first and then Graham Gay scored from a set piece.

The Rovers were awarded a free kick near the edge of the penalty area and Gay floated the ball over the defence and out of the reach of the keeper. So from being only let down by the Magpies found themselves 3-0 adrift, but to their credit they came storming back.

Pat Casey hit the corner of the crossbar and uphill, and then Glen Davies, who had come on as substitute not long after Pellatt had been carried off, broke through and squared into the path from the edge of the penalty area.

Four minutes later the excitement really mounted as this time Davies himself held off challenges to drive the ball hard and true along the ground into the net from the corner of the net to make sure that the Rovers took the points.

While perhaps the standard of football was not all that might have been desired, nevertheless there was plenty of entertainment for a good sized crowd who were enjoying the welcome sunshine at the same time.

Press cutting from the match.

JAMES COOK

My first memory of Forest Green Rovers is fairly vague, against a far superior Fairford Town team who ran out easy winners, 3-0. The main memory I have of the match is Derroll Loveday, the FGR hero of the time, having to be stretchered off. I remember at the time thinking that this was a fabulous name for a footballer, easily matching our domestic footballers' names – Bobby Charlton, Georgie Best and Frannie Lee – if not as exotic as say Pelé, Jairzinho or Carlos Alberto. I was already interested in football, mainly due to the England team in the 1970 World Cup and the dazzling brilliance of the Brazilian winners of the same tournament – to this day the most exciting team I have ever seen.

It was a few years after this initial introduction to FGR that I began to take a keener interest. Some friends and I decided to go to watch a reserve match against Newent Town in the Gloucestershire Northern Senior League – for a laugh as much as anything. And laugh we did. From the outset we developed a method of watching and enjoying the game that would last as long as our small group of six to ten lads would endure. We picked on one of the opposition players and gave him dog's abuse at every possible opportunity.

In our first match, it was Mel Smith the Newent defender and, I think, captain. In the tannoy introduction, as soon as his name was announced, he was dubbed 'Smelly' Smith. I guess, for a thirteen-year-old, the possibility of abusing an adult with impunity was a rare opportunity and delight. Mr Smith was, I think, a little taken aback with the attention at first but, to his credit, he took the abuse in good part and got his own back by scoring one of the goals in a 4-1 defeat of FGR reserves.

AGM Season Summary

The playing season was reasonably successful, the highlight of course winning the Senior Amateur Cup and perhaps to a lesser degree the Stroud Charity Cup for the third successive year. Our fourth position in the County League, it was felt, could have been improved on with a bit more effort by some players. Our club-record run in the FA Amateur Cup was also a good achievement.

The leading scorer last season was again Derroll Loveday, with a total of 34 goals in the league and cups, with 30 for Jan Burridge. Congratulations were extended to D. Loveday, J. Dangerfield and M. Francis, who again played for the county team. Congratulations also to Derroll for being the first County League player to score a hundred goals in the league. Last year saw the introduction of a new venture, the 250 club. During its short life it had so far contributed £450 to the parent body. Given time to get established this could be a great asset to the club.

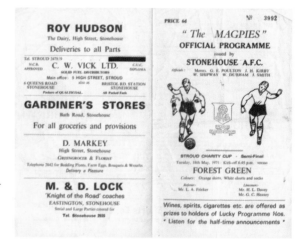

Forest Green finished behind Cinderford Town, Bristol St George and champions Cadbury Heath. Derroll Loveday was again top scorer for Forest Green Rovers with 19 league goals, behind Andy Leitch, who was top scorer for champions Cadbury Heath with 33 league goals.

Forest Green Rovers 1st XI, June 1972. Back row: P. Goring, P. Nurding, Eddie F, unknown, C. Bird, J. Dangerfield, A. Newport, G. Day, D. Loveday, unknown, D. Waller, K. Mortimer, unknown, A. Morris. Middle row: A. Dyer, B. Sabatella, J. Lavis, H. King, R. Gingell, A. Moore, S. Gannaway, A. Hartley, B. Coates, S. Evans, A. Townsend, J. Burridge, D. Huxford, unknown, B. Lewis. Front row: R. Hudd, H. Waterworth, R. Davis, G. Smith, D. Brown, J. Duff, B. Russell, W. Truman, L. Chapple, H. Gannaway, D. Gannaway.

1972/73

The season kicked off with a friendly against Wantage, arranged after Forest Green's very successful FA Amateur Cup outing the previous season. Andy Bish arrived at The Lawn.

ANDY BISH

I was born and bred in the East End of London. As a schoolboy I played representative football for West Ham and Essex, playing alongside Frank Lampard Snr and Trevor Brooking before signing for Spurs. I progressed through the youth teams to the Football Combination as a professional and qualified as an FA coach, and also helped to train the Spurs schoolboys where, among others, Glenn Hoddle shone through at the start of his career at the club.

After five seasons with Spurs I decided to move away from London to college in Gloucestershire, where I qualified as a PE teacher. I first played at Cheltenham Town in the Southern League before being signed by Peter Goring. I made my home debut against Matson in a 4–2 win. I had decided to travel to the match from Stroud on a bus, but got the wrong one and ended up in Minchinhampton. I explained to the driver that I was late for the match and he suggested that I walked down the hill as it wasn't far to Forest Green. Thankfully a car stopped and I hitched a lift. That was the last time I got a bus to the game.

After causing a stir at the end of the previous season, John Dangerfield signed on again for the first team. Derroll Loveday and Tony Townsend were both selected to play for the county in October but, by Christmas, results in the league were not up to standards set in previous seasons.

ADRIAN BROWN

Peter Goring was a smashing fellow. Every Saturday after the game you always knew if Pete wasn't happy because he'd have his hand in his pocket and he'd rattle his change. He'd look over at me if we'd lost. Everyone had to get out of the dressing room. Nobody changed and he'd be rattling; any minute now I thought, and bang, up the cups would go in the air.

And then he'd let his temper cool, and then he'd say, 'Well, I've got that out of my system Adie. Come on. We'll get changed and go and have a beer.' He'd say start a slate; but then I think some players took advantage of it because they used to go over and say, when Pete hadn't even arrived from the dressing room, it's on the slate. He always paid up, but they took advantage sometimes. Peter was a very nice fellow.

Forest Green Rovers 1972/73. Back row: Archie Moor, Brian Coates, Steve Gannaway, Seth Evans, unknown, Mike Portlock, Rod Gingell. Front row: Chris Bird, John Dangerfield, Graham Day, Eddie Feigherey, Dave Walker.

At the AGM in June 1973, the season was summarised as follows:

The playing season has been most frustrating and disappointing, the Firsts finishing ninth in the County League, their lowest position since joining the league. Our Seconds, although making a reasonable start to the season, had to fight hard in the end to avoid relegation. There was a noticeable lack of effort from some players, which, in my opinion, contributed to the final positions of the teams, but despite this we reached four cup finals, winning one, losing two and of course one still to be decided.

The leading scorer was again Derroll Loveday with 28 goals.

It is interesting to note that twenty-seven players were used for the First XI and no fewer than forty-five for the Second XI. Perhaps another factor that contributed to our lowly positions.

BRIAN COATES

I used to stop after the match. I was one of those that would have a pint, that would socialise. We had the new clubhouse. I can remember all the old boys – Harold King and Wes Stokes, and there was Doug Brown. They were all very good committee men and if there was anything to do, I can remember them going up a ladder to change the bulb in the lights. We always used to muck in.

That's got it where it is today. If you look at the other teams in the area, and the kind of league they were playing in, it's amazing what Forest Green Rovers have achieved. I would have never dreamt they would be building a new ground, especially up the road. They've moved on again. We won the County Cup, and they used to always have a local cup, the Berkeley Hospital Cup and things like that. We used to win every year, nearly.

Andy Leitch was again league top scorer with 43 goals for the champions Cadbury Heath, retaining their title from the previous year.

1973/74

Peter Vick was elected a life member at the beginning of the season for all the work that he had done with the club since joining in 1936. Training started in early July. Friendlies were organised against Western League Taunton Town, and Wantage again, and in the FAA Cup, Forest Green beat Avon quite comfortably 2-0 before losing to Yate Town 1-0. The FA Vase replaced the FAA Cup the following season.

John Dangerfield finally followed in his brother's footsteps, moving to Cheltenham Town as a professional in September 1973. The team lost Derroll Loveday as well and performances on the pitch reflected this.

Forest Green played Stonehouse on Monday 15 April 1974, following a 1-0 victory over Bristol St George two weeks before. The goal against Bristol St George was Brian Coates' hundredth goal for the club in competitive matches. The once-mighty Stonehouse were struggling at the bottom of the league and finally finished fourth from bottom. In the seasons

Forest Green Rovers 1973/74. Back row: Colin Walker, Alan Newport, Brian Coates, Seth Evans, Micky Carroll, John Murphy, Andy Bish, Tony Burgess, Alan Morris. Front row: Archie Moor, Chris Bird, Tony Townsend, John Evans, Ron Newley.

Forest Green Rovers reserves 1973/74. Back row: unknown, unknown, unknown, Mike Townsend, ? Wood, Martin Webster, Colin Walker, Billy Sabatella. Front row: Bob Cowley, Dave Walker, Brian Underwood, Terry Patterson, John Gray.

to come, they continued to struggle, finishing bottom of the league seven times in fourteen years before finally withdrawing from the County League in the summer of 1988.

The season ended as the year before, with Forest Green finishing in mid-table in the County League. Andy Leitch was again top scorer for Cadbury Heath with 32 goals in the league, helping them to become champions for the fourth year in succession, and Geoff Medcroft also appeared in the top-scorers list in fourth place, with 19 goals for Sharpness.

Bill Truman summed up the season at the AGM in June 1974:

The playing season had been one of mixed fortunes. The First XI had made a disastrous start to their league programme but finally finished in eleventh place. The Second XI, for the second year running, had struggled to maintain their position in the Senior League Division One and the secretary felt the manager was not helped by the attitude of some first-team players who considered themselves beyond reserve-team football.

The bright spot of the season had been the winning of both the Senior and Junior Stroud Charity Cups.

Congratulations were extended to Brian Coates on scoring his hundredth goal for the club. J. Burgess was the leading scorer with 12 goals and C. Walker 10. When one considered a few seasons ago two players scored about 30 goals each, perhaps the lack of a marksman contributed to our struggle throughout the season. Tony Townsend made most appearances, 46 in all, and had played in all County League matches and First XI cup matches.

1974/75

The club's last season in the County League kicked off with Peter Goring still in charge. John Evans had joined the club mid-season the previous year and Derroll Loveday returned to the club for another season. Geoff Medcroft also joined from Sharpness.

Forest Green Rovers first team, August 1974. The last season in the County League. Back row: Billy Sabatella, Dave Walker, Brian Coates, Seth Evans, Andy Bish, Mick Carroll, Geoff Medcroft, Peter Goring. Front row: Chris Bird, Keith Mortimer, Tony Townsend, John Evans, Derroll Loveday.

Five Forest Green Rovers players were selected for a county trial in September 1974: Mickey Carroll, Tony Townsend, John Evans, J. Wilkes and Derroll Loveday giving quite an indication of the strength of the team.

Forest Green's first game in the FA Vase was against Yate Town again, this time winning 1-0. Rovers were given a bye in the next round, Avon withdrawing, and then lost away to Chipping Norton Town 3-1. The club ran a fifty-seater coach to the match, charging 25p for children and 50p for adults for the privilege of travelling with the team.

Up until this point, advertising at and around the ground was non-existent. The committee was very impressed with the set-up at Chipping Norton and immediately opened discussions regarding the placement of advertising boards around the pitch perimeter. The committee was also impressed by the format of the Chipping Norton programme. By the end of the season, the club announced that they had advertising space at the ground in the local press and were charging 50p per square foot for the privilege of the advert, or £12 per board.

In order to assist with rising costs anticipated in the Hellenic League, the social club increased its rent from £1,000 to £1,700 a year and the supporters' club upped its contribution to £1,500 a year. The Hellenic League visited the club at the beginning of March and were entertained as VIPs in the social club. Rothmans, the Hellenic League sponsors, gave help with programmes as well as other substantial benefits dependent upon results. It was agreed that fifty per cent of any winnings would go to the players, based on their appearances, with thirty per cent to the club and twenty per cent to Mr Goring.

John Evans made it into the county team for the third time that season with Alan Morris as trainer in a match against Dorset. The county team was again training on Forest Green's ground.

JOHN DUFF

The Hellenic League were based in Oxford, and the chairman was quite ambitious to spread it both east and west. They were talking to clubs in 1974. It was Fairford who probably put the recommendation that Forest Green would be an acquisition. Obviously we had a look at them, they had a look at us, and we debated joining the Hellenic at our committee meetings and then voted. There was only two against joining the Hellenic League, which was quite exciting; another step up the ladder.

The game away at Matson on 12 March, which Rovers lost 4-2, brought specific comment from the committee that they were disgusted with Matson's performance but praised the Forest Green players for their sportsmanship under extreme provocation.

The captains pause for a photo, looking more like characters from a *Monty Python* sketch, Tony Townsend on the right.

DERROLL LOVEDAY

I took part in a game against Matson towards the end of the County League years. I think Matson had either one or two sent off and at least seven booked. Tony Townsend had his leg broken and I had my shinpads kicked right out through my socks. It was strange really because some of them were very good players but they were absolutely manic against us, and they were like it every season. They would go over the top. Nobody looked forward to playing Matson.

JAMES COOK

The last few games in the County League were fairly uneventful, and FGR finished low down. The only other real memory I have from the County League days was a GNSAC semi-final against Almondsbury Greenway, a team that would replace FGR in the County League. A hard-fought match at The Lawn ended in a 2-2 draw after ninety minutes, but in a disastrous extra time period FGR lost 7-2!

The club's round up of the season was as follows:

The playing season had been one of frustration, the First 11 having spells of brilliant football only to go back into their shells, but despite this had ended up a creditable sixth in the league. The cup competitions were disappointing, having lost their grip on the Senior Charity cup for the first time in many years. The Second 11 had a disastrous season. Having struggled for two years they were finally relegated to Division Two, but all credit to them for the way they fought back to try and avoid the drop. Division Two football is not good enough for a Club of this standing and perhaps we had now learned a lesson, for it appeared their predicament had been ignored for far too long. Congratulations to them for winning our only cup, the Berkeley Hospital Cup Senior.

Geoff Medcroft was the leading scorer with 29 goals. Tony Burgess led the reserves with 12 goals. Congratulations to John Evans for playing in all County matches.

The cost of running the club in its last season in the County League had risen to £2,592. More than half of this had been covered by £1,100 received from the supporters' club, £500 from the 250 Club and £100 from the social club.

Forest Green/Sharpness XI with TSV Sevlingen. A combined team from Forest Green and Sharpness visited Germany for a number of tours following a successful visit under the Stroud banner in the 1970s.

DERROLL LOVEDAY

After the first tour to Duderstadt in 1971 we arranged for the Germans to come over to us, but Forest Green didn't want anything to do with it. We tied up with Sharpness and half of them stayed with us around Forest Green and the other half down at Sharpness.

I remember that we arranged a boat trip down to Upton-on-Severn. The captain made more money on that one day on the small boat than they would make in a week on the big boat from wedding parties and the like.

Forest Green and the committee wouldn't do anything to help us with the tour, not a penny. They wouldn't even allow us to use the social club; down at Sharpness and Stonehouse they laid on buffets, food and the like and we had a great time.

When we brought them over to Nailsworth all the Germans went down to the Wade Inn with us and the same thing happened as on the boat trip. We were invited in for free all week and Brian Wade was very happy with the money he made. The Forest Green committee lost out there.

We had a very successful tour in 1975 with Alan Morris. They were great years and there must have been at least eight or nine Forest Green players on the tours.

Part IV

1975–2014

CARLISLE UTD

SCARBOROUGH

BARROW

MORECAMBE

YORK CITY

HALIFAX TOWN

SOUTHPORT

DONCASTER ROVERS

ALTRINCHAM

NORTHWICH VICTORIA

CHESTER CITY

BOSTON UTD

SHREWSBURY TOWN

BURTON ALBION

KING'S LYNN

TAMWORTH

KETTERING

HEREFORD UNITED

CAMBRIDGE UTD

CHELTENHAM TOWN

STEVENAGE BOROUGH

GLOUCESTER CITY

FOREST GREEN ROVERS

DAGENHAM & REDBRIDGE

NEWPORT COUNTY

SUTTON UTD

MARGATE

BATH CITY

NEWBURY TOWN

WOKING

DOVER ATHLETIC

BASINGSTOKE

ALDERSHOT TOWN

TAUNTON TOWN

SALISBURY CITY

CRAWLEY

YEOVIL

FAREHAM

EXETER CITY

WEYMOUTH

17

The Hellenic League: 1975–1981

1975/76

Forest Green kicked off in the Hellenic League, moving up the football ladder for the second time in eight years. For the first time, they moved into the world of sponsored football against teams from beyond the county border.

BRIAN COATES

We did very well in our first season. We used to get bonus points for goals scored and Forest Green was always one of the top-scoring sides in the Hellenic League. I moved back from centre forward to half-back but I had been there fifteen years by then.

ANDY BISH

After the club joined the Hellenic League I formed an under-18 youth squad with the agreement committee. The youth team won all their three competitions. During one game, The Lawn was shrouded in fog. I remember the referee allowing the game to play but each time a goal was scored he had to run over to the bench to report to the managers who had put the ball in the net. We won 4-2. The last youth game of that season was at Eastville in the final of the County Youth Shield. A Mike Bruton hat-trick helped defeat Henbury. During the season Mike scored 69 of the team's goals. With his scoring exploits he broke into the first team and they themselves became the highest scorers in the Hellenic League with 82 goals.

JOHN EVANS

Peter Goring always believed in attacking football but that season was one for the record books. We finished high up in the league and were top scorers by a long way. I remember regularly playing with four attackers and all four players were in the top six scorers in the Hellenic League. We also won the County Cup that year and I was fortunate to score a hat-trick at Cheltenham Town's Whaddon Road in a 4-2 win in the final.

JOHN DUFF

The standard of football rose dramatically, without doubt, because not only were we playing in probably another six or seven different counties, as opposed to just playing in Gloucestershire, we were also getting involved in the competition sponsored by Rothmans, who sponsored the Hellenic League, and were going out to the Western League, the Northern League and the Isthmian League. And the Channel Islands, where we must have travelled on three or four occasions.

We had some great local players, like Johnny Townsend, Brian Coates, Seth Evans, John and David Dangerfield (he went off to Swindon Town). We had several players came to us from Leyhill Prison. They weren't prisoners – they were prison officers, and they contributed.

The season kicked off with a series of friendlies during August against Bristol Crusaders, Red Dragon, Oxford City away, Westfield, Stonehouse and Gloucestershire Police. Peter Gosling and Kevin Prue were both signed from the Yate Town.

DERROLL LOVEDAY

The Hellenic League was a completely different standard, a big step up from the county game. The first game that we played was against last year's champions, Thatcham. They came down and the first half I remember they played us off the park and we were actually run ragged, but it was still 0-0 at half-time.

The second half, we came out and thought 'God, we will be really up against it,' but early on in the game, I was on the right wing and Johnny Evans was playing up front, and I kicked one across from right down by the touchline and it sailed over the goalkeeper and into the net. We thought we'd scored, but Johnny Evans was offside so it was disallowed. But that didn't half give us a lift and we went on to win the game 5-0. It was a fantastic game, a brilliant team performance. Burnham were always a good side too. It was a very good league I must admit.

The first Hellenic League programme.

JAMES COOK

The first season in the Hellenic League saw a tense relationship between our teenage entourage and some of the older supporters at the club. I genuinely think the players enjoyed the support we gave them and our home form gave us the belief that some of the success we achieved was down to the supporters urging on the team. Unfortunately, the noise we made – particularly with the tuneless drum and loudhailer – did upset a few of the old boys. One particular league game played in that first season had to be played on a Sunday. The game was against Clanfield Town and one of the committee members politely requested that we kept the noise down so that the club received no complaints from the local residents. We seethed (quietly) at this but generally acceded to the request. We lost – our only home defeat of the season. Clanfield finished ahead of us on goal average and my point about our support is proven.

There were certain people at the club who never accepted us as anything other than a nuisance. Others warmed to us after a while and one or two welcomed youth to the club as the way forward. One of the people I always thought was in the latter camp was Les Chester. Les was definitely what you would call a character. I do not think I ever heard him criticise FGR or opposition players. Les's penchant was for baiting referees. He seemed to have a dossier in his head on all refereeing mistakes ever made because a referee could be barracked on to the pitch based on previous performances before he had a chance to do anything new wrong. I guess the fact that Les was as audible as we were earned our respect, and he earned our respect by showing us kindness. Les invited us on to the team coach for our first proper away game with a cautionary, 'As long as you behave yourselves'. We, of course, repaid the team by cheering them on to their first away win of the season – admittedly against a lowly Bicester Town (1-0, John Evans with the winner). We now thought we were becoming a real part of the club and several of us would do what we could to get to every game.

The squad was further strengthened in September when Jim Utteridge arrived from Moreton Town. The social club secretary appealed for more barmen on a Saturday afternoon to serve the increased attendance at matches.

Rovers drew Blyth Spartans from the Northern League in the Inter-League Cup. They were one of the top ten amateur giants of the age. The game, on Saturday 11 October 1975, was played in front of a then modern-day record crowd. Blyth had just had the most successful season in their history. They lost only three matches in the entire previous season, to Preston North End, Southbank and Bishop Auckland in the FA Cup, FA Trophy and Northern League Cup respectively. They held Preston to a 1–1 draw at Blyth, Bobby Charlton and Nobby Stiles included, losing the replay. They had won the Northern League, having played 36 games, drawing 6 and losing 0. Next on their list were Forest Green Rovers.

BRIAN COATES

Before the game we were thinking they were on a different planet, such a famous team; probably like we were Bristol Rovers and they were Arsenal or somebody, one of those sort of type of games. I think we were all a bit nervous, but they had some very good players. They were a good side and we had a great crowd. There was a big crowd, probably the biggest I saw at Forest Green in my day.

JAMES COOK

In preparation for the match; we made bedsheet banners exulting our local heroes. We manufactured a drum from an old oil tin to make a din that would upset anyone in the Nailsworth valley and, just in case it didn't, we made a loudhailer out of an old police cone we managed to 'find' somewhere. In addition to helping with the general accoutrements for the cup tie, I got busy hand-sewing FGR AFC RULES OK down the front legs of a perfectly good pair of black jeans – the letters had to be white so another bed sheet was sacrificed.

The build-up to the match was electric but the game itself, for once, more than matched the hype. At the time a good crowd at FGR would have been 250. The lure of Blyth Spartans brought out a crowd of 900, including a coachload from the North-East. None of these people could have predicted what followed. We were highly delighted to discover that Blyth Spartans chose to play in a horrible all-yellow strip. This made our job of finding a song with which to bait them all the easier. 'We all hate bananas' greeted their entrance on to the pitch.

The first half was lively enough with Blyth Spartans taking an early lead. FGR slowly played their way into the game and just before half-time equalised with a well-struck free-kick from Geoff Medcroft. The half-time score was 1–1. From the kick-off in the second half Blyth Spartans took the game to FGR and scored 3 goals in quick succession to lead 4–1. This was the moment that my father's Geordie mate decided the match was over and it was time for a pint in the club. However, FGR started to get back into the match and, with 20 minutes to go Peter Goring (FGR's manager at the time) made a decisive change. FGR's young centre-back, Mike Bruton, was pushed up front to support the strikers, Kevin Prue and John Evans. Mike had more than impressed in the County Youth League, scoring a plethora of goals including a record 13 in a match for FGR Youth against Uley. Whether Blyth had eased down or whether the sheer strength of this six-foot-plus teenager had taken advantage of ageing legs is still not clear to me, but FGR were transformed as a team. Waves of attacks ensued with Bruton bullying his way down the left-hand side of the Blyth Spartans defence and cutting back cross after cross. Prue, Evans and Bruton himself helped themselves to goals to stun their opponents and take the game into extra time. The drama continued in extra time when Brian Coates – a hard-working defensive midfielder and a particular favourite with our little group – forced another cross from Bruton over the goal line in the first minute of extra time. This was when my father's Geordie mate returned from the club saying, 'You canna leave 'em for five minutes, can ya man?' To Blyth's credit they did not lie down like many teams did at The Lawn that season and fashioned an equaliser before the break in extra time. But there was still time for Kevin Prue to go agonisingly close seconds from the end of the game. Final score: Forest Green Rovers 5, Blyth Spartans 5.

The tie had to be decided on the day so penalties it was. It should be remembered that penalties had not been included in any major competition in the past – the only time we had encountered it was probably in the Watney Cup or the Anglo-Italian Cup (anyone remember these?). FGR and Blyth Spartans certainly were not familiar with the format and much head-scratching ensued. The referee seemed more interested in stopping the partisan crowd behind the goal selected for the shoot-out from putting off anyone from the opposition, issuing a threat to have any penalty missed retaken if we booed – imagine that today!

Suffice to say Spartan spirit shone through and the penalty shoot-out was nowhere near as exciting as the game (Blyth won 3-1), although poor old Chris Bird, the FGR full-back, was asked to take his penalty three times. Missed, scored, missed ended a magnificent game in a less than magnificent manner, but the game itself secured a place for FGR in my consciousness forever. Blyth went on to play in the FA Cup fifth round in the next season, beating Stoke City on the way. They were quite a side.

JOHN EVANS, SUPPORTER

There were lots of new faces behind the goal that night. In an amazing climax we drew level just before the final whistle and I remember we ran on to the pitch and wrapped a scarf around their goalkeeper's neck. Our team had just drawn with one of the biggest non-league teams in the country.

DERROLL LOVEDAY

We got out there and we were giving as good as we got, but they were a good footballing side but we went down 4-1 and then I was substituted for the only time in my life in a competitive match. That didn't go down too well with me I must admit. We pulled it back well though and got level at the end of normal time. I remember it going to penalties and standing there on the touchline. I was the normal penalty taker and I was kicking myself that I couldn't take the thing because I was off the pitch. I don't think it would have made much difference but I certainly didn't like it at the time.

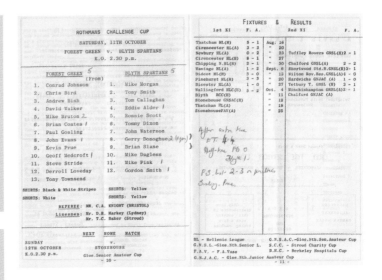

In the following month's issue of the Rothmans news:

One moment you're up, at the next you're brought down to earth with a bump! That's football! We all know about the way the game plays havoc with the emotions of the committed but what must Forest Green Rovers be feeling like after a hectic month of cup football? A 5-2 league cup win against Wallingford was followed by the epic 5-5 'defeat' in the Rothmans knockout cup against Blyth Spartans and a 5-1 win over Stonehouse in the Gloucestershire Senior Cup. Fifteen home goals in three weeks ! No wonder the fans are pouring into the lovely Lawn ground. But in the vitally important FA Vase match the following week a second game with Stonehouse was lost 1-2. However, their free-scoring forwards will no doubt strike again and their challenge to Moreton Town at the top of the league will be intensified.

Forest Green were certainly not finding life in the higher league a struggle and had taken to it like a duck to water. The club hired two fifty-three-seater coaches for the Burnham match at the end of November, charging supporters 75p and children 35p. Kevin Prue and John Evans played for the league against London Universities, winning 2-1, and featured in a 3-0 win against the Western League. John and Kevin had also shared 4 goals the previous November, playing for Gloucestershire against the RAF.

Forest Green Rovers players and committee, 1975/76. Back row: Pete Hill, John Evans, Steve Gannaway, Charlie Jones, Mike Bruton, Fran Walker, Brian Ponting, Geoff Medcroft. Standing: Alan Morris, Peter Goring, Tony Townsend, Paul Gosling, Chris Bird, Derek Huxford, Dave Walker, Brian Coates, Conrad Johnson, Phil Chandler, Ian Brown, Andy Bish, Derroll Loveday, Kevin Prue, Merv Painter, Dave Robinson, Geoff Smith. Seated: Don Gannaway, Harold Gannaway, Rod Gingell, Ron Davis, Wilf Riley, Bill Trueman, John Duff, Doug Brown, Harold Waterworth, Les Chester, Peter Pearch, Phil Wood. Front row: Duncan Edwards, Kevin Brown, Nicky Vowles, Stuart Freeman, Paul Dursley, Ian Pitcher, Mark Spill, Mel Ackland, Terry Scuse, John Tregonning.

Towards the end of the season, and with 6 games in hand over the top team, Forest Green were leading the goalscoring table with John Evans on 18, Kevin Prue on 16 and Jeff Medcroft seventh-highest scorer with 11.

DERROLL LOVEDAY

One of my memories from my playing days at Forest Green was a game at home to Chipping Norton. The manager, Peter Goring, had us in the changing rooms talking tactics and handing around the shirts, and to my surprise he gave me the goalkeeping jumper. I looked at him, and then he told us our keeper's car had broken down near Salisbury and he couldn't make it here in time. As usual, when we ran out on to the pitch the crowd always gave us a good welcoming cheer, until they saw who was in goal, and then you could hear a pin drop. I thought 'Well, that's a good confidence boost.' In the end I think we won 2-1.

Rovers' away match against Hungerford Town in March was played under floodlights on a Wednesday night to assist Hungerford with their fixture congestion. The fifty-three-seater coach departed at 5.30 p.m. with a large band of energetic teenagers on board, going away for the first time for a night match that finished in a 1–1 draw.

At the end of the season, in June 1976, Bill Truman presented the most upbeat report of his tenure:

> *The First XI brought great credit to the club on their first season in the Hellenic League, finishing fourth. The Second XI had done extremely well in winning the Division Two of the Northern Senior League at the first attempt since being relegated and the youth side had swept all before them, including in the County Youth Shield.*
>
> *Mike Bruton made most appearances, 55 in all, and had scored 82 goals, 69 of those for the youth. Of the others, Tony Townsend played 41 games, Peter Gosling 40, Jeff Medcroft 40. None of the regular first-team squad had played less than 35 games.*
>
> *Commenting on our first season in the Hellenic League, the secretary said the high standard we had set could be a burden to us. We would be expected by the league and by our supporters to maintain this next season. The most disappointing thing about the league had been the poor standard of referees and linesmen.*

The club had spent a total of £5,610 during the past year. Gate money had more than doubled from £312 to £635, a fraction of the running costs.

TIM BARNARD

I remember feeling very grown-up when we all travelled away midweek to Hungerford. We'd all met up and got on to the team coach, smuggling some alcohol on board and were very vocal by the time we reached Hungerford.

Our small band headed off behind the goal to cheer the team on with the traditional Forest Green chants, including the old favourite 'Rovers!' (bang bang bang), 'Rovers!' (bang bang bang) on the metal sheets at the back of the stand. It was a case of Rovers bang bang crash as one of the panels of the back of the stand came away from its bearings. No serious damage was done, the game ending in a draw and milling about in the social club after the game we felt very grown-up.

1976/77

The season kicked off with a hard act to follow. John Dangerfield was now rehabilitated at the club, although Derroll Loveday had moved on. Peter Goring was allowed an extra £7 per week for players' expenses for the forthcoming season by the committee.

Rovers drew with Bristol St George in the FA Vase, beating them in a replay 6-1, and then lost to Worrall Hill 2-0 in the next round. In the Rothmans Knockout Cup, Forest Green beat Bridport from the Western League 2-1 away and were then drawn away against another Northern League team, Tow Law Town. The coach went on Friday and returned on Sunday.

A second coach with supporters was to leave at 5.30 a.m. on Saturday morning and return the same evening, with a fare being set at £2.50. Rovers lost 4-2 but certainly provided memories for the players and supporters, especially considering that two years previously, they had very rarely played outside of Gloucestershire.

The playing squad was strengthened theoretically with the addition of Ron Radford, the scorer of Hereford United's famous goal in the FA Cup, but no sooner had he arrived, than the talk among the committee was that he was unlikely to play for the team because he was heavily involved in the renovation of his house.

Results were not quite living up to last year's standards and Peter Goring was called before the committee in February. In March, Forest Green's ground was chosen to stage a match between the Hellenic League and Northern League to take place in May, following in the tradition of the GFA using The Lawn for its main amateur fixtures.

The report at the AGM on Monday 9 June did not make such good reading. Forest Green finished eleventh of sixteen:

> *Following a previous good season this one has been most frustrating and disappointing for the First 11, having to fight hard in the end to avoid relegation. The reverse was said of the Second 11. After winning the Second Division title they achieved a rare success by gaining the Division One Northern Senior League championship. Tony Townsend had, for the third season running, played in every first team game, 43 in all, followed by Chris Bird, Brian Coates and G. Davies on 41. The highest scorer was J. Gray with 18 goals, 17 for G. Davies and 16 for Kevin Prue.*

1977/78

Alan Morris left the county in August 1977 having served the club extremely well since originally being appointed as player-manager back in the 1960s. Forest Green finally entered the FA Cup, beating Larkhall 3-2. In the league, results were not going the club's way and certainly not living up to the heights of the first season in the Hellenic League. In September 1977 Peter Goring was given the dreaded vote of confidence.

JAMES COOK

By the end of the 1970s we were all confirmed Forest Green nuts. In 1978 a friend and I decided that, because there was no coach, we would walk the twenty miles to the match. We started out at about 8 a.m. and, barring one lift of a few miles into Cirencester, we walked all the way, getting there at about 1 p.m. Again we were rewarded with a rare away win (1-0, Kevin Prue scored – I think) and lifts home by a couple of committee members, strangely enough in separate cars – I guess they must have thought we were crazy!

Having played teams from the Northern League and the Western League in the previous years of the Rothmans Knockout competition, Forest Green entertained Oaklands, a team from the Channel Islands, at Forest Green in a match in November 1977, winning 2-0.

Weston were the next opposition in the FA Cup, Forest Green losing 2-0, the only game lost that month. In the FA Vase, Forest Green beat Chippenham 3-2 and then beat Malvern away 3-1 before meeting Almondsbury Greenway in the third round in December, losing 2-1. Mike Bruton suffered an horrendous leg-break and was in Standish Hospital in October 1977. He had two operations for his injury. The committee finally confirmed that they would travel to St Martins in Guernsey in February for the Knockout Cup match on Saturday 11 February, travelling out on the Friday and returning on the Sunday. Mike, still recovering from his injury, accompanied the team on the tour, all his costs being met by the club. Forest Green beat St Martin's 2-1, leading to a happy trip back to Guernsey in April for the next round.

Rovers finished twelfth of sixteen, not a glorious season in the league, a far cry from their inaugural season two years before.

THE SMILES of these Forest Green players, officials and supporters were even broader after their cup victory Channel Islands on Saturday. They are pictured leaving for Guernsey at Nailsworth last week.

Rothmans Overseas National Knock-out Cup

GEOFF BOOKS ROVERS THEIR RETURN TICKET

ST. MARTIN'S (GUERNSEY) 1   FOREST GREEN ROVERS 2
(After extra-time)

FOREST GREEN'S stop-start quarter-final ended when they booked a return Channel Island ticket at the weekend.

But Rovers were fortunate to hold on to their cup lives and Dick Maycock played superbly in goal to spoil St. Martin's hopes. Chairman John Duff said in Stroud on Monday: "We realise we were fortunate.

"We had the break but we were a little bit lucky." Rovers join Whitby Town and Bideford in the draw, with the remaining place going to either Mangotsfield or Evenwood.

Mike Bruton returned for his first senior game since last April with Mel Jeffries unable to travel. Ian Wilkes was substitute in a team that read: Maycock, D. Walker, B. Coates, M. Carroll, A. Bish, M. Bruton, T. Townsend, P. Gosling, J Dangerfield, G. Davies. G. Medcroft. Sub: I. Wilkes.

All the early pressure came from Forest Green and in the third minute Paul Gosling's long throw was met by Brian Coates and the ball missed its target by inches.

On an enormous pitch, St. Martin's, the premier Guernsey side, came back into the game. Mick Carroll saved Rovers with a clearance off the line. Then in the 19th minute, an attack down the left flank saw a hard low centre which was driven home by LeRiches to make it 1-0.

John Dangerfield was dangerous when in posses-

It was very, very close indeed and it could have gone either way."

Manager Peter Goring agreed that Rovers were somewhat lucky to be going back to Guernsey for the semi-finals and finals on April 7-9.

brought down in the area. From the spot, Glyn Davies blasted past the keeper.

Rovers finished the half with further shots from Tony Townsend, Dangerfield and Bruton.

A deadlock set in after the break, but Maycock was called upon to make two great saves. Andy Bish also shone, with all the forwards trying hard.

Mike Bruton faded and was replaced by Wilkes. Extra time was called upon with the scores level and five minutes into the first period, Rovers pro-

duced the best move of the match.

Ian Wilkes and John Dangerfield swapped passes, and Dangerfield crossed for Geoff Medcroft to head home the winner.

Wilkes was carried off injured with five minutes to go leaving Rovers with ten men to hold off St. Martin's final onslaught.

After the disasters of two weeks ago, when Rovers were stranded at Southampton, Mr. Duff added: "We were extremely impressed by the arrangements and the hospitality of the home club."

F. HAND & SON
Horsley
Glos.

to cater for all sections of the community — for ... Clubs. Football Clubs, etc. as well as specializ... parties for Senior Citizens and Schools.

It is our pleasure to help you with arranging theatre ... antonine bookings, visits to night clubs, etc.

Further afield why not let us help you arrange a ... booking for a day tour, or even perhaps for a tour ... rope?

- Whatever your requirements why not ring us and ... all be delighted to be of service.

**Tel.
Nailsworth 2722**

FOREST GREEN ROVERS A.F.C.
OFFICIAL PROGRAMME

Top: Forest Green Rovers 1977/78. Back row: Peter Goring, Steve Gannaway, Phil Chandler, Pat Hennessey, Brian Coates, Jim Lavery, Charlie Jones, Glynn Davis, Tony Lewis. Front row: Micky Carrol, Chris Bird, Paul Gosling, John Dangerfield, Keith Mortimer, Tony Townsend, Adrian Brown

Above: The first game against Channel Island opposition, Forest Green Rovers *v.* Oaklands, November 1977.

BRIAN COATES

We played St Martins over in Guernsey. It was the quarter-finals and we beat them over there. About two or three weeks later we had to fly back over again to play in a semi-final. They was holding the finals there; we lost to Mangotsfield in Guernsey. We had a really good time there and it got really professional when we were flying away there to play football!

ANDY BISH

I can still picture Forest Green goalkeeper Dick Maycock winning the raffle in the old government hotel in St Peter Port and, on reaching over for his prize from the resident DJ, he fell flat on his face and demolished the whole disco in the process!

JAMES COOK

After the success of 1976, the next few years were fairly lean. We won the GNSA Cup again but the league form was nothing better than average and our better players were being lured away. But Peter Goring and Tony Lewis took us to the brink of the 1978/79 Hellenic League championship, missing out by only 2 points – being defeated by Fairford (yes, them again) on the last home game of the season. The feat achieved in this season was winning ten league games in a row. Unfortunately the eleventh game was the defeat against Fairford, which probably cost the title. We finished 2 points behind Newbury and 1 behind Fairford.

1978/79

Peter Goring was in charge for his tenth season. In the FA Vase Rovers beat Avon Bradford 12-1, Kenny Gill scoring 6 goals in the game, and then drew 1-1 with Yate at home before beating them 3-1 in a replay. Forest Green then took on Almondsbury Greenway again, losing 5-0. Almondsbury went on to reach the FA Vase final that year. Kenny Gill, Bill Silto and John Dangerfield played in a league representative match at Hungerford in November.

Off the pitch, the club looked into the possibility of franchising a lottery company as a means of raising further funds. The contract was received in February and a portable cabin was installed at The Lawn, which became the Goldliner Lottery headquarters.

By the end of April, and another season almost over, the committee voted by ten votes to three to invite Mr Goring to be manager for his eleventh season at the club. He had guided Rovers back to third position, below Fairford and Newbury Town who were champions that year.

1979/80

The Goldliner Lottery was now up and running, with £1,000 prizes on offer and a large uptake around the area. Rovers received their share of a total of £21,826 in October, income unheard of in previous years.

At the beginning of the season, friendlies were arranged at The Lawn with Gloucester City and Portway of Bristol. In the FA Cup, Forest Green drew Clandown, winning 3-2, then moving on to play Weston-super-Mare, again losing 3-1. In the FA Vase, Forest Green drew a team simply called Park and won 1-0, followed by Northfield, who were beaten 3-0.

After a meeting between John Duff and Peter Goring at the beginning of October, Peter resigned as manager. He felt the team were not responding to him and that a new manager would do better. The Peter Goring era was over, just as additional funds were beginning to come into the club. Tony Lewis was appointed caretaker manager.

As well as the appointment of a new manager, thoughts turned to what to do with the lottery money. First on the list was floodlights. In January 1980, long discussions took place as to whether it was in the club's best interests to stay in the Hellenic League. The merits of the Western League or the Midland Combination were discussed. It wasn't clear whether Rovers needed to join the Western League for progression to the Southern League, which was the aim of the club. Ultimately, consensus of opinion was that a strong team should be built in the Hellenic League with a view to applying for Southern League status in 1981/82. The club was aiming high again.

In the league, Rovers finished sixth in a league of sixteen.

ADRIAN BROWN

What's always crossed my mind is what would Peter Goring have done, or what could he have done if he'd have had the money that later managers like Bob Mursell had? Forest Green had started the lottery, the Goldliner, and they had a shop in Nailsworth where the video shop is, and they were doing very, very well and they made a lot of money. I've always thought that, what if?

BRIAN COATES

I remember Peter Goring leaving in 1979. We used to be pretty close. I finished up a couple of games with the reserves and that was it, I had to call it a day. Nice chap; he was a pretty good manager and he had won the FA Cup with Arsenal.

Forest Green Rovers at the beginning of the 1980/81 season. Back row: R.A. Brown (trainer), B. Coates, G. Medcroft, R. Maycock, M. Bruton, M. Carroll, A. Lewis (coach). Front row: D.F. Walker, J. Dangerfield, C. Bird, A. Townsend, P. Gosling, G. Davies, K. Mortimer.

1980/81

Forest Green Rovers appointed Tony Lewis as their manager after a spell as caretaker. Results got steadily worse until Rovers were one place off the bottom of the league in October and looking at relegation rather than glory. Tony was sacked and new manager Bob Mursell arrived in October 1980 full of gusto, having the persona of a big-time football manager, and set about checking out all of the players currently at the club. By the end of the season, with 6 games left to play, Forest Green faced the runaway leaders of the Hellenic League, Newbury Town, at home. Rovers won by 4-0 with goals scored by Steve Millard, Colin Williams (2) and John Dangerfield.

ANDY BISH

Success eluded Tony Lewis and the committee informed him that his services were no longer required. I became caretaker manager for 2 games until Bob Mursell was appointed with Roy Hillman as his assistant. New players came and went as the foundations for future success were laid. Bob's team talks were long and detailed, with the players locked in the changing rooms for a rollicking if they hadn't performed. It was a complete change in management style from Peter's days. With only a few local players left, the team started to lose its family feel and even training became separate in Bristol.

JOHN DUFF

Peter Goring had moved on, regretfully. He was followed by Tony Lewis. He did well for a little while but found it a bit much. I was on holiday and had a phone call from one of my colleagues. 'We understand that Bob Mursell's left Gloucester City and can we talk to him?' I said 'Yes, go ahead.'

We went on the Saturday to Maidenhead and Mursell was there, I was impressed with him and said, 'Here you are Bob, take over.' He started to change the team, and I know there was great concern among the players. Andy Coburn, who incidentally later became chairman of our club, was most upset and thought that he wouldn't last long when Bob come in. His reputation was as a hatchet man who brought the toughies in, and he did just that. He went round the district and he knew these players, and he got them in. John Turner from Matson was a prime example.

By 1981 players were coming from further afield, but they were feathering their own nests a bit as well because Forest Green was becoming a force, a well-organised club. The facilities at Forest Green were excellent; better than most.

Forest Green Rovers 1980/81, towards the end of the season. Back row: Nick Rock, Andy Bish, Jeff Board, Steve Dolling, John Turner, Tim Bayliffe. Front row: Brian Sheasby, Steve Boseley, John Dangerfield, Colin Morris, Williams, Tim Davis, Russell Dunn.

The first team had seen thirty-six players passing through. John Dangerfield, Nick Rock, Brian Sheasby, Keith Mortimer, John Turner and Steve Boseley had been with Rovers since the beginning of the season. Andy Bish, Steve Gannaway and Alan Newport had been there for ten years and were still regularly featuring. But the team also included new signings Steve Millard, David Dixon and Brendan Guest.

The lottery tickets were selling thick and fast and provided the revenue stream to fuel Forest Green's progress. In Bob Mursell, the club appeared to have a pilot to see the club through to a higher level. The season's top scorers – Nick Rock, John Dangerfield and Brian Sheasby – also made valuable contributions.

F. HAND & SON

Horsley
Glos.

e cater for all sections of the community - for
Clubs, football Clubs, etc. as well as specialist-
arties for Senior Citizens and Schools.

is our pleasure to help you with arranging theatre
oming bookings, visits to night clubs, etc.

ther afield why not let us help you arrange a
oking for a day tour, or even perhaps for a tour
e?

Whatever your requirements why not ring us and
be delighted to be of service.

Tel.
Nailsworth 2722

FOREST GREEN ROVERS A.F.C.

OFFICIAL PROGRAMME

LAWN LINE UP

HELLENIC LEAGUE PREMIER DIVISION

Monday 20 April 1981 - KO 3 PM

FOREST GREEN ROVERS/NEWBURY TOWN

(FROM)	(FROM)
Steve DOLLING	Pat MOONEY
Malcolm KING	Steve FOSTER
Russell DUNN	Dennis BUTLER
Andy BISH	Ray PITHERS
Dave DIXON	Charlie FENNY
Keith MORTIMER	Alan PRIOR
Brendan GUEST	Alan McNAB
Steve BOSELEY	Brendan McKEVITT
Steve MILLARD	Paul DYER
Brian SHEASBY	Tony INGRAM
Nick ROCK	Simon EIGHTEEN
Colin WILLIAMS	Martin HUNT
John DANGERFIELD	Chris GWYN
John TURNER	Paul MEASHAM

Referee : R A RIGHTON (Cirencester)

Linesmen : J Little (Nailsworth)
H Stunt (GLOUCESTER)

Colours : Forest Green Rovers All Green
Newbury Town Amber/Black

For a report of today's game read the Stroud News and Journal.

Forest Green Rovers thank them for their continued
excellent coverage of our matches. Hopefully the
rest will join in when they realise what they are
missing.

EASTER PARADE

On Easter Monday we are pleased to welcome as
visitors the "cream" of the Hellenic League -
Newbury Town. They have had a tremendous season
and by the time they reach us today they could
have clinched the championship. If this is the
case let us hope for an exciting, open game with
plenty of thrills for what could be our biggest
gate of the season.

Newbury had their first defeat of the season
only 9 days ago at home to Thame United when the
visitors won by 3-1. Despite this defeat it has
been a brilliant season for their club as they
have totted up win after win.

We sincerely welcome their players, officials
and supporters for this holiday fixture and
trust the game will round off the Easter holiday
in the right spirit whatever the result.

We went to press too early to include details of
our game against Hazells but it was good to return
to the winning trail away to Flackwell Heath. A
victory clinched the double over the Buckingham-
shire club this was added to other "braces" against
Wallingford Town and Abingdon United.

Dave Dixon powered his second goal in only three
matches since signing from Gloucester City and
skipper John Turner notched his ninth for the club.
In addition Brendan Guest continued to add to his
form with a hand in both goals.

Unfortunately I missed my first game since joining
the club but I am told that it was a very good
performance by our lads. Malcolm King returned to
the side in goal and got better as the match
proceeded until he was a picture of confidence by
the end. The back four of Russell Dunn, Andy Bish,
Dave Dixon and Keith Mortimer kept it tight at the
back . Our midfield quartet of Steve Boseley,
Brian Sheasby, Steve Millard and Brendan Guest

...ING ON.......

d well, especially as it was the first occasion that
ve employed four men in the middle of the park, and
Turner and Colin Williams blended up front.

Dolling, Reg Rix, Alan Newport, John Dangerfield,
Gannaway and Kevin Hollywell were all players who
appeared in the first team this season who lined up
the reserves who are fighting to avoid relegation.
eam gained a deserved win under the guidance of Bob
ll. Bob fully realises the importance of keeping the
d team in the higher division, this will mean less of
up for those players called into first team action.

illman took charge of the first team at Flackwell Heath
was the second time this season that Roy has been
ager" for the day at opposition's grounds and the team
responded with two wins. Perhaps he should have control
often (only joking Bob !).

Wilcox was called into the senior squad for the first time
stitute, although he did not get a game the experience
stand him in good stead for the future.

aturday we play our final home match of the season against
gdon Town. As they are one of the teams we can leapfrog
league a win is important. We then visit them the
owing Tuesday night (29 April).

ber to keep buying your Goldliner Lottery Tickets, this
tal revenue to the club. We appreciate the hard times of
oment but 25p will not break the bank.

ou fancy a drink, visit the Forest Green Supporters Club
the game. Prices are very favourable and the company
ood.

annot let the season pass by without mentioning the
ladies who run the refreshment hut on match days. I can
for the Bovril and Terry for the coffee. Again prices are
. Thankyou ladies, long may you be around.

ve already indicated our pre season plans, read the local
(especially the Stroud News) for all details.

HERE'S BOBBY

Good afternoon !.

I hope that your Easter break has been enjoyable. We are
intending to provide you with some good entertainment this
afternoon and I cannot think of better opponents to play
than Newbury Town. Their record speaks for itself and I
assure all of you that Roy and I are working towards
building a team next season to challenge their championship.

I decided to stay at the Lawn with the reserves last week
but Roy was generous in his assessment of our performance
at Flackwell. This is the result we were looking for to
indicate that our rebuilding is working. Despite the
fact that we again conceded a sloppy goal the character
was present to enable us to win the game with a real
battling performance.

We must realise that to win league titles we have to play
with much more patience, especially away from home. This
will ensure that our goals against is dramatically improved.

If you study the list of players that have appeared in the
first team this season you will find it totals 36. This
was partially caused by the changes I made when I arrived
at the club. Not only did I bring in new players but have
also tried several permutations to give all of the senior
players a chance. I now know the players who can do a good
job for Forest Green, they will form the nucleus of my
plans for next season.

In addition the transfer lists will soon be published and
it is certain that there will be some useful players
available. I have already talked to players and other
managers and have a strong belief that I already know
who I want. You can rest assured that next season's
squad will be a strong one. If this is backed up with
a good reserve side then we can realistically challenge
anyone. We have the extra incentive of knowing that a
good season will ensure Southern League football the
following season. Your support is vital, without it the
task is much harder. There are exciting times ahead for
us all-get behind us right now, you won't regret it.

Bob Mursell

Forest Green Rovers Youth Team
1980/81. Runners up Stroud Youth
League, Winners Stroud Youth League
Red Cross Cup. Back row: Sean
Ludlow, David Maryon, Mark Cowley,
Sean Little, Jeremy Duff, Craig Benton,
Adrian Evans, Rob Furley, Mike
Woollett. Middle row: Lyndon Smith,
Eddie Brandenburg, Peter Pearch,
John Duff, Andy Bish, Richard
Pearch, Richard Ind. Front: Chris Kite,
Paul Meredith.

...TILL EIGHTH

S	TEAM	P	W	D	L	F	A	PTS	HAT
1	NEWBURY TOWN	22	19	2	1	60	18	40	56
2	Hazells	26	14	7	5	47	31	35	43
3	Moreton Town	26	12	8	6	62	29	30	40
4	Thame United	24	12	8	4	41	17	32	44
5	Fairford Town	28	15	2	11	48	38	32	36
6	Flackwell Heath	26	12	6	8	42	25	30	38
7	Abingdon Town	24	11	7	6	43	31	29	41
8	FOREST GREEN ROVERS	24	11	5	8	40	46	27	39
9	Maidenhead Town	27	10	5	12	40	52	25	31
10	Bicester Town	28	6	11	11	37	54	23	27
11	Kidlington	27	8	6	13	32	51	22	28
12	Didcot Town	26	6	9	11	27	43	21	28
13	Northwood	26	6	8	12	33	45	20	28
14	Wallingford Town	28	8	4	16	42	60	20	24
15	Morris Motors	28	6	6	16	34	55	18	22
16	Abingdon United	30	5	4	11	31	75	14	14

he above league table does not include last Saturday
r some midweek matches played recently.

t seems apparent that Wallingford Town's recent run
t good results will save them from relegation. Morris
otors and Abingdon United seem doomed for the drop.

ewbury could well have clinched the title by today.

ive months ago the league had a different look, since
hen the positions were :- Newbury 21 pts 13 games
airford 21-15, Hazells 20-14, Maidenhead 19-16,
hame 17-12, ROVERS 14-13, Wallingford 8-14,
oreton 13-14, Flackwell 12-13, Abingdon T 11-11,
icester 11-14, Kidlington 11-13, Didcot 11-16,
orthwood 8-12, Morris M 8-13, Abingdon U 8-16.

hat would have been our position if we had not.....
ell I suppose they all say that don't they.

SO FAR

NAME	APPS	GLS	NAME	APPS	GLS
John Dangerfield	29(1)	7	Jeff Board	7(1)	1
Nick Rock	29(1)	11	Malcolm King	7	0
Brian Sheasby	29(2)	7	Terry Haile	6	0
Keith Mortimer	28	0	Steve Millard	4	0
John Turner	21		Dave Dixon	3	2
Colin Williams	21(1)	12	Brendan Guest	3	0
Steve Boseley	20	0	Alan Newport	3(3)	1
Reg Rix	19(2)	0	Steve Gannaway	2(3)	1
Russell Dunn	18(1)	1	Duncan Edwards	1	0
Steve Dolling	16	0	John Hawkins	1	0
Tim Davis	14(1)	0	Ian Dando	0(1)	0
Andy Bish	14(1)	0	Kevin Hollywell	0(1)	0
David Walker	9(2)	0			

The following have also appeared
A Coeburn 18(1)-1, J Murphy 15-0, P Rugman 13-0,
G Kelly 12-1, T Bayliffe 11-2, A Croker 9(1)-0,
R Ford 6-0, J Cox 5(1)-0, A Ireland 3-0, S Lockett 3-0,
R Cason 0(1)-0.

LEAGUE RESULTS 1980/81

16 Aug	Thame U	H	1-1	22 Nov	Moreton T	A	2-3
20 Aug	Fairford T	A	2-0	13 Dec	Didcot T	A	2-2
23 Aug	Thame U	A	1-4	20 Dec	Abingdon U	H	2-0
27 Aug	Moreton T	H	0-6	27 Dec	Fairford T	D	0-2
6 Sep	Bicester T	A	1-2	17 Jan	Flackwell H	H	3-2
20 Sep	Morris M	A	2-2	24 Jan	Kidlington	H	4-3
11 Oct	Maidenhead T	A	2-0	7 Feb	Kidlington	H	4-3
25 Oct	Wallingford	H	7-3	14 Feb	Didcot T		2-0
25 Oct	Northwood	H	3-3	21 Mar	Bicester T	H	2-1
1 Nov	Abingdon U	A	2-0	28 Mar	Maidenhead T	H	1-4
8 Nov	Wallingford	A	3-0	4 Apr	Hazells	H	0-1
15 Nov	Morris M	H	3-1	11 Apr	Flackwell H	A	2-1

Matches remaining

Home- Newbury Town, Abingdon Town.

Away- Newbury Town, Abingdon Town, Northwood.

The Hazells(A) result not included.

18

Double Success – The Vase and the League: 1981–1982

1981/82

The season kicked off with an unprecedented series of friendly matches against Yeovil Town, Bath City, Bristol Rovers, Swindon Town and Hereford United. Newport County came to The Lawn having just had a good run in the European Cup-Winners' Cup, which ended with a defeat at home to Carl Zeiss Jena. They had finished in a comfortable mid-table position in the old Third Division. The Newport team included Paul Bodin, while the Bristol Rovers team included Shaun Penny and Gary Mabbutt. The new Forest Green team was as unfamiliar to the home supporters as to the away teams, and included nine new signings.

Ken Hallam and Andy Leitch were among them. Dave Moss, a goalkeeper, at well over six feet tall, was another to join from Salisbury Town. Kenny Norman followed Bob Mursell from Gloucester City, having had spells at both Torquay United and at Swindon Town.

John Duff's fourteenth season as chairman at the club was one he might only have dreamt of when the club were playing Northern Senior League football at the start of his reign. Before a ball had been kicked, the Rovers knew that a good season could well lead to Southern League football.

The club entered the FA Vase again and played their first tie in October.

ANDY LEITCH

I was going nowhere at Yeovil Town when Bob talked me into joining Forest Green. We talked about many things, and Wembley was one of them, as Almondsbury had reached Wembley a couple of years before. He thought we had a chance; but I think it was more daydreaming than really believing that made me sign up.

STEVE DOUGHTY

I was playing for Frampton United and we were playing Forest Green Rovers in the semi-final of the Stroud Charity Cup. We beat Forest Green 2-1 and I scored both goals. After the game Bob Mursell made a few enquiries about the following season and got in touch with me and my Dad a bit later on, enquiring about whether I would be interested in joining Forest Green. Gloucester City, Cheltenham Town and Bath City were all interested. I was leading scorer in local football for three years.

We met Bob at the Prince of Wales and, truthfully, he said that if I signed for Forest Green, he would make sure that I got a Hellenic League winners' medal and an appearance at Wembley in the FA Vase. My Dad looked at me and I looked at him and we both thought 'Oh yeah!' But that was enough for me to sign on the dotted line for the following season. He had ambition.

The standard of football was a complete gulf away from what I had been used to at Frampton United, it was massive.

Bob Mursell knew so many players with ex-league experience and I had just come in from Frampton, which was just a local village side. Everybody else in that side had league experience apart from me. I learnt a great deal from them very quickly and I just gained more experience every week really, learning off them. It was a massive step up from Frampton to Forest Green, but I thought I did okay with it.

ANDY LEITCH

We'd had a very good pre-season, trained hard and had some good results in friendly matches against some very good opposition. We were all ready for our first match and turned up at training on the Tuesday evening and had a really hard session, so when Thursday night training started, I thought it would be a little bit of stretching then sprinting, and finishing with a little five-a-side game and then perhaps tactics for the Saturday.

How wrong I was. Bob and Roy had us running all night, like pre-season all over again, and come Saturday morning I had a job to get out of bed. I think I was too tired to be excited about our first game and, looking round our team, all our players seemed to be knackered. It was like we were all wearing lead boots. The first half was a disaster, we were losing 1-0 and not looking like scoring. We were given a roasting at half-time but we still couldn't get going, but then Doughts snatched a late equaliser that we didn't really deserve. It wasn't a good start if we were going to win the league. It was a really bad performance, but some good came of it – we never trained anywhere near as hard as that on a Thursday night ever again!

Saturday 10 October 1981: FA Vase Preliminary Round: Worrall Hill home.

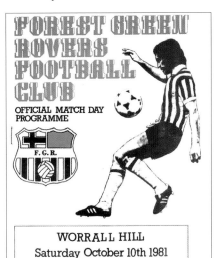

MIKE BURNS

The final of the FA Vase was nearly seven months away and it seemed very strange to hear Steve Millard saying in the dressing-room before the game that Wembley was the prize for winning this one. I hadn't played against Worrall Hill for nearly fifteen years when I was last in the County League, and I was surprised to see one or two players who I had previously played against still playing for them. We ran out easy winners, winning 5-1, and I scored my first goal for Rovers in that game.

Forest Green Rovers *v.* Gloucester City, 30 September 1981. While the official opening of the floodlights had not yet occurred, this game was played under lights. Micky Burns is the only player who has spotted the ball!

Forest Green Rovers v. Wolves, 19 October 1981. The mighty Wolverhampton Wanderers brought a full first team to the official switching on of the floodlights. Forest Green were good but not that good, they lost 6-1.

HUNGRY WOLVES SAVAGE BRAVE FOREST GREEN

FOREST GREEN ROVERS 1, WOLVERHAMPTON WANDERERS 6

IT WAS virtually a full strength Wolves' first team went some way to matching the brilliance of Forest Green's new floodlights on day evening.

In a friendly to the official opening of Rovers' £25,000 lights, the visitors 37 as to get their first

a damp, murky g a crowd of about urned out to watch atch.

es were without Gray, under suspens and Kenny Hibbitt, as injured.

the team included Clarke, Joe Gallradshaw.

any fears that the might be reluc-a hit top gear were lispelled as, after a tart, they began to up some skilful, one-soccer which at had Rovers floun-

st Green made a break in the first a which threatened Wolves' goal. The s soon retaliated but

lacked finishing power in the early stages and when they did let fly Rovers' 'keeper Dave Moss was in charge of the situation.

Matthews put Wolves ahead, however, in the 37th minute and four minutes later Richards blasted a long range effort which deceived Moss and rocketed into the top, left hand corner of the net.

Wolves' class began to tell in the second half when they had most of the possession.

Clarke made it 3-0 in the 66th minute from close in when he steered home a superb cross from Eves, one of Wolves' five second half substitutes.

And then the goals began to flow as Brazier, Clarke and Gallagher locked Rovers with four more.

Despite their battering Rovers refused to give up and in the dying minutes got a consolation goal when Nick Rock popped up to score with a smart header from close in.

The match was well refereed by Brian Stevens with Brian Norman and Tony Gannon as linesmen. Following the game a reception for players, officials and guests was held at Flickers, Nailsworth. Forest Green had been given a boost for their clash with Wolves by a 3-1 win over Northwood in the Hellenic League last Saturday.

They went ahead through Mike Burns, but Clark equalised after half an hour.

In the last 12 minutes, however, Rovers swooped with a vengeance and two goals from leading scorer Andy Leitch ensured that they took home both points.

FOREST GREEN ROVERS FOOTBALL CLUB

OFFICIAL MATCH DAY PROGRAMME 25p

F.G.R.

STOKE CITY
Monday 7 December 1981
Kick Off 7 30 pm

LAWN LINE-UP

FOREST GREEN ROVERS	STOKE
Dave MOSS	Peter FOX
Kenny NORMAN	Ray EVANS
Peter HIGGINS	Peter HAMPTON
Ken HALLAM	Alan DODD
John TURNER	Denis SMITH
Brendan GUEST	Bren O'CALLAGHAN
Mike BURNS	Adrian HEATH
Dave DANGERFIELD	Paul BRACEWELL
Andy LEITCH	Lee CHAPMAN
Steve DOUGHTY	Peter GRIFFITHS
Steve MILLARD	Paul MAGUIRE
Keith HARDCASTLE	Paul JOHNSON
Keith MORTIMER	Loek URSEM

Man in the Middle _____ Eric READ
Man with the Red Flag _____ R SCUDAMORE
Man with the Orange Flag _____ R HAMER

The lottery money funded new floodlights. Wolverhampton Wanderers brought a full-strength team to The Lawn for the official switching-on on Monday 19 October 1981. Rovers lost 6-1. Wolves were the seventh league team to play Rovers that season and would not be the last. Stoke City visited on Monday 7 December for a friendly, including emerging youngsters Lee Chapman, Paul Bracewell and Adrian Heath and were the first team with shirt advertising to play at The Lawn.

Saturday 14 November 1981: FA Vase First Round: Ledbury Town home.

ANDY LEITCH

Every game on the way to the final was a hard game. Probably one of our only 'not so tough' games was the final itself. I think our hardest game was the first round proper tie against Ledbury Town, who had signed a lot of ex-league players and were hoping to progress up the leagues. We were feeling confident that we could beat any of the local teams. If we didn't know what a hard game Ledbury was going to be before kick-off, we did after twenty-five seconds – 1-0 down at home. We struggled all half to get back into the game but then, just before half-time, we conceded a penalty; a disaster. Up stepped ex-Newport County player Brian Preece to slam the ball against the post. I think that was a defining moment in our season. Had that gone in I think that would have ended the FA Vase for us that year.

In the second half, we got right back into it. We were awarded a penalty, but our joy turned to despair when J.T. slammed his kick against the post. We never lost belief and kept battling until Doughts managed to scramble an equaliser. With us happy to be forcing a replay by then we sneaked the winner. I think this game gave us the belief and mental strength that we needed many more times in some very tense FA Vase games that would follow, to get us through to Wembley.

Wednesday 16 December 1981: FA Vase Second Round: Chippenham Town home.

MIKE BURNS

This game had been previously cancelled and got played the next Wednesday under our new floodlights. Without disrespect to Chippenham, we were confident that we knew that they didn't have the players that would trouble our defence. We slammed in 4 goals, 3 of these being scored by Andy to make it a memorable evening for him. Once again Doughts weighed in with a goal and it was obvious that the two big men were going to prove a vital factor in our quest for a good FA Vase run.

Programme sales were poor even with success on the pitch and this free handout was the best that the club could do for the second round match; it included a moan about small crowds.

Wednesday 20 January 1982: FA Vase Third Round: Almondsbury Greenway home.

Today's Line Up

Forest Green Rovers V Chippenham Town	
All Green	All Blue
Dave Moss	1 K Nash
Brendan Guest	2 R Pratt
Peter Higgins	3 B Mortimer
Ken Hallam	4 I Monnery
John Turner	5 P Stevens
Mike Burns	6 C Moss
Steve Millard	7 R Radcliffe
Dave Dangerfield	8 M Ashe
Andy Leitch	9 M Glanville
Steve Doughty	10 C Meech
Kenny Norman	11 M Bohane
Nick Rock	12 G Learmouth

Referee   B March(Street)

Linesman(Red Flag) R Mc Milan(Worle)

Linesman(Yellow Flag)B Rollings (RAF Locking)

FOREST GREEN ROVERS

F.A. CHALLENGE VASE - 2ND ROUND

Forest Green Rovers v Chippenham Town at The Lawn

on Saturday 12 December Kick Off at 3 P.M.

-0-

-0-

Hopefully this FREE sheet will give you all the information you need for today's match. Unfortunately recent programme sales have been disappointing and therefore unprofitable to produce for each match.

Last Monday

Hopefully all of our supporters present today were at the game against First Division Stoke City. In a splendid display of football we were beaten by 4-0, including a penalty and an own goal.

The only disappointments of the evening were, firstly, the gate of only 1027. This was understandable in some way due to the lousy weather. However I feel that this is only a part excuse. There is plenty of cover at The Lawn and I cannot recall allowing rain to deter me from a game of football. Maybe football fans are a different breed today.

The one thing sure is we will not make a profit on the game having printed programmes for an anticipated crowd of 2000. Souvenir programmes, including two inserts, one a photograph of Stoke the other a leaflet all about The Potters is still available for only 25p from the office.

The second disappointment was the injury to Paul Maguire, the Scottish striker of Stoke City who had already scored twice. The first goal was a real 30 yard rocket past Forest Green guest keeper David Mogg.The second was a penalty which also caused the thigh injury to the Stoke lad.

Our physio, Peter Tennant, helped get Paul to Gloucester Hospital where he was detained for two days before being transferred to Shrewsbury Hospital. We wish Paul a speedy recovery and a quick return to the City team. Bob and I went laden with a basket of fruit to visit Paul and spent a very enjoyable hour, especially in the circumstances, talking soccer(what else ?).

Richie Barker took the whole thing philosophically and said it could have happened just as easily on the training ground.

Publicity

One thing is for sure the Paul Maguire incident got Forest Green a lot of publicity, including the national press. It was a shame that we got it for the wrong reason but all publicity is good.

Next week

THAME UNITED

We are again at home next week for something like the eighth consecutive week when we entertain Thame United, who finished third last season, in the Hellenic League.

GATES

I must confess to a real disappointment concerning the size of our gates this season. With a good side being placed at the top of the league we should be getting more not less than last season which is the case.

As I have already said we must now seriously consider whether to continue our talks with other First Division teams if we cannot attract more people. No one can accuse Rovers of not trying to please their followers but we ain't gettin' much back.

Another important side issue of Monday was the presence of Southern League Officials and many Directors of other clubs. To solidify our case for entry next season it would help to be able to show healthy attendance figures.

GREENLINER

Make sure you buy your GREENLINER tickets regularly and if you want a job, how about becoming a GREENLINER agent. Contact Frank Sims on Nailsworth 4860.

MIKE BURNS

The better chances fell to Almondsbury and more than once we sighed with relief, but then Andy scored with a good header in the seventy-sixth minute and we were convinced that we were on our way through to the next round. But then John Turner made a mess of a backpass and John Bond nipped in to equalise for Almondsbury.

We played out extra time switching from end to end and then, in the dying seconds, Doughts shot from the edge of the area and the ball rebounded from the upright. I had followed up the shot, convinced that it was going in, when it rebounded into my path, and with the keeper slow-moving, I managed to slot it past him. Maybe now this was going to be our lucky year.

Jimmy Jenkins, who had featured in the Bath City team played at the beginning of the year, joined the club in January.

F.A. CHALLENGE VASE – THIRD ROUND
ALMONDSBURY-GREENWAY
SATURDAY, 9 JANUARY 1982 K.O. 2pm

Saturday 30 January 1982: FA Vase Fourth Round: Odd Down home.

MIKE BURNS

Their manager, Paul Gover, a former Bath City colleague, had watched our game against Almondsbury and had obviously worked on tactics to stem our flow. We struggled throughout the game, although we eventually won 3-1 with goals from Andy, Doughts and a John Turner penalty.

Saturday 20 February 1982: FA Vase Fifth Round: Shortwood away.

MIKE BURNS

The draw against Shortwood was probably one of the worst we could have had. Local interest was high as Shortwood and Rovers have a very, very long history. I am sure that it affected our league performances because everyone seemed to be talking about the game at Shortwood, and it was in the lead up to this game that we hit patchy form in the league. Pat Casey certainly had enough time to prepare tactics and watched us in a number of games, during which we struggled.

There was a definite feeling within the locality that the winner of this tie could go all the way to Wembley and some locals were even saying it was a pity that the two teams had to meet at this stage.

During the second half, once again Steve Doughty scored a vital goal that was enough to send us through to the next round. Our fans were delighted at this result and it certainly gave them bragging rights. I think this result gave them as much pleasure as any other during the season.

FOREST GREEN ROVERS F.C.

F.A. CHALLENGE VASE – 4TH ROUND

FOREST GREEN ROVERS v ODD DOWN

Saturday, January 30th 1982 K.O. 3.00pm

Dave Moss	G	Richard Carey
Kenny Norman	2	Martin Schwartz
Peter Higgins	3	Richard Bell
Ken Hallam (Capt)	4	Roger Brown
John Turner	5	Adrian Broom
Dave Dangerfield	6	Steven Reynolds
Jimmy Jenkins	7	Donald Symonds
Mike Burns	8	Steven Lambert
Andy Leitch	9	David Hobbs (Capt)
Steve Doughty	10	Paul Cheesley
Steve Millard	11	Mark Bryan
Keith Hardcastle	12	Nigel Lee

COLOURS: Black and White Stripes, All Yellow
Black Shorts

REFEREE: M.Baldwin – Chippenham

LINESMEN: S.Cox – Devizes
J.Crowder – Melksham

Welcome to Odd Down, their players, officials and supporters. Apologies for lack of match programme but the four matches in eight days and 'normal' pressure of work have taken their toll.

Graham Day joined the club quite late on in February. He met Don Megson at Bristol Rovers and later he went to play for Portland Timbers in America. It was seven years that, in Graham's own words, money couldn't buy; he made a name for himself playing against such famous names as Pelé and Cruyff. Wherever Rovers played, the opposition were always in awe of someone who had played in such famous company. I'm not sure that the Hellenic League or Forest Green can boast of many players who modestly claimed that their most difficult opponent was Pelé.

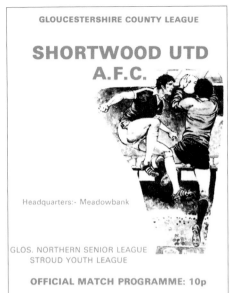

GLOUCESTERSHIRE COUNTY LEAGUE

SHORTWOOD UTD
A.F.C.

Headquarters:- Meadowbank

GLOS. NORTHERN SENIOR LEAGUE
STROUD YOUTH LEAGUE

OFFICIAL MATCH PROGRAMME: 10p

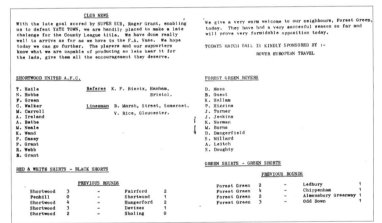

CLUB NEWS

With the late goal scored by SUPER SUB, Roger Grant, enabling us to defeat YATE TOWN, we are handily placed to make a late challenge for the County League title. We have done really well to arrive as far as we have in the F.A. Vase. We hope today we can go further. The players and our supporters know what we are capable of producing so lets hear it for the lads, give them all the encouragement they deserve.

We give a very warm welcome to our neighbours, Forest Green, today. They have had a very succesful season so far and will prove very formidable opposition today.

TODAYS MATCH BALL IS KINDLY SPONSORED BY :-
ROVER EUROPEAN TRAVEL

SHORTWOOD UNITED A.F.C.

T. Haile	Referee K. F. Biesix, Hanham,
N. Hobbs	Bristol.
P. Green	
C. Walker	Linesman B. Marsh, Street, Somerset.
M. Carroll	V. Rice, Gloucester.
A. Ireland	
A. Bathe	
M. Neale	
K. Wand	
P. Casey	
P. Grant	
R. Webb	
R. Grant	

FOREST GREEN ROVERS

D. Moss
B. Guest
K. Hallam
P. Higgins
J. Turner
J. Jenkins
K. Norman
M. Burns
D. Dangerfield
S. Millard
A. Leitch
S. Doughty

RED & WHITE SHIRTS - BLACK SHORTS

GREEN SHIRTS - GREEN SHORTS

PREVIOUS ROUNDS

Shortwood	3	-	Fairford	2
Penhill	0	-	Shortwood	1
Shortwood	4	-	Hungerford	2
Shortwood	3	-	Devizes	1
Shortwood	2	-	Sholing	0

PREVIOUS ROUNDS

Forest Green	2	-	Ledbury	1
Forest Green	4	-	Chippenham	1
Forest Green	2	-	Almonsbury Greenway	1
Forest Green	3	-	Odd Down	1

Top left: Shortwood v. Forest Green Rovers, 27 February 1982. The crowd look cold!!

Middle left: Shortwood v. Forest Green Rovers, 27 February 1982, Forest Green Rovers attack, with the Forest Green floodlights on top of the hill in the background.

Saturday 13 March 1982: FA Vase Quarter-Final: Willenhall Town away.

MIKE BURNS

We had a number of injuries in the run-up to this game and Bob was worried about that. He jumbled all our numbers up to confuse the opposition. I went on wearing number 3 and Andy Leitch number 6. On the morning of the match we were to train at the ground and then go by coach to Wolverhampton. John Turner had other ideas and missed a training session, and so Bob dropped him, which meant that David Dangerfield would play having been told that he was out of the side earlier that morning.

The crowd must have been well over 1,000. We got a free-kick and Brendan Guest slammed the ball against the crossbar and Doughts was on hand to bundle the ball over the line. One-nil up in the first minute – what a start! As the first half wore on, Willenhall threw everything against us and Dave Moss stopped everything that was coming at him.

During the second half Willenhall kept up constant pressure and only Dave Moss stopped them scoring three or four times. Gary Matthews eventually equalised and now Willenhall were very confident. I'm sure that Dave Moss kept us in the game in the second half and then we were into extra time.

Our confidence lifted for the first time since the opening few minutes and we started to match Willenhall; we both had chances to score but we were happy enough to play out the time and take them back to The Lawn for a replay. With 3 minutes to go a mix-up in the Willenhall defence let me in for our winner. To say that I was excited as I ran to the touchline was an understatement! We couldn't hide our excitement as we played out the remainder of the match to secure a very fine victory, and I had just scored the winning goal.

Willenhall couldn't believe it; the previous year they had lost unfortunately at Wembley and now, having controlled most of the game, they were once again on the losing side. Their misfortune was our luck and at the end of the game chants of 'Wemberley, Wemberley' were ringing out from our dressing-room.

JOHN EVANS, SUPPORTER

We took several coachloads of fans as well as those who went up by car. Upon arriving at the ground we were greeted by the police, who gave us a pre-match warning about our behaviour. Steve Doughty put us ahead in the first few minutes, a dream start! One of their fans turned to me and said 'Mere hiccup pal!' Willenhall then put us under tremendous pressure and if it wasn't for Dave Moss I think we would have been dead and buried. Their main striker was the then England non-league front man Gary Matthews and he levelled the score.

As extra time wore on we clearly looked the fitter side and, when Micky Burns came up with the goods in the dying seconds of the match, we were all ecstatic and a small pitch invasion followed. As we were escorted off the pitch I saw the fan who had bantered with me after the first goal. I said 'More than a mere hiccup now, eh!?' I remember we celebrated until the next day but I haven't got a clue where. We were just 2 games away from Wembley – unbelievable!

Saturday 3 April 1982: FA Vase Semi-Final first leg: Blue Star away.

MIKE BURNS

We travelled up on the Friday night and stayed in Newcastle and, on the way to the ground in the morning, my feeling of nervousness was the most I had ever experienced. We were now so near to Wembley and if we got a hiding it was all over. We would give everything we had, although we would be quite happy with a draw or even a 1-0 defeat.

In the dressing-room you could see that we were all nervous but you could also see a look of determination on everybody's face. Peter Tennant reduced the tension when, just as we were about to leave the dressing room, he commented 'Treat it just like any other semi-final for Wembley!'

After 15 minutes no goals was suiting us more than Blue Star, then the break we had been hoping for suddenly came. I played the ball to Andy Leitch out on the right touchline, and there appeared to be little danger as Andy set off towards the Blue Star defence. It looked as if Andy had lost the ball when, at the last moment, he poked it through the defender's legs and his centre carried over the keeper's head and somehow dropped in at the far post. Lucky? I don't think so; he had already scored 28 goals.

Blue Star really seemed confused when we let them have the ball in their own third of the pitch, but we were closing quickly in midfield and were very tight in defence. They were creating nothing and then a square backpass by their full-back was intercepted by Steve Doughty, who took the ball into the penalty box and picked his spot for 2-0.

Then Kenny Hallam, in his keenness, tripped the Blue Star winger when there was no apparent danger. There were no complaints from us and Dave Moss stood no chance with the penalty. 2-1 was good enough for us.

I walked out for the second half with Peter Higgins, whose first-half performance I thought was the best he had ever produced for Forest Green, and we knew that we were only 45 minutes away from a tremendous upset. Their manager was going ballistic and had a slanging match with their striker, who he then took off and then we could really sense that we could win the game.

Midway through the second half came what, to me, would be one of the highlights of my career. At this particular point we were quite happy to settle for a 2-1 win, which would have been a dream result twenty-four hours earlier. I received a pass from Steve Millard just inside our own half and I flicked it forward and I was away towards the Blue Star goal. As I approached the box Dave Ward tripped me. I stumbled but just managed to keep my balance enough to enable me to beat the goalkeeper with a firm shot into the corner of the net. As I lay on the ground, I couldn't stop myself beating the floor with my fists as I looked up towards our fans. The feeling of joy was one that I cannot relate accurately enough. I was literally shaking for about ten minutes.

It came as no surprise when a Steve Doughty header was handled on the line, and up stepped Peter Higgins to crash home a penalty for his first goal for Forest Green.

The whistle went and we had won 4-1, a result no one would have dared hoped for. It was a strange feeling in the dressing-room, elated and overjoyed but still not at Wembley. Tonight was to be our night and the joy was obviously shown on the faces of everybody and, above all, the supporters whose noise had been superb. I don't think the supporters could really believe it.

ADRIAN BROWN

Blue Star away – tell me about that. I remember walking out in our tracksuit tops for Forest Green. 'Who's Forest Green?' they shouted. I said, 'You'll soon find out.' The crowd was packed out. We won 4-1 but the goal I remember was in the second half. Micky Burns got the ball just by the halfway line and his little legs was going round and round like I don't know what, and he went all the way and smashed it home; I can remember turning round and saying, 'Who's Forest Green now then!?' They remembered me, walking back. Not nastily, you've got to take a bit of fun!

JOHN EVANS

The trip up for the semi-final first leg was, at the time, the furthest Forest Green had travelled for a match; it was an eight hour or so haul up to Blue Star in Newcastle. Geordies are legendary for their love of football and we were well up for it that day, especially having had so long for pre-match drinks on the coach. Little did we know that we were in for an absolute footballing treat. Most of their side was made up of players that won the vase the year before with Wycombe, so they were red-hot favourites.

Rovers played better that day than at any time I'd seen them play before, and I have yet to see a Rovers side play better. There was a lot of banter between the fans, some of it not so friendly, before and during the game. We totally outclassed them and ran out 4-1 winners. We weren't allowed into their clubhouse after the match and, although we'd been allowed drinks on the way up, someone decided that there was to be none on the return journey, which went down like a lead balloon. We eventually got back to Nailsworth in the wee small hours. The coach driver dropped us off at the Crown in Inchbrook, which the landlord had kept open for us, following a telephone call from the motorway service station. The party went on all day Sunday!

TIM BARNARD

I remember arriving back in Nailsworth from university in London on the Friday afternoon in my Triumph Herald and meeting everybody in the Crown for a boozy evening of anticipation. Rover coaches had apparently laid on a fleet to take everybody up to Newcastle and I had assumed that tickets would be available. In the end, there had been a cock up and there simply weren't enough coaches to carry all those wanting to go up to Newcastle. The news about the coaches didn't filter round until we were in the fish and chip shop after the pub, which left only one solution: drive up to Newcastle for the match.

So five of us set off early in the morning for the long drive up to Blue Star on the north side of the Tyne. Five people in a Triumph Herald gets very cosy after a few minutes, let alone a few hours. We arrived at the ground around 2.30 p.m. and I for one had a headache, probably a mixture of the hangover, the early start and the driving. It certainly wasn't planned to be like this.

We sat down in the club at Blue Star to get a breather for a few minutes and then it was out to a packed ground to join up with the lads, already out-singing the Blue Star supporters. It was an unbelievable experience. I think everybody expected that it would be a hard game and that we would be lucky to come away with a result but, by half-time, feelings were turning to the possibility of a trip to Wembley. Having had a headache before the game, and having almost lost my voice during the game, my head was throbbing when it got to five o'clock and the thought of the long drive home.

We got as far as Nottingham before the engine seized up. Checking the oil was the furthest thing from my mind. After a long wait into the early hours and time to relax for the first time that day, the AA finally arrived and we were chauffeur-driven back to Gloucestershire, truly elated and dreaming of Wembley. There was no way that we were going to lose by that many goals at home.

Opposite above, left: Forest Green Rovers' cheerleaders ready to spur Steve Doughty into action.

Saturday 10 April 1982: FA Vase Semi Final second leg: Blue Star home.

MIKE BURNS

It was Easter Saturday and the TV cameras were there. Bob dropped Steve Doughty and brought back John Turner. Steve had scored in each of the 4 previous games and I think we didn't attack as perhaps we should have done. We played well, Peter Higgins went close with a free-kick and Andy had one effort just wide of the post. Blue Star gradually got on top and, after a defensive mix-up, we let them in for a goal, which they desperately needed. We were now very much under pressure and their striker, who had been substituted the previous game, slammed a shot from thirty-five yards against our crossbar. Had that gone in we could well have been really in trouble.

All in all, our first-half performance had been very poor but, in the second half, we created three good chances, two of which fell to Jimmy Jenkins and one to Steve Millard. All in all we played much better. As the minutes ticked by I knew then that we wouldn't lose and, as the final whistle neared, the crowd started to chant 'Wemberley'.

Rovers Impulse, Forest Green's own cheer leaders who hope to be in action at Wembley before Saturday's FA Vase game.

JOHN EVANS

Blue Star still brought quite a few fans down to The Lawn for the second leg and were worthy 1-0 winners at our place. A few of them even stayed the night to celebrate with us. I've always had respect for any Geordie football fans since that day. So the dream was to become a reality; mighty Forest Green Rovers were going to play at Wembley Stadium in the FA Vase final.

ROB COOK

My earliest memories of watching Forest Green – to tell you the truth, it was 50p to get in at half-time but you could get through the fence at the back path near the school when nobody was looking. I remember the Blue Star game because the roads were absolutely packed, and it was the biggest crowd that I'd ever seen. I watched Steve Doughty playing that game and had seen him play that season and thought, 'That's who I want to be, playing for Forest Green when I'm older.'

The crowd queue to get in for the big game.

Blue Star, home. Andy Leitch thinks the ball has crossed the line.

Blue Star, home. Steve Millard on the ball as spectators look on from the windows.

Saturday 8 May 1982: FA Vase Final at Wembley: Rainworth Miners Welfare.

ANDY LEITCH

The big day had finally arrived. It was nine months since we beat Worrall Hill in the first preliminary round, and now we were off to play the biggest game of our lives at Wembley.

After a quiet night in our Maidenhead hotel, I think a couple of us had a relaxing drink. I was up quite early for a hearty breakfast. I knew I'd have to eat well early, as I would be too nervous to eat later on. After breakfast we had a team meeting and went through all that was wanted of us and all our tactics for the day ahead. We then went to Maidenhead's ground for a warm up and to go through the set pieces, nothing too strenuous, and then back to the hotel for a light lunch.

We were soon in the coach, dressed up to the nines in our jackets and trousers. We drove straight up the tunnel and went into our dressing room, the north one, where England had been when they beat West Germany in 1966. We thought this a lucky omen. We had had a trip around the day before so the sightseeing was over and this was the business side of the trip. We were there to win.

We got changed and warmed up and soon we were summoned to the players' tunnel. Rainworth were already there and looking at them gave us a psychological advantage, as they looked very nervous. We burst into song, with a chorus of, 'WEMBERLY, WEMBERLY, WE ARE THE FAMOUS FOREST GREEN ROVERS AND WE'RE PLAYING AT WEMBERLY!'

We then walked from the tunnel on to the pitch, from the silence to the roar, shook hands with all the dignitaries, and here we go. When we beat Blue Star in the semis a few of their players told us to enjoy the day as it went so quickly. They were certainly right. We won the toss and chose to kick off. Bob had wanted us to keep the ball for as long as possible, a good ploy till John Turner lost the ball on the edge of the area, but it was scrambled away safely.

The first half was flashing by. We had looked dangerous without creating much, when one of the set pieces we had been practising all morning, without success, came into operation. Brendan swung the ball out to Steve Millard wide on the left wing, he went past his marker, cut and squared the ball into the box. It was a perfect ball into my path just outside the six-yard box. Without thinking I sidefooted the ball into the net. One-nil up, and my name up in lights on the Wembley scoreboard. I was in seventh heaven. What could be better?

The half was coming to a close when I was hacked down by a defender, who was booked. I was alright but I stayed down 'injured' to make sure Adie Brown would get on to the Wembley pitch.

After half-time we were in control, but needed another goal. Rainworth put us under a bit of pressure, and after they had had a few half-chances we were looking a bit unsteady to say the least. Next came a moment I'll never forget. Mickey Burns intercepted a pass and tried to thread a pass through to me. There were two Rainworth players in front of me and they looked odds on to win the ball but, for some unknown reason, or instinct, I had the feeling that they were going to miss the ball, so I ran where I thought the ball might go. The two defenders both went for and missed the ball, and it was a race between me and the keeper. My long legs have been good to me throughout my career and once more they won the day for me, as I toe-poked the ball past the advancing keeper into the corner of the net for 2-0 and game over.

Rainworth were finished and I and a couple of others missed chances before Kenny Norman ran down the line with about 5 minutes to go. He turned a deaf ear to our pleas for a centre and chipped the ball superbly over the keeper for one of the finest goals ever seen at Wembley. And I'm not just saying that. The game finished 3-0. I looked up at the scoreboard and saw my name in lights for 2 goals, one each end, a phrase I was to use many times in my stories of Wembley over the next few years.

The final whistle blew, and before we knew it we were up the steps to pick up the FA Vase and our medals. We had our photographs taken here there and everywhere, talked to the TV reporters, then took the FA Vase to show our fans. Boy, did we enjoy every moment.

Top: Steve Doughty, Steve Millard, Peter Higgins celebrate with Andy Leitch after his first goal.

Centre: The largest crowd ever to watch Rovers at the time enjoyed their Wembley away day.

Bottom: Dave Moss clears under pressure.

Left: Goalscorers Andy Leitch and Kenny Norman with the Vase.

MIKE BURNS

Time was flying by and I remember so many people saying 'Make the most of it, it will fly by.' I have some wonderful memories of that day but, after we went 2-0 up, what happened next is something that will live long in Kenny Norman's mind. Ken made a wonderful run down the touchline and showed great composure, then chipped the keeper with a shot from something like thirty yards. What a moment for him. He was skipper for the day and, although not the scorer of many goals, he had scored as good a goal as you would ever see at Wembley. I remember looking up and seeing a banner that read 'Kenny Norman eats three Shredded Wheat.' It was definitely all over now at 3-0.

The referee blew his whistle and my first reaction was to hug Steve Millard, who was the nearest player to me. Can you imagine that two months before Steve was on a heart machine and at one time it seemed as if he may never play football again? Yet there we were, two months on, ready to go up the steps and collect our winners' medals. I must confess to having a few tears in my eyes as I came down the steps. Years of memories flashed through my mind and I wondered why football has been so good to me.

The Vase in Rovers' hands. Back row: Graham Day, Brendan Guest, Andy Leitch, Kenny Norman, Dave Moss, Steve Millard, John Dangerfield, John Turner. Front row: Jimmy Jenkins, Steve Doughty, Bob Mursell, Peter Higgins, Keith Hardcastle, Micky Burns.

Forest Green's trip to Wembley warranted special trains direct from Stroud to Wembley for the day.

JOHN EVANS

The build-up to the final in the local news and press was fantastic for the club. Suddenly we had new fans coming to The Lawn to find out about the local heroes. What I also remember is that a few days before the game souvenir sellers from London were in Nailsworth selling flags and scarves. For us Rovers fans it was incredible that something like this could happen in the town. Nailsworth suddenly had a buzz to it.

On the eve of the game I remember buying a big cigar and a bottle of champagne to take with me to the final. Losing just wasn't an option. We never entertained the idea – the players were in top form in the league and practically unbeatable. The morning after the night before started with hair of the dog and we met up at The Lawn to get on the coaches. Our coach was full of singers and shouters so the atmosphere on board was great and the drink started to flow. I had made arrangements to meet in the Greyhound pub outside Wembley Stadium and when we drove past we noted the place was full of their supporters inside and out. We got off the coach and walked back to the pub to meet Tim Barnard. Within minutes of us getting there, fighting broke out. I didn't even get a pint. I hasten to add that we didn't start it. Some of their borrowed fans started throwing glasses and pool balls and all hell let loose. I can remember dragging my then girlfriend out of the fracas and starting to walk back towards the stadium. There were several other minor skirmishes outside the ground and I couldn't even get a programme for the game due to the trouble.

Once inside the ground it was singing and shouting time. It was a great feeling being there. It was incredible to be there with Forest Green, the pride of Gloucestershire! We were simply too good to them. Straight after we'd scored, trouble started among their fans, the police got involved and several people from both sides got ejected from the ground, only to appear again a few minutes later. The process repeated itself after the second goal. The third and decisive goal was a cracker, worthy of being scored at Wembley. Kenny Norman lobbed their keeper from way out and we went absolutely berserk. I can't put into words how I felt when I lifted the FA Vase. There are some moments that you can't really do justice to when you describe them. This was one of them.

Ian Ridley—Forest Green 3, Rainworth MW 0

The violent vase

The sun shone and there was a spring in the step as we walked down Olympic Way, for once not ankle deep in discarded hamburgers. An unchanged stroll around the ground as a record player blurted out Rainworth's Road to Wembley by Carlo Santana (not that one) added to the sense of well-being. It was not to last.

The FA Vase final, an event that should be a celebration of achievement for the smallest of the smaller clubs, became confirmation that for many, soccer, at whatever level, is an excuse for drunken, loutish behaviour.

There were 26 arrests outside the ground, 18 attached to Rainworth Miners' Welfare and eight to Forest Green Rovers. In a crowd of 12,500, a disappointment to all, that represents a disturbing ratio. The surprise was that there were no arrests inside the ground where the unpleasantness detracted from the touching scenes before and after the game of the players and managers, like little boys let loose in a sweet shop.

The Metropolitan Police must have been in tolerant mood for all as well as having to break up scuffles caused when Rainworth followers infiltrated Forest Green

ranks, they were kept busy removing the bench seats broken up by both factions.

Rainworth, of the Nottinghamshire Football Alliance, were billed as the real amateurs of the final. Not so many of their followers who seemed to be disillusioned Mansfield Town supporters with a nice line in professional bigotry. True, their team were defeated, but they gave a game display against better organised opponents, who move up into the Southern League next season. Three bookings — for Rainworth's Slater and Forest Green's Guest and Millard — for over-exuberant tackles could scarcely have fuelled their bad behaviour.

Rainworth, for whom Radzki was a skilful leader, imaginatively used a sweeper and then threw seven forward when attacking. It was undermined, however, by a naive offside trap, which was beaten easily by Leitch in the 24th and 63rd minutes and Norman, the captain, in the 71st with a goal worthy of any cup final; a clever chip after he had burst through from his right back position.

Forest Green Rovers: Moss; Norman, Higgins (Dangerfield, 80min), Day, Turner, Burns, Guest, Doughty, Leitch, Millard, Jones.

Rainworth Miners' Welfare: Watson; Hallam, Hodgson, Slater, Stirland, Oliver, Knowles (Robinson, 72min), Raine, Radzki, Bean, Comerford.

Referee: K. Walmsley (Blackpool).

A heroes' welcome

Rovers returned to a heroes welcome from supporters at a special reception held at the Hare and Hounds at Westonbirt.

At the reception, organised by the XI Forest Green Supporters' Club, the Mayor of Nailsworth, Mr. Francis Arkell, paid tribute to the skill and application of the players and manager.

"You have all done Nailsworth proud," he said.

'FANTASTIC' SAY THE FOREST SUPPORTERS

Forest Green supporters were unanimous in agreeing that the Club's stunning 3-0 victory was well-deserved in every way.

Former Sharpness manager, Ernie Calder, now living in Wickwar, made the trip and said Rovers' positive approach was a vital factor in their success.

"They never looked in trouble. Rovers should have been 2-0 up in the first fifteen minutes, but they paced themselves well and deserved to win" he said.

"Rovers were the more professional side and had the right approach on the day. They came here to win and that's what it is all about."

Mr. Calder said the win was a great boost for local football and should benefit the Stroud League in particular, with more youngsters eager to play competitive football.

"Forest Green have got a hardworking committee and are well organised on and off the field. Success breeds success" he added.

Nailsworth newsagent Mr. John Rowley travelled to Wembley with his two sons Marc and Steven and all agreed they had enjoyed a fantastic day.

"Forest Green were by far the betterside", said Mr. Rowley "Andy Leitch took both of his goals well and what a great score by Kenny

Norman. We've had a great day".

Tony Elliot who works with Micky Burns, Jimmy Jenkins and Peter Higgins at Wick said "i am very pleased for the three of them. It was a great team effort. Rovers showed the better touches and deserved to win" he said.

The Millard family were out in strength to follow the fortunes of Rovers' forward Steve. Brother-in-law Nigel Byatt of Downend, Bristol said Rovers' victory was convincing, and Steve's father Nick of Longwell Green showed no bias when he said goalkeeper David Moss and defender Graham Day were outstanding for Rovers.

"But it was our Steve who laid on the pass for the first goal" he said.

Before the match Badminton Picksons skipper John Burns predicted a 3-0 win for Rovers and after the game he said the performance of his elder brother Mike had almost brought tears to his eyes.

"This is one of the proudest days of my life. I thought Rovers did themselves proud. it is a great achievement for thei clubs in the Hellenic league and proves it can be done. We are in the Vase next year and I would like to think we could follow Forest Green's achievement" said Mr. Burns,

---

Will he stay with Rovers?

With the FA Vase now safely locked away in the Forest Green boardroom the focus of attention will once again be Rovers' manager Bob Mursell.

Mursell, manager at The Lawn for the past 18 months, shocked the club two weeks ago by announcing that he may quit at the end of the season.

Mursell claimed that the pressure of business commitments could force him out of the game.

He was also linked with Bath City but Forest Green deny they have been officially approached by any club with regard to Mursell's availability.

Rovers are naturally anxious for Mursell to stay with the club. He has masterminded the spectacular rise which has taken the Nailsworth side to the FA Vase and the Southern League within a year and a half.

As one club official admitted on Saturday night: "Bob Mursell is this club's most valuable asset. All our success is due to him." There were rumours that Mursell would be signing a new two year contract after Saturday's final but that failed to materialise. However, a decision on his future is expected sometime this week.

Above: The Rainworth infiltrators that Ian Ridley refers to were followers of nearby Nottingham Forest out to cause trouble on the day.

Above right: A video was made of the match for sale but a copy has not been located.

Below right: The whole team attended a reception at Nailsworth town hall with the Vase, pictured with the mayor, 'Bunny' Arkle and manager Bob Mursell in the front.

The season was to be remembered for the club's fantastic run in the FA Vase, but at the same time the league title was secured and Southern League football confirmed for the following year.

Wednesday 12 May, Kidlington away.

MIKE BURNS

We made a number of changes that day but we still won 2-0, with goals from Brendan Guest and Andy Leitch. We were always doing enough to win but most of the decisions against the home side were met with cries of, 'No wonder they got to Wembley'.

Saturday 15 May, Abingdon Town home.

MIKE BURNS

The last day of the season came and it was also to be my last game. I had decided to retire. We had a good crowd to see the League Shield presented and many photographs were taken of us with the Shield and the FA Vase. The game was not a classic but we won 2-0 with a Doughts double, and it was good to end the season with a win.

At the end of the season, Nuneaton Borough won the Southern League Midland Division with Kidderminster Harriers in third position, Gloucester City in fifth and Cheltenham Town in a lowly sixteenth place.

Forest Green's season was summed up by secretary Graham Collins at the AGM:

I have pleasure in submitting my annual report for the 1981/82 season. This season must go down as the most momentous and important season in the club's long history. The main features of this historic season were winning the Premier Division Championship of the Hellenic League, winning the FA Challenge Vase at Wembley Stadium, being elected to the Southern League, the official switching on of the floodlights at The Lawn, the appointment of a full-time commercial manager.

Forest Green Rovers double winning side. Back row: Peter Pearch, Brian Hobbs, Roy Hillman, John Turner, Andy Leitch, Dave Moss, John Duff, Graham Day, Brendan Guest, Steve Doughty, Peter Tennant, Bob Mursell, Mike Lewis. Front row: Jimmy Jenkins, David Dangerfield, Kenny Norman, Keith Hardcastle, Mike Burns, Peter Higgins, Adrian Brown.

Above left: Forest Green Rovers reserves 1981/82. Back row: Andy Painter, Charlie Jones, Rob Clark, Rob Bruton, Malcom King, Sean Little, Richard Pearch, Mark Brazneill, Andy Brazneill, Alan Dodd. Front row: Ollie Sandell, Dave Norris, John Dangerfield, Andy Bish, Nick Rock, Kevin Hollywell, Dave Tilley. Keith Hardcastle, Rob Emmerson. Andy Bish was player-manager.

Above right: Following on from the Vase win, the club entered a float in the Stroud Show that summer. You can just hear the theme tune to *Match of the Day*!

19

Another Step Forward in the Southern League: 1982–1988

1982/83

Forest Green Rovers entered the Southern League for the first time in its history. They played friendlies to match those of the previous year, beating Bath City 3-0, Swindon Town 3-0 and losing to Yeovil Town 2-1, Cardiff City 1-0 and Birmingham City 2-1.

ANDY WHITING

We kicked off in the Southern League with around 350 spectators watching and ended up losing 2-0 to Bridgend Town. There was plenty of excitement awaiting us, with Southern League football against the likes of Cheltenham Town, Gloucester City and Bromsgrove.

Following our first home defeat, I remember we played Dudley Town and won 1-0, with the goal scored by former Bristol City stalwart Gerry Sweeney, who had joined Rovers over the summer. We played Cheltenham Town at home that year and a 700 crowd watched us win 5-3 with goals from Martin Wheeler (2), Andy Leitch (2) and Steve Doughty. We really felt the big-time football had now arrived.

We were great that year and we went on a 5-match winning streak, which didn't end until mid-October with a 2-0 defeat at Aylesbury United. We were top of the league most of the season but rumours were rife at the time that the club did not want Premier Division football so soon after the step up from the Hellenic League and everything began to fall away for the last few games.

We went over to Cheltenham on Bank Holiday Monday in early May and crammed into Whaddon Road to watch what was going to be the promotion decider. There was a huge contingent of Rovers fans who had travelled over, but we ended up disappointed, losing 3-0 on the day.

The team that faced Birmingham City at the beginning of the 1982/83 season. Back row: Dave Rogers, Dave Moss, Steve Doughty, Andy Leitch, Graham Day, Peter Higgins. Front row: Martin Wheeler, Kenny Norman, Bobby Brown, Gerry Sweeney, David Dangerfield.

ANDY BISH

I finished the year after the Vase and, looking back on my ten years at Forest Green, I can honestly say that I'm very proud to have been a Forest Green player. I had a happy and memorable time playing in the best stadium in the area, on the best playing surface bar none and with some of the best supporters and committee members you could ever wish to meet.

JOHN DUFF

Bob Mursell was always making noises about wanting to leave, and I must have met him four times to persuade him to stay. He was a bit flighty, Bob, and after about four occasions with me trying to tell him that this was his scene, it was getting a little bit that I'd had enough. He phoned me and he said 'John, I've had an offer to go to another club, a professional club,' and I said to him then 'Bob, I think you'd better go.'

His assistant, Roy Hillman, took over and did an excellent job. We were in our first year in the Midland Division and headed it. We looked like winning it and, unfortunately, we didn't have the confidence in Roy to be hard enough to be a successful manager and we thought therefore we ought to prepare for the next year, when we were going to be promoted to the Premier Division. So I asked Roy to step down, which, with hindsight, was quite a mistake. We appointed Steve Millard and Micky Burns and failed to make it to the Premier Division, beaten by Cheltenham and Sutton Coldfield to the promotion spots and the rest is history. Well, it may not have been, if we had stuck with Roy.

SOUTHERN LEAGUE MIDLAND DIVISION

GREENLINER

OFFICIAL MATCHDAY MAGAZINE OF FOREST GREEN ROVERS F

SOUTHERN LEAGUE CUP – SECOND ROUND REPLAY

A. P. LEAMINGTON   25p

TUESDAY 12 OCTOBER 1982 KICK OFF 7.30 PM

Forest Green played against Cheltenham Town for a League game for the first time since the 1930s and entered the FA Vase in the second round, and the run started to take on the feel of the previous year, beating Avon Bradford 2-1, Wadebridge Town after a replay 5-1, Shortwood 2-0 in January, and then AFC Totton 1-0, all under the guidance of Roy Hillman. The winning streak came to an end, both in the league and in the cup after the appointment of Steve Millard. Forest Green fell at Burnham in the quarter-final of the FA Vase, losing the game 4-0.

Above left: Roy Hillman, manager after Bob Mursell left, at the Shortwood game in the FA Vase fourth round.

Above right: Action in the middle against Shortwood in the FA Vase, a repeat of the previous year's meeting, this time one round earlier.

Right: Forest Green Rovers v. Totton in the FA Vase fifth round, February 1983. Forest Green playing in green shirts sponsored by Coffer Sports.

STEVE DOUGHTY

I remember the Cheltenham game on the Easter Monday, I think it was, and we were challenging for the championship. We lost 2-0 in front of about 2,500 fans. It was a really big game, certainly the biggest crowd I played in front of for a league game. Steve Millard used to be very vocal in the changing rooms with his team talks, very committed. He wound us up for the Cheltenham game but, on the day, Cheltenham were the better side and you can't argue with that. We gave it everything but on the day they were better than us. They deserved to go up.

ADRIAN BROWN

After the FA Vase year, we had a team that virtually picked itself. Graham Day, and we had Bristol City players, Gerry Sweeney for one. He was a real good professional, and he gave it his all.

   One of the biggest disappointments for me was Dave Rogers, a great big tall man. I can remember his first game for Rovers; he went down and on I went. He had a mark on his foot and wanted to come off. 'I want the club doctor,' he said. I said 'You're not at Bristol City now son.' Anyway we subbed him. Now John Turner would have looked and laughed at you, but when I seen that I thought, 'We watched you on the television last year playing in what was the First Division for Bristol City.'

   That was one thing that went wrong under Steve Millard. Some of them was just along for the ride, and I don't say it was Stevie's fault. He was trying to get good players in. When you think of the class of player we had from the First Division, that was the Premiership then, wasn't it?

JOHN EVANS

I remember drinking and chatting in the bar with Graham Day and Gerry Sweeney, who were having a go at each other about being City or Rovers, as was the norm for those two. Graham turned to me, knowing that my loyalties lie with the Rovers. He said jokingly 'Do you know what John, there are two things that I hated as a kid: jocks and Bristol City and the b—s both!' We laughed for ages. I had several heated discussions in the club towards the end of the season and even came to blows with the late Steve Millard on one occasion, after accusing him of deliberately throwing games.

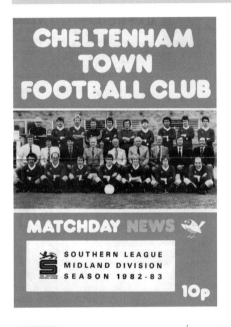

ALAN WOOD

NEWSDESK

TEAM CHECK

Opposition in Focus

Duncan Berry (No.7) lashes his shot through a crowd of players to give the Robins a 1-0 lead against Aylesbury.

Appearances & Goalscorers

```
:·—————————————Lawn Line Up═════════


   Forest Green Rovers      Bromsgrove Rovers

    Black & White Striped Shorts      Red Shirts
    Black Shorts.                     White Shorts.


     Dave MOSS             1      Steve POMROY
     Kenny NORMAN          2      Danny McCORMACK
     Peter HIGGINS         3      Jeff RUMJAHN
     John TURNER           4      Benny BROWN
     Dave RODGERS          5      Dave FRANCIS
     Bobby BROWN           6      Andy REECE
     Phil PURNELL          7      Andy WILLIAMS
     Jeff MEACHAM          8      Bill BENNETT
     Andy LEITCH           9      Mark STANTON
     Steve DOUGHTY        10      Brendon DRUMMOND
     Dave DANGERFIELD     11      Andy ALLEN
     Dave WILTSHIRE       12      Ian JEFFS.



     Today's Officials
     Referee     :   Mr. C. Peake. (Gloucester)
     Linesmen    :   Mr. V. Vines (Chippenham) Red Flag.
                     Mr. M. Price (Cirencester) Yellow Flag.


    DM Graphics, Brombecombe 862979
```

Another visitor to The Lawn in the first Southern League season was the referee Mr C. Peake, later to become heavily involved with the club.

Graham Collins summarised the season as follows at the AGM in June:

Last season must be recorded as a successful season. Obviously, it was a big disappointment to all of us that we only finished third, thereby missing out on promotion by one place, after having been in top position for almost all of the season. Indeed, it was only in the very last week of the season that we lost our place in the top two positions in the league table.

We reached the quarter finals of both the FA Vase and the GFA Trophy. The 4-0 defeat at Burnham in the quarter-final of the FA Vase was particularly disappointing. The club participated in the Western Counties Floodlight League for the first time.

Forest Green Rovers finished third, behind Sutton Coldfield Town and Cheltenham Town. Gloucester City, meanwhile, finished in mid-table in the Premier Division.

1983/84

JOHN DUFF

By the summer of 1983, it was felt that the financial responsibilities of the club and the vulnerability of the trustees who were responsible for it were getting too great, and we therefore ought to form a limited company limited by guarantee. This project was really pushed through by Brian Hobbs who was the then secretary, having come from Gloucester City. A hundred maximum members, our liability was five or ten pounds – I can't remember now.

Dave Moss and John Turner stayed with the club, as did Kenny Norman, who had been voted Player of the Year the season before. Only four of the FA Vase-winning side remained in the first team. Brian McNeill, another ex-Portland Timbers and Bristol City player, joined the club in February. The playing kit also changed from ultra-wide black-and-white stripes to white shirts with black pinstripes and black shorts.

STEVE DOUGHTY

I really enjoyed playing against my heroes in the Aston Villa team up at Forest Green, and I scored with an overhead kick to win 4-3 in a pre-season friendly. And being a Villa fan I also enjoyed the pre-season from the year before, scoring against Tony Coton for Forest Green against Birmingham City in another friendly.

Following on from the cheerleaders the season before, Kenny Norman and the squad trained over the close season, trying out a new aerobics regime.

Forest Green entertained Aston Villa in August 1983, losing 4-3, having drawn 2-2 against a first team from Cardiff City the week before.

Forest Green Rovers 1983/84 pictured before the Redditch game in February 1984. Earlier in the season a deal had been done with Valley Ford, the first big money (relatively speaking) sponsors of Forest Green sporting their new pinstripe shirts. Back row: Steve Millard, Nigel Ryan, Mike Malpass, Jeff Meacham, Dave Moss, John Turner, unknown, Kenny Gill, Adrian Brown. Front row: Jamie Salt, Pete Fryer, Bobby Brown, David Dangerfield, Kenny Norman.

Left: Redditch clear off the line during a league tussle in February 1984.

Opposite: Forest Green Rovers 1984/85. Back row: Gary Mockridge, John Turner, Dave Bruton, Mike Bruton, unknown, Mike Malpass, Jeff Meacham, Kenny Gill, Adrian Brown. Front row: Mike England, John Evans, Bobby Brown, Steve Milllard, Kenny Norman, Jamie Salt, unknown.

STEVE DOUGHTY

I think of the season after the Cheltenham game, and a lot of the players were getting that much older. The side drifted a little bit and we started to bring new players in and it wasn't the same. Those two or three years after the FA Vase we were on a good understanding and then a few left, and new players came in. It didn't quite gel like it had before, it wasn't there. We did okay – we had some good players, but it wasn't the same buzz.

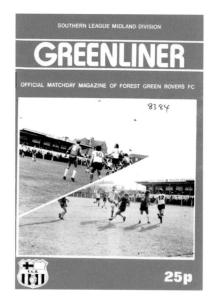

SOUTHERN LEAGUE MIDLAND DIVISION

GREENLINER

OFFICIAL MATCHDAY MAGAZINE OF FOREST GREEN ROVERS FC

83 84

25p

The season did not quite live up to the highs of the previous two seasons and Forest Green Rovers finished up in a mid-table, eleventh place. The club entered the FA Trophy for the first time, losing to Weston-super-Mare 1-0 after a replay, following a 2-2 draw away in the first preliminary round. Rovers lost to Witney Town, again after a 2-2 draw, having previously beaten Wimborne Town in the FA Cup preliminary round. Gloucester City and Cheltenham Town were both now in the Premier Division, finishing ninth and eighth respectively.

1984/85

Dave Moss, Kenny Norman and John Turner, along with Steve Doughty, were still in the squad from the FA Vase year; John Evans returned to the club having rejoined from Cheltenham Town. Another player from the early Hellenic League days, Mike Bruton, also rejoined Rovers as a striker to play alongside his brother Dave, who had also joined Forest Green from Gloucester City in the summer. Bobby Brown, Kenny Gill and captain Mike Malpass all stayed on from the previous season.

Steve Doughty was top scorer for the season, during which Shaun Penny and Mark Rymall also joined. Rovers slipped to fourteenth of eighteen teams, finishing one place below Rushden Town, while Cheltenham Town won the Premier Division to move into the Alliance League and to play football on a national basis for the first time. Gloucester City finished third from bottom in the Premier Division and were relegated. FGR and City would compete in the same league for the first time since the 1930s.

The glossy programme had been replaced with a cheaper version.

ANDY WHITING

Year after year, we would finish in the bottom half of the table, and I think that the big game that used to stand out was the fixture against Newport. I don't think we ever beat them at home, but we used to do well against them at Somerton Park before it was demolished. They used to play in the league and in European games and just to play them always felt like a big game.

Above left: In July 1984 the Greenliner lottery was still going strong, with winners regularly picked and a steady income for the club to continue along its upward path.

Above right: Forest Green Rovers *v.* Moor Green, February 1985. Forest Green playing in their new pin stipe kit.

1985/86

The newly extended social club was ready for business and was officially opened on 31 August to members only. The season opened with a 3-2 win over Merthyr Tydfil with goals from Kenny Gill, Shaun Penny and Chris Townsend. Mike England left the club for Bristol Rovers and Gary Emmanuel to Bristol City. Dave Moss, Kenny Norman and Jeff Meacham all moved on as well

Forest Green were finding it difficult to hold on to players and the next to leave was Kenny Gill, who was sold to Newport County. The decision was not popular, as revealed by the minutes of 14 October 1985.

> *W. Riley stated that he considered it a retrograde step to sell Kenny Gill to Newport County. The chairman stated that a rushed decision was required and it was regretted that not all members of the board could be contacted to express their opinion. Every effort would be made for any future sales to be placed before the whole board before a decision was reached.*

JOHN DUFF

I remember Kenny Gill going to Newport County for £2,000, and they couldn't afford to pay us until they'd played an FA Cup match away at Newcastle. It took so long to get paid that the next occasion they came for someone, Mike Malpass our centre half, I said no, so no deal was done on that one. We didn't really transfer any other players. In fact we were in the habit of recruiting, but usually recruiting players who were past it for league football but were certainly good enough to get us to go where we were looking to go.

Forest Green Rovers v. Coventry Sporting, November 1985. Forest Green go ahead.

STEVE DOUGHTY

The Gloucester City games on Boxing Day were always big games. They were the highlight of the season each year, home and away. They were very physical, always a big crowd home and away. There is a lot of fierce rivalry, quite friendly off the pitch but for 90 minutes it was all blood and guts, no quarter asked and no quarter given. Playing in front of a big crowd like that at Forest Green or Gloucester always helped us to lift our game, especially when the supporters got behind us, and especially in the local derbies.

Shaun Penny was top scorer at the end of the season, closely followed by Steve Doughty, but again the overall performance had not been impressive. Forest Green finished fourteenth, in the same position as the previous year, but this time in a league of twenty-one teams with Gloucester City in ninth place.

Forest Green Rovers 1986/87. Back row: John Relish, unknown, Clint Gobey, Mike Malpass, Steve Doughty, unknown, unknown, Richard Crowley, Kenny Gill, Steve Millard. Front row: Simon King, Ian Doyle, Shaun Penny, Steve Strong, Nigel Gillard, Graham Day.

1986/87

John Relish joined at the beginning of the season to strengthen the team, which also included Graham Day, returning to Forest Green following his FA Vase triumph in 1982. Steve Smith continued in goal. Towards the end of the season, John Eastment joined the club from Merthyr Tydfil. He became a driving force behind the idea of an image change for Forest Green Rovers. Bristol Rovers played their Combination matches at The Lawn this season, bringing Forest Green many compliments regarding the playing surface and facilities at the ground. Many future stars of the Premier League passed through The Lawn during this period as Bristol Rovers entertained First Division reserve teams.

ANDY WHITING

Bristol Rovers Reserves played at Forest Green for three seasons and during those years a host of well-known stars graced The Lawn: Glenn Hoddle, Paul Ince, Charlie Nicholas, Paul Merson, Niall Quinn, Perry Groves ... the list is endless.

The crowds were among the best in the Football Combination with well over 1,000 there for the visits of Tottenham and Arsenal. It was a great experience for all of us. My own top eleven who played at The Lawn includes Ossie Ardiles, Lou Macari, Glenn Hoddle, Paul Ince, Gerry Francis, Nigel Martyn, Graeme Le Saux, Matt Le Tissier, Joey Jones and Charlie Nicholas. What a line-up, even though it lacks defenders.

Tottenham arrived the second season with no kit and ended up wearing the white shirts of Forest Green Rovers. Tony Parkes, who had earlier played in a European final and made a penalty save, played both games, along with Tony Galvin, Paul Moran, Neil Ruddock, John Chidozie and Chris Hughton.

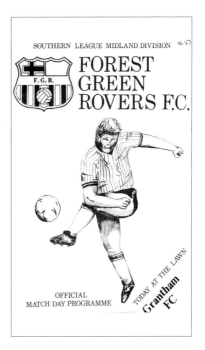

SOUTHERN LEAGUE MIDLAND DIVISION

FOREST GREEN ROVERS F.C.

F.G.R.

OFFICIAL MATCH DAY PROGRAMME

TODAY AT THE LAWN
Grantham FC

On the pitch, the season proved to be reasonably successful, with home and away wins against Gloucester City, Rushden Town and Bilston Town. Off the pitch, the minutes of the AGM in July 1987 record that the club was in debt for the first time in its history to the tune of £1,600 for the year ended. The frugal committee were not around to keep a stranglehold on spending. Southern League football required a much higher level of income, which had been comfortably achieved with the Greenliner Lottery, but that was now losing its appeal and the club's income was being severely hit.

Forest Green finished slightly better this year in ninth place, two places below Gloucester City, with Shaun Penny, Steve Doughty and John Relish top scorers of the season.

1987/88

Steve Millard was in charge in August for his sixth season at The Lawn and Forest Green's sixth season in the Southern League, but he moved to Gloucester City later in the season with a derby game against Gloucester a few weeks away.

Forest Green Rovers v. Bath City, in a friendly at the beginning of the 1986/87 season, with the extended social club in the background; it had opened the season before, paid for by the lottery.

Forest Green Rovers 1987/88. Back row: Steve Millard, Greg Steele, Steve Westerburg, Richard Bryant, John Macey, Steve Doughty, Mike Malpass, Steve Scarrot, Mark Rymal, Steve Tregale. Front row: Shaun Penny, Phil Bater, Peter Hayes, John Relish, Steve Summers, Martin Williams, Graham Rogers, Craig Morgan (mascot).

STEVE DOUGHTY

Steve Millard left Forest Green under something of a cloud soon after the start of the season, because he went to Gloucester City and he took Mike Malpass and a couple of other players and left us managerless. So Shaun Penny and me were made temporary player-managers and one of my first games in charge was Gloucester City away. I think we lost 4-0. It was literally one Friday night I was told what happened and I was sitting there making phone calls trying to raise a team until 11 p.m. because we just didn't have a team.

The season kicked off in August against Hednesford Town with a 4-0 win and with Forest Green participating in the Welsh Cup for the first time with a visit to Worcester City.

John Evans took over as manager with John Macey, hauling the club away from the relegation zone to end the season in a very respectable ninth place. Rovers beat Torrington and Barnstaple in the FA Cup before going out to Merthyr Tydfil. In the FA Trophy, Rovers saw off Minehead Town and Cwmbran Town before losing to Gloucester City.

Forest Green's last home game of the season, against Merthyr Tydfil, gave John Duff the opportunity to point out a few home truths about the support for the club, just as he had done back in 1982. While Merthyr were getting crowds well in excess of 1,000, Forest Green's average crowd had dropped to 174, one of the lowest averages for the Midland Division. Sponsorship for the club was not forthcoming from Nailsworth itself, with eighty per cent of the sponsorship coming from outside the district. With such low crowds, off-field income was vital to the running of the club. Merthyr won the Midland Division, beating Forest Green 3-0 at home and 2-1 at The Lawn. Forest Green again finished in ninth place, with Gloucester City two places above them, exactly the same positions as the previous season. Steve Doughty was top scorer.

Rovers carried off the David Russell Memorial Trophy in a game against Shortwood in March in front of more than 600 spectators, far above the average crowd for that season. The fixture showed once again that people would come to watch a competitive clash between the two local teams.

STEVE DOUGHTY

The club should have gone on and on and on after the FA Vase but, instead of going that way, it went the other way. It was all set up to move on and up and we'd finished third back in 1983. We weren't good enough. The side should have been built on but it wasn't. We did okay but we should have built and got a few more players in, but it tailed off instead. We went through a very long poor patch really. There are so many players that I played with up there. Jeff Meacham, he was a great player, Gerry Sweeney was a great player, John Relish was quality when he came, Paul Collicutt was quality, they were all experienced players that came in, Mike Malpass, Richard Crowley.

Above: New sponsors are brought on board by Allen Grant and John Duff, 29 August 1987.

Above left: Steve Doughty is presented with the David Russell Memorial Trophy after the floodlit game against Shortwood, March 1988.

Above right: Floodlit action from the Shortwood match March 1988.

20

Stroud FC: 1988–1992

1988/89 – Still Forest Green Rovers

By 1987, income had dropped off dramatically but the same level of football was expected. John Evans was manager with John Macey assisting him. Karl Bayliss had also joined the club with Kevin Roberts in goal.

The previous year's accounts showed that the club had a debt of approximately £15,000 with an annual deficit of £4,000. Something had to be done to cut the running costs or increase the income to avoid a financial crisis. The directors of the club were just as ambitious as they had been at the beginning of the decade, and looked for new solutions to the club's financial situation.

A directors' meeting on 29 February 1988 considered the following suggestions:

a   Use Forest Green Rovers' freehold as surety for borrowing monies etc, which in turn could be invested in property.
b   Enter into agreements with a developer, such as Beazer Homes, to build new greenfield stadium and gift it to FGR in return for the existing ground.
c   Sell freehold of social club to the social club, or another organisation.
d   Consider return to County League, and try to pay off outstanding debts over five to six years.
e   Sell ground to property investment trust and lease back.

Nobody wanted to see Forest Green return to the County League, although the committee of bygone eras may have done that rather than see the club in debt. The company used the ground to borrow against but, by April 1988, Forest Green's bankers were threatening to call

Above: Forest Green Rovers, 1988, shortly before the proposed
name change to Stroud became public. Back row: Terry Johnson,
John Macey, Brian Lewis, Ted O'Leary, Paul Collicut, Kevin Roberts,
Gareth Howells, unknown, Russell Wilton, Steve Tregale, Jim Blyth,
John Duff. Front row: Mark Rymall, unknown, Norman Parselle,
Richard Smith, unknown, Karl Bayliss, Nick Ackland, John Relish,
Craig Morgan (mascot).

Right: The programme for the 1988/89 season.

BEAZER HOMES LEAGUE – MIDLAND DIVISION

FOREST GREEN ROVERS F.C.

OFFICIAL
MATCH DAY PROGRAMME

in the overdraft unless the club could demonstrate that it was
reducing its debt.

The extremely ambitious directors formed a wholly owned
property development subsidiary company called Goldrem
in July 1988, and bought into their first development in
September. The social club rent was increased to £8,000 per year and it became responsible
for paying off the mortgage previously taken out to cover increasing debts. It was providing
heavy financial support to the company.

The first Goldrem development was highly profitable and returned the club to a trading
profit for the year. A mood of optimism was in the air and the directors set out their targets
for the forthcoming five years:

1   Achieve promotion to Premier Section within two years.
2   Develop ground to comply with grading standards C, and if possible B, within three years.
3   Attain Alliance football within five years.

In addition to the property arm of the company, an even more ambitious move to change the
name of Forest Green Rovers to Stroud Football Club was put forward.

JOHN DUFF

John Eastment had joined our committee. He was the chairman of the Southern League. John
had a falling out with Merthyr, and we were pleased to offer him a directorship at Forest
Green. We knew it was one of convenience and we thought it would be not only good for the

Southern League to have the chairman continue but also for Forest Green to be seen to have the chairman coming from our club.

He was very much in favour of a bigger name in the Southern League and we were trying to increase the support. Stroud was better known than Forest Green and certainly known better than Nailsworth. David Weager was in favour for the same reason. We all were at the time really, with the possibility of greater local sponsorship.

There was also talk that if we changed our name to Stroud, then there was a possibility that a certain large local building society may have been induced to come on board. I don't think there was ever anything from them in writing.

Right: Forest Green Rovers, February 1989. Back row: John Macey, John Evans, Dave Webb, Paul Collicut, Steve Doughty, Kevin Roberts, Gareth Howells, Brian Lewis, Ted O'Leary, Steve Tregale. Front row: John Relish, Russell Wilton, Richard Smith, Mark Rymall, Norman Parselle, Danny Iddles.

Below right: Forest Green Rovers *v.* Hednesford, at the end of the season, one of the last games as Forest Green for three years, March 1989.

At the end of March the football club sent out a notice of an Extraordinary General Meeting to all company members to try to keep them on board with the name change. The property development company was seen as the replacement for the lottery income and had been very successful in its first transaction. They felt that Goldrem would produce funds to provide the club with an increasing source of income for years to come, while sponsors would be more willing to back a Stroud club. Don Gannaway and Jeff Small both left the board, unable to support the name change.

JOHN EVANS

I had returned as manager and thoroughly enjoyed my time in charge, with many happy moments with Doughts, John Macey, Paul Collicutt and John Relish, and I like to think I did well on an extremely tight budget. It was something of a surprise then, when Martin Morgan rang me up to tell me I was no longer manager of Forest Green Rovers, I was manager of Stroud FC. I have got to be honest, things became more difficult then and I think a lot of heart went out of the club. To have made that decision in the centenary year seemed very odd to me but there we are.

While Forest Green finished twelfth, Gloucester City were promoted to the Premier Division. In reality, on the footballing side, having competed in the Southern League Midland Division for seven years, little progress had been made. The very high standards set at the beginning of the 1980s were simply not being met. Crowds were down, sponsorship was down, income was down and the club was struggling.

Amongst the fans, there was despair also that the name of the club was being changed in its centenary year.

1989/90 – Stroud FC

STEVE DOUGHTY

The name change was a complete disaster. They couldn't attract players there. The name of Forest Green was great in non-league with the history that they had. I just think that the name change was a stupid decision. I was still playing, John Evans was the manager at the time, but it just got rapidly worse in that period with him in charge. They couldn't attract the quality of players that they had had in the past. Steve Millard had gone, all of those type of players were gone, the players from the past were gone and it was a struggle. It really was a struggle to try and get it back.

JOHN DUFF

I stayed on for the 1989/90 season, but I thought it was time that maybe someone else with fresh ideas came in. In twenty-one years, I'd progressed the club from a Northern Senior side to a Southern League club and a cup-winning trip to Wembley.

I thought we'd changed the club enough to put it on a pretty good footing, so I stood down. David Weager was there for hardly two years, and then he had his problem.

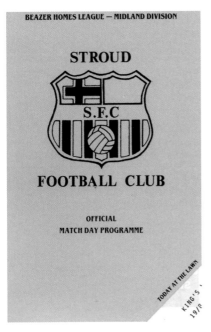

Above: Stroud FC, including Steve Doughty and ex-player John Evans as manager. Back row: Jeff Evans, Unknown, Paul Collicut, Doug Foxwell, Steve Doughty, Kevin Roberts, Ted O'Leary, Mike Kilgour, Steve Tregale, Gary Marshall, John Evans. Front row: Chris Hyde, Nigel Gillard, Dave Webb, Richard Smith, Mark Rymall, Dave Seal, Russell Wilton, Craig Morgan (mascot).

Left: Match programme for the first season as Stroud FC.

The season kicked off with a game against King's Lynn. John Evans brought in Jeff Evans, an ex-manager of Bath City, as assistant at the beginning of the season. Most of the team from last year had stayed, and the first home match of the season was sponsored by ex Rovers player in the 1970s, Andy Coburn's, company.

TREVOR HORSLEY

Andy Coburn was working in one of the units opposite where I'm based in Stonehouse, and invited me along as his guest. They were a sponsor on the night and that was the start of it. Andy knew I was interested in football. He wasn't a director then, I think he was just a sponsor.

The club was being plunged into financial crisis by the property crash, with Goldrem building up a very large debt on a development that it could not sell, and the fans had turned away from the club as a protest against the name change. By April 1990, the lack of support meant that cash to pay weekly bills was not always available and a shortfall of some £8,000 on the annual budget was created from a lack of sponsorship. The financial problems were hitting crisis proportions.

On the footballing side, Mike Kilgour joined and it was agreed that the club should enter the Welsh FA Cup again for the coming season. Swindon Town and Bristol City played pre-season friendly games at The Lawn. The playing budget remained the same as the year before.

By the end of the season, John Evans had left to be replaced by Jeff Evans, before Bobby Jones was appointed late in the season to take the reins. The first season under the 'Stroud' banner saw the team finish in tenth place, slightly better than the year before, with Rushden Town finishing in runners-up spot in the Midland Division. Gloucester City finished ninth in the Premier League.

TRYSTAN SWALE

I don't think anybody could believe it at first, the idea of a name change. After ninety-nine years of progress Forest Green Rovers would be denied its centennial season. At best it was an ill-timed decision, at worst a kick in the teeth to those who had brought the club so far under its true banner. The correspondence pages of the local press simmered with resentment but everybody at the club appeared to be unmoved.

Many supporters just simply stopped going, following the lead of the supporters' club, which chose to direct its funds away from the club for the only time in its history.

STEVE DOUGHTY

I remember the season before I went to Newport, we met Slough Town in the FA Trophy. Jeff Evans was the manager. We decided that we would have a pre-match meal and the players came round to my house and we had beans on toast for ten players. Then we walked up to the ground. And from the moment the match started, it went just completely downhill. Maybe it was the beans!

Every time they attacked they scored. We just couldn't get off the pitch quick enough at the end. It was definitely one of those days. We came up against a better side and everything they touched went in and everything we'd tried turned to dust. It just didn't happen.

Above: Stroud v. Spalding, January 1990.

Opposite: Stroud v. Burton Albion, FA Trophy second round at the snow covered Lawn. Stroud won 3-2.

1990/91

David Weager was chairman at the start of a season that did not go well in the league, but it was definitely memorable for its cup runs.

STEVE DOUGHTY

I went to Newport County with John Relish. Forest Green had told me that there was going to be a testimonial but it never materialised. John Relish went to Newport County as manager and I decided to go with him. There were a lot of things promised by Forest Green. I had been there nearly ten years, there was going to be a testimonial, everything was done, everything was arranged for it, so I was told, and it all fell through towards the end.

ANDY WHITING

The pre-season started with Bobby Jones as manager. We thrashed Conference team Cheltenham Town 6-3 in a pre-season friendly, which put everybody in good spirits. But after 11 games, Stroud were languishing at the bottom of the league along with Alvechurch but, after struggling most of the season, we managed to pull clear with a couple of games to go.

As well as the Welsh Cup games, another fantastic performance that season was against Premier League Burton Albion in the FA Trophy second round. I well remember the game being played on a snow-covered pitch with an orange ball. We took a 1-0 lead through a long-range effort from Martyn Williams, which the goalkeeper couldn't hold on to, and Martyn followed up his own shot into an empty net. Just before half-time, the Brewers got an undeserved equaliser. They then went ahead just after the interval, but Shaun Penny equalised with time running out. Simon Haynes was brought down in the area by their substitute who was sent off in the process and Shaun made no mistake from the spot to send Burton packing.

We went to Northwich Victoria for the quarter-final in the oldest-surviving football ground in the world at that time, the Drill Field. Despite a two-goal defeat, the team performed well against a side fifty-three places above them. Martyn Grimshaw did have the ball in the home net, but it was ruled out by the referee. This was the furthest that we had ever progressed in the FA Trophy.

TRYSTAN SWALE

It's the Welsh Cup matches that stand out, the two second-round matches against Conference high-fliers Kidderminster Harriers. They squandered a 2-goal lead and returned up the M5 with a 3-3 draw. The replay on the following Tuesday was witnessed by a just a handful of travelling supporters, but was surely one of the club's most impressive results at the time. Within a blistering opening quarter, Stroud had gone 2 ahead, both goals coming from the tricky runs of winger Richard Brown, who was turning in the performance of his career. Having halved the lead, Harriers threatened to shatter Stroud hearts after being awarded a penalty, but Richard Forsyth's spot kick struck the base of goalkeeper Glen Thomas's left-hand post and bounced to safety. Both sides traded goals during the second half, but we weathered a late battering to clinch a famous win.

We then beat Chirk and Llandarcy near Port Talbot, both 3-0, to become unlikely quarter-finalists against Wrexham. Despite being managed by Brian Flynn and fielding a side featuring a young Chris Armstrong (late of Millwall, Crystal Palace and Tottenham), Wrexham had to come from behind to a speculative strike from Martyn Grimshaw. We hit the crossbar and the inside of the post inside the final ten minutes, and were understandably aggrieved at not at least having a replay against supposedly superior opposition.

Left: The Stroud team to play Wrexham in the Welsh Cup quarter final, 15 February 1991. Back row: Mike Kilgour, Martin Grimshaw, Richard Dunn, Stewart Martyn, Phil Shrimpton, Kenny Gill, Simon Payne, Russell Dunn. Front row: Mark Rymall, Martin Williams, Nigel Gillard, Russell Wilton, unknown. Front: Craig Morgan (mascot), Andy Lord (mascot).

Below: Action from the cup tie against Wrexham, the first time Stroud/ Forest Green played Football League opposition in a competitive match.

RICHARD GRANT

The Wrexham game stood out that season. I was only about ten but was going around the ground selling raffle tickets. Virtually every fan still going to the games was doing something to help make money for the club that night.

But the thing I remember about the game was watching almost in slow motion as Mark Rymall, near the halfway line, just turned and kicked the ball back into his own half. It was so short that Chris Armstrong just ran on to it and tucked it away, before he got transferred to Tottenham. We were so close to a famous result.

Having had a fantastic run in the cups, the league form had dropped off altogether. The club was going nowhere under their new name and finished in eighteenth place in a league of twenty-two teams. Off the pitch the name change had not brought about the sponsorship and prosperity that they had hoped for. By the end of the season, only three players from the squad had any kit sponsorship at all. Gloucester City finished runners-up to Farnborough Town in the Premier Division, narrowly missing out on national football for the first time in their history.

1991/92

TREVOR HORSLEY

I was first asked to become a director in 1991. I came on board when we used to have the odd meetings in the old wooden shed opposite by the changing rooms. The first meetings were quite interesting because they had all kinds of problems and they wanted to cut the playing budget. So it started from there really, and at the next one we had a working party on the Saturday morning and the Inland Revenue turned up to put a restraint order on the floodlights so we couldn't use them. We had to pay for them to lift the restraint order, and it just continued from there really.

The first few years, you know, weren't very nice; having to argue with solicitors and telling them you weren't going to pay the Inland Revenue. The brewery wanted to wind us up. We just had an accumulation of problems that needed resolving.

Stroud reverted to the traditional black-and-white striped shirts not worn since the 1970s, pointing the way towards a reversion to tradition, and a potential name change back to Forest Green Rovers.

STEVE DOUGHTY

Tim Harris, then manager of Stroud, said, 'Do you fancy coming back?' So I came back, but it was never the same. I didn't stay long with Tim Harris at the end of the Stroud era. I think that I played one game under Frank Gregan but that was a bit of a farce. I enjoyed my time up there, I really did, until it all went a bit sour. I gave my all for the club, I played in goal, I'd played out, I played when I was injured because we were short of players when I shouldn't have done. I remember one game when we were so short of players and both Mike Malpass and me were injured and we had to toss up to decide who would play in goal and who would play outfield. That's how bad it had got.

Stroud v. Bath, friendly, September 1991. Not a spectator in sight, not even in the social club.

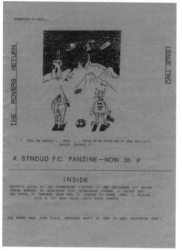

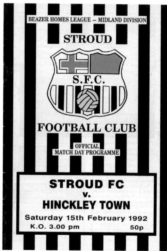

Far left: A fanzine was started by disgruntled supporters, entitled 'The Rovers Return'.

Left: The black-and-white stripes returned to the programme and the team.

Most fans were not happy with the name change at all and those who still attended matches voiced their protests at the name of Stroud and lobbied for the name to be changed back to its rightful one. A fanzine was started, cutting very close to the knuckle on every level. After two issues, the producers were threatened with legal action and it ceased production.

The last season under the name of Stroud FC saw the team finish nineteenth of the twenty-two-team league, narrowly escaping relegation. Gloucester City could not reach the heights of the season before and finished twelfth in the Premier Division. Cheltenham Town, meanwhile, were relegated from the Alliance League into the Premier Division. By the end of 1992, Forest Green Rovers was in debt to the tune of £100,000. The new directors started to turn matters around but the annual income was still approximately £25,000 less than its annual outgoings by 1992.

COLIN PEAKE

Andy Coburn rang me to say that the then club secretary, Peter Wainwright, had suffered a heart attack and they did not have anyone in the club who could do the football secretary's job. I said I would help out to the end of the season and took over the reins.

The first match was at home to Racing Club Warwick and the weather was atrocious. We were leading 2-0 when the visitors were awarded a penalty on the hour. Watching from the old directors' room, I made the comments that I hoped they scored. Basing my comment from previous experience of whistleblowing, I pointed out that if they scored the opposition would still be in the game and would not pressure the referee into calling the game off. The penalty was duly missed and 2 minutes later the game was abandoned. Hopefully I proved to many in that one instance that at least I knew what I was talking about.

Being a police officer, I was asked to set up an inquiry into how the club had come to be indebted to the point where its existence was threatened. This was the first time I came into contact with Trevor Horsley. I didn't know what to make of him at first but soon saw in him a man who I could work with. Trevor agreed with me that the club had to rediscover its identity and to this end we completed the paperwork to rename the club Forest Green Rovers.

CERTIFICATE OF INCORPORATION

ON CHANGE OF NAME

No. 1731483

I hereby certify that

STROUD FOOTBALL CLUB LIMITED

having by special resolution changed its name,

is now incorporated under the name of

FOREST GREEN ROVERS F.C. LTD.

Given under my hand at the Companies Registration Office,

Cardiff the 25 MAY 1992

M. ROSE

an authorised officer

Above left: Trevor Horsley and Andy Coburn bring the name back to its home, May 1992.

Above right: Certificate of Incorporation on Name of Change. Forest Green Rovers was back.

TREVOR HORSLEY

Me and Andy decided that the Stroud name was all wrong, and they had changed it to Stroud just before the centenary, which didn't make a lot of sense to me. So we changed it back to Forest Green and then we went on and celebrated the centenary with Portsmouth. With hindsight it should never have changed in the first place.

Tim Harris was manager. It was the start of his first season and obviously we had problems. We were in the Midland Division – as Stroud – and we changed the strip back to black and white. Tim did a reasonable job, I think there were a budget then of about £800 a week. And we asked him, at our second board meeting, to cut it, and he cut it and we managed to get within budget.

Tim moved on. I think we appointed Glen Thomas then as caretaker manager. I think his first game were Newport County away in a cup competition. Glen stayed with us for the rest of that season, and eventually broke his arm at Tamworth away, towards the end of the season. Then we decided that we were going replace him at the end of the season. It were only a caretaker role – goalkeepers don't make very good managers, we've since found out. We just avoided relegation that year.

21

The Rovers Return: 1992–1996

1992/93

Forest Green Rovers chairman Andy Coburn and a new board of directors, including Colin Peake, hoped to bring the romance back to the club. Trevor Horsley became a vice-president for the time being. Rovers dropped out of the FA Trophy and re-entered the FA Vase for the first time in ten years. The centenary was celebrated belatedly with the visit of Portsmouth's first team.

Glen Thomas was replaced by Geoff Medcroft as manager, another Rovers player from the 1970s, in an attempt to keep the players local and operate the club on an extremely tight budget. The policy saw Rovers bottom of the table with just 1 point after 9 games. Geoff couldn't stay and was replaced by Pat Casey, with John Evans returning as his coach, to steer Forest Green Rovers to safety.

Pat and John had completed a very successful season at Shortwood United in 1992, winning the Hellenic League Premier Division, the Gloucestershire Senior Cup and the Stroud Charity Cup, but Shortwood had hit a glass ceiling and couldn't progress further.

Just as John Duff had bemoaned the lack of support for the club in the 1980s, a plea was made by Colin Peake in November 1992 to bring back the lost supporters.

JOHN EVANS

A few years after managing the Stroud team, I was back as coach with Pat Casey as manager. Times were really tight behind the scenes with debts being paid off.

We kept the club in the Southern League somewhat against the odds, and it was in this period that I encountered my most embarrassing moment. Pat asked me to go on as sub at the age of forty-one for Forest Green at Rushden & Diamonds in the last game of a season. They needed a point to win the league. We were 4-0 down after 20 minutes. Their new electronic scoreboard kept flashing 'Champions' and I thought it could be 10-0. The crowd started chanting 'Who ate all the pies?', but we only lost 5-1 in the end, so only 1-1 when I was on then! Then the floodlights failed with 5 minutes to go and the ref was going to abandon the game. I persuaded him to blow up early so we did not have to replay the game.

The romance of the FA Vase didn't last beyond the game against Tiverton, with Forest Green Rovers losing the match 6-0 at home. But the TV cameras were back at the ground to witness the spectacle.

JAMES COOK

After moving to Aberdeen in 1988 my FGR match days have been restricted to big games. Michelle and I would leave work at 5 p.m. and, with one food stop, drive the 530 miles and crash out in Stroud around midnight. Friends and family would be greeted at the social club before the game. These days we stop halfway overnight, maybe a sign of old age.

My worst ever visit has to be the fifth round FA Vase match against Tiverton. After a dreadful start and lucky only to be 1-0 down at half-time, I uttered the immortal words, 'We can't play any worse than that'. Forty-five minutes later the score was 6-0. Imagine travelling well over a 1,000 miles for that!

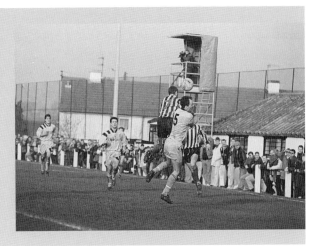

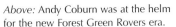

Above: Andy Coburn was at the helm for the new Forest Green Rovers era.

Top right: Forest Green Rovers *v.* Tiverton, FA Vase fifth round, 6 February 1993.

Middle right: The centenary team that faced Portsmouth. From left to right, back row: Chris Gardner, Gareth Howells, unknown, Andrew Gardiner, Nick King, Mark Patterson, Andy Pinkney, Wayne Hams, Adrian Tandy, Geoff Medcroft. Front row: Tony Francis, Lee Davies, Gary Marshall, Russell Wilton, Tony Goodwin, Ryan Parker, Jason Benson, Andy Lord (mascot).

Lower right: Rovers are back, action from July 1992, Karl Bayliss looking on.

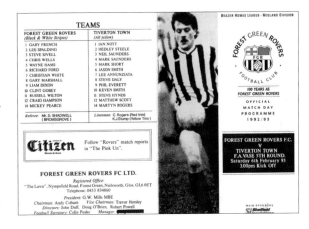

Above left: Forest Green Rovers in a celebratory mood against Halesowen in January 1993. Pat Casey and John Evans had instilled winning ways back into the team. Gary Marshall is congratulated after scoring.

Above right: Pat Casey in a pensive mood despite the win v. Halesowen in January 1993.

By the end of the season, Forest Green Rovers only narrowly escaped relegation, finishing nineteenth of twenty-two in the same position as the Stroud team the year before. Cheltenham Town finished runners-up, with Gloucester City finishing in thirteenth place in the Premier Division.

1993/94

Off the field, Andy Coburn had been replaced by Doug O'Brien, who remained as chairman until January 1994, when Trevor Horsley took over the reins. Pat Casey and John Evans had to try and improve on the year before, but still on an extremely tight budget, as the club set about resolving the financial problems. The playing budget was cut to the bone with the brief again to avoid relegation.

Rovers re-entered the FA Vase, meeting Barnstaple at The Lawn. They played an ineligible player, which led immediately to disqualification from the competition. No romance this year. Forest Green had beaten Barnstaple the previous year in a preliminary round of the FA Cup before losing to Newport AFC in the first qualifying round at home 2-1. In the FA Cup this year, it was very much the same story, as Rovers drew Odd Down away in the first qualifying round, managing a 2-2 draw before losing the replay 3-1 against the Western League team. Of more significance to the club as a whole was the emergence of a new driving force in the form of Trevor Horsley. Rovers finished fifteenth of twenty-two in the Midland Division.

TREVOR HORSLEY

We advertised at the end of season for the manager. We interviewed all day long from memory, and we had some very good candidates, but the one that stuck out among them all was Frank Gregan, head and shoulders. We appointed Frank, offered him the job that day.

1994/95

The key concern at the club, other than the poor performances on the pitch, was to service the debt and to create a revenue stream to allow finances to grow. The club was sponsored this year for the first time since the end of the 1980s, which helped to bring in much-needed revenue.

FRANK GREGAN

I was one of six shortlisted candidates that had been interviewed earlier on in the day by the board. My wife took the phone call the afternoon of my interview and had to drive to the golf course to tell me I had got the job.

I had just had a very successful season at Andover and I held a minor scouting role at Arsenal. Trevor and the board obviously had seen enough to take a chance and give me the job. I think it's safe to say that Colin Peake was in my corner. The irony is that I never got on particularly well with Colin when I worked at Forest Green. I think it was probably just a clash of two strong personalities. Nowadays I am able to reflect and realise just how hard he worked both on behalf of myself and the club, and I have a great deal of respect for the man.

My appointment was confirmed on 1 June 1994 but the *Citizen* was unimpressed. 'Frank who?' was the headline on the back page. If the *Citizen* weren't impressed by me, I dread to think what the players must have thought. The first time I met them I was forty-five minutes late. I got lost on the way to the ground.

ROB COOK

I joined the club in 1994, having played over at Shortwood for a while under Steve Doughty. One of Frank's favourite training sessions was to send us down to the bottom of the hill and get back as fast as you can. I didn't mind this and thought it was easy, but others hated it. Sometimes as punishment he would send us all down and ask us for the price of an onion bhaji from the Indian restaurant to make sure we went to the bottom. Some players would beg Alex Sykes, Don Forbes or myself to tell them so they didn't have to go all the way to the bottom of the hill.

Left: Forest Green Rovers *v.* Swindon Town at the beginning of the season. The changing room roof had been painted in the club's colours.

Below: Forest Green Rovers 1993-1994. Back row: Pat Casey, Liam Dixon, Martin Churchward, Tim Bayliffe, Paul Collicult, Richard Ford, unknown, Steve Jones, John Evans, Adrian Tandy. Front row: Chris White, Clint Gobey, Gary Marshall, Russell Wilton, unknown, unknown.

Forest Green v. Yeovil, a pre-season friendly 1994, one of the first matches with Frank Gregan in charge. Allan Kennedy scores.

FRANK GREGAN

My first game in charge was a pre-season friendly against Walsall, managed by Kenny Hibbitt. We drew 2-2 and shortly afterwards I had my first dilemma as the Rovers manager. It was the first of hundreds that I would encounter thereafter. The team captain was Russell Wilton, an experienced and well-respected player in the Gloucestershire area. He was also a big favourite with the fans. He wanted a pay rise and he also gave me the impression that he was not really enamoured with my appointment. I remember him saying, 'I've got nothing to prove to you,' which I thought a little strange as I was his manager. He wanted an extra £15 a week and I was not prepared to give him it until I've seen more of him. I asked him if he would really leave the club for such a small amount of money and he replied that he would. I shook his hand and said, 'Don't slam the door on your way out!'

It didn't take Russell long to get his own back when his new club Cinderford dumped us out of the FA Cup after a replay at Meadow Park, Gloucester. We struggled that first season. It really was a building job, there was so much work to be done. With all due respect to the players I inherited, very few of them were up to the task. Those that were included Phil Underhill, Richard Ford, Garry Marshall and Andy Hoskins, all of whom performed admirably during the first term. By the end of the season we had added Alan Kennedy, Nick Hendy, Steve Book, Tommy Callinan, Karl Bayliss, Rob Skidmore and Kasey Johnstone.

The team didn't finish any higher in the division than it had the year before, but some solid work had been done recruiting good-quality players, and the board had stumped up a record transfer fee of £5,000 for Karl Bayliss. My first year report as the Rovers manager probably read, 'Showing potential but we'll have to do better!'

Rovers finished eighteenth of twenty-two teams but, behind the scenes, foundations were being laid to take the club forward again. In an attempt to spark more interest and to avoid playing the same teams year in, year out, Forest Green Rovers applied for and successfully transferred to the Southern Division of the Southern League at the end of the season, bringing about more local derby fixtures and, with shorter travelling distances, the potential for larger crowds.

1995/96

The switch to the Southern Division brought about local derbies against Yate Town, Clevedon Town, Weston-super-Mare, Trowbridge Town and Cinderford Town, the latter being old rivals from pre-war days. The club as a whole benefited tremendously from this switch, with a thirty-seven per cent increase in the sponsors' club revenue and a dramatic increase in sponsorship and interest from local companies. Towards the end of the season, Colin Peake became managing director full time at the club.

Forest Green Rovers 1994/95. From left to right, back row: Richard Ford, Gary Marshall, Andy Hoskins, Neil Fulton, Steve Book, Tony Bennett, Rob Skidmore, Nick Hendy. Middle row: Micky Pearce, Dave Honeybill, Pete Amor, Tony Islesley, Frank Gregan, Paul Collicutt, Gerald Mauler, Colin Peake, Glenn Thomas. Front row: Rob Cook, Alan Kennedy, Phil Underhill, Tony Blandford, Doug O'Brien, Trevor Horsley, Roger Cowley, Allen Grant, Alan Theobold, Ian Willmott, Paul Bloomfield.

Forest Green Rovers v. Bath City, pre-season friendly 1995, Dave Maynard on the ball with Karl Bayliss looking on.

Forest Green Rovers v. Cheltenham Town, 1995. In a pre-season friendly, Tommy Callinan scores as Karl Bayliss looks on.

Forest Green
Rovers *v.*
Exmouth 1995.

Paul Hiron
celebrates a
goal with Dave
Maynard early
in the season.

ANDY WHITING

I became a director that year. We had to play Poole Town. They were rock bottom; 1 point all season I think. All the roads were very icy. We eventually got to the ground very late and Forest Green's game was the only game nationwide that had survived the weather that night.

Trevor managed to wind me up good and proper. Colin Peake couldn't make it, he usually did the radio commentary from his mobile phone and he asked if I would do it for him. I was a bit nervous but said I wouldn't mind. And then I had a phone call apparently from Radio 5 saying would I mind if my commentary went out live on the BBC as Rovers was the only game on that night. I think at that point I wanted the ground to swallow me up, until I saw Trevor and the other lads watching me take the phone call!

It was a very close game and I think we came back from a goal down to win 2-1. Before we left I think everybody was expecting at least a 10-0 win.

Opposite: Work started on the new stand in January 1996, with supporter Ron Gardener in the picture.

FRANK GREGAN

We were treated to the more salubrious surroundings of Sittingbourne and Weymouth this year. The changing rooms at Sittingbourne were massive and we held a small sided game in there prior to going out for the warm up. I remember a few years later one of the players saying that Sittingbourne was the best ground they had ever played at and Nigel Spink piping up with 'The San Siro isn't bad either!'

I also remember that we came up against Cinderford Town in the FA Cup during the year. We drew with them at home, drew with them away and then lost the second replay 3-1 back at The Lawn. We had also been knocked out of the FA Cup by Cinderford the year before. I had a microphone shoved up my nose and the reporter hit the nail on the head with the pointed question, 'You must have been disappointed with that result?'

It took great willpower to prevent myself from bursting into a Victor Meldrew-type tirade. 'No, no, of course not. I'm ecstatic at getting knocked out of the cup like that. One of my favourite fantasies is that we will turn up for a big game, play like a bunch of fairies and get battered. It's good that we've gone out now. Who wants to go on to Old Trafford in the third round anyway? Imagine all that noise, I'd have a headache for weeks and the money we make on the run like that, what about the worry of how to spend it?'

Of course, I didn't. I was representing the club and consequently I strung a few placating sentences together spattered with a couple of decent cliches, 'concentrate on the league', 'let's see where both teams finish in May', and then went away to the dressing room and had a frank and meaningful discussion with the players.

The season finished with us eighth in the table with a total of 74 points from 42 games, a huge improvement on anything in recent years. Mike Kilgour had joined from Salisbury, Chris Tomlinson was on board, John Scott was also in the side. We were getting close to a side that could challenge for promotion. Only a couple more players were needed to complete the jigsaw.

Off the pitch, Trevor Horsley and the directors drew up plans for a new grandstand, incorporating new player-changing facilities and a boardroom. The contractors for the project, Tudor Builders, became the shirt sponsors for the season. The £170,000 project was ready to accommodate 300 spectators in August. The building work was a very public sign of Trevor's vision to push the club forward and leave the last ten years finally behind it.

22

Reach for the Top: 1996–1998

1996/97

TREVOR HORSLEY

We had only increased the budget slightly from the first year to the second year. It was his managerial skills as well as the team spirit we had that saw the results improve. Whatever people say about him, without Frank Gregan we wouldn't be where we are today. And nobody can ever take that away from him.

The team was again sponsored for the season, continuing Trevor's drive to increase the income of the club. In September, Forest Green beat Waterlooville 3-2 and were hanging on to third place in the league behind Cinderford Town and Havant Town.

Early in January, in a top-of-the-table clash, Forest Green beat Havant 3-2 having been 2-0 down at half-time, to move to within 1 point of them.

ALEX SYKES

One of the most memorable games of that season was beating Havant 3-2. They were top of the league at that time and 2-0 up at half-time. They thought it was easy and that we were done with. I remember Tommy Callinan coming off at half-time getting loads of stick from their midfielders and him saying that we were far from done with. He wound us up at half-time and with Frank's team talk we went on to win the game. The party in the clubhouse afterwards was as big as winning the league. Even the directors were dancing on the tables and I remember one putting his head through the roof tiles. As was the spirit at the time, all the players, directors and supporters alike were all mixing together and celebrating. The spirit was second to none.

Forest Green Rovers moved to the top of the table with a 4-0 win over Bashley in February and stayed on top for the rest of the season with some fine wins, including a 3-1 away to Weymouth.

Paul Hunt had joined the club earlier in the season and was knocking in goals in virtually every match, including an injury-time winner against Witney towards the end of March, which moved Rovers 8 points clear at the top. This was followed by a 3-1 win against Cirencester Town in front of a crowd of 623, the biggest of the season.

PAUL HUNT

I was at Andover with Frank Gregan when he was first there. He moved on, I stayed there and still did okay and then I went to Cirencester but didn't score many goals. Forest Green were

Forest Green Rovers directors in 1996, set to take the club forward to new levels, pictured in the new stand, open to spectators in time for the new season. Back row: Dave Honeybill, Robert Powell, Roger Cowley, Gerald Mauler, John Cooper, Steve Hearn. Middle row: Mike Hollyoak, Pete Amor, Andy Whiting, Allen Grant. Front row: Doug O'Brien, Trevor Horsley, Colin Peake.

Forest Green Rovers v. Waterlooville, 21 September 1996. Forest Green won 3-2 with goals from Scott, Tomlinson and Moore.

Above left: Frank Gregan won the manager of the month award in February 1997.

Above right: Forest Green Rovers on the march, against Erith and Belvedere in 1997.

in the same league and I played against them and had a great game. Two weeks later Frank tapped me up and said he wanted me to come to Forest Green. 'I don't want you to destroy us like you did the first game,' he said. I played against them, done really well again; two weeks later he signed me on. So that's how I joined Forest Green.

Fareham away: the match that secured the championship fourteen years after entering the Southern League.

Rovers secured a place in the Dr Marten's Premier League, beating Dartford 2-1 in mid–April and, in the following game, away to Fareham Town, Rovers claimed the championship.

Stroud News & Journal:

Fareham Town 0 Forest Green Rovers 1 – another little piece of history

A headed goal in the seventy-ninth minute by captain Mike Kilgour fittingly not only defeated Fareham Town 1-0, but also clinched the championship for Forest Green Rovers with 2 games to play. At the final whistle, the large contingent of travelling supporters joined the players on the pitch in jubilant celebrations for the little club's highest achievement in their 107-year history.

With Dave Mitchell sidelined with a chest infection, manager Frank Gregan drafted in John Scott to the midfield and Richard Ford joined Alan Kennedy on the bench. A free-kick by Gary Smart was helped on by Kilgour and Karl Bayliss turned to fire home a shot that was charged down on the line. As Rovers pressed for the opener, Kilgour rose to a smart corner only for keeper Andy Fisher to tip his header over the bar.

From the resulting corner, Rovers appealed for what seemed an obvious handball but to the dismay of the 100-plus travelling supporters, referee Mr Carver waved play on. Moments later Paul Hunt shielded the ball well before laying it back to Chris Smith, whose rocket shot was parried away by the keeper.

After the break, Fareham forced Rovers back continuously at the start of the second half and Rovers were almost beaten when Lee Pinhorne put in a cross that was missed by Kilgour, and Book had to save well down low from Mark Gough's header. On sixty-five minutes Alex Sykes floated a cross into the path of Tommy Callinan, who missed the ball by inches with the goal at his mercy and, within minutes, substitute Alan Kennedy crossed to Hunt, whose cross-goal header stuck in the mud on the goal-line and Fareham managed to get back to clear the danger.

In the seventy-ninth minute Smart took a corner on the left and captain Kilgour rose majestically at the far post to claim the winning goal, his fourth of the season and probably his most important for the club.

On the final whistle Rovers were champions of the Southern Division and, as the tannoy played Queen's We are the Champions. *Some players left the field in joyful tears of relief, while others just stayed with the supporters and soaked up the atmosphere.*

Rovers were looking forward to the last game of the season at home to Tonbridge Angels. The game itself was a 3-3 draw and brought to an end the most successful league campaign in Forest Green's history, undefeated at home with 18 wins and 3 draws for the season. What a turnaround from the Stroud days five years before!

PAUL HUNT

We played Witney away. We were 2-0 down and we beat them 3-2 at their place. When we played Witney here, we beat them 3-2, but we won the Southern Division away at Fareham. We all went back to a hotel in Southampton for some serious celebrations!

FRANK GREGAN

And so there it was, three seasons after taking over, we had achieved our first goal: promotion to the Southern League Premier Division. The presentation evening held by the league was another good party. Gresley Rovers' directors were there that night; they had won the Premier Division but were unable to be promoted because of ground grading restrictions. Tommy Callinan and a Gresley director were having a heated discussion about the difference in standards between the two divisions. I remember the Gresley director mocking Tommy, 'So you think you'll do well next season at the higher standard then?' 'Do well?' laughed Tommy, 'We'll win it!' 'That's it Tommy,' I thought, 'Let's sneak up on the rails unannounced!'

Top left: Jubilation after the Tonbridge game. Back row: Don Forbes, John Scott, Kevin Lee, Rob Skidmore, Rob Cook, Chris Smith, Tommy Callinan, Dave Mitchell, Nick Hendy, Chris Tomlinson. Front row: Karl Bayliss, Alex Sykes, Mike Kilgour, Gary Marshall, Allan Kennedy, Frank Gregan, Dave Tyrrell.

Above right: Mike Kilgour with the Southern Division Shield.

Above left: Forest Green Rovers, ready for the big push in the last game of the season in the Southern Division. Back row: Frank Gregan, Richard Ford, unknown, Don Forbes, Rob Cook, Tommy Callinan, Steve Book, Chris Tomlinson, Dave Mitchell, Nick Hendy, Karl Bayliss, Dave Tyrrell. Front row: Allan Kennedy, John Scott, Gary Smart, Mike Kilgour, Alex Sykes, Gary Marshall, Chris Smith.

TREVOR HORSLEY

The team spirit and camaraderie were there and Frank and me very seldom had a difference of opinion; I think we fell out twice in six or seven years, which is, for a manager-chairman relationship, quite amazing. He were very good at his job, and he were a good man manager. His team talks were phenomenal, and if he couldn't lift them there was nobody else who could really.

Additional income was now being generated by various initiatives, including hospitality boxes in the new stand, many different sponsorship deals and a significant shirt sponsorship deal with Sheffield Insulations, a company with which Trevor Horsley did business.

As Forest Green finished champions of the Southern Division, Cheltenham Town finished runners-up in the Premier Division, with Gloucester City in third place. The move up also brought higher running costs and the need to employ more stewards for fixtures.

1997/98

Behind the scenes, the directors of the club were determined to push it forward and ensure that it had a firm foundation, but the club's ambition lay higher than the Premier Division.

TREVOR HORSLEY

Frank and me had a little chat about the Premier League in the summer. We went away on a pre-season tour in Belgium. Me and Frank said if we get off to a flyer we can go straight through. But we didn't make it public. Obviously we had a belief that if we got a flyer, then the rest would be history.

The Premier Division team, ready for a new challenge. From left to right, back row: Dave Tyrrell, Alan McDougal, Mark Hallam, Chris Honor, Rob Cook, Justin Shuttlewood, Martin Woodhouse, Don Forbes, Shaun Rouse, Tim Banks, Tommy Callinan, Mike Kilgour. Front row: Tom Jones, Paul Hunt, Grantly Dicks, Paul McLoughlin, Frank Gregan, Gary Smart, Alex Sykes, Matt Coupe, Toby Jackson, Steve Winter.

The campaign opened with a 2-0 win against Cambridge City at The Lawn and was followed by a draw against Dorchester Town. Seven more wins and a draw with Crawley Town clearly showed the intent of Forest Green to fight it out at the top of the Premier Division.

TREVOR HORSLEY

I can remember early in the season going to Gresley, and I asked the barman for a tape measure because they had the trophy on the wall. He said 'What d'you want that for?' I said, 'I just want to measure the trophy to make sure we can get it in our cabinet.' And we said then that we wouldn't make the fatal mistake that Gresley had done because they wasn't able to go up because of their ground.

The fine run finally came to an end at home to Burton Albion in October, bringing to an end a string of 30 matches unbeaten at home since 20 March 1996. With promotion to the Conference now a distinct possibility, work started to upgrade The Lawn, including a 200-seat extension to the stand and new covered terrace to the Nympsfield Road end. The works had to be completed by 1 April if Rovers were to stand a chance of promotion.

Rovers run out at Gresley, on their march to the top. Gresley had been refused entry to the Conference the year before because of ground grading problems.

ROB COOK

I was groundsman from 1996 to 2000 and loved the job, and many people will tell you the ground never looked so good. I wasn't playing because of a foot injury and Trevor told me that I had to dig fifty-two holes for crush barriers through the limestone. I was not a happy camper but I got on with digging five to six a day and, on completion, the club sent me for an MRI scan only to find that my foot had been broken all along. I bet Wayne Rooney would not have had to put up with that!

After a patchy spell in November, during which Rovers dropped to third in the league, a bumper crowd of 1,333 watched Forest Green draw with Gloucester City on Boxing Day with the headline 'Tigers mauled by Rovers'. Two more wins saw Rovers back within 4 points of Merthyr at the top of the table. The average crowd had risen to 505, well above the average of 189 in the 1995/96 season, and the many sponsorship initiatives were also paying dividends to fund a bigger playing budget. Success on the pitch was being matched off it.

Rovers moved back to the top of the table with a 3-2 win over Crawley Town at the end of January. The belief in the squad was second to none and the race to the Conference was now hotting up after a 4-1 demolition of Gloucester City, with Forest Green wearing their red-and-white away kit, and winning for the first time wearing it in six attempts.

By the end of March, Merthyr had been told by the Conference that their ground would not comply with the grading rules and they would be barred entry. The work being undertaken by Trevor and the board was reaching a crescendo to meet the Conference deadline before Rovers had their grading inspection.

TREVOR HORSLEY

We had the Football Conference down looking round and they wrote a letter to us saying that we'd never make it and we won't ever finish in time, threatening us really. I wrote back to them via a solicitor and just said, please retract your statement because we will be there and we will do what you want us to do. So we did the stand and we did the terrace opposite, we did behind the goal and when they came to do the inspection, they didn't like it.

When they arrived for ground grading I wouldn't let them go out. I remember I locked them in the boardroom, I wouldn't let them go out. I made them watch a DVD of where we wanted to be and what we were trying to achieve. They were trying to get out and I just wouldn't let them go. So I made them wait; we had quite a few people outside just waiting to see what the result were, and we got the thumbs up, and then we went on and obviously then we had to keep it going on the pitch.

Forest Green Rovers *v.* Rothwell Town, 17 January 1998. Work on the ground continued with the construction of a new covered terrace at the Nympsfield Road end to ensure that The Lawn complied with Conference ground requirements at the time. Matt Coupe leads a break out, Mike Kilgour looks on.

COLIN PEAKE

Behind the scenes the club was having a right battle with the then chief executive of the Football Conference. By any standards we were not guaranteed a promotion place and it seems the Conference only wanted clubs in their membership from big towns and cities. Little old Forest Green Rovers was a culture shock waiting to happen and we as a club knew that if our application was not perfect they would find any excuse to deny us our rightful entry.

Forest Green faced Merthyr at Easter and they crashed to a 4-0 defeat, leaving Merthyr 1 point clear at the top. The defeat wasn't part of the plan but there were still 4 games left till the end of the season, including the rearranged Merthyr game at The Lawn for 29 April. The defeat at Merthyr at Easter was now past history and all eyes turned to the Wednesday night clash, with Rovers hoping to break their modern-day ground record with a crowd in excess of 2,000. On the day a crowd of 2,891 turned out to witness a spectacular game, Rovers winning 3-1 and only requiring a draw on the last day of the season against Bath City to secure Conference football for the club.

ALEX SYKES

The most memorable game that season obviously was that one against Merthyr. I remember the build-up was nothing like the past few seasons. Suddenly TV and radio were descending on The Lawn and the crowd I remember being second to none both in number and in voice.

That was followed up by the game against Bath. At the time I was still a student and my housemates decided to follow Forest Green that season, and on that sunny Saturday they had nowhere better to be than drinking cider at Forest Green. On the last day they all decided it would be a good idea to wear Hawaian shirts and stand right behind the goal. When I scored the second against Bath I went straight over to them and they were made up to find it on the local news on the Sunday night.

Forest Green Rovers v. Merthyr Tydfil
Wednesday 29 April 1998
*Many times this season people have predicted Forest Green's weakness would be shown to be their defence
but, as every other week, this remained unproven.*

*The Welshmen had the better of early exchanges, but were unable to show any profit. The best chance of
the opening half-hour fell to Ian Mitchell after good play down the left flank, but he was foiled in the box.
Minutes later, a goalmouth scramble led to the ball being hacked off the line as several Merthyr players tried
in vain to pounce. The crowd stepped up the atmosphere another notch. At the other end Mark Hallam had a
header blocked, and Steve Winter volleyed wide. The first goalkeeping action of note came from the experienced
Gary Wager, saving low from a Hallam header, following a corner from the impressive Alex Sykes.*

*The remainder of the first half saw the visitors resorting to hopeful crosses, dealt with comfortably by the
home defence. As the whistle blew a number of fans moved towards the opposite end before checking, unable
to scratch that familiar itch.*

*Colin Addison's Merthyr team talk concentrated on the positive and urged his players to produce more of
the same. Dean Clarke received a second yellow card and, as he left the field, Rovers' fans' confidence didn't
just grow, it visibly surged. Rovers sensed blood and, shortly after Tommy Callinan had a header kicked off
the line. Paul McLoughlin and then Winter both missed chances. Then, after a mistake by Roger Gibbins,
McLoughlin was left to cut towards the near post where he drove a close-range cross shot into the net right in
front of the Lawn End. Within minutes a long ball right of the Merthyr defence found Sykes, who tricked his
way through a glut of defenders and shot home. Even the most nervous Forest Green fans started to believe
Conference football could happen.*

*Steve Winter rounded off the scoring with a calm finish to slay the dragon. Merthyr ended the game with
a consolation goal. The atmosphere, the image and the game had proven worthy of a title decider, there was no
doubt that this was the football that all supporters dreamt of.*

PAUL HUNT

I really had an understanding with Mark Hallam up front, we scored a lot of goals. I scored 20-odd
goals, 27 goals that year. I was about the top goal scorer, we had the Golden Boot of the year. And
good crowds here at The Lawn, it really makes a difference when the supporters are up for it as
well. My highlight that year was getting Supporters' Player of the Year, and just playing really well
that year.

That game we played against Merthyr here there were thousands, and it was the best atmosphere
I've seen here up to that point. It was tremendous. The bigger and noisier the crowd the better the
boys play. It's simple, it's entertainment isn't it? The bigger the crowd the better I play because I've
always been a crowd pleaser. If you can't be a crowd pleaser there's no point in playing. That's one
thing I'll always remember playing here for because, one thing I always did, if I scored a goal, I
shared it with the fans, and it was tremendous.

COLIN PEAKE

Merthyr Tydfil ran us close all season long and the largest attendance ever for a league fixture at
The Lawn in modern times saw the clubs meet in the penultimate fixture of the season. My main
worry that night was the safety of those attending and I often think back to a director from Merthyr
who complained he didn't have a seat to watch the game. 'Watch it from the terraces,' was my
reply, 'or not at all.' Afterwards I found the reason he didn't have the right ticket was because
his manager – one Colin Addison – had taken them all for his family and friends. Our fans went
home happy with the 3-1 victory and the title was within our grasp. It was for us to lose not for
someone else to win.

TREVOR HORSLEY

I can remember we lost the Merthyr fixture over Christmas because of the weather. So I said to Frank I wanted it played in January. He said, 'Don't play in January, that'll be the one that wins the league, you want to play in April.' I said 'We need it now, we need some money on the gate.' And he said 'No, it'll be the biggest crowd you've ever had here, it'll be the one that decides it.' Well we'd been to Merthyr over Easter, and we'd got beat; and we had them to come back to our place, and in fairness Frank got that right as well. He said that'll be the one that wins it.

The Merthyr game was easily the club's biggest win since the FA Vase days in 1982. The game entered folklore in true 'Roy of the Rovers' style. But the title still wasn't secured – that had to wait until Saturday when Rovers beat Bath City with a goal in each half from Gary Smart and Alex Sykes. In total, 1,700 joyous supporters turned out to see Gary Smart handed the giant championship shield and the players collect their medals. It was an emotional day for both the players and the directors, with many of the Rovers squad experiencing the highlight of their career. For Trevor Horsley and Colin Peake, promotion to the Conference was the first part of their ultimate aim of Rovers, playing football at the highest level in the best possible facilities.

The transformation of the club both on and off the pitch since 1992 was simply phenomenal, the stuff that dreams are made of. Rovers finished top scorers with 93 goals from a team bristling with attacking talent.

Top: Before the kick off for the Merthyr game, the ground is packed for the championship decider.

Middle: An attendance of 2,891 crammed into The Lawn on the Wednesday evening.

Above: Forest Green players celebrate the victory against Merthyr knowing that the title is within reach.

COLIN PEAKE

At the Bath game, as I introduced each player by name and asked our management team to step forward to receive their mementos, Mike Kilgour held aloft the largest trophy in football. It was a proud moment in my life and I am sure many others. Even more importantly though, for Trevor and Pete Amor, the shield fitted perfectly into the new cabinet.

Forest Green would play national football, week in, week out, for the first time in its history, against such famous names as Hereford United and Doncaster Rovers.

Forest Green Rovers beat Bath City to be crowned champions of the Dr Martens Premier Division, national football beckons for the first time in the club's history.

Alex Sykes and Steve Winter celebrate taking the club into the Conference.

RICHARD GRANT

The Premier Division season was by far the best I've ever seen. We weren't expected to do anything and were favourites for relegation, but we just walked it. We went into every game knowing that even if we went 2 goals down we would still score 4. We were just that prolific up front. Gregan's team basically, apart from the back four and a goalkeeper, were all strikers, which meant that we were fantastic attacking. We were scoring so many goals it didn't make a difference letting some in. We could afford to lose a couple of goals each game.

FRANK GREGAN

Gary Smart had joined us the previous year. Smartie was a brilliant player and his ability to create his own space suited our 3-5-2 formation. We played Gary in the hole behind the front two and his link-up play was tremendous. Steve Winter had come in from Torquay and Paul Hunt had his best ever season in football. I have known 'Oggy' a very, very long time. He was brilliant. We had an unbelievable spirit, and invariably it was based around laughter. There were some great stories that season in the dressing room.

I suppose sometimes you have to be there. It just doesn't sound as funny when you read these tales, but believe me we had some great fun. 'Shutty' was an undertaker as well as goalkeeper, and I remember he had a face like a bulldog licking a nettle at training one night. I pulled him aside at the end and confronted him, saying his attitude was not what I expected and what was his problem.

'My problem is,' he said, 'that a lady died about eighteen months ago and her husband decided to move to Scotland. He is now missing his wife. So, because you can't dig a body up in daylight, I have to get up at 3 a.m. and dig up her grave. After eighteen months I'm expecting the coffin to have started rotting and I will have to transfer it into another coffin. All this in the dark, on my own, in the middle of the graveyard. In a nutshell, my problem is, I'm not looking forward to work in the morning.' I bet Alex Ferguson never had to cope with a problem like that with one of his players!

23

The Conference: 1998–2006

1998/99

The dream had come true. National league football, and what better way to start the season than a game against Manchester United, albeit a youth eleven, and another crowd. Rovers managed a 4-1 win, with David Healy pulling a goal back for United. Further friendlies included the 10-0 defeat of Uley in their centenary celebration, 100 years after Forest Green had first played Uley in the Dursley League.

On the footballing side, Mark McGregor joined from Endsleigh in the Hellenic League, along with Rob Murray from AFC Bournemouth and Danny Bailey. Martin Boyle, Grantley Dicks and Gary Marshall all left Rovers.

The opening game of the season saw Rovers take on Rushden & Diamonds, backed by Max Griggs and his Dr Martens shoe empire. A crowd of 1,120 turned up to see Rovers lose 2-0 but certainly not disgraced. In fact, Forest Green should have bagged a hatful of goals in the first half. Rovers then drew with Farnborough Town 2-2 to pick up their first Conference point.

COLIN PEAKE

Rushden & Diamonds were our first Conference opponents. It was all a bit surreal and, despite the 2-0 loss, it was a shot in the arm for Max to say afterwards that he respected all that we had achieved. It had cost him a personal fortune and we had done it on grit and determination. He described us as a 'real football club'. Praise indeed and Max has always been welcomed at the club.

The first competitive league fixture against Cheltenham Town since 1983 was now only a week away. On the night, Rovers were outplayed by a very strong Cheltenham Town team including ex-Rovers keeper Steve Book, Neil Grayson, Jason Eaton and Dave Norton. Cheltenham went 2 goals up before Steve Winter scored in the eighty-seventh minute. Chris Honour became the third Forest Green player to be sent off in the first 4 Conference games.

As a sign of the standard of opposition that Forest Green would be up against, newly relegated Doncaster Rovers signed Tunisian under-21 international Dino Maamria to strengthen their squad, in an attempt to bounce back into the Football League. After 5 games Rovers were second from bottom with 1 point and then drew with bottom club Woking 1-1. Rovers' seventh game was away to Doncaster Rovers.

TREVOR HORSLEY

Well, having got to the Conference, it were just a matter of making sure we stayed in there. We'd been quite fortunate because when we won back-to-back promotions we'd managed to negotiate deals for two years for players, so each time we progressed forward the budget weren't going up as much as it might have done because of Frank's good management.

I can remember going to Doncaster on our first away win. We'd been under the cosh for 88 minutes and we won 1-0. The team spirit coming back on the bus was unbelievable. We had to get out of there pretty quick because it's not a nice place to be, Doncaster, when you've won 1-0. We had some characters in them days like Matthew Coupe dancing on the bus coming back; we've had some great times together.

Forest Green Rovers 1998/99. From left to right, back row: Adie Mings, unknown, Rob Cook, Chris Burns, Shaun Chapple, Billy Clarke, Steve Perrin, Justin Shuttlewood, Don Forbes, Dave Meyhew, Wayne Hatswell, Jason Drysdale, Ian Hedges, Bob Baird. Front row: Chris Honor, Paul Hunt, Steve Winter, Mike Kilgour, Frank Gregan, Marc McGregor, Alex Sykes, Andy Pratley, Adie Randall.

PAUL HUNT

We didn't win the first 6 games, and then we played at Doncaster, away, and we were in the changing rooms and suddenly there was a little knock on the door. Who comes in? Mike Summerbee – massive player, and he looks around and he says 'Where's Paul Hunt? There he is.' I had a little chat with him, he walks out the door and the boys were looking over and I said, 'Boys, you either know him or you don't,' and with that we played the game.

Sykesy, he put me through, and there I was, one on one with possibly the best goalkeeper in the world at one time, Neville Southall. What do I do? There were 4,500 people calling me 'gyppo' because I've got long hair, singing, 'Where's your caravan?', and I was one on one with formerly one of the greatest goalkeepers in the world. What do I do? I slip it past him of course, and we won 1-0. I ran the whole length of the pitch with me hands to me ear saying 'Where's your caravan?' to them, and we won 1-0. That's what kicked our season off.

Neville Southall collects the ball for Doncaster Rovers, Forest Green's first win of the season.

After a further win against Kettering, Rovers then played Kidderminster away and drew 2-2.

PAUL HUNT

Kidderminster away – you ask Mr Peake about the best goal he's ever seen. We was 2-1 down, we took kick-off. I took one touch, nutmegged one, gone past two, gone past three, gone past four, come to the fifth player, looked to me right and me left, couldn't see anyone. I thought I got to go on my own. I took one touch and banged it in the top corner; but the best part about it was I ran, jumped over the railings, put me arms aloft, looked at all the fans and said 'yes' and then I realised I was in the wrong end! I jumped back over and ran up the other end. Two each – great game.

RICHARD GRANT

Shaun Penny scored one of the best goals I've ever seen and that was in the Stroud era, playing in those horrible blue shorts. He was in the six-yard box and he had two defenders behind him with his back to goal, and another two defenders beside him. He had the ball at his feet and he somehow flicked it up on to his toe and then did an overhead kick straight into the back of the net. Brilliant.

But the best goal that I have ever seen was Paul Hunt's goal at Kidderminster. We had just conceded a goal and, from the kick-off, he went past about four players, went out towards the wing and then he just hit this amazing ball cutting in from just outside the penalty area. He was almost on the touchline when he kicked it and it just flew right into the top corner. I had my girlfriend with me at the time and she wasn't really a football person, and she looked at me and her jaw just dropped. She said, 'Is it like this every week?' Fantastic.

Rovers then managed to put some daylight between them and the drop zone with a further win at home against Welling, which was followed by draws against Hednesford and Southport.

The game against Southport also brought national publicity when *The Sun* newspaper decided to follow Forest Green to the game and put a full-page article in the paper in October. Rob Cook was Man of the Match against Southport and also scored the goal in the 1-1 draw. Rovers then lost 2-0 to Rushden & Diamonds away in the third qualifying round of the FA Cup. Rob Cook marked his 100th appearance for Rovers with 2 goals in the 3-1 win over Northwich Victoria and then Forest Green set out on the Trophy trail with a 4-1 victory over Boreham Wood.

Rovers' Christmas fixture list included Yeovil Town at home on Boxing Day and Hereford United on 28 December. The Yeovil game was lost to the weather and it was left for nearly 2,000 people to watch Rovers beat Hereford 2-1. An away win against Welling followed before attention turned again to the FA Trophy, when a crowd of more than 800 turned up to see Forest Green Rovers beat Witney Town 4-0 with an Alex Sykes hat-trick.

The cup form continued in the league with a 3-1 win over Leek Town and then a 4-0 thrashing of Yeovil on their own ground, with goals from Sykes, McGregor and 2 from David Meyhew ending fourth-placed Yeovil's 14-match unbeaten run and stretching Rovers' own to 5 straight wins. Rovers had eight teams below them in the league. Attention then turned back to the FA Trophy and a trip to Weymouth, where Forest Green booked their place in the last sixteen with a dazzling double strike in the second half from Marc McGregor, winning the game 2-1. Frank Gregan snapped up Wayne Hatswell from Cinderford Town to strengthen his squad, which was fast gaining a reputation for having the biggest heart although it belonged to the smallest club in the Conference. They then beat Hitchin Town in the FA Trophy 2-1 with 2 more goals from David Meyhew to reach the quarter-finals.

At the end of March, Forest Green faced Southport at The Lawn in front of a 1,240 crowd in the quarter-final of the FA Trophy, with as much publicity as their trip to Southport at the beginning of the season. Mark McGregor scored his twelfth goal of the season, and his first at The Lawn, to see Forest Green to the semi-final.

Above left: Paul Hunt in action at Southport.

Above right: Rob Cook in action against Witney Town.

All eyes turned to the FA Trophy semi-final against St Albans. Rovers drew the first leg away 1-1, remaining bloodied but unbowed, having led from the second minute when Jason Drysdale smacked home a penalty. They were kept in the game by substitute goalkeeper Steve Perrin, who had replaced Justin Shuttlewood when he suffered a shoulder injury in the first half. In the league Rovers reached their 50-point target in a 1-1 draw against Barrow.

The home leg of the FA Trophy semi-final against St. Albans had been switched to a Sunday to ease crowd congestion, and a record 3,002 crowd turned out to see Forest Green go 2 goals down before Alex Sykes pulled one back on the stroke of half-time.

ALEX SYKES

After scoring a number of goals in the run-up to the semi-finals against St Albans, I still consider one of my career low lights to be getting dropped in the first leg. I was top scorer in the competition that year and couldn't understand Frank's logic. I did get my revenge though with the first goal of ours, and we managed to pull off a massive fightback to get to Wembley. Looking back now, I can honestly say that it's a great honour to have played for Forest Green at Wembley and I couldn't have wished to have done it with any other club.

FRANK GREGAN

Half-time against St Albans in the second leg of the semi-final was one of my more inspirational team talks. We were getting a bit of a pasting and looked out of the tie trailing 2-0, but a Syko goal just before half-time gave us hope. The players still looked despondent in the dressing room and I knew that I had to give them a lift mentally rather than tactically. We were 45 minutes away from Wembley. They had been so much better than us in the first half and all they had to show for it was a slender 1-goal lead. My final statement was, 'If I had told you during pre-season that come April you would be 1 goal behind at half-time, at home in the second leg of the FA Trophy semi-final, to a side from a division below, how many of you would have thought the task beyond you?' St Albans had a goal disallowed in the second half and Steve Perrin made two brilliant saves late on, but it proved to be our day. Goals from Ian Hedges and Gary Smart gave us a 3-2 win and the club's first appearance in an FA Trophy final. I was delighted for everyone at the club, but the person who probably best summed up what that Rovers side was all about was Mike Kilgour, a real football man who had made the most of what he was given and never failed to give his all.

PAUL FURLEY,
BBC RADIO SPORTS DESK

It was all square after the first game and then we went 2-0 down, starting with an own goal. It all looked dead and buried until Alex Sykes scored just before half-time. I remember Colin Peake coming round behind the goal of The Lawn and then stand with the fans to try to generate noise, shouting 'Come on, get them going again!' Unorthodox, but it worked. What a fantastic game. We won 3-2 and were on our way to Wembley.

Above left: Gary Smart scores the winner to take Rovers to Wembley for a second time in their history.

Left: Who would have predicted a return to Wembley at the beginning of the season?

Opposite page:

Above left: The players line up before the match in pensive mood.

Above right: David Meyhew's effort is blocked by the keeper.

Below left: Marc McGregor breaks down the line.

Below centre: It was not to be Rovers' day.

Below right: FA Trophy final programme.

In the run-up to the semi-final, Rovers fans had been dreaming of meeting Cheltenham at Wembley for the final, only to see Kingstonian create an upset. So Forest Green were to face Kingstonian instead, who Rovers had beaten twice in the league. Forest Green visited Whaddon Road in the League and came away with a point after equalising in the eightieth minute through Matthew Coupe.

The league season ended with Rovers in a very respectable twelfth place and then all thoughts turned to the FA Trophy final.

Stroud News & Journal:

Rovers' second visit to Wembley

After the formalities, the final kicked off with both sides making a nervous start, Marc McGregor earning an early talking to from referee Alan Wilkie for his challenge on Mustafa inside the first minute. It was Rovers who seemed likely to draw first blood. On five minutes, Drysdale played a dangerous ball through to Sykes on the left and his cross, aimed at Meyhew, was cut out before the former Bristol Rovers player could cause problems. Six minutes later, McGregor's firm challenge allowed Sykes to launch an ambitious shot from distance that ended up well wide.

Chris Honor then teed up Meyhew twenty yards out, who in turn set up Sykes on the edge of the box. The young striker turned well but fired his shot wide. Rovers should then have taken the lead on seventeen minutes when McGregor slipped his lead along the left and appeared to be held back by Matt Crossly as he surged into the penalty area. He shrugged off the challenge and, with the goal at his mercy, watched on in disbelief as Farrelly pushed his eight-yard effort wide. At the other end, Kingstonian also went close when Mustafa connected with Jeff Pitcher's telling cross from the left but could only direct his shot wide of Shuttlewood's post.

The game became more open and Kingstonian's Gary Patterson was booked for hacking down McGregor on thirty-six minutes. Two minutes later Rattray almost had the misfortune to head into his own net following Sykes' dangerous cross; his clearance was only inches over Farrelly's crossbar. Just before half-time, Kingstonian squandered a golden chance to take the lead.

Half-time: Forest Green 0, Kingstonian 0.

Rovers created another priceless opening for themselves when McGregor charged down Crossley's attempted clearance on the right and charged towards the box. He squared the ball via Meyhew's dummy to Sykes, whose shot was blocked by a sea of red-and-white shirts.

Seconds later, Sykes was cursing his luck as Kingstonian took a forty-ninth-minute lead. Only Shuttlewood will know what he was doing when he flapped at Mark Harris's hanging free kick, allowing Mustafa to sweep the loose ball into an unguarded net for the softest of goals.

Rovers dominated after the goal and relaxed into their best spell when Sykes fed a good ball through to Meyhew down the left, but his low centre was driven too close to Farrelly. While Rovers were streaming forward, there was always the chance of a counterattack and Gary Patterson's delightfully chipped pass found an unmarked Pitcher who shot wide. Rovers made a final throw of the dice on seventy-six minutes, bringing on Gary Smart in favour of Bailey, but Kingstonian went close again two minutes later with Rattray heading Patterson's cross just wide.

Rovers poured forward in the closing stages with Smart almost setting up Sykes, but the pace of the ball into the penalty area was just too heavy for the striker. McGregor then saw his injury time shot tipped wide as Farrelly barely managed to clear the resulting corner.

On the day, the Rovers' contingent of almost 10,000 in the crowd of more than 20,000 saw Kingstonian win 1-0, leaving Forest Green Rovers to fight another day and still dream of becoming the first team to do the FA Vase and FA Trophy double.

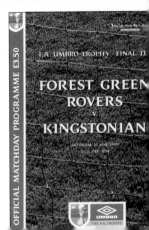

COLIN PEAKE

The team had changed in certain areas but Frank Gregan gave all the players the chance to prove themselves at a higher level. They were not found wanting and the 'little club on the hill' made history by becoming the first to play in the final of the FA Vase and FA Trophy at the home of football – Wembley Stadium. Losing that day was hard but everyone in the area was so proud of how far we had come. Twelfth in the Conference was way above the bookmakers' forecast for certain relegation.

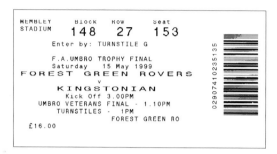

Off the pitch, it immediately became apparent that the club would need to keep one step ahead of yet more ground grading rules introduced by the Conference board. Further issues were raised regarding the standard of stadium accommodation on a number of fronts. Consultants considered many different permutations and combinations but the existing site simply wasn't big enough to redesign and reconfigure the facilities to meet the new grading rules. One of the major problems related to sight lines from the seats in the new stand, which had effectively been built one story above pitch level so that the view of the near touchline was very restricted. Rules are rules, and under the new ones, such a structure would simply not be acceptable.

An opportunity arose to purchase part of the Stroud College site next to The Lawn, which the college had now decided was surplus to requirements. The directors saw an opportunity to expand the site of the existing Lawn ground and worked closely with the Town Council to develop proposals to bid for the site and to develop it for community use, which obviously included the club.

At the end of the day, Stroud College obtained outline planning permission for residential development on the site and walked away from any discussions with the club or the town council. The decision was immediately appealed against. Either the directors could leave things as they were and accept their fate, or move to a new site. The former was not an option. The club also opened the Lawnside Fitness Suite in April and the club's website had been launched at the beginning of the season, having been set up by John Duff's son Jeremy, who had become a director that season.

1999/00

Having finished twelfth in the league and runners-up in the FA Trophy, it really felt as though Forest Green Rovers belonged in the Conference by right. Dennis Bailey joined the club for £15,000 from Cheltenham Town, joining along with Billy Clark from Exeter and Adie Mings. Adie Randall joined from Salisbury. Paul Hunt returned from injury in time for the beginning of the season. On paper, Forest Green had an even stronger squad than the previous year.

The first game of the season was lost away to Doncaster Rovers 3-2. Further losses to Scarborough, Telford and Southport mirrored the poor start to the season before, before Forest Green again beat Kidderminster Harriers, this time 3-2. Four more defeats followed, before Rovers gained a point away at Welling in which Rovers were 'robbed' by a late penalty. Northwich Victoria were then beaten 5-1 and then Stevenage Borough 3-2, with 2 goals coming from Paul Hunt and the third from Dennis Bailey.

ROB COOK

I remember Paul Hunt had a knack of nutmegging players, and he also liked a bet. Anyway, sometimes he would say I bet you I will nutmeg five players today and the bet would usually be £10. One game, I remember he says I'm going to nutmeg the linesman today. As he was on the bench I thought this was easy money. As the players ran out of the tunnel to start the game the referee ran to the middle and the two linesmen ran to check if the nets were okay. I heard Oggy shout 'Oi Cooky!' and I turned to look at him to see him toss the ball up in the air and hit it on the half volley towards the linesman, who was sprinting to the goal thirty yards away. The ball passed through his legs, but clipped his heel and he went tumbling over like he had been shot. We couldn't stop laughing. I didn't mind paying up my debt on that one!

Rovers were still bottom of the league when they lost to Hednesford in October, before facing Worcester City in the FA Cup fourth qualifying round.

FRANK GREGAN

I remember when we reached the FA Cup first round proper for the first time in the club's history after a 5-2 away win against Graham Allner's Worcester City. We were drawn at home to Guisley and our coach, Chris Smith, and I travelled to Yorkshire to run the rule over our opponents. I left home at noon for an evening kick off and after a curry in a Garforth Indian restaurant with the chairman Trevor Horsley and braving a freezing cold northern wind watching a very poor Guisley display, I got home at about 3.30 a.m. 'We'll murder them,' was Chris's confident prediction and he was proved right. We were coasting and went 6-0 up with about five minutes to go. Chris grabbed me by the arm in the dugout, waving a betting slip. 'I've got £3 on at a 100/1 on us winning 6-0 gaffer,' he screeched with excitement!

Having produced 6 first-round goals for *Match of the Day* in the pouring rain, Rovers faced Torquay United in the second round, the second competitive match against a league team in the club's history, but the first under the name of Forest Green Rovers.

The furthest that Forest Green had ever progressed in the FA Cup up until this season was the third qualifying round; another milestone had been achieved in the development of the club. In a blaze of publicity, *The Sun* newspaper, which had taken an interest in Forest Green the year before, called Forest Green the team from the 'Royal Triangle', making reference to the close proximity of Prince Charles, Princess Anne and Princess Michael, all of whom live close to Forest Green.

Another crowd nearly 3,000-strong witnessed another chance for Paul Hunt to beat Neville Southall, who had joined Torquay from Doncaster Rovers the season before. On the day, having played superb FA Cup football for 75 minutes, Forest Green lost to 3 late goals in 10 minutes. A poor header out of defence landed at the feet of Torquay's Brandon, who blasted in a twenty-five-yard shot before, 4 minutes later, the second was scored from a volley inside the penalty area and the third from a follow-up after the original strike had been well saved by Perrin. Torquay went on to play QPR while Forest Green were left to rue the chances that they had earlier in the match.

Dave Norton helped Forest Green to a 3-0 win over Yeovil after Christmas Day, with Marc McGregor scoring twice. Yeovil got their revenge on 3 January with a 1-0 win, before Forest Green again drew with Altrincham 1-1. Still rooted to the bottom of the table, Forest Green faced Hendon in the FA Trophy with a poor first-half performance, before receiving another half-time team talk from Frank Gregan and winning the game 4-1. The win was followed by a confidence-boosting 1-0 victory against Rushden & Diamonds to move the club off the bottom at Welling's expense.

Rovers attack the Torquay goal.

As the season wore on into February, Forest Green faced Sutton away in the FA Trophy, hoping to repeat last year's feat. It was not to be and the game was lost 3-0. By this time, Rovers had suffered 15 defeats in 25 Conference matches and seemed destined for the drop.

A 5-2 victory over Telford, who had parted company with their manager Alan Lewer the day before, lifted Forest Green out of the relegation zone on goal difference from Woking, Welling and Sutton. A further vital victory was secured against Southport and, by the end of March, Forest Green were one of five teams hoping to avoid relegation when a 3-1 win against third-placed Dover Athletic raised further hope. Rovers lost 3-2 away at Sutton United, the league's bottom team, and 5-0 at Scarborough, leaving only 4 games to escape the drop.

FRANK GREGAN

Every FGR fan remembers 'the Kettering game', but the drama started a couple of weeks prior to that game. We lost at home to Welling in a crucial game at The Lawn on Easter Monday and Trevor and I drove to a pub straight after the game just to get away from the club and sat in absolute dejection contemplating the future. We both thought we were down, our chances looked slim.

They continued to look slim when we were drawing at home to Doncaster, in a game we had to win the week before the end of the season, with 10 minutes to go. Syko popped up with a crucial goal and we won 1-0 to keep the hope on a life-support system. We looked dead and buried when we played Kiddy midweek. They had been crowned champions and a full house was helping them celebrate the title. We were 3-0 down midway through the second half and staring the Southern League firmly in the face. Chris Burns hit a screamer to give us hope and, trailing 3-2 in injury time, we were awarded a penalty. McGregor scored and unbelievably we were still alive. A crucial side issue was a falling out I had with Oggy at Kidderminster. He was returning from a long-term injury, had come on as a sub and had changed the game. He was his normal self, buzzing everywhere and making things happen. However, at 3-2 down the ball went dead for a goal kick and I was going mental for us to retrieve the ball and get it back in play as quickly as possible. Oggy collected the ball and, when the keeper held his hand out to get it off him, Oggy 'custard pied' him and dropped the ball and 'megged' him.

Vintage Oggie, very, very funny in a normal situation, but it was neither the time nor the place. It wasted valuable seconds when we were staring relegation in the face. I was fuming and let him have it with both barrels after the match and was adamant he would take no part in the Kettering game.

A couple of nights later Altrincham played Kingstonian and again an Alty win would see us relegated. I couldn't go, I had no control over the game and didn't want to be there when we went down without being able to influence the situation. I went to watch a game at Clevedon with Chris Smith, purely to get out of the house, and Smudge used the time wisely, convincing me I was cutting my nose off to spite my face to not use Oggy against Kettering. Trevor went to Altrincham and I kept in contact by mobile phone. The result was going our way when the fourth official held up the board indicating 4 minutes of stoppage time. Chris Smith was driving up the M5 when I passed on the message. He went berserk – how could there possibly be 4 minutes of stoppage time? There was no way that the watch had been stopped for anywhere near that length of time. We had been watching a game 200 miles away and had no idea how many times the physios had been on the pitch but still he managed to rant and rave about the injustice of it all until the 4 minutes had expired and Trevor passed on the message that we were still alive – just!

Against Kettering our fate was still not in our hands. Trevor had a man at all the games that could have a bearing on us and with about half an hour to go and our game standing at 0-0 he came behind the dugout and kept me informed. Their goal was leading a charmed life and we were doing everything but score. Smudge was badgering me to get Oggy on, the crowd were screaming for him but I was determined to wait. He was chomping at the bit but we were running them ragged and the longer it went on the greater his impact would be against a tiring defence. Fair play to Trevor, he was white as a ghost and every time a shot flew just wide and I'd look at him in anguish I thought he was going to burst into tears! But never once did he interfere, all he kept doing was updating the scores for me. Oggy's impact was massive – he scored 1 and set up the second for McGregor and yet again all the other results went our way. There are a load of tales of sides celebrating promotion and relegation matters without having the full facts, most notably Gloucester City at Bromsgrove under Brian Godfrey and Steve Millard, who celebrated for a full forty-five minutes before finding out they had been pipped for a place in the Conference by Farnborough! The moment the whistle went I headed back to the dressing room. Trevor had told me the scores but I wanted them validated. I was alone, sat on the shower floor with the cold shower flowing, listening to James Alexander Gordon reading the scores and, at four minutes past five I knew the Great Escape had just been re-enacted!

TREVOR HORSLEY

All I can remember was I had somebody at Altrincham, I had somebody at Hednesford, and I had two mobiles and I were stood by the dugout. And I'm stood there and flipping Frank went and kicked the dugout and I dropped both me mobiles, so I was trying to get back live to the two kids that I'd sent to each ground and couldn't get a line back. And we didn't really know until 5 minutes after the final whistle whether we were certain or not.

Frank Gregan, the architect of Forest Green's rise through the ranks in the 1990s.

PAUL HUNT

Kettering at home. This is where the fans play a great part; everyone kept singing 'Oggy, Oggy, Oggy, we want Oggy.' I had been injured a lot at the time as well – and Frank Gregan was looking at me. 'Go and get warmed up,' and every time I warmed up the crowd got excited, and then I'd sit back down again. Ten minutes from the end, 15 minutes from the end, I can't really remember now, he said to me 'Go on, on you go son, get me the winner,' and all I can remember was Chris Burns played me the ball, I took one touch inside on my left peg, which is never my best one; and I just swerved it in the bottom bag. From there on it was just, well, it was madness. Well, it was better than winning a cup, because I'd met the girl of my dreams at Forest Green, and I'd helped them along, staying up in the league they're still up now. I'd kept them up in this league, done my job, what I was paid for, and it's the best feeling I've ever had with football to be fair.

Left: Sheer elation, Paul Hunt fires his shirt into the crowd after the Kettering game.

Opposite: Forest Green had been to Wembley and won the Vase, lost in the Trophy final the season before, but the Kettering game was something else.

PAUL FURLEY, BBC RADIO SPORTS DESK

I think my most memorable goal has to be Oggy's goal against Kettering on the final day of the season. I saw stars in front of my eyes jumping around realising that, with 6 minutes to go, Oggy might have saved us, so long as Altrincham only drew, and they did. Marc McGregor scored a second just a couple of minutes later, but Oggy's goal was the key.

I remember BBC Radio Gloucestershire's 'Ballistic' Bob Hunt jumping out of the commentary seat, describing it thus: 'Burns finds Hunt. Hunt, edge of the area now, gonna set it up for a shot is Hunt, shoots AND IT'S IN! HUNT HAS SCORED FOR FOREST GREEN ROVERS! A TYPICAL GOAL FROM OGGY HUNT! He took his time, he beat Paul Cox, he put it in the inside netting. It's Forest Green Rovers 1, Kettering Town 0, 6 minutes to go!'

Off the pitch, other sites for a new stadium in the area were considered, particularly one site in Stonehouse and a second site along the Avening Road just outside Nailsworth. The Stonehouse site fell foul of planning restrictions, where it was felt that such a significant development could lead to further offspring developments, and also a high value was put on the land at the last minute. It would not be financially viable to develop that site. The Avening Road site was not ideally situated for a stadium development and fell to technical issues regarding access to the site and highway upgrading issues both along the Avening Road and in Nailsworth. Both potential sites were not viable. A new option had to be found.

2000/01

At the start of the season, Nigel Spink signed as goalkeeper. At the same time Marc McGregor was sold to Nuneaton Borough for £35,000, joining Alex Sykes, who had received an offer from Nuneaton in the close season.

ALEX SYKES

I remember the greatest wrench of my Forest Green career was Frank telling me that I could go elsewhere if I could find a club. After four and a half years with Forest Green I felt so settled and for him to tell me I could leave after being involved with their rise, I was gutted. I got a call from Brendan Phillips who said he would like to meet me to chat about going to Nuneaton (I had already turned down Stevenage, thinking I would be at Forest Green for at least another year), so I met Brendan and he offered me terms. Me leaving Forest Green actually took all of twelve seconds when I called Frank on his holidays in Spain and informed him that I had been approached by Nuneaton. He said 'All the best,' and in such a short time, that was that.

Pre-season friendly matches didn't produce a win and Forest Green travelled to Boston and drew 0-0 before losing at home to Stevenage and then drawing at home with Doncaster Rovers 2-2. Off the pitch, planning permission was obtained for a new stand on the Nailsworth side of the ground to meet further Conference ground grading requirements. A win against Kingstonian in the eighth game of the season catapulted Rovers to thirteenth with goals from Adrian Foster, Billy Clark and Alex Meechan. The game was followed by a thrilling 4-4 draw against Dagenham. At 3-3 in the last 10 minutes, Wayne Hatswell scored a goal at both ends, not his last own goal at The Lawn.

League worries were forgotten when Bath City were soundly beaten 3-1 in the FA Cup fourth qualifying round. Rovers' reward was a first-round tie against Morecambe in November, which proved to be one of Wayne Hatswell's last games for the club. Forest Green lost 3-0 but the game produced one of the most famous goals scored by a Rovers player when Wayne spectacularly slammed an attempted clearance into his own net. The goal has been shown many times since on *Match of the Day* as Gary Lineker's favourite. The result against Morecambe also brought about the end of Frank Gregan's time in charge at Forest Green, with Trevor Horsley admitting that he had 'endured his worst day in football' having to part company with the architect of the club's footballing success.

FRANK GREGAN

Forest Green sacked me in November 2000 but the board meeting that probably sealed my fate took place in June that year. 'Give me an extra thirty grand and I will guarantee that we will not finish in the bottom six,' I said. 'Anything less and we are in for an almighty struggle again.' I am still to this day not privy to their negotiations but the meeting lasted nearly three hours after which I was told there was no increase. I always said I didn't want the biggest budget, I just wanted a competitive one. Give me a bottom-six budget and I'll give you a mid-table team, I used to tell the board. Give me a bottom-two budget and I'll scrap like hell to keep you out of the bottom three. I was told by the board in June, 'We accept it will be a struggle, just keep us out of the bottom three.'

I had had a meeting with Trevor and Carol Embury straight after the Morecambe game and I was the proverbial turkey voting for Christmas. I made it clear that I thought a change was necessary. It was still an awful meeting on the Monday morning between Trev, Carol and I. It was certainly emotional. I was greatly saddened leaving a club that I loved. You hear that from chancers all the time – 'I love the club' – but believe me, I did. It was a massive wrench. Even to this day, a director at Weston collects all the scores in our division and we sit down in the boardroom and go through the day's events that affect our football club. When we are finished, without asking, he tells me two other results. Newcastle United and Forest Green. Enough said.

My exit package was tied up quickly between Carol, Trev and myself. However, the board intervened again. I took a call from Trevor at home, he told me he was on speakerphone and the rest of the board were listening in. He said they were unhappy with my pay-off and only prepared to pay X amount. The shortfall was large. 'That's not what we agreed Trev,' I said. There was a short pause and the gruff Yorkshire voice came down the line. 'I'll make sure you get what we agreed, I'll pay it myself.' Anyone who has ever done business with Trevor will know how hard he is and never gives an inch if he doesn't want to. I think that action summed up what kind of job he thought I had done for him over six and a half years.

I am certainly not bitter. Not in the slightest. I feel a great deal of pride about our achievements while I was there and have the greatest affection for the club. But the overriding emotion I have is gratitude. I am so grateful to have been given the opportunity to manage the club. That opportunity has allowed me to live my dream.

Billy Clarke clears from Cheltenham's Neil Grayson in the Senior Cup at the start of the season.

Nigel Spink and Dave Norton were appointed player-managers and they got off to a winning start with a 2-1 win over Dover, both goals being scored by Wayne Hatswell before he was finally sold to Oxford United for an initial payment of £35,000. By the turn of the year, Paul Hunt was eying a return from his latest injury after a second knee operation in eighteen months and Rovers lost to Boston on a frozen pitch at The Lawn on New Year's Eve. Leon Cort joined Rovers' defence on loan from Millwall and Alex Meechan signed a contract to move back to Forest Green.

Rovers were fourth from bottom in January when they beat Barton Rovers 6-1 in the third round of the FA Trophy. Rovers moved on to meet Matlock Town, drawing 2-2 and then winning 3-1 in the replay. Under new management, Frankie Bennett became the latest player to fall out of favour and was placed on the transfer list. He had made 9 starts under Frank but only 2 for Nigel and Dave. Rovers then beat Rushden & Diamonds 2-0 to face Worksop Town in their second quarter-final in two years. They also slipped back into the relegation zone as Kingstonian drew level with them on points.

Martin Foster made his loan move from Doncaster Rovers permanent in March, bolstering the midfield. He played in the quarter-final against Worksop, whose team included forty-year-old Chris Waddle in front of a crowd of 1,448. Rovers were originally informed that their visitors would be bringing two coaches but the number had shot up to eleven once it became clear that Chris Waddle had joined the club. On the day, only nine coaches turned up. The other two coaches had gone to Forest Green in Surrey, a short drive from Gatwick Airport. The mistake led to further national newspaper coverage with a story of coaches going missing in the 'Royal Triangle'.

In the league, Rovers won 3-2 against Kettering to move up to fourth from bottom on the same day that Kingstonian lost to Rushden & Diamonds. The Kettering game saw Mark Cooper make his debut having moved from Hednesford, and he scored his first goal for the club after 25 minutes with a thirty-yard screamer.

The first leg of the Trophy semi-final was played at The Lawn against Hereford in front of nearly 3,000 fans. Hereford had the half-time advantage but Frankie Bennett levelled with a superb chip after 62 minutes. Hereford then went back into the lead 12 minutes from time but Alex Meechan levelled 2 minutes later with a penalty, having been brought down by Tony James.

Having drawn with Hereford at home in the first leg of the semi-final 2-2, attention turned to the second leg. The large contingent of Forest Green fans was treated to one of the best displays ever seen from a Rovers team, when Hereford were simply overrun by a scintillating display of attacking football. Forest Green won the match 4-1 and moved into the final at Villa Park against Canvey Island, a team from the Ryman League, making Rovers favourites to pick up the Trophy.

Stroud News & Journal:

It was an epic performance. Forest Green defended well against an onslaught from the Bulls and Steve Perrin was in superb form; his save after five minutes from Ian Wright was a turning point. Rovers kept their shape at the back, and when they had the opportunity to attack they did it in style. The finishing was clinical and Frankie Bennett, who was brilliant when he came on at half-time in the first leg, was the hero when he rifled home from just inside the box after a Stuart Slater corner was poorly cleared.

Rovers continued to soak up the pressure but went further ahead with Bennett instrumental in the move with a fine run down the right and a weighted cross into the box. Striker Adrian Foster placed a low header against the post but Alex Meechan was on hand to blast the ball home. Hereford lost their impetus in the second half and it became a niggly affair with a string of bookings, but it was still Rovers who managed to apply the pressure.

Rovers seemed to have made the game safe on fifty-nine minutes when Chris Burns netted in a goalmouth scramble following a Meechan corner. Hereford pulled a goal back three minutes later but any hope of a comeback was short lived as Adrian Foster made the game completely safe and booked Rovers a place in the final at Villa

Park with a super goal nine minutes from time. Slater made the initial run, playing a one-two with Adrian Foster to allow him to go for goal and rifle home. The goal was very special to Adrian Foster, who had taken a lot of abuse from the Hereford supporters when they were relegated from the Football League.

Rovers ran out to a packed house at Edgar Street, and then produced one of their best-ever performances.

ALEX SYKES

I was cup tied, on loan from Nuneaton when we went to Hereford and won 4-1. Myself and Jason Eaton were jumping up and down like madmen in the stand. I remember in previous meetings with them that I would get loads of stick from their fans who remembered who I was, so even though I wasn't involved on the pitch, I was ecstatic that we beat them so convincingly.

After getting on the coach to leave, a couple of their less pleasant fans attempted to get on the bus to cause trouble, while also giving Tony Daley abuse. I had never heard Tony ruffled in any way before, both by opposing fans or opposing players who used to taunt him. This occasion was slightly different though – after I heard one fan really laying into him Tony retorted 'At least I haven't got a mortgage to pay.' The lads in the squad loved it because, as anyone who knows Tony will tell you, he is the least big-time Charlie ever, such a top gent, and for him to say that was hilarious.

TREVOR HORSLEY

The best games under Nigel Spink and Dave Norton were the semi-finals against Hereford. They had come to our place and got the draw and thought they'd done it. It were disappointing at home because we'd had a bit of trouble that day, not on the ground but in town, a lot of Hereford lads causing trouble, and it weren't a nice day, the home game.

But then, when we went to Hereford, what spurred us on was when we got to the ground, we looked at the Hereford programme and they had an advertisement in there selling merchandise for the final. So I just said to Spinksy and Norton; we've got to make the most of this because they think they've won. And so we put it up, all over the dressing room, and when the players arrived we had them all up just as a motivator. Frankie Bennett tore them apart. And we had a bit more trouble after because there were a lot of bad feeling towards Dave Norton and Adrian Foster, who used to play up front for them. It were just a nice feeling to get out of there. And then we're off to Villa Park – two appearances in an FA Trophy final! It's quite good going for a village side!

ANDY WHITING

There were so many stories going around that Hereford had opened up the shop to sell FA Trophy final merchandise before we'd even played the second leg. I don't think more than 500 Forest Green fans went to the game, it wasn't a very nice day weatherwise, but my abiding memory of that day was Frankie Bennett, who caused absolute mayhem and completely ran the show and overwhelmed Hereford. I will never forget that game as certainly the best game that I've seen. To beat Hereford like that, as underdogs, was a very special day.

Rovers were still in severe danger of being relegated when they travelled to Chester City and won 1-0, then drew with Hereford at home in the league 1-1 and again with Hednesford 1-1, stretching Forest Green's unbeaten run to 6 games. They then gained a superb victory away at Morecambe 2-0.

Alex Sykes had returned to the club a few months earlier and he scored 1 of the goals in the 2-0 win over Southport that clinched Conference football for another season. It had gone right down to the wire again, with only 2 further league games to follow. Adam Lockwood scored the other goal, having played 9 games for Forest Green since joining on loan from Reading as a replacement for Leon Cort who had returned to Millwall. His presence in the team coincided with Forest Green's unbeaten run at the end of the season. They then drew with Nuneaton and beat Kingstonian on the last day of the season to complete an 11-match unbeaten run. Rovers finished in sixteenth place at the end of the season. Mark Cooper had finished the season as skipper but Frankie Bennett didn't feature in the last few games, having played his role in getting Forest Green to their second FA Trophy final.

The Aston Villa romance of having joint managers and Tony Daley being an ex-Villa player was latched on to by the press. Canvey Island, from the Ryman League, were the first non-Conference team to appear in a final for some time.

Stroud News & Journal:

On the day, Forest Green simply didn't perform. It was supposed to be a dream return to Villa Park for the Villa contingent. Few would argue that Canvey didn't deserve the victory; they had bite and attitude in their approach to the game; Rovers had five of their regular first team cup tied.

In the early stages, Rovers battled it out, giving as good as they got, but they couldn't deal with a simple set piece, one that they would normally have dealt with blindfolded, and they were cruelly punished from Canvey's first corner of the match. It was taken short, and ended in a cross into the box that Ben Chenery cruised on to the end of, unmarked, to nod the Gulls in front after sixteen minutes. It was as easy as that, Steve Perrin didn't stand a chance. There were too many unforced errors. Adam Lockwood, who had been a rock towards the end of the season, had Rovers' nerves jangling after he headed a cross inches wide of his own goal. Spink and Norton brought on Frankie Bennett at half-time with Tony Daley switching back to his favoured left flank, but it was Canvey who again went close ten minutes into the second half, missing an open goal.

Towards the end of the game Rovers came alive and a frenzied final ten minutes followed with Paul Hunt brought on as a substitute. Nothing Rovers did could break the Essex side down, even when Adam Lockwood was pushed up front. The FA Vase and FA Trophy double would have to wait for another year.

Nobody could say that Forest Green's first three seasons in the Conference had not been eventful.

Above left: Rovers supporters in expectant mood before kick off.

Above right: Rovers supporters made up the majority of the crowd.

Middle left: The Villa Park squad. Back row: Nigel Spink, Billy Clarke, Ian Hedges, Adrian Foster, Matthew Ghent, Steve Perrin, Adam Lockwood, Chris Burns, Tony Daley, Rob Cousins, Paul Hunt. Front row: Jason Drysdale, Frankie Bennett, Stuart Slater, Luke Prince, Alex Meechan, Martin Foster, Dave Norton.

Left: Steve Perrin under attack from Canvey.

TREVOR HORSLEY

We went to Villa Park as favorites. We'd done us homework on them and we knew how good a team they were, and we had to stop one player playing, Stimpson, who became the Grays boss. Unfortunately they didn't stop him playing on the day and too many of our people froze. It was disappointing really that Frankie Bennett didn't play from the start because I thought he'd done enough to get a place, but the gaffer chose not to give him a place, and we probably paid for that. We should have probably started with him because his pace were phenomenal and he could deliver.

So disappointing really, but still delighted to get there twice. Third time lucky, it has to be then!

FRANK GREGAN

The second appearance in an FA Trophy final was a surreal experience for me. I'd left the club in November and watched from the stand at Villa Park in May as we went down 1-0 to Canvey Island. What made the situation bizarre was that I had signed the entire team that played that day with the exception of Adam Lockwood. It was my team that day, yet I was no longer in charge of them. It was not a pleasant experience.

2001/02

Nigel Spink was manager when more than 1,000 spectators turned out to watch Forest Green play a Manchester City XI in Frank Gregan's testimonial, with the team including a young Joey Barton. New arrivals Carl Heggs and Simon Travis added strength in depth to the Rovers squad.

Off the pitch, the new Barnfield Terrace was completed. The planning appeal lodged by Stroud College went against the club in August, finally putting an end to any hope of expansion at the existing ground. The club had hit a glass ceiling with their facilities and could not meet the latest ground grading rules regarding sight lines.

After 12 games, Forest Green had 19 points in the bag and a mid-table position before old habits returned, losing to the league's bottom side Stalybridge Celtic 2-0 at home.

Off the pitch, John Clapp joined the board as an executive director, having resigned as a director of Bristol City two months previously, where he had been a director for eight years. Rovers jumped at the opportunity to benefit from his experience in both football and business, and his contacts with Bristol City.

Kayode Odejayi made his debut for the club against Telford United in a 0-0 draw on 20 October on loan from Bristol City and, in the same month, goalkeeper Steve Perrin was called into the England semi-professional squad, following in the footsteps of Marc McGregor two years earlier. In the FA Cup, Forest Green Rovers beat Fisher Athletic 3-1 before meeting Macclesfield away in the first round proper. Rovers drew 2-2, with Mark Cooper equalising from the penalty spot 9 minutes from time after Kayode Odejayi was brought down. The replay that followed at The Lawn was watched by more than 1,700 fans, despite being on the *Match of the Day* highlights, and ended with a 1-1 draw and a penalty shoot-out that would go down in history, setting the record at the time for the longest penalty shoot-out with twenty-three attempts. Rovers were cruelly knocked out 11-10 on penalties and lost out on the £20,000 prize money. But the blow was sweetened by the appearance on *Match of the Day* for which a small fee was paid.

Stroud News & Journal:
In an extraordinary shoot-out, every player including the goalkeepers from both sides took a penalty. Alex Meechan missed from Rovers' second kick but Ricky Lambert had his effort saved by Steve Perrin immediately afterwards. The unfortunate miss came from midfielder Kevin Langan, who blazed his second spot kick over the bar. Experienced striker Lee Glover was the Macclesfield hero, when he coolly stepped up to slot the ball past Perrin. Nigel Spink rightly felt hard done by with the result after a superb performance. Rovers had been the better team over the two games.

Margate at home November 2001, Steve Perrin in action again in less luxurious surroundings.

Rovers' 10-match unbeaten run in open play ended with a 3-0 defeat at Farnborough, which was Odejayi's last game on loan for Forest Green for the time being, having been edged out of the team by Carl Heggs. The Boxing Day match saw Yeovil Town held to a 1-1 draw, and then came a 6-1 defeat away to Boston. Rovers then beat Aldershot Town in the FA Trophy after a replay to set up a second meeting, again against Worksop Town, winning 1-0. Mark Cooper had given Rovers the lead with yet another scorching free-kick, this time skimming across the drenched turf from more than forty yards out. Rovers then bowed out of the competition, losing 3-2 away to Stevenage in the fifth round.

Results towards the end of the season tailed off quite dramatically as Forest Green plummeted to within 2 points of the drop zone, before they beat Barnet away 1-0 with a penalty from Mark Cooper, with 2 games of the season left. Cooper then assured Forest Green's Conference survival by scoring 2 to beat Northwich Victoria in the penultimate game. Forest Green finished eighteenth, 7 points above the relegation zone.

THE NEW STADIUM

Forest Green's hopes of securing the land adjacent to the The Lawn disappeared in April when the High Court slammed the appeal inspector's decision to refuse Stroud College permission to change the land use on the school site to housing. Permission was granted and it was quickly sold off.

The club's thoughts turned to the possibility of siting a new stadium on the surplus playing fields at Highwood. The idea received positive support from the town council, Nailsworth Primary School and Gloucestershire County Council, who actually owned the playing fields. The town council employed a consultant to look at potential proposals in more detail and a thumbs-up was received. Further discussions followed to establish whether the county council could consider selling some of the surplus playing-field site to the football club. The answer was yes.

2002/03

Under Nigel Spink, Rovers lost the first 5 games of the season. Jon Richardson and Neil Grayson joined the club along with Kayode Odejayi in time to face Chester City. Experienced midfielder Gary Owers had also joined at the beginning of the season.

Nigel Spink was shown the door after another defeat at home to Chester. The team's form at the beginning of this season and the end of the last had resulted in only 2 wins in 15 games, including 11 defeats, not good enough to keep Rovers in an increasingly professional league.

Above: Forest Green Rovers 2002/03. Back row: Matt Coupe, Alan McLoughlin, Carl Heggs, Neil Grayson, Kevin Langan, Gary Owers, Steve Jenkins. Middle row: Steve Lock, Paul Birch, Alex Meechan, Luke Jones, Lee Pritchard, Steve Perrin, Ellis Glassup, Jamie Impey, Simon Futcher , Rob Cook, Darren Perrin, Dave Tyrrell. Front row: Trevor Tierney, Danny Allen, Lee Russell, Adie Adams, Nigel Spink, Martin Foster, Alex Sykes, John Cant, Nathan Lightbody.

Right: Neil Grayson challenges for the ball against Hereford United, August 2002.

ANDY WHITING

Nigel got relieved of his duties against Chester City at home. Colin Addison watched from the stands when we beat Burton Albion in the following game for our first points of the season, and then he took over the reins.

I remember Brian Clough being at the game in Burton and I had taken David Smith up to watch Forest Green. David was obviously a well-known referee from the 1970s and Brian Clough recognised him and came over to us. They had a long chat together about their time in football. They obviously had a great respect for each other.

TREVOR HORSLEY

We just were going nowhere and I think we'd gone so many games without a win, and there were probably times when we should have won. That's when we got Colin Addison in. He was a difficult person, great manager, great motivator. I would like to have worked with him ten years prior to that when he were a bit younger because I would imagine that me and him could have worked together very well. He brought in Paddy Mullin with him, and they did very well; worked hard at it.

Colin Addison, who not so long before had been manager of Atletico Madrid, was installed to guide Forest Green to safety. Rovers were still bottom after 10 games, with only 6 points, and then travelled away to Farnborough. Forest Green's new strike partnership of Neil Grayson and Kayode Odejayi, the old and the young, both netted goals in a 3-0 victory complemented by a spectacular effort from Alex Sykes. A 4-4 draw against Barnet saw Rovers move out of the relegation zone, with Alex Meechan scoring 2 goals to peg Barnet back towards the end of the game.

Forest Green's form picked up as the season wore on. In the FA Cup, Rovers played Ford United in the fourth qualifying round, winning 2-1. Their reward was a home tie against Exeter City, which was destined to become the first live TV game beamed from The Lawn into everybody's homes for Sunday lunchtime viewing on the BBC. Unfortunately, the game itself was not a great spectacle and ended 0-0 with a replay to follow at St James' Park.

The following Saturday, Forest Green travelled to Barnet and gave what must have been one of their most inept performances so far in the Conference. Kayode Odejayi managed to give the ball away when not even under pressure, leading to an early goal for Barnet and the whole

Right: Colin Addison congratulates Rob Cook after the Gravesend game.

Far right: Kayode Odejayi in action against Gravesend in September soon after joining the club.

of the rest of the team seemed to be under a spell that said 'thou shalt not play football'. The game was lost 2-0, but had it been lost 7-0, Forest Green couldn't have complained.

Three days later down in Exeter, for the FA Cup replay, the story could not have been more different. Forest Green came out from the kick-off and took the game to Exeter and played one of their most memorable matches in front of a large contingent of Rovers fans. For most of the match, it looked as though Rovers were the better team and then, right at the death, Steve Flack popped up at the back post to score a winner for Exeter, breaking the hearts of the Rovers' travelling support.

A Boxing Day win over Yeovil 2-1, with the winner from Odejayi, and a draw away at Hereford, set Rovers up for the New Year. The match at Hereford saw Rovers play in red again, having to borrow the home side's away kit after the referee insisted on a change because of a colour clash. In the FA Trophy, Forest Green beat Barnet 4-2 at the beginning of January in the third round, followed by Gainsborough Trinity and Dover Athletic before facing Havant & Waterlooville at home in the quarter-final in March. Rovers lost the game 2-1 having appeared to become overconfident. The dream of a semi-final meeting against Gloucester City remained just that, as they also bowed out against Aylesbury in the quarter-final.

Rovers' fans were not too disappointed because, in the league, it appeared that Forest Green stood a real chance of finishing in the top half for the first time in the Conference, especially after a fine 6-1 victory over Nuneaton with 8 games to go. And this is exactly what they did, ending in ninth position, their best ever finish.

TIM BARNARD

I had been following reports of the possibility of developing a new stadium proposal within Forest Green with interest. I am a structural engineer and deal with development proposals from feasibility stage to completion on a daily basis.

The one thing I did want to do was to help the club if it went ahead with the proposal. I initially offered our services to Colin Peake and then met Trevor Horsley for the first time before the match at Gravesend that season to talk through the proposals in more detail. If they were up to seeing it through, then so was I.

An initial meeting was arranged by Colin Peake to meet all of the local authority officials, who would have an input into the planning process early in May 2003 and, with twenty-five people attending the meeting, it was immediately clear that the planning process would be a delicate balancing act from the start.

2003/04

Denny Ingram and Gareth Stoker joined the squad as Ken Boulton took over as chairman to allow Trevor Horsley to concentrate on the ground relocation plans. The pre-season's friendlies in July included traffic questionnaires, as design work on the new stadium plan went ahead in earnest.

Two of Forest Green's first 5 matches included 5-goal hauls for the opposition, one of them a 5-2 loss to Exeter City at home. Steve Brodie joined on loan from Chester, bringing scintillating attacking form to Rovers but, after 7 games, only 7 points had been gained. By the end of September, things hadn't improved when Scott Morgan lashed out at his teammate Martin Foster in a home defeat at Halifax, and immediately left the club. Jamie Moralee and Richard Kennedy had also joined Rovers from Barry Town, who had just gone bust.

Forest Green's league position the year before had earned them a first-ever appearance in the LDV Vans Trophy, in which they were drawn against Brighton & Hove Albion on Monday 13 October. Brighton became the highest-positioned league opposition played to date and, although the game was lost 2-0 with goals from Leon Knight, Forest Green did not disgrace themselves in any way against a team two divisions higher than them.

Gary Owers left the club to manage Bath City at the beginning of November, as Forest Green lost 3-1 in the FA Cup fourth qualifying round at home to Aldershot. Alex Sykes travelled the other way, having been on loan at Bath, as Rovers again lost to Aldershot, this time 3-0 in the league.

As Christmas approached, Forest Green had already conceded 5 goals on three occasions before they infamously faced Hereford on Friday 19 December at The Lawn, losing 7-1. Colin Addison made his exit following that game to be replaced by his assistant Tim Harris, who took over as caretaker manager.

TREVOR HORSLEY

Things weren't going so well for Colin that season. I think the culmination of that were the Hereford game. To try and take on a footballing side like Hereford in your own back garden and lose seven; that were the lowest point of my involvement with Forest Green. I just couldn't let it go on any longer and we had to change it.

Whether we got it right or not, I don't think we did. In fact, there are several times when I don't think we got it right; perhaps we should have took more of a gamble on going for a bigger name.

Forest Green defeated Chester City 2-1 at The Lawn in January, a game that they were fully expected to lose to the league leaders. On the day, Forest Green proved the better team, Scott Rogers scoring the winner, and the result convinced the directors to appoint Tim Harris on a permanent basis. On the previous Saturday, Forest Green beat Sutton United 4-0 in the FA Trophy and went on to meet Dover in the fourth round, losing in a replay 2-1.

As the season wore on, Forest Green's form dropped off and Rovers finished in eighteenth place, 9 points above the relegation zone. Talk towards the end of the season was once again dominated by the need to survive in the Conference.

Northwich Victoria finished bottom of the league, below Leigh RMI, and the bottom three teams were spared relegation as both Margate and Telford United left the league and Lewes failed ground grading rules and weren't promoted.

Above: Neil Grayson scores against Sutton, January 2004.

Right: Martin Foster in action against Barnet, March 2004.

The New Stadium

TREVOR HORSLEY

I had always wanted to try and improve The Lawn but, looking at the position we'd got ourself in, there was no way we could ever do that at the existing ground. The Conference weren't happy with our ground but, because we have always had such an exemplary safety record, they let us stay.

TIM BARNARD

As the season wore on, so the number of meetings with different officials from the various local authorities increased. A strategy was drawn up with the aim of submitting a planning application by October 2003, and achieving planning approval by May 2004. The sheer volume of work required made the task an uphill struggle.

Back in 2002, the idea of volunteering to help out felt only right. By the end of 2003, it felt like a matter of life and death to see the club through what for any organisation is a very difficult and risky time. An archaeological dig, bat survey, badger survey, reptile survey, traffic studies and many more things were commissioned in support of the application.

As well as developing proposals for the stadium, plans were also drawn up to maximise the value of the existing ground, and planning permission was sought for residential development at the existing ground. The key to the whole development was to ensure that sufficient funds could be generated from the sale of the ground to see the new stadium come to fruition. In actual fact, both applications were lodged with Stroud District Council in January 2004 and there then followed many more anxious hours, paying yet more consultants to answer questions raised by the authorities.

The application was finally reviewed by the planning committee at their meeting in July 2004, where it received their unanimous backing. I felt an overwhelming sense of relief, nothing more, that the first major hurdle had been crossed but, less than twenty-four hours later, the application was pulled in by the Home Secretary for review through his Government Office for the South-West. Stroud Council had a restraining order placed on them by the government not to issue the approval certificate until all the submitted information had been reviewed by their team of experts.

I remember going down on the train with my family for our annual holiday in Cornwall that August simply wondering whether we had crossed every 'T' and dotted every 'I', or whether all of these last year's efforts would be in vain. In actual fact, at the end of August, still in St Ives, I received a phone call from Stroud Council to confirm that the Government Office had confirmed that all was in order and gave them the go-ahead to issue the approval. The new stadium was now more likely than not to become a reality.

2004/05

Martin Foster left the club to join Halifax to be near his home in Yorkshire, following the birth of his first child. Tim Harris started the season as manager with Trevor Horsley back in the driving seat as chairman. Forest Green got off to their worst ever start, losing their first 7 games, ending with the defeat 4–0 away at Halifax. This was the last straw for the board and Alan Lewer was brought in as manager to try and turn Rovers' fortunes around. From day one, Alan's task was an uphill struggle but the first signs of daylight were seen in his first game in charge at home in a 1–1 draw with Farnborough. The first win of the season came away at Woking in October in Forest Green's twelfth game of the season. Rovers were firmly rooted to the foot of the table. Three further defeats in the league were followed by a surprise 3–1 win away at York City on 6 November.

Having had the worst possible start to the season in the league, Forest Green Rovers drew Thame United in the FA Cup, with Jefferson Louis featuring up front against his former team. There was a real sense of satisfaction among both supporters and players as Forest Green progressed to the next round, winning 5–0.

Forest Green moved to the first round of the FA Cup again, this time drawing AFC Bournemouth at home. The game proved to be more of a spectacle than when Rovers had faced Exeter and a reasonably entertaining match was drawn 1–1, Jefferson Louis scoring the equaliser with a great header. The replay followed in Bournemouth's new Dean Court stadium. In the event, Forest Green gave a really good account of themselves, scoring a fantastic goal through Des Lyttle towards the end of the match, although they ultimately lost 3–1.

Northwich Victoria received a 10-point deduction but fought back admirably throughout the latter part of the season, gaining a sufficient number of points to avoid relegation. Northwich's success on the field moved Forest Green into the third relegation slot above Leigh RMI and Farnborough, and a 1–0 win away at Carlisle at the beginning of April gave some sense of hope to follow the despair of the previous week, when Rovers lost away at Northwich 2–1.

Everything depended on beating Hereford United to pull away from the relegation zone but it was not to be and the game was lost 3–1. Following a further defeat at Morecambe and a draw at home to Canvey Island, Forest Green finished in twentieth place and were technically relegated from the league. Alan Lewer left the club following the game against Canvey Island.

Rovers were reinstated in the summer, having already decided to play in Conference North, when the decision was taken to relegate Northwich from the Conference because of company irregularities. Forest Green were spared to fight another day in the Conference, just as Northwich had been the year before.

Forest Green Rovers 2004/05. From left to right, back row: Jason Ford, Adie Adams, Simon Bryant, Scott Rogers, Michael Green, Matt Bown, Ben Cleverley, Ryan Trowbridge, Ray Brown. Middle row: Nick Cornwall, Charlie Griffin, Ian Holloway, Matt Gadsby, Danny Greaves, Steve Perrin, Andy Thompson, Tom Jordan, Matt Aubrey, Stuart Martyn. Front row: Luke Jones, Steve Cowe, Mark Beesley, Alan McLoughlin, Tim Harris, Steve Lock, John Richardson, Alex Sykes, Darren Davies.

TIM BARNARD

Having obtained a 'Resolution not to refuse' the new stadium from the council, there then followed perhaps the most frustrating part of the whole process as the two legal agreements to accompany the planning certificates were effectively negotiated by no fewer than eight sets of solicitors, all soliciting in the best interests of their clients. I don't think I have ever felt so frustrated in my life, effectively becoming a messenger to chase one solicitor up to ring another solicitor, to then have a chat and agree to change a section of wording, which then had to be agreed by all the other parties. The whole process simply went round in circles for months and even calling the various parties together for meetings seemed to have no effect. At the same time, legal bills mounted up to a figure in excess of £100,000. Every single time a clause was redrafted by one party or another, the time charge clock ticked on eight solicitors' clocks.

Delicate negotiations also continued with potential purchasers, and an agreement was finally reached with Redrow Homes to sell the site and for Redrow to issue Forest Green Rovers with a cost-free licence to continue to play at The Lawn until the new stadium was complete. The money was therefore in the bank to enable the job to proceed without affecting the day-to-day finances of the club. Quite an achievement.

In May 2005, the last legal agreement was signed and the planning approval certificate issued within twenty-four hours. Work literally began the next day in the hope that the pitches could be seeded and germinated before the onset of winter 2005.

2005/06

Following Alan Lewer's departure after the last game of the season, the board appointed former Rovers player Gary Owers as manager, fully expecting to play in Conference North in 2005/06. He set about building Forest Green's first full-time squad to ensure that Rovers bounced straight back into the Conference National League.

The situation was turned on its head when Northwich Victoria reached an agreement with the authorities to drop out of Conference National in order to avoid any further punishment to do with company irregularities associated with the football club. Rovers were therefore given a reprieve and re-entered the Conference National. By the time of the decision, the squad had already been tailored to compete in the lower league, leaving Gary Owers in the unusual situation of being promoted before a ball had been kicked.

Unusually, Rovers kicked off the season on a high note, with a 1-0 home win against Cambridge United. This was followed by a draw away at Tamworth and gave everyone cause for optimism. Further points were picked up against Halifax and Exeter, before Grays Athletic visited The Lawn in early September for one of the most entertaining games seen on top of the hill for a long time. Rovers lost 2-1 in the last minute.

Results continued to see-saw from good to bad with another notable win at home to Morecambe in October, Forest Green's Portuguese striker Bruno Teixeira scoring the winning goal in an increasingly rare appearance. But it was midfield inspiration, Paul Wanless, who was keeping Rovers afloat with goals at important moments to see a lower mid-table position achieved towards the end of the year.

After Christmas, Forest Green entertained Dorchester Town in the FA Trophy, winning the match 3-1. Former Rovers favourite Andy Leitch travelled up with the coach from Dorchester to witness another good cup win. League form improved with the arrival of striker Guy Madjo and the loan signing of winger Johnny Hayes from Reading. Altrincham were soundly thrashed 5-0 and Tamworth, the next opposition at The Lawn, were expected to be beaten to move Rovers to a mid-table position. Nothing could have been further from the truth,

Top left: Scott Rogers challenges for the ball against Tamworth, April 2005.

Top right: Forest Green Rovers 2005/06, the first full-time squad. Back row: Christian Sylvester, Scott Rogers, Jon Beswetherick, Marvin Brown. Middle row: Keith Marfell, Abdou Sall, Paul Wanless, Ryan Clarke, Matt Gadsby, Ryan Harrison, Adam Garner, Sekani Simpson, Mick Byrne. Front row: Mark Danks, Mark Beesley, Ian Foster, Gary Owers, Shaun Taylor, Jon Richardson, Darren Davies, Damon Searle.

Left: Paul Wanless celebrates his second goal against Halifax, August 2005, chased by Adam Garner.

Below: Bruno Teixeira celebrates his goal against Stevenage on the last day of the season.

however, as The Lambs won the bruising encounter 3-1 and Rovers started to head inexorably towards the bottom of the table. Two more defeats were followed by another 5-goal haul to relieve the gloom, this time against fellow strugglers Scarborough.

By the end of March, Rovers' position was dangerously close to the two automatic relegation slots and a 3-0 home defeat by Dagenham & Redbridge warned of impending doom if things did not improve quickly. Four consecutive draws in April left Rovers deep in the relegation mire and a defeat away at Burton Albion saw Forest Green with just 2 games left to avoid the drop. The penultimate game away at Woking was lost, despite the home team being down to ten men for much of the encounter. As a result, Rovers were glued to the bottom of the table, needing to win their last game of the season. But for them to avoid relegation, the results of both Scarborough and Tamworth also needed to go in their favour.

The stage was therefore set for the last ever game at The Lawn. Forest Green entertained Stevenage Borough, who themselves had to win in order to secure a place in the play-offs. On a beautiful sunny afternoon, Rovers raised their game and cruised to a 2-0 victory, with a strike in the first half from fans' favourite Bruno Teixeira and a second-half header from Julian Alsop.

Miraculously, both Scarborough and Tamworth drew their final games, allowing Forest Green to leapfrog them and to avoid relegation on goal difference. Relieved fans joined celebrating players on the pitch for the final time, rekindling memories of the last-minute reprieve against Kettering in 2000.

So, after a topsy-turvy season, Rovers survived to fight another day and to play their ninth consecutive season in the Conference at the new stadium.

Below left: Julian Alsop scores the last ever goal at The Lawn and secures Forest Green's place in the Conference for another season.

Below right: Generations, old and new, watch the last game at The Lawn.

Above: Who wrote the script? Another dramatic end to another season.

One hundred and seventeen years after their formation, Forest Green Rovers left their home to move 400 yards up the road to 'The New Lawn', a stadium fit for the Football League to enable the club to progress once again.

24

Life at The New Lawn

2006/07

The cliffhanger on the last day at the old ground was forgotten as Gary Owers took charge of the first league game at The New Lawn on 12 August against Dagenham and Redbridge. Just over 1,000 people turned up to watch Rovers lose 1-0, and 3 further defeats in a row ushered in a returning sense of gloom for the season to come.

The first win came on the last Saturday in September against Stafford Rangers 2-1, with Adriano Rigoglioso scoring 1 and Allan Russell the other in front of 945 supporters.

COLIN PEAKE

Colin Gardner was chairman and he called me and said, 'Can you give me your view about what's going on?' Who did I think, with my football experience, would do a good job. I didn't know whether he would come this far south, but the name I suggested was Jim Harvey.

Jim Harvey.

JIM HARVEY

I remember watching the first game and we lost at home. Paul Wanless was in charge, and I thought, Oh goodness me this is not a good team, and it was going to be hard work. But those boys were just playing with a lack of confidence and, for me, without instruction; so it was a case of 'alright, let's get the instruction into the boys and then see where we can improve the team'. So slowly but surely the changes came in, not wholesale changes because in that squad that I inherited there was Darren Jones, Alex Lawless, Simon Clist, Kevin Nicholson, Michael Brough; there was some good players and all of a sudden they were much better than what they had been showing when I first arrived.

But any sense of optimism was put on hold on Friday 6 October when recently relegated Oxford United beat Rovers 5-1 in front of a Rovers' club record league attendance of 3,021.

With feet firmly back on the ground, Rovers then enjoyed a 7-match unbeaten run in the league before losing 2 games on the trot at home in December. John Hardiker joined at the end of November, providing extra strength at the back but the following week Rovers went out of the FA Trophy to Yeading, having already been beaten by Stevenage in the FA Cup fourth qualifying round.

JIM HARVEY

John Hardiker and Adriano Rigoglioso were both from Morecambe Academy. I had sold John from Morecambe to Stockport for £150,000, and he did a very good job for me again at Forest Green. Ryan Robinson was at the setup in Morecambe and then I brought Ryan down. So those two boys, together with Ryan Robinson and the others, all did a good job for us.

January proved to be a turning point, beginning with a 3-2 home win against Weymouth. Fans turned out in numbers before the game to help ensure the match went ahead in very wet conditions. Three further wins in the month brought 12 valuable points. The improvement in form coincided with a clear-out in January, with Alex Meechan moving to Chester City, and Danny Carey-Bertram arriving.

February and March saw mixed results. The highlight was a 2-0 win at Oxford United, with both goals scored by Carey-Bertram on 10 March. A further win against Exeter City at the end of the month brought welcome cheer but, by the beginning of April, Rovers were still only 4 points above the relegation zone after a 0-0 draw with Grays athletic at The New Lawn in front of 782 people.

Mark Beesley celebrates with Michael Brough after scoring against Weymouth on a wet afternoon at The New Lawn.

JIM HARVEY

So as time went on and I got to know the players' ability and they got to understand their jobs in the team, then we gained some momentum and, if I'm correct, at the end of that first year we finished fourteenth which, from the disastrous start when everything was rock bottom, was ok.

The average attendance was up to more than 1,200, including the bumper crowd for Oxford United's first visit to Forest Green Rovers. As summer approached, the future from the outside looked bright for all concerned with FGR but off the pitch little was being done to market the facilities and to get people up to The New Lawn for non-football activities. The financial projections for the new stadium had suggested a £1 million turnover, although no detail of how this might be achieved had been set out. The expected revenue on moving to the new ground simply hadn't materialised. In January 2007, a consultant was commissioned to write a business development action plan in order to tackle the shortfall in projected revenues.

For some years, the Club had been considering a move to a shareholding company and in February an EGM was called by the club to discuss proposals to enable direct investment in FGR (the move didn't ultimately take place until 2010). The old constitution was no longer appropriate for such a large football club, and prevented proper investment. In the summer, Club Chairman Colin Gardner issued a 'Use it or Lose it' plea to fans to come and use the facilities at The New Lawn. The accounts showed a loss for the year up to £415,000 on a turnover of £1.2m, up from £850,000 at the old ground and now with substantially higher running costs.

2007/08

As Jim's first full season in charge approached a top half finish was now the hope from supporters for the forthcoming season.

JIM HARVEY

Jamie Pitman was player coach after Paul Wanless left. Jamie was excellent and we brought an ex-player and friend of mine, Ian Rogerson, to do the physio's job, so the three of us were living in Hereford and we travelled across so that was very good.

I got Anthony Tonkin in and Stuart Fleetwood to play alongside Mark Beesley who had been at the club for some time. And this is to me what management's all about: you have to work with the players that you have and you have to understand what they have to offer. Now Mark Beesley, he was a goalscorer, but he was better than that; he could play and find a pass and he was clever, you know the number 10 role, well that was Mark Beesley. So now it's just getting those boys to hook up.

The first game, away at Oxford United, saw a 1-0 reverse, but this was followed by 3 wins on the trot and a draw on August Bank Holiday Monday against Torquay United, leaving Rovers riding high in the Conference. Jonathan Smith also joined the club soon after the start of the season.

Stuart Fleetwood was scoring for fun, assisted by Mark Beesley, and had 11 goals to his name by the end of September, including a brace in the win against Stevenage Borough and a hat-trick against Cambridge United on the following Saturday. The performances on the pitch were well above the norm but attendances still struggled, with only 719 and 1,179 people turning up to see Rovers for the games mentioned.

Rovers then went unbeaten in October including an FA Cup 4th qualifying round replay win against Eastleigh at The New Lawn, setting up a 1st Round home tie against Rotherham United. The match took place on Sunday 11 November at The New Lawn, resulting in an entertaining 2-2 draw in front of 2,102 spectators. Jim Harvey's Rovers then made history in the replay on 20 November, beating Rotherham 3-0 for FGR's first ever win against Football League opposition.

A remarkable win at Rotherham creates a little bit of club history.

JIM HARVEY

It's not so much a philosophy for cups, I would look to dominate possession and if you can do that then you have a better chance of creating opportunities. So we had a draw at home to Rotherham, and at the time, Mark Robins was on something like a 15-match unbeaten run in his league and he was getting rave reports. So to draw at home was excellent, but the performance away; that was tremendous. We ripped them apart and I remember that there was a fellow from Sky TV at the match, he came to me and said, 'I've never seen a team play as well as your team have played, the organisation, their football, their style it was magnificent.' That was just a tremendous performance.

Rovers then faced Swindon Town in the 2nd Round on 1 December for the first-ever competitive meeting between the two clubs. More than 1,000 Rovers supporters made the short journey to Swindon to watch a thoroughly entertaining 3-2 defeat to the Robins in blizzardy conditions.

The quality of football being played won plaudits nationally and the 29 goals of Stuart Fleetwood by the end of December brought him to the attention of a number of Football League clubs. The partnership between Fleetwood and Mark Beesley was the best that the club had ever had in the Conference.

JIM HARVEY

And equally, I remember the local derby with Swindon in the following round, because of the torrential rain and sleet and all our supporters were getting soaked, it was horrendous, but again we put in a real lively performance, and then they scored late on, which was disappointing. We were playing superb football and I think we would have been confident about going and playing against anybody at that time. You know there was a nice balance, the atmosphere was good and we were playing some excellent football. It's all about your boys understanding how you're going to play, it reaps dividends. Now the likes of Fleetwood, he's just finishing off the work that the whole team has done. That's it. So now he's getting recognised and now somebody else wants him to go to them.

JIM HARVEY

You want to be developing Stuart Fleetwoods and Mark Beesleys and moving them on for good money and then reinvesting again. You know you don't find them overnight, but that is the job, that is what has to happen. We had the academy set up at Morecambe, and you'd have someone in the system to come through. That's the way it worked at Morecambe but I wasn't there long enough at Forest Green to see that happen.

Rovers travelled to meet league leaders Aldershot towards the end of January and came away with a 1-0 win courtesy of Beesley's goal in the first minute. Mark made 1 further appearance for Rovers on the following Saturday at home against Exeter City in a 1-1 draw, and then moved to Cambridge United for a 5-figure fee, funds much needed by the club.

COLIN PEAKE

My only disappointment back then was that Stuart did not wish to sign another contract. I know there is always this argument about how long the contract is and the club has been criticised in the past for not putting players on long contracts, but then recently of course everyone's been moaning that they've been put on too long contracts, so you can't really win.

   He went to Crewe and had a chance to sign and work with Dario Gradi, which would have been his wisest move. We had £250,000 on the table for him to sign. But then Charlton Athletic offered a lower fee to us, but Stuart was going to get paid a lot more money, so off he went to Charlton.at the end of the season. And as we all know he never really played a game for Charlton Athletic. If Stuart had gone to Crewe that would most probably have changed the whole history of the club, you know, because a six-figure sum like that would have been invested in certain areas which would have helped sort some of the problems.

   And with Mark, it was a case again of people starting to notice Mark, and Cambridge United came in, were rebutted, and then came in again to the extent where after a while it was 'the player wants it', is more important than what the club wants. He wanted to go and felt that Cambridge probably gave him the better chance of winning something than Forest Green did and that's why Stuart's performance tailed off: his goal provider had gone.

The Conference League Cup was reintroduced for the 2007-08 season as the Setanta Shield, to coincide with live TV coverage provided by Setanta, and a 1-0 win saw off Hampton and Richmond Borough in the club's first appearance, before falling to Woking in round 5. In the League at the end of March, Rovers beat Burton Albion 3-1 on Bank Holiday Monday in front of the TV cameras, and with 6 games remaining, a play-off place remained mathematically possible. But optimism waned after two consecutive draws against relegation threatened Halifax and Northwich, and a home defeat to Rushden. A further win against Farsley Celtic and then 2 draws left Forest Green Rovers in 8th place, and 10 points off a play-off position with 71 points. The highest-ever league position had been achieved and supporters went away for the summer full of optimism.

COLIN PEAKE

I just think that that was a great time, and probably one of the best times that I experienced during my time at the club and it went really, really well.

In March 2008 another EGM had been called, to again discuss the proposed move to a company limited by shares. The cost of short-term loans was reported as badly affecting cash flow, and discussions were taking place with mortgage providers to secure more favourable terms. The proposed share offering for the new company was to have a minimum purchase of £1,000, hoping to raise a substantial sum for FGR.

The club's accounts again stated that, 'The new premises are expected to provide more scope for income generation and the directors are looking forward to improved results for the company over the next few years,' but no improvement in sales was materialising.

2008/09

Off the pitch, Chairman Colin Gardner resigned due to ill health in October 2008, having overseen the club at The New Lawn, with Trevor Horsley taking the reins at the club once again. Stuart Fleetwood signed for Charlton Athletic and Michael Brough departed in the summer. Jim turned to Andy Mangan and Kaid Mohammed, two strikers with league experience to fill the void up front. Lee Fowler, Curtis McDonald and Connell Platt also joined the club.

Mangan, Mohammed and Fowler all scored in August and, with a 1-0 win away to Histon on Saturday 30 August thanks to John Hardiker's goal, Rovers were top of the Football Conference for the first time in their history, albeit only after 6 games of the season. The sense of optimism was strong but it was not to be. Jamie Pitman moved back to Hereford United and Jerry Gill stepped in at the beginning of October as player coach, but Rovers plummeted, not winning again in the league until a 1-0 victory over Mansfield Town at the end of November. A run of 9 defeats and 3 draws left Rovers lying 21st at the beginning of December.

JIM HARVEY

Jamie Pitman left just after the start of the season, he saw the opportunity at Hereford. People I think at the club were saying that things fell apart because Jamie wasn't there because he was making all the noises and all this. No, Jamie didn't do any of the coaching, he would take the warm up and stuff like that. But losing Jamie as a player and disrupting the rhythm and losing him out of the team at that stage was a real blow to us and it took us a wee while to recover from that again.

A dour 0-0 draw against Ashford town in the FA Cup 4th Qualifying Round didn't signal much, but Ashford were dispatched 4-0 in a replay at The New Lawn at the end of October. A 1st Round 1-0 victory against Team Bath saw Rochdale arrive at the end of November for the 2nd Round. They were dispatched 2-0 to give Rovers a second-ever victory against a Football League team. With Rovers in their 4th season as a full-time squad, Derby County were drawn to play at The New Lawn in the New Year, bringing a Championship club to Forest Green Rovers for the first time in its history.

In the meantime two much needed wins against Ebbsfleet and Barrow in December left Rovers 20th in the league. All attention turned to the Derby County match, with supporters helping out on the day to ensure that the game went ahead in freezing conditions in front of a capacity crowd of 4,836, on 3 January 2009.

In a cracker of a game, Rovers took a 2-0 lead with a wonder strike from Jonathan Smith and a second well-worked goal from Alex Lawless, but the lead slipped away before half-time with thoughts turning to what might have been had the defending been a little better. But soon after the restart, Paul Stonehouse broke free on the left and scored to put Rovers 3-2 up to the

Paul Stonehouse puts Rovers 3-2 up against Derby at a packed New Lawn.

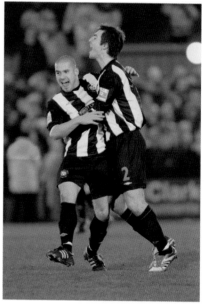

joy of the home support. Unfortunately, it was not to be as Derby first drew level and then broke the club's heart at the end of the game, despatching a penalty after Darren Jones was sent off, to win the game 4-3.

Stonehouse and Lawless celebrate the 3rd goal.

JIM HARVEY

I thought we should have won that game. Derby County for their money and everything that they've got, I think that we outplayed them on the day. They had one or two individuals who are possibly better than that and that's just turned it round for them, Chris Commons is at Celtic now. But our team play was a lot better than theirs. What's that saying the sum of the whole is greater than the parts. That was very much what we would apply to my teams, well managed and well structured and then the individuals shine in that framework.

On the player front, Simon Clist left the club on the last day of the Transfer window signing for Oxford United for a nominal fee, and in the FA Trophy, Rovers dispatched first Redditch and then Hednesford, before bowing out to Stevenage, losing 4-0 away on 21 February.

JIM HARVEY

Well, budget cuts had been ongoing, you know, things just deteriorated slowly all the way through, the budget was dropped, and I was just aware that things, well where I thought when I first arrived things were all ok, well they weren't. So Simon was just another case of things starting to go downhill, although it was a good move for Simon, I couldn't argue with that, but it was starting to break up a little bit, you know, the momentum.

Rovers made good progress in the Setanta Shield competition beating Oxford United, Torquay United and Woking to reach the final against Telford, which was televised live at The New Lawn on 9 April. After a hard-fought game and a 0-0 draw, the match went to penalties with Rovers missing their first 3 to hand the cup to Telford, in front of a crowd of 2,323 at The New Lawn.

COLIN PEAKE

Having lost such a good goal scorer as Stuart Fleetwood and then bringing in Andy Mangan, who also finished top of the scoring charts with 30 to his name, to have a Forest Green Rovers player with the golden boot in the football conference two seasons on the trot and two different players, was a tremendous achievement and attribute to Jim's management.

The second-highest scorer, Jonathan Smith, had 11 goals, proving just how reliant Rovers were on Andy Mangan.

The last game of the season away at Grays caused controversy off the pitch. Upwards of £50,000 had been staked on the game at bookmakers at odds of 22:1 on Grays losing at half-time but ultimately winning the match. Two bookmakers independently suspended betting on the fixture and called in the Gambling Commission who later concluded that there was insufficient evidence to warrant any prosecutions. The 2-1 defeat meant that Rovers' season ended on a low note, finishing 8 points above the relegation in 18th place with 52 points, a far cry from the highest-ever league finish the season before, but with historic Derby County match to look back on.

COLIN PEAKE

I went into Stroud that season with David Drew to see Dale Vince. We came up with this name called the 'Green Arena'. Dale listened to us and then when we cut to the chase; it was a no-go.

DALE VINCE

Colin Peake first contacted me sometime before I got involved in the summer of 2010 when he came to Ecotricity looking for sponsorship and I said we weren't really interested. He wanted £50,000 I think for the east stand. I said no (it didn't make any sense) but I was interested at the time about the structure of the club, and I asked who owned it and how that worked because I might be interested in buying into the club rather than sponsorship, and he said it was a private members club basically, so that was a no-go.

2009/10

During the close season things visibly took a downturn. The club accounts showed turnover up again to £1.65 million with a small profit, but a 'revaluation adjustment' was showing a £1.5 million loss. The financial situation was far from clear. In a pre season fans forum, Jim Harvey warned supporters not to set their sights too high, with budget cuts in place. Alex Lawless and goalkeeper Ryan Robinson both departed, with Terry Burton moving up to first-choice keeper. Lee Fowler and Jerry Gill left after failing to agree personal terms and Lee's brother Mike arrived from Salisbury City in July only to suffer a triple ankle fracture and ligament damage days later in a pre-season game against Exeter City.

JIM HARVEY

In the summer of 2009, I couldn't get a final budget from Trevor, I had meetings and then he actually went through all the players and, you know what their contracts were, and I was just asked to reduce, reduce, reduce. The budget by that time was half of what it was when I joined.

So I was really aware, but ok, that's all you've got and I will work with that to the best that I can, but support me Trevor, tell the people so that people don't say 'Harvey what are you doing?' Explain to them, but he didn't do that. I think the club should have made it a little bit more open to the fans that summer, but it didn't happen. That's no good.

To add to the woe, last season's top scorer Andy Mangan was one of five men convicted of, and banned for, betting thousands of pounds on the outcome of the Accrington Stanley *v.* Bury match before he had arrived at FGR, in May 2008. Mangan, then at Bury, received a five-month ban in July from an FA commission, meaning that Rovers had lost their top scorer until after Christmas. Finally, to make matters worse, before a game was even played, Jim Harvey was dismissed for an alleged breach of contract, leaving Rovers manager-less and with budget cuts confirmed.

JIM HARVEY

George Rolls, he had sacked his manager at Cambridge and he rang me and said he was interested in me and Jerry and I said that if that was the case then what he needed to do was to square it off with Trevor. Trevor's got wind of this conversation and acted and that's the height of it. He said there was a breach of contract and I was told to leave the club there and then and leave the ground on the spot. When I left, there was still a year to go on the contract.

I loved my time at Rovers. The supporters and the people like Ken Bolton, they were real characters and lovely people and I really enjoyed my time there. I was just disappointed with the way that it finished off, that was wrong, it shouldn't have gone like that, but these things happen and you move on.

David Brown was appointed caretaker manager, but with little time to prepare he lost the first 6 games before a battling 0-0 draw away to Oxford United at the end of August provided a glimmer of hope. Sean Rigg had joined on loan ten days before to solve the striker problem, scoring on his debut in an away defeat at Rushden and Diamonds. But any hope of an upturn was dashed a week later with a 7-0 thrashing by Cambridge United, old boy Mark Beesley rubbing salt into the wound with a late goal.

With 8 games gone and 1 point on the board, David Hockaday was tasked to steer Rovers away from impending doom. Ollie Thorne and Jeffrey Imudia arrived and for the remainder of September Rovers went unbeaten with 4 draws and 2 wins against Grays Athletic and Chester City, now managed by Jim Harvey. Sean Rigg came in and scored for 4 games in succession, and by the end of September Rovers had clawed themselves up to 19th place, before a serious knee injury for Jeffrey Imudia meant that he couldn't play for the club again. No momentum could be found in October with 3 games lost, the only win coming against Mangotsfield 2-1 in the FA Cup 4th Qualifying Round. The 1st Round tie against Mansfield Town was won 2-1 in a replay and the 2nd Round tie away to Bath City at the end of November saw Mark Preece and Jonathan Smith score in a 2-1 win to set up another appearance in the 3rd Round, away to Notts County.

Things did not improve in the league and wins against Rushden and Diamonds and Salisbury City in December still couldn't lift Rovers out of the bottom four. A 0-0 draw away at Tamworth saw FGR end the year in the drop zone.

COLIN PEAKE

David Brown was a nice lad. The budget wasn't brilliant. We had a player who wasn't going to be playing for us but we had to pay him under the regulations, so that really didn't leave a lot to play with, but it didn't really work out. There was a process to replace him and it tied into our dealings with Hartpury College. I was approached by the board, because Hartpury College had come in with a scheme. Team Bath had risen to the higher echelons in non-league football, and Hartpury wanted to do the same thing. They wanted to run Forest Green Rovers and use it as part of their curriculum to attract better players to the college. The guy who'd run Team Bath had moved to Exeter City to take over their youth team. So I contacted Exeter and we put in an official club approach. But he declined. We were headhunting as opposed to advertising. As it turned out, the whole project with Hartpury died a death; the board didn't wish to give away the club and have it there in name only.

The second choice was Gary Haylock, the manager at Hayes and Yeading. He was interviewed on the Monday and offered the job, and on the Tuesday he came down with Hayes and Yeading for a match, and he turned the job down when he came. He was under contract at Hayes but we went through the whole process properly with the club.

Then came David Hockaday. And to cut a long story short, when he came in I thought he was a reasonable choice as manager based on his experience and his time as Watford assistant manager.

Rovers finally travelled to Notts County on 19 January for the belated 3rd Round tie, but went down 2-1 that evening with Isaiah Rankin scoring the goal, having joined in December. A much-needed 3-1 win away at Hayes and Yeading in front of just 291 people at the end of January saw a debut for Reece Styche, who bagged 2 goals which moved Rovers to 20th place, just above the relegation zone. Andy Mangan completed his ban and immediately moved to Wrexham. On the goalkeeping front, Terry Burton was injured towards the end of January and in mid-February, Coventry City reserve keeper Danny Ireland took over. By the end of February, Rovers were in 22nd position when further bad news arrived. A 1-1 draw with Cambridge had followed a 4-match losing streak in February which also saw the home tie against Chester City cancelled with hours to go after they couldn't pay for transport. Three weeks later, the Conference removed Chester from the competition and the 3 points that Rovers had earned against Chester earlier in the season were erased. Rovers were back in the relegation zone, their 27 points from 32 reduced to 24 from 31, with only 13 games remaining.

A 2-1 home win against third-placed York City on 6 March brought hope, but losses at Luton and Gateshead followed. A 2-0 away win at Kettering saw the start of a mini revival for Rovers, with 3 further wins moving Rovers up to 20th, out of the relegation zone, and 36 points from 37 games by the end of March. But April saw losses to relegation contenders Eastbourne and Tamworth, and to top of the table Stevenage, before home wins to Crawley and Histon left Rovers in charge of their own destiny.

Sean Rigg puts Rovers ahead against Grays.

Danny Powell is congratulated by David Brown in the win against York City.

As with the previous season, Rovers faced Grays Athletic, already relegated and playing their youth team. A win would see Rovers safe for another season. Terry Burton returned in goal following injury to Danny Ireland and in an uneventful first half, Reece Styche was brought down in the area and David Brown stepped up to give Rovers the lead at half time. Other results that day were not going Rovers' way, with Eastbourne taking the lead against Oxford United, and Gateshead also winning 1–0 against AFC Wimbledon. Histon were also drawing with Barrow, but still a draw would be enough to keep Rovers up. However, as the game drew to a close, Grays first equalised and then took the lead with 4 minutes to go, sending Forest Green down with all three relegation contenders leapfrogging Rovers on the day to escape relegation. Supporters were left dumbstruck as to how the game could have been lost.

COLIN PEAKE

To be fair to David, I felt sorry for the guy, he worked very hard in the first year, I couldn't argue with his professionalism, he was working with a squad he had inherited and yes he didn't have a very good budget. I felt very sorry for him on the last day, I thought we missed opportunities all the way through the match that we wouldn't normally. Jonathan Smith always holds his hand up and says, 'I missed an open goal', which would have changed the whole game.

The Conference AGM in June saw Salisbury City demoted to the Southern League, having broken the strict financial rules, and thus Rovers were left to fight another day in the Conference. But Rovers had their own financial problems. The club constitution had finally changed after an inaugural shareholders meeting in February 2010, and the disastrous financial position was laid out for all to see. A statement to shareholders read, 'The Board had perhaps taken for granted that the new stadium facilities would sell themselves,' and also cited additional costs associated with the stadium build. The projected revenues had simply not materialised. Underpayments of PAYE and VAT were revealed with insufficient cash to meet each month's wage bill. Three options for FGR were set out at a shareholders' meeting: to go into administration; find a buyer for the club; or to raise more capital. A total debt of around £1.5 million was set out, including £322,000 of personal loans and £850,000 of commercial loans with four different bodies. The main problem was cash flow and the club just survived until the end of the season with all supporters pulling together to contribute to fighting funds. The Club's FA Cup winnings from the run up to the Notts County match were handed straight to the Inland Revenue to help pay some of the money owed.

2010/11

The club had stumbled across the finishing line the previous season and David Drew was appointed Chairman of FGR at a special meeting in June, to try to find investors or a buyer for the club. Rovers needed substantial investment to survive.

COLIN PEAKE

There were lots of things that were put into place to save the club; we had a company working for us who I don't think ever came up with a buyer for the club and I was talking to one or two people including the guy who eventually went into Swindon, so we were talking to a few different people with a few different fingers in the pie.

DALE VINCE

It was pretty big local news, Forest Green going bankrupt and/or getting relegated and Colin invited me to go up to a pre-season friendly match, which I did. I thought it was a lovely place and lovely people actually. And Colin told me the club just needed something like £30,000 to get through to September for cash-flow reasons, which didn't seem too bad. I was looking at a local football club with a long history and some good people behind it and it just seemed a shame for it to go bankrupt for the want of £30k. We are a local company and it seemed the right thing to do, it wasn't a fortune, I'm a football fan, so it was a good fit.

And then it kind of moved on from there, August came and went and the club needed more money and then at some point about September or October I think, there was a realisation, as we dug deeper, that it was actually a big sum of money required, perhaps twenty times the original sum and so we struck a deal to put that sum of money in, and that was the sum to keep the club alive, for the season. The club was about to fall off a precipice and it's amazing to me, even now, how close to disaster it was and how big the problem and cash hole was – and no one really seemed to know it.

In the meantime, David Hockaday moved into his first full season in charge after technically failing to keep Rovers up, and was given an opportunity to bring in his own players from the start of the season.

David Hockaday, retained as manager.

DALE VINCE

We got involved that summer and within a short period of time it seemed like everybody wanted to sack David; that was made very clear to me by Trevor and many on the board. In truth, I don't think the board were honest with the fans, I think if they had been told that David Hockaday had a budget thirty per cent less than the previous relegation season then I don't think the people would have been so negative. He took a pay cut as well, there were no proper training facilities and the team only played together on a full-size pitch at league matches, and we were part-time. The way I saw it, David simply hadn't been given a proper chance to do the job and I thought he deserved that. I also think that if the board doesn't give the manager the tools to do the job then it can only look to itself, not let the manager carry the can. It's no problem if that's all the board can give the manager, but the fans should know, it's about taking responsibility and being honest.

The majority of the first team departed, with James Bittner arriving as first-choice keeper, as well as James Norwood, Jan Kuklowski, Luke Jones, Ian Herring and Gavin Caines, to play alongside Mike Fowler, who had recovered from his ankle injury the year before.

A mid-August 3-0 home win against Wrexham, followed by a draw with Gateshead and a win against Hayes and Yeading, indicated a solid team, but by mid-October Rovers had not added to their 2 early victories and had plummeted to 23rd place after a 6-1 thrashing at Luton Town. Results improved, starting with a 2-1 win against York City at the end of October, and 2 wins and 3 draws followed, lifting Rovers to seventeenth by the end of December.

DALE VINCE

I went to a few monthly board meetings from the beginning of the season, and they were an experience I can tell you. Each month the board members turned up and said the same things and went away, then came back and said the same things again. More or less, what was missing was someone actually doing things. My options were to walk away or to roll my sleeves up and get stuck in and make it work, and for that I clearly needed to be the chairman. I needed to reform the board and I really needed to reset the whole structure of FGR. I'm not criticising anybody at Forest Green at all because, as a volunteer-led football club from its very early days, we've come an awful long way, and fair play to everybody that played a part in that, and a village club in the Conference Prem is no mean feat. But it had probably come as far as a volunteer-led club could.

Nobody had a clue how much money was being lost on things like the catering and on the bars or anything. For some years, as you know, I was a traveller and I thought that travellers were some of the most out-to-lunch people you might ever meet, happily so in many cases, but I tell you what, Forest Green took that to a whole new level. It was the most dysfunctional organisation I've ever been part of. Again no disrespect, just telling it how I saw it.

COLIN PEAKE

Initially there was going to be a small board, perhaps of three people who would be responsible for the football side but then it all seemed to totally change and we got to a situation where there was no discussion in the board about football whatsoever, football was just going to be a matter between the chairman and the manager, with nobody else's input. And personally I thought that was dangerous, because I just think the manager can tell you anything that he wants.

Chris Stokes arrived at FGR in November but wouldn't make his debut until mid-February. Maidenhead United had been dispatched 1-0 in the FA Cup 4th Qualifying Round at the end of October, but defeat in the 1st Round at home to Northampton Town in November cut short any lingering thoughts of another good cup run. Rovers also exited the Trophy against Cambridge United in Round 1 in December, leaving only the League to 'concentrate on' for the New Year.

Off the field, Ecotricity now had a controlling stake in the new company structure and aimed to use Forest Green Rovers to promote Green Issues and bring their Eco message to football fans. In February, eyebrows were raised with a decision to stop selling meat at the club. A wave of publicity engulfed Rovers, shocking many fans. FGR were on the map but not for footballing reasons.

On the pitch, a 1-0 home win against high-flying Fleetwood was the only highlight in a run of 9 defeats, 6 draws and 3 wins from New Year until the end of March, with Rovers slipping to 22nd place and into the dreaded drop zone.

In a further move to bring Green issues to football, Rovers installed a large-scale solar panel array on the south stand, with the panels provided by former Manchester United player Gary Neville who had set up a charity with Dale Vince called Sustainability In Sport.

Adam Quinn, Reece Styche, Luke Jones and Ross Dyer line up against Northampton Town in the FA Cup.

With 6 games left, Rovers were staring relegation in the face for the second season in a row, with no real improvement in form despite an almost complete renewal of the playing squad. Steve Guinan arrived from Northampton Town together with Robbie Matthews and Curtis McDonald from Newport County, and a 3-0 win away to Histon and a 1-0 home victory against Altrincham at the beginning of April brought hope and 44 points after 42 games.

With 1 game to go, Rovers had 46 points before travelling away to Tamworth. As with the season before, Rovers' destiny was in their own hands and a win would see them survive, but after just 3 minutes Tamworth were 1-0 up after very slack defending. Matt Somner equalised early in the second half to give Rovers hope, but on 77 minutes disaster struck when Jake Sheridan's cross/shot drifted over James Bittner to give Tamworth the lead and put Rovers in the relegation position. With 3 minutes to go, Rovers were rescued when Kettering scored goals in the 87th and 90th minutes to beat Southport, leaving Rovers above Southport on a goal difference 1 better than Southport and out of the relegation zone. A close shave. David had asked to be judged on his own team at the start of the season, with many fans judging that David should leave.

DALE VINCE

I think we may have ended the year with a £500,000 budget. We survived on a goal difference that season, what a day that was at Tamworth.

2011/12

Changes continued apace with a new club badge adopted to replace the old Barcelona-style emblem that had been at the club since the 1970s, and it was another move that was not popular with both fans and former directors. The new way of doing things at Forest Green proved

FGR 2011-12.

too much for former Chairman Trevor Horsley, who resigned from the Board of Directors in June and withdrew all sponsorship, citing a lack of influence at FGR. A twenty-year era came to an end which had seen Rovers rise from the Southern League lower divisions to become a Conference stalwart, and playing in a Football League compliant stadium. A great debt was owed by the club to Trevor for the work that he did to transform Rovers into what they had become. New Chairman Dale Vince showed faith in David Hockaday when few others did, and David took charge for a third season with an increase in budget, and the offer of long contracts to many of the squad.

DALE VINCE

David more or less got to start properly, I would say. I don't remember the details, but the budget definitely went up each year.

Luke Jones left the club, as did Gavin Caines, Ross Dyer, Steve Guinan and Craig Armstrong. In came Al Hassan Bangura, who only five years before had been Watford's player of the season in their Championship promotion campaign. Kieron Forbes and Chris Todd also arrived for the start of the season, as did Jamie Turley, Luke Graham and James Rowe, the latter having been released by Reading and impressing in a pre-season trial.

The season kicked off with a televised game against Stockport County on the new Premier TV channel, which had taken up the mantle of showing live Conference Football. An entertaining 1-1 draw followed, but was marred by a hamstring tear injury to Chris Todd, ending his season before it had really started. A 1-1 draw away at Luton followed and a 6-1 demolition of Alfreton Town on their own ground seemed to signal an upturn in fortunes.

But, as the season wore on results remained patchy. A home win against Bath City at the end of August was not repeated until a 2-1 win against AFC Telford at The New Lawn on 18 October, with FGR in 14th position. Matty Taylor arrived at FGR in September from lower league North Leigh, which showed David Hockaday's emphasis on younger players. Eddie Oshodi then arrived in October, having been released by Watford, to shore up the defence.

Any thoughts of a cup run were dispelled by a dismal 2-1 defeat away at Arlesley Town in the FA Cup 4th Qualifying Round at the end of October and subsequent defeat to Newport in the FA Trophy 1st Round after a replay. In the league, a run of 4 further wins and 3 draws moved Rovers up to 9th in mid-December, although losses to Lincoln City and Kidderminster saw Rovers in 11th place at the turn of the year.

Sam Russell arrived from Darlington in January when many of the Darlington squad were released for financial reasons, and immediately took over as first team goalkeeper, while Jamie Collins signed from Aldershot Town. Results were again mixed in January, although a 1-0 win at The New Lawn against Wrexham and a narrow home defeat to Fleetwood the following week gave cause for optimism. Further wins against Gateshead, Kettering and Cambridge maintained a mid-table 11th position at the beginning of March, and a 3-0 home win against Luton, and a 2-1 away win at Wrexham at the end of the month saw Rovers move to 10th spot.

Yan Kuklowski celebrates his hat-trick with Jared Hodgkiss in the 3-0 win against Barrow in March.

Further wins against Barrow, Ebbsfleet and Bath City moved Rovers up to 8th by Bank Holiday Monday with 3 games to go. A subsequent defeat away at Gateshead and a 2-0 home win against Darlington saw Rovers hold 8th position with 1 game to go, but a 1-0 away defeat to York City meant the position couldn't be held, with Rovers finishing in 10th spot; their third best-ever finish.

COLIN PEAKE

One of the problems that you get into as soon as it becomes known that you are a cash-rich club, you all of a sudden are put under pressure by agents and everything else. We had a policy at Forest Green previously that we wouldn't deal with agents, you know, and it's probably only when David Hockaday came to the club that we started to get involved with agents and again that's fraught with danger because you get held to ransom over different bits and pieces and it all adds up on a daily basis to create not the best working environment that you want.

I saw in the fans that the club expectation was going through the roof. All of a sudden the club had money and a decent budget, and sometimes instead of spending that money wisely, it wasn't always spent as wisely as it could in my opinion. Not all the signings were poor but there were a number of players signed who quite frankly were being paid more money than we could have paid for a player of a similar calibre who would have signed for less. I left the club that May.

2012/13

Off the pitch, controversy continued as the black-and-white stripes of Forest Green Rovers, worn on and off since 1919, were replaced with a bright green shirt provided by Adidas. The move again split fans' opinions, with many asking again, 'Why Change?' Talk of making the play-offs was a hot topic among fans in the close season after the summer signings of Magno Vieira, O.J. Koroma, Ben Wright, alongside Ed Asafu Adjaye, after he was released by Luton Town. Aaron Racine impressed in a pre-season friendly against Manchester United, arranged with Gary Neville as a fundraiser for Sustainability In Sport, and joined for the season. Financially, the club appeared to be stable and had a far higher budget than ever before in its history.

A 1-1 draw at home against Cambridge United was followed by 5 wins and a draw, leaving Rovers top of the table, before a 1-0 defeat to Grimsby Town at Blundell Park on 8 September saw Rovers surrender top spot. A 1-1 draw against Alfreton Town followed at The New Lawn in front of gold-medallist rower Peter Reed, and 3 further wins followed, the latter shown live on Premier Sports TV against Lincoln City at The New Lawn. Rovers were top of the table once again at the end of September.

Ben Wright scores Rovers' 2nd in a 4-1 win against Ebbsfleet to see unbeaten Rovers top of the Conference.

But a winless run in the league in October saw Rovers drop to 6th, a run only broken with a 4-1 win over Dartford in the FA Cup 4th Qualifying Round Replay, which set up a home 1st Round tie against Port Vale at the beginning of November, which was lost 3-2.

Rovers then travelled to Dartford in the league on 6 November, returning with a 1-0 win that saw a move back into a play-off spot at Dartford's expense. Further wins against Stockport and Nuneaton, and draws with Barrow and Macclesfield saw Rovers unbeaten in the league in 6 games, before a 3-1 defeat at Braintree on 18 December lost them the chance to move back up to second place. Prior to the Braintree match, Rovers had bowed out of the FA Trophy in the 2nd Round to Gainsborough Trinity, having despatched AFC Totton in the 1st Round.

Electric innovations and a change of image.

Rovers lost 2-1 to Newport County on Boxing Day, which saw FGR drop out of the play-off spot for the second time that season, but things improved on New Year's Day when Rovers snatched a 5-0 away win in Newport to leave the league leaders scratching their heads, and Rovers back in 4th place. From the Newport game up to mid-February, there was only a single defeat away to Stockport County, and 4 further wins and 3 draws, including 0-0 against Wrexham and 1-1 against Luton Town. Rovers maintained 4th position and had a real hope of securing a top 5 finish for the first time.

But a play-off 6 pointer against Kidderminster Harriers at The New Lawn on 19 February was lost 1-0, and a further defeat away to Woking saw Rovers drop out of the play-off berths into 6th place. A draw away at Cambridge at the beginning of March was followed by another home defeat, this time to fellow play-off contenders Grimsby Town.

Off the pitch, and in another cloud of publicity, Ecotricity did a deal with Nissan to bring a fleet of electric cars to FGR in March. The players were all given cars in an effort to help bring the Eco message to a wider audience, although it may have led to them taking their eye off the ball.

Rovers gradually lost ground on the top 5, but after a 2-1 home defeat to leaders Mansfield, with 7 games to go, Rovers were still in 6th place. As Easter weekend approached, Rovers had a real chance of a play-off berth if a bit of momentum could be found. Wes Burns joined from Bristol City together with Reece Connolly, the latter scoring in a 2-0 win away at Ebbsfleet on Easter Saturday. But this was followed immediately by a 0-0 draw at home on Easter Monday against already relegated Telford, while Grimsby Town pulled further away in 5th spot.

The motivation of the team was brought into question after a run of 5 straight defeats to the end of the season. Perhaps things were just a bit too comfortable for the players. Rovers finished 10th for a second season running: the chance for a best ever league finish gone.

DALE VINCE

I don't think long contracts affected the players badly, but you know there is a possibility that the cars did; we have considered it – we can't be sure whether it was just coincidental timing, it wasn't dead on, it was only approximate timing, the drop-off you know, but it is possible.

2013/14

With the disappointing end to the previous season on everyone's mind, the squad was added to with the arrival of Anthony Barry and former Rovers player Andy Mangan from Fleetwood, Conference stalwart Matthew Barnes Homer, Danny Wright from Wrexham, and Marcus Kelly also joined. Rovers were installed as favourites to win the league with such a large squad and such firepower. An 8-0 thrashing of 10-man Hyde United at The New Lawn for the opening game of the season appeared to justify the position.

After 8 matches, Rovers were lying 3rd and a mid-week journey to Welling in mid-September didn't appear to pose a problem on paper, but Rovers lost 5-2 for their second defeat of the season. This was closely followed by 2 further defeats away to Cambridge and at home to Tamworth. Rovers slipped into the bottom half of the table: not part of the plan. A 1-0 home win against Gateshead brought respite at the end of September, although worse was to come, and a 3-1 away loss at Grimsby Town, only a month after the Welling game, saw Rovers having lost 7 out of 8 games and in lowly 16th, only 4 points away from the relegation zone.

The string of defeats signalled the end of the David Hockaday era, one of Forest Green Rovers' longest-serving managers after more than four years in charge but with little to show for it. Assistant Manager Gary Seward took temporary charge the following Saturday for the

Danny Wright celebrates his goal against Alfreton Town in front of the main stand at FGR.

FA Cup 4th Qualifying Round visit of Bishops Stortford to The New Lawn, but a 1-0 loss and no sign of any change in form saw Gary depart on the following Monday.

Youth team Boss Scott Bartlett took charge of first team coaching for the visit of Dartford on 2 November and a 1-0 win resulted, much to the relief of all concerned.

After the departure of David Hockaday, Adrian Pennock, the former assistant manager at Stoke City under Tony Pulis, was a surprise choice as manager and stood alongside Scott Bartlett in the dugout for a 1-0 home win over Nuneaton ten days later. Adie took sole charge on the following Saturday with Lincoln City leaving The New Lawn on the end of a 4-1 defeat. A sense of cautious optimism returned to FGR. Rovers had seven strikers in their squad who were not producing goals and Adrian let it be known that he felt the playing squad was too large, and sidelined a number of players who had only ever played bit parts in the team. At the same time he brought in young striker James Alabi from Stoke City to try his luck up front, but his loan period proved fruitless.

Scott Bartlett, unbeaten as caretaker manager.

The nosedive in October had been halted, but by Christmas Rovers were still 14th after a 3-1 win on Boxing Day at The New Lawn against Aldershot. Two televised games against Hereford United in January added only a single point to the tally and Adrian Pennock signalled his intention to bring experience to the squad with the arrival of Lee Hughes at the beginning of the month. Reece Styche moved on loan to Wycombe Wanderers. But still no consistency could be found.

The early part of the year saw many games postponed and by March, 8 games had to be fitted in. A 2-1 win against Grimsby Town at the end of the month saw Rovers move up to 6th place, a position not occupied since the disastrous trip to Welling at the beginning of the season. But it was not to be; Rovers ended in 10th place for the 3rd season running, having turned to thirty-six players during the course of the season. James Norwood finished top of the goal-scoring charts with 18 for the season.

As the club moved towards its 17th consecutive season in the Conference, much had been learnt by Chairman Dale Vince. The playing squad was altered, including the loss of Yan Kuklowki who had become FGR's top scorer in the Conference era with 14 goals in the season, bringing his tally to 48 in 157 appearances. It was now Adrian Pennock's task to oversee the fulfilment of the ambitions of Forest Green Rovers FC.

Adrian Pennock, manager for FGR's 125th season.

DALE VINCE

Our budget peaked that season, it was bigger than intended at the start, there were adjustments to make to the squad that David never got round to. But the thing is budgets change during the year, you get players in and players go out and if the timings of those moves slip then you go over budget. Looking at the season coming we will be operating with a 6-figure budget, a smaller one than last season for sure. Adie, our new manager has a different approach to what players are paid, and that's what he's set out to do.

25

The Future

JOHN DUFF, PRESIDENT

The question that's often asked is, 'Where are we going?' The answer as always is 'anything is possible'. But we need to be patient. It took us thirty years to progress from the Gloucestershire Northern Senior, on to the Hellenic, and then Southern Leagues, to reach the Conference. We've now had sixteen years as members of the Conference, some hanging on by a whisker, but it's seen us establish a launching pad to move onwards and upwards again. It's a difficult league to be promoted from but I am sure we can do it one day. I wish good luck to our shareholders, manager and team.

DALE VINCE, CHAIRMAN

I don't do short term, no matter what world it's in, football is no different. I think and plan very long term, that's what I'm about. Our plan isn't just to get to League 2, it's bigger than that. We have a Ladies' Team and the Youth set up, and want to see these thrive as well. I think that the further we travel up the leagues of English football the louder our Eco message will be and the more people will pay attention to what we're doing and therefore the more this works, and the more fun we can have as well along the way. Life is really short, at least that's what I think, and it's best to make an adventure of it so that's what I'm up for, I'd like to see Forest Green in the Championship; that's the goal. I'm often asked if I plan to change the name of the club, the answer is absolutely not. Forest Green Rovers is a great name, the perfect name.

Sustainability doesn't exist in the Conference, not for a club with our gate, so the first part of our plan is to get into League 2 where there is considerably more money from the FA, more sponsorship and more TV revenue, but without such a big increase in budget actually. Those at the top end of this league are as competitive in my opinion as the bottom of the football league and budget wise the top few teams in our league have probably got bigger budgets than the bottom half of League 2.

Off the pitch, it's a slimmer organisation; it's much more focused. We've got a lot of activity at the club on non-match days now, business events, conferences and that kind of thing, but this kind of activity suffers from the same problem that the football side does and that's location: its not the easiest place to get to. I think the place has been transformed and that's really important whether you're coming to the club for a conference or coming to the football, because you just get this feel about the place that it's going somewhere.

COLIN PEAKE, LIFE MEMBER

Whatever lies ahead for the future of Forest Green Rovers, there will be the same challenges as I saw in my time at the club over more than twenty years, maybe in a different guise, and what you do need is a lot of enthusiasm and a lot of belief from everybody associated with the club. You need to spend wisely to achieve results. Getting into the Football League would be the right thing to do.

When I first came to the club we didn't have a Supporters Club because the Supporters Club got fed up with the name change and everything else. The club was going downhill. One thing the club needs in order to be successful is togetherness and that will help bring consistency. It's time for all supporters to get behind the club and equally to be embraced by it, to help push the club forward in its next era.

Players old and new at the Presidents Day in March 2014. Andy Leitch (centre), scorer of the Wembley winner in 1982, flanked by Luke Rodgers and Lee Hughes, both additions to the 2014 squad under Adrian Pennock.

FGR Statistics in the Conference 1998–2014

The following statistics have been prepared by Heather Cook and show Rovers' journey in the Conference since joining in 1998.

Many players have passed through the club in the Conference era and all appearances have been recorded by Heather.

The tables show the league positions, scores promotion, and relegation for the season.

The scores are stated in the tables with FGR's score first, home and away.

All Time Leading Goalscorers

Yan Kuklowski   49
Alex Meechan   46
James Norwood   39
Reece Styche   35

All time goalscorers

Yan Kuklowski 49
James Norwood 39
Reece Styche 35
Alex Meechan 46

Results

L 278
W 207
D 216

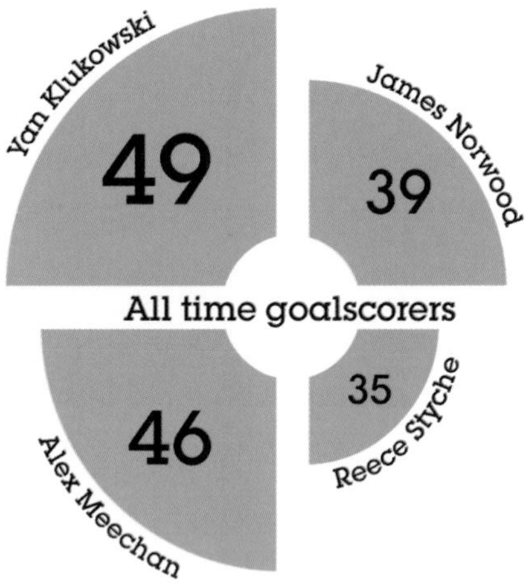

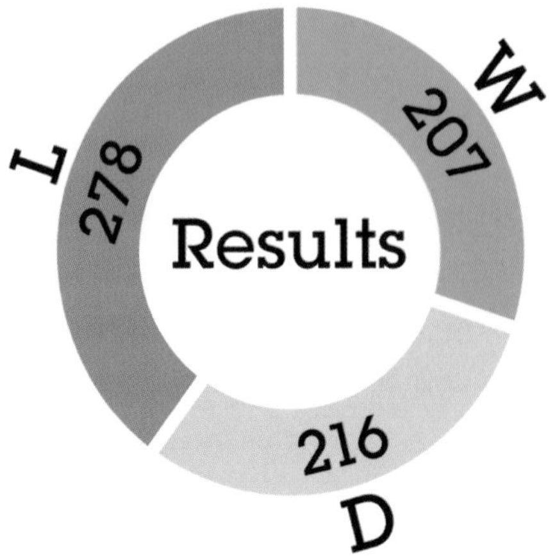

League position and points won

There was only one promotion spot in the Conference Premier until the 02/03 season and only 22 teams until 06/07.

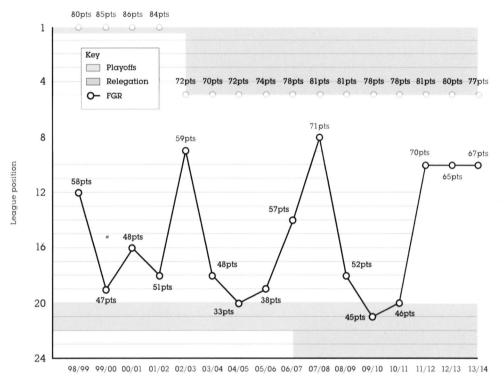

League Goals scored and average attendance

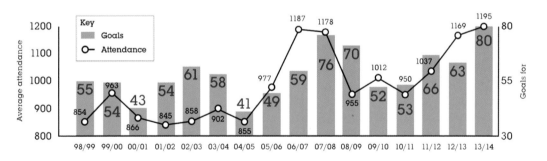

	1998-99	Res	H-A	P	W	D	L	F	A	Pts	W	D	L	F	A	Pts	POINTS
P	Cheltenham Tn	1-2	1-1	42	11	9	1	35	14	42	11	5	5	36	22	38	80
2.	Kettering Tn	1-0	1-2	42	11	5	5	31	16	38	11	5	5	27	21	38	76
3.	Hayes	1-2	3-0	42	12	3	6	34	25	39	10	5	6	29	25	35	74
4.	Rushden & D	0-2	0-4	42	11	4	6	41	22	37	9	8	4	30	20	35	72
5.	Yeovil Tn	1-2	4-0	42	8	4	9	35	32	28	12	7	2	33	22	43	71
6.	Stevenage B	1-2	1-1	42	9	9	3	37	23	36	8	8	5	25	22	32	68
7.	Northwich V	3-1	0-1	42	11	3	7	29	21	36	8	6	7	31	30	30	66
8.	Kingstonian	1-0	1-0	42	9	7	5	26	19	34	8	6	7	25	30	30	64
9.	Woking	0-2	1-1	42	9	5	7	27	20	32	9	4	8	24	25	31	63
10.	Hednesford Tn	1-0	1-1	42	9	8	4	30	24	35	6	8	7	19	20	26	61
11.	Dover Athletic	0-1	1-1	42	7	9	5	27	21	30	8	4	9	27	27	28	58
12.	**FGR**			**42**	**9**	**5**	**7**	**28**	**22**	**32**	**6**	**8**	**7**	**27**	**28**	**26**	**58**
13.	Hereford Utd	2-1	0-4	42	9	5	7	25	17	32	6	5	10	24	29	23	55
14.	Morcambe	2-2	1-3	42	9	5	7	31	29	32	6	3	12	29	47	21	53
15.	Kidderminster H	5-0	2-2	42	9	4	8	31	22	31	5	5	11	24	30	20	51
16.	Doncaster R	0-0	1-0	42	7	5	9	26	26	26	5	7	9	25	29	22	48
17.	Telford Utd	1-1	1-2	42	7	8	6	24	24	29	3	8	10	20	36	17	46
18.	Southport	1-0	1-1	42	6	9	6	29	28	27	4	6	11	18	31	18	45
R	Barrow	1-1	1-2	42	7	5	9	17	23	26	4	5	12	23	40	17	43
20.	Welling Utd	3-2	2-0	42	4	7	10	18	30	19	5	7	9	26	35	22	41
R	Leek Town	3-1	2-0	42	5	5	11	34	42	20	3	3	15	14	34	12	32
R	Farnborough Tn	0-0	2-2	42	6	5	10	29	48	23	1	6	14	12	41	9	32

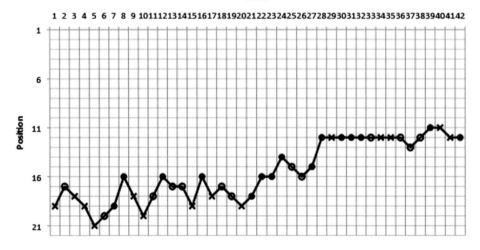

1998-99

	LA	LS	LG	CA	CS	CG	TA	TS	**TG**
Don Forbes	39			12			51		
Alex Sykes	36	5	8	10	1	9	46	6	**17**
Justin Shuttlewood (G/K)	34			11			45		
Ian Hedges	32	2	3	11	1	2	43	3	**5**
Danny Bailey	27	2		10			37	2	
Jason Drysdale	28	1	3	9		2	37	1	**5**
Rob Cook	28	9	5	7	3		35	12	**5**
Chris Honor	29			6	1		35	1	
Mike Kilgour	25		1	9			34		**1**
Nathan Wigg	25	8		6	2		31	10	
Marc McGregor	20	11	12	8	1	3	28	12	**15**
Paul Hunt	22		8	4	1	4	26	1	**12**
Matthew Coupe	17	13	2	5	2		22	15	**2**
David Meyhew	15	1	5	7	1	3	22	2	**8**
Gary Smart	16	17	1	3	5	1	19	22	**2**
Steve Winter	16	5	3	2	4		18	9	**3**
Mark Hallam	13	4	3	1	1		14	5	**3**
Dean Birkby	8	6		3	3	2	11	9	**2**
Jim Rollo	7	15		2	3		9	18	
Shaun Chapple	8	7		1			9	7	
Steve Perrin (G/K)	7	1		1	1		8	2	
Chris Smith	3	9		2	3		5	12	
Andrew Catley	2	3		2	3		4	6	
Ben Hobson	3	2					3	2	
Terry Westlake (G/K)	1						1		
Tommy Callinan	1						1		
Toby Jackson		3						3	
Richard Evans		1						1	
David Mogg (G/K)		1						1	

1999-00		P	W	D	L	F	A	W	D	L	F	A	Pts	GD	Res H-A	
P	Kidderminster	42	16	3	2	47	16	10	4	7	28	24	85	35	3-2	3-3
2.	Rushden & D	42	11	8	2	37	18	10	5	6	34	24	76	29	1-0	2-3
3.	Morecambe	42	10	7	4	46	29	8	9	4	24	19	70	22	1-2	1-1
4.	Scarborough	42	10	6	5	36	14	9	6	6	24	21	69	25	0-1	0-5
5.	Kingstonian	42	9	4	8	30	24	11	3	7	28	20	67	14	0-3	1-0
6.	Dover	42	10	7	4	43	26	8	5	8	22	30	66	9	3-1	0-4
7.	Yeovil	42	11	4	6	37	28	7	6	8	23	35	64	-3	3-0	0-1
8.	Hereford	42	9	6	6	43	31	6	8	7	18	21	59	9	0-1	0-1
9.	Southport	42	10	5	6	31	21	5	8	8	24	35	58	-1	1-0	1-2
10.	Stevenage	42	8	5	8	26	20	8	4	9	34	34	57	6	3-2	1-1
11.	Hayes	42	7	3	11	24	28	9	5	7	33	30	56	-1	0-1	0-3
12.	Doncaster	42	7	5	9	19	21	8	4	9	27	27	54	-2	1-0	2-3
13.	Kettering	42	8	10	3	25	19	4	6	11	19	31	52	-6	2-0	0-1
14.	Woking	42	5	6	10	17	27	8	7	6	28	26	52	-8	0-0	1-2
15.	Nuneaton	42	7	6	8	28	25	5	9	7	21	28	51	-4	1-2	3-2
16.	Telford	42	12	4	5	34	21	2	5	14	22	45	51	-10	5-2	0-2
17.	Hednesford	42	10	3	8	27	23	5	3	13	18	45	51	-23	3-0	0-1
18.	Northwich	42	10	8	3	33	25	3	4	14	20	53	51	-25	5-1	0-0
19.	**FGR**	**42**	**11**	**2**	**8**	**35**	**23**	**2**	**6**	**13**	**19**	**40**	**47**	**-9**		
R	Welling	42	6	5	10	27	32	7	3	11	27	34	47	-12	1-2	1-1
R	Altrincham	42	6	8	7	31	26	3	11	7	20	34	46	-9	1-1	1-1
R	Sutton Utd	42	4	8	9	23	32	4	2	15	16	43	34	-36	1-2	2-3

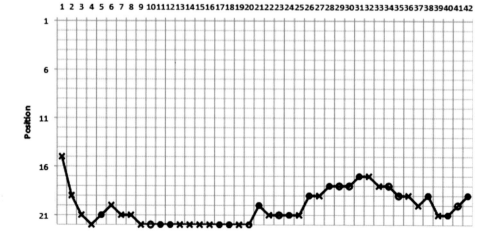

1999-00

	LA	LS	LG	CA	CS	CG	TA	TS	**TG**
Billy Clarke	36	1	3	5	2	1	41	3	**4**
Chris Burns	33		5	8			41		**5**
Dennis Bailey	34	5	9	5	1	1	39	6	**10**
Alex Sykes	30	9	7	8	1	6	38	10	**13**
Jason Drysdale	32	1	2	6		1	38	1	**3**
Wayne Hatswell	30	4	2	5	1		35	5	**2**
Marc McGregor	25	3	12	8	1	4	33	4	**16**
Steve Perrin G/K	26	1		7			33	1	
Tony Daley	26		4	5		1	31		**5**
Don Forbes	18	9		6	1		24	10	
Rob Cook	13	4	1	6	2	2	19	6	**3**
Justin Shuttlewood G/K	16			2			18		
Dave Norton	18		1				18		**1**
Mike Kilgour	12	3		5			17	3	
Paul Hunt	10	18	4	3	3	3	13	21	**7**
Chris Honor	12	1		1	1		13	2	
Adie Randall	9	2	1	3	2	2	12	4	**3**
David Meyhew	8	14		3	2	3	11	16	**3**
Adie Mings	8	11		1	1		9	12	
Bradley Thomas	8	7	1	1			9	7	**1**
Frankie Bennett	9		1				9		**1**
Steve Winter	3	3					3	3	
Dave Barnett	3						3		
Shaun Chapple	2	1					2	1	
Chris Smith		2		1	1		1	3	
Andrew Catley		2		1			1	2	
Nathan Lightfoot				1	1		1	1	
L. McMullen				1	1		1	1	
G. Little					1			1	

2000-01		P	W	D	L	F	A	W	D	L	F	A	GD	Pts	Res H-A	
P	Rushden & D	42	14	6	1	41	13	11	5	5	37	23	42	86	0-0	0-0
2.	Yeovil Town	42	14	3	4	41	17	10	5	6	32	33	23	80	0-1	0-2
3.	Dagenham & R	42	13	4	4	39	19	10	4	7	32	35	17	77	4-4	1-3
4.	Southport	42	9	5	7	33	24	11	4	6	25	22	12	69	2-0	1-1
5.	Leigh RMI	42	11	5	5	38	24	8	6	7	25	33	6	68	3-1	1-1
6.	Telford United	42	13	1	7	33	23	6	7	8	18	28	0	65	1-1	0-1
7.	Stevenage	42	8	7	6	36	33	7	11	3	35	28	10	63	2-3	1-3
8.	Chester City	42	9	8	4	29	19	7	6	8	20	24	6	62	1-1	1-0
9.	Doncaster	42	11	5	5	28	17	4	8	9	19	26	4	58	2-2	0-3
10.	Scarborough	42	7	9	5	29	25	7	7	7	27	29	2	58	2-3	0-1
11.	Hereford United	42	6	12	3	27	19	8	3	10	33	27	14	57	1-1	1-3
12.	Boston United	42	10	7	4	43	28	3	10	8	31	35	11	56	0-3	0-0
13.	Nuneaton	42	9	5	7	35	26	4	10	7	25	34	0	54	0-0	0-2
14.	Woking	42	5	10	6	30	30	8	5	8	22	27	-5	54	0-0	0-2
15.	Dover Athletic	42	9	6	6	32	22	5	5	11	22	34	-2	53	2-1	2-1
16.	**FGR**	**42**	**6**	**9**	**6**	**28**	**28**	**5**	**6**	**10**	**15**	**26**	**-11**	**48**		
17.	Northwich	42	8	7	6	31	24	3	6	12	18	43	-18	46	1-0	0-0
18.	Hayes	42	5	6	10	22	31	7	4	10	22	40	-27	46	1-2	0-1
19.	Morecambe	42	8	5	8	35	29	3	7	11	29	37	-2	45	0-0	2-0
R	Kettering Town	42	5	5	11	23	31	6	5	10	23	31	-16	43	3-2	3-1
R	Kingstonian	42	3	5	13	19	40	5	5	11	28	33	-26	34	3-1	1-0
R	Hednesford	42	2	6	13	24	38	3	7	11	22	48	-40	28	0-2	1-1

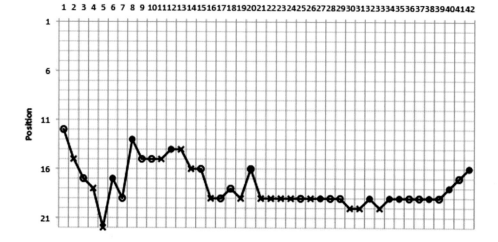

	LA	LS	LG	CA	CS	CG	TA	TS	TG
Robin Cousins	40	1		13		1	53	1	1
Billy Clark	38		3	12		2	50		5
Chris Burns	32			11		1	43		1
Alex Meechan	31		13	9	1	5	40	1	18
Jason Drysdale	30			9	2	1	39	2	1
Steve Perrin G/K	26			11			37		
Adrian Foster	27	5	8	8	1	2	35	6	10
Tony Daley	23	7	2	8	1	1	31	8	3
Stuart Slater	20	1		10		1	30	1	1
Dave Norton	25		1	4			29		1
Wayne Hatswell	19		5	4			23		5
Ian Hedges	14	9		7		1	21	9	1
Martin Foster	15	1	1	6		1	21	1	2
Leon Cort	12			4			16		
Frankie Bennett	10	8	1	5	3	5	15	11	6
Nigel Spink G/K	14			1			15		
Adam Lockwood	10		1	3			13		1
Nathan Lightbody	9	8	1	3	1	3	12	9	4
Dennis Bailey	9	12		2	3	1	11	15	1
Jason Eaton	11	1	2		1		11	2	2
Mark Cooper	11		1				11		1
Luke Prince	4	3		4	1		8	4	
Danny Bailey	6	1		1			7	1	
Alex Sykes	7	1	2				7	1	2
Mark Shaw	5	1					5	1	
Darren Middleton	4	3					4	3	
Martyn Sullivan	3	1	1		1		3	2	1
Matthew Ghent G/K	2			1			3		
Bradley Thomas	2	7					2	7	
Steve Cambell	1	5		1	1	1	2	6	1
Mike Kilgour	1	1		1	1		2	2	
Kevin Nicholson	1			1			2		
Paul Hunt		2		1	1		1	3	
Tony Dobson		2		1			1	2	
? King				1			1		
Steve Clarke				1			1		
Dean Birkby		3						3	
Ian Olney		2						2	
Danny Allen					1			1	
Don Forbes					1			1	

2001-02		P	W	D	L	F	A	W	D	L	F	A	GD	Pts	Res H-A	
P	Boston United	42	12	5	4	53	24	13	4	4	31	18	42	84	0-3	1-6
2.	Dagenham & Red	42	13	6	2	35	20	11	6	4	35	27	23	84	2-4	1-1
3.	Yeovil Town	42	6	7	8	27	30	13	6	2	39	23	13	70	1-1	2-2
4.	Doncaster Rovers	42	11	6	4	41	23	7	7	7	27	23	22	67	0-2	1-5
5.	Barnet	42	10	4	7	30	19	9	6	6	34	29	16	67	2-2	1-0
6.	Morecambe	42	12	5	4	30	27	5	6	10	33	40	-4	62	3-1	0-2
7.	Farnborough Town	42	11	3	7	38	23	7	4	10	28	31	12	61	1-0	0-3
8.	Margate	42	7	9	5	33	22	7	7	7	26	31	6	58	3-3	1-1
9.	Telford United	42	8	6	7	34	31	6	9	6	29	27	5	57	1-1	0-0
10.	Nuneaton Borough	42	9	3	9	33	27	7	6	8	24	30	0	57	1-2	1-2
11.	Stevenage	42	10	4	7	36	30	5	6	10	21	30	-3	55	0-0	1-4
12.	Scarborough	42	9	6	6	27	22	5	8	8	28	41	-8	55	2-2	1-1
13.	Northwich Victoria	42	9	4	8	32	34	7	3	11	25	36	-13	55	2-0	2-2
14.	Chester City	42	7	7	7	26	23	8	2	11	28	28	3	54	0-2	3-2
15.	Southport	42	9	6	6	40	26	4	8	9	13	23	4	53	2-1	1-5
16.	Leigh RMI	42	6	4	11	29	29	9	4	8	27	29	-2	53	1-2	2-1
17.	Hereford United	42	9	6	6	28	15	5	4	12	22	38	-3	52	1-1	0-0
18.	**FGR**	**42**	**7**	**7**	**7**	**28**	**32**	**5**	**8**	**8**	**26**	**44**	**-22**	**51**		
19.	Woking	42	7	5	9	28	29	6	4	11	31	41	-11	48	2-1	4-3
R	Hayes	42	6	2	13	27	45	7	3	11	26	35	-27	44	2-1	1-1
R	Stalybridge Celtic	42	7	6	8	26	32	4	4	13	14	37	-29	43	0-2	1-2
R	Dover Athletic	42	6	5	10	20	25	5	1	15	21	40	-24	39	2-1	2-1

Scarborough deducted 1 point.

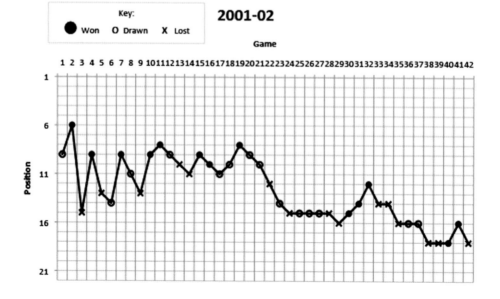

Player	LA	LS	LG	CA	CS	CG	TA	TS	**TG**
Alex Meechan	40	2	8	7		2	47	2	**10**
Steve Perrin G/K	39	1		7			46	1	
Martin Foster	38			7			45		
Mark Cooper	37		17	7		4	44		**21**
Steve Jenkins	36		2	7			43		**2**
Simon Travis	31	4	3	7			38	4	**3**
Robin Cousins	31	2	1	7			38	2	**1**
Jamie Impey	31	1		5	1	1	36	2	**1**
Carl Heggs	28	2	10	3	1	2	31	3	**12**
Kevin Langan	24	1	1	5			29	1	**1**
Paul Futcher	18	9		6		1	24	9	**1**
Mark Shaw	21	4	1	2		1	23	4	**2**
Lee Howey	15		2	3		1	18		**3**
Alex Sykes	11	1	1				11	1	**1**
Danny Allen	9	6	1	1	2		10	8	**1**
Matthew Coupe	8	2		2			10	2	
Trevor Tearney	7	6		1	1		8	7	
Kayode Odejayi	5	1	1	3		1	8	1	**2**
Tony Daley	6	6		1	2	1	7	8	**1**
Geoff Hopkins	6	2					6	2	
Bryan Small	5						5		
Chris Ward	5		1				5		**1**
Nathan Lightbody	3	8	3	1	2		4	10	**3**
Adi Adams	2	7		2			4	7	
David Lee	3	3	1				3	3	**1**
Jason Pearcey G/K	3						3		
Luke Middleton		6		1		1	1	6	**1**
Ellis Glassop G/K				1			1		
? Chambers				1			1		
D. Impey				1			1		
Chris Freestone		1						1	
Luke Jones		1						1	
Steve Clarke					1			1	
? Davies					1			1	
Andy Sandell					1			1	
? Haydon					1			1	

2002-03		P	W	D	L	F	A	W	D	L	F	A	GD	Pts	Res H-A	
P	Yeovil Town	42	16	5	0	54	13	12	6	3	46	24	63	95	2-1	0-1
2.	Morecambe	42	17	3	1	52	13	6	6	9	34	29	44	78	1-0	0-4
P	Doncaster	42	11	6	4	28	17	11	6	4	45	30	26	78	1-2	0-1
4.	Chester City	42	10	6	5	36	21	11	6	4	23	10	28	75	0-2	1-0
5.	Dagenham & Red	42	12	5	4	38	23	9	4	8	33	36	12	72	5-2	1-3
6.	Hereford Utd	42	9	5	7	36	22	10	2	9	28	29	13	64	1-3	1-1
7.	Scarborough	42	12	3	6	41	28	6	7	8	22	26	9	64	0-0	0-3
8.	Halifax	42	11	5	5	34	28	7	5	9	16	23	-1	64	0-2	1-1
9.	**FGR**	**42**	**12**	**3**	**6**	**41**	**29**	**5**	**5**	**11**	**20**	**33**	**-1**	**59**		
10.	Margate	42	8	9	4	32	24	7	2	12	28	42	-6	56	4-1	0-3
11.	Barnet	42	9	4	8	32	28	4	10	7	33	40	-3	53	4-4	0-2
12.	Stevenage	42	7	6	8	31	25	7	4	10	30	30	6	52	0-3	0-0
13.	Farnborough	42	8	6	7	37	29	5	6	10	20	27	1	51	3-1	3-0
14.	Northwich	42	6	5	10	26	34	7	7	7	40	38	-6	51	1-0	1-2
15.	Telford	42	7	2	12	20	33	7	5	9	34	36	-15	49	1-1	1-0
16.	Burton	42	6	6	9	25	31	7	4	10	27	46	-25	49	2-0	3-2
17.	Gravesend & N	42	8	5	8	37	35	4	7	10	25	38	-11	48	2-1	1-1
18.	Leigh RMI	42	8	5	8	26	34	6	1	14	18	37	-27	48	4-1	0-1
19.	Woking	42	8	7	6	30	35	3	7	11	22	46	-29	47	3-2	0-1
R	Nuneaton	42	9	4	8	27	32	4	3	14	24	46	-27	46	6-1	2-3
R	Southport	42	6	8	7	31	32	5	4	12	23	37	-15	45	0-2	2-2
R	Kettering	42	4	3	14	23	39	4	4	13	14	34	-36	31	1-0	3-2

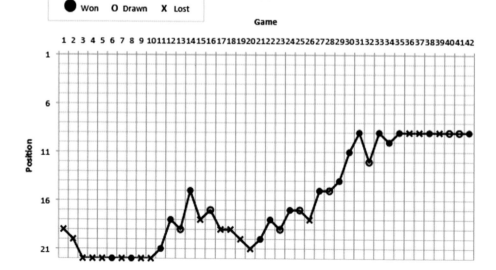

Key: ● Won   O Drawn   X Lost

2002-03

Game

Player	LA	LS	LG	CA	CS	CG	TA	TS	**TG**
Steve Perrin G/K	40			7			47		
Kayode Odejayi	37	1	13	8		3	45	1	**16**
Martin Foster	38		1	7		1	45		**2**
Gary Owers	35	1		8		2	43	1	**2**
Steve Jenkins	36	1		6			42	1	
Jon Richardson	34	1	4	8		2	42	1	**6**
Neil Grayson	30	8	15	5	2	5	35	10	**20**
Alex Meechan	27	8	12	7			34	8	**12**
Alex Sykes	31	2	5	3			34	2	**5**
Kevin Langan	28	2		5			33	2	
Matthew Russell	20			7			27		
Matthew Coupe	18	1		2			20	1	
Lea Russell	14			3	1		17	1	
Steve Cowe	9	8	3	1			10	8	**3**
Allen McLoughlin	10	2					10	2	
Danny Allen	6	6		1	1		7	7	
Ben Cleverley	6	2		1	1		7	3	
Carl Heggs	4	5	1		1		4	6	**1**
Rob Cook	3	16	1		3		3	19	**1**
Paul Futcher	2	5		1	2		3	7	
Jamie Impey	3						3		
Justin Shuttlewood G/K	2						2		
Steve Tweddle		4	1	1	2	1	1	6	**2**
Adi Adams	1	5			1		1	6	
Trevor Tearney	1	3					1	3	
Chris Giannangelo G/K				1			1		
Luke Jones		1						1	
Ellis Glassop G/K		1						1	
Lee Pritchard		1						1	

2003-04		Pld	W	D	L	F	A	W	D	L	F	A	GD	Pts	Res H-A	
P	Chester City	42	16	4	1	45	18	11	7	3	40	16	51	92	2-1	0-1
2.	Hereford United	42	14	3	4	42	20	14	4	3	61	24	59	91	1-7	1-5
P	Shrewsbury Tn	42	13	6	2	38	14	7	8	6	29	28	25	74	1-1	0-2
4.	Barnet	42	11	6	4	30	17	8	8	5	30	29	14	71	1-1	0-5
5.	Aldershot Town	42	12	6	3	40	24	8	4	9	40	43	13	70	3-1	0-3
6.	Exeter City	42	10	7	4	33	24	9	5	7	38	33	14	69	2-5	2-2
7.	Morecambe	42	14	4	3	43	25	6	3	12	23	41	0	67	1-2	0-4
8.	Stevenage B	42	10	5	6	29	22	8	4	9	29	30	6	63	3-1	1-2
9.	Woking	42	10	9	2	40	23	5	7	9	25	29	13	61	2-2	1-1
10.	Accrington St'y	42	13	3	5	46	31	2	10	9	22	30	7	58	2-1	1-4
11.	Gravesend & Nt	42	7	6	8	34	35	7	9	5	35	31	3	57	1-2	1-1
R	Telford United	42	10	3	8	28	28	5	7	9	21	23	-2	55	0-0	2-0
13.	Dagenham & R	42	8	3	10	30	34	7	6	8	29	30	-5	54	1-3	2-5
14.	Burton Al'n	42	7	4	10	30	29	8	3	10	27	30	-2	51	1-1	3-2
15.	Scarborough	42	8	9	4	32	25	4	6	11	19	29	-3	51	4-0	2-2
R	Margate	42	8	2	11	30	32	6	7	8	26	32	-8	51	1-2	0-2
17.	Tamworth	42	9	6	6	32	30	4	4	13	17	38	-19	49	2-1	0-1
18.	**FGR**	**42**	**6**	**8**	**7**	**32**	**36**	**6**	**4**	**11**	**26**	**44**	**-22**	**48**		
19.	Halifax Town	42	9	4	8	28	26	3	4	14	15	39	-22	44	1-2	1-0
20.	Farnborough Tn	42	7	6	8	31	34	3	3	15	22	40	-21	39	1-1	3-1
21	Leigh RMI	42	4	6	11	26	44	3	2	16	20	53	-51	29	2-2	2-1
22	Northwich V	42	2	8	11	15	38	2	3	16	15	42	-50	23	0-0	4-0

Burton Albion deducted 1 point.

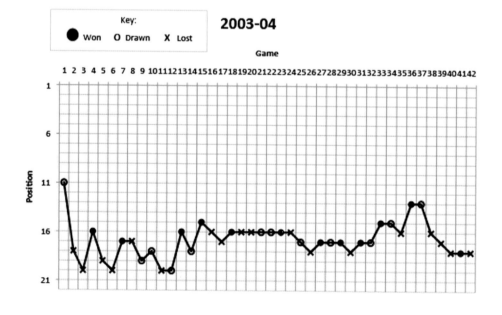

Player	LA	LS	LG	CA	CS	CG	TA	TS	TG
Martin Foster	42		3	6		1	48		**4**
Steve Perrin G/K	42			5			47		
Denny Ingram	32		2	6		2	38		**4**
Jon Richardson	33			5			38		
Damon Searle	31		4	7			38		**4**
Scott Rogers	27	12	9	5	2	1	32	14	**10**
Gareth Stoker	24			5			29		
Neil Grayson	24	1	9	4		5	28	1	**14**
Steve Cowe	21	13	6	5		1	26	13	**7**
Lee Phillips	19	2	2	4	1		23	3	**2**
Alex Meechan	22		6				22		**6**
Alex Sykes	16	8	3	3	3		19	11	**3**
Gary Owers	14		1	1			15		**1**
Kevin Langan	11	5	1	3			14	5	**1**
Richard Kennedy	11	2	1	3	1		14	3	**1**
Darren Jones	10			3			13		
Steve Jones	11						11		
Steve Jenkins	10	1					10	1	
Jamie Moralee	6	4	2	1			8	4	**2**
Hugh McAuley	6	7		1			3	7	
Steve Morgan	7						7		
Steve Broady	7		3				7		**3**
Tom Jordan	5			1			6		
John Cant	4	7	1	1	2		5	9	**1**
Michael Green	5						5		
Paul Moore	4	2	1		1		4	3	**1**
Ian Fitzpatrick	4	1					4	1	
Matt Aubrey	2	6		1		1	3	6	**1**
Jimmi Lee Jones	3	2					3	2	
Matt Russell	3	1					3	1	
Adi Adams		4		2	1		2	5	
Dave Gilroy	2	3					2	3	
Chris Giannangelo G/K				2	1		2	1	
Keith Simpson	2	1					2	1	
Sam Bowen	2		3				2		**3**
Luke Jones		9		1	3		1	12	
Danny Allen				1			1		
Rob Cook		1						1	
Ian Clarkson					1			1	
Martin Bown					1			1	
Stratford					1			1	

2004-05		P	W	D	L	F	A	W	D	L	F	A	GD	Pts	Res H-A	
P	Barnet	42	16	2	3	56	20	10	6	5	34	24	46	86	0-2	1-3
2	Hereford	42	10	7	4	28	14	11	4	6	40	27	27	74	1-3	1-2
P	Carlisle Utd	42	12	5	4	39	18	8	8	5	35	19	37	73	0-3	1-0
4	Aldershot	42	13	3	5	38	22	8	7	6	30	30	16	73	0-0	2-1
5	Stevenage	42	13	2	6	35	21	9	4	8	30	31	13	72	1-1	2-2
6	Exeter City	42	11	5	5	39	22	9	6	6	32	28	21	71	2-3	0-2
7	Morecambe	42	12	5	4	38	23	7	9	5	31	27	19	71	0-3	1-3
8	Woking	42	11	6	4	29	19	7	8	6	29	26	13	68	1-3	1-0
9	Halifax Twn	42	13	4	4	45	24	6	5	10	29	32	18	66	0-0	0-4
10	Accrington	42	11	6	4	43	26	7	5	9	29	32	14	65	1-0	2-2
11	Dagenham	42	12	4	5	39	27	7	4	10	29	33	8	65	1-4	2-2
12	Crawley	42	13	4	4	35	18	3	5	13	15	32	0	57	1-1	2-4
13	Scarborough	42	9	12	0	42	17	5	2	14	18	29	14	56	0-1	0-0
14	Ebbsfleet	42	7	7	7	34	31	6	4	11	24	33	-6	50	3-2	1-4
15	Tamworth	42	10	3	8	22	22	4	8	9	31	41	-10	50	1-1	0-4
16	Ebbsfleet	42	7	7	7	34	31	6	4	11	24	33	-6	50	1-5	0-0
17	Burton	42	6	7	8	25	29	7	4	10	25	37	-16	50	3-2	1-4
18	York City	42	7	6	8	22	23	4	4	13	17	43	-27	43	1-1	3-1
19	Canvey Is.	42	6	10	5	34	31	3	5	13	19	34	-12	42	2-2	1-2
R	Northwich V	42	9	5	7	37	29	5	5	11	21	43	-14	42	1-3	1-2
20	**FGR**	**42**	**2**	**9**	**10**	**19**	**40**	**4**	**6**	**11**	**22**	**41**	**-40**	**33**		
R	Farnborough	42	4	5	12	20	40	2	6	13	15	49	-54	29	1-1	1-1
R	Leigh Gen.	42	2	2	17	18	52	2	4	15	13	46	-67	18	1-1	0-2

Tamworth deducted 3 points.
Northwich deducted 10 points.

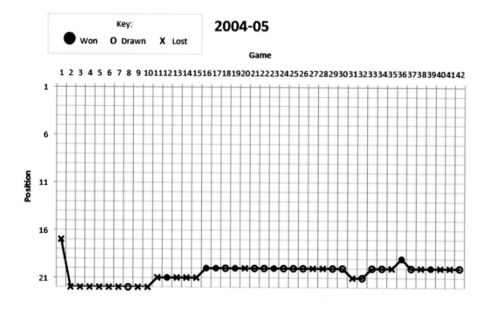

Player	LA	LS	LG	CA	CS	CG	TA	TS	TG
Matt Gadsby	36	2	3	6			42	2	**3**
Charlie Griffin	33	6	17	8	1	3	41	7	**20**
Des Lyttle	36			5	1	1	41	1	**1**
Scott Rogers	28	9	1	6			34	9	**1**
Chris Davies	27	2		7	1		34	3	
Jon Richardson	28	2		6		1	34	2	**1**
Adam Garner	24	2	1	8		2	32	2	**3**
Mark Beesley	25	7	9	2	4	3	27	11	**12**
Damon Searle	26		2	1	1		27	1	**2**
Dean Williams G/K	20			5	1		25	1	
Stuart Roberts	16	3		5		1	21	3	**1**
Steve Perrin G/K	19			2			21		
Jon Beswetherick	8	2		5		2	13	2	**2**
Andy Harris	12		1				12		**1**
Ben Cleverley	8	7	1	3	1	1	11	8	**2**
Michael Green	7	6		4			11	6	
Steve Reed	7			4		2	11		**2**
Jon Holloway	9	1		1	1		10	2	
Hugh McAuley	8	2		1	1		9	3	
Jefferson Louis	7	1	1	1	2	2	8	3	**3**
Richard Appleby	4	3		4			8	3	
Ryan Williams	7		1	1			8		**1**
Andy Watson	4	3		2			6	3	
Alex Sykes	6						6		
Paul Warhurst	6		2				6		**2**
Lewis Haldane	6						6		
Richard Hodgson	5	2	1				5	2	**1**
Steve Cowe	5	1					5	1	
Mo Harkin	5	1					5	1	
Andy Rapley	5						5		
Liam Burns	2	1		2			4	1	
Tom Gould	4						4		
Julian Alsop	3		1	1			4		**1**
Mark Danks	3	15			1		3	16	
Lee Davis		4		3	1	2	3	5	**2**
Rob Betts	3						3		
Craig Loxton	3						3		
Danny Greaves G/K	2			1			3		
Robert Gill	2	4					2	4	
Andy Rushbury	2	1					2	1	
Michael Alexis		2		1	1		1	3	
James Turner	1						1		
Nurudeen Bello				1			1		
Adi Adams				1			1		
Mike Husband				1			1		
Kenny Schofield G/K				1			1		
Marvin Brown		4						4	
Luke Jones					1			1	
M Bown		1						1	

2005-06		P	W	D	L	F	A	W	D	L	F	A	GD	Pts	Res H-A	
P	Accrington	42	16	3	2	38	17	12	4	5	38	28	31	91	1-1	0-2
P	Hereford Utd	42	11	7	3	30	14	11	7	3	29	19	26	80	2-2	1-1
3	Grays Athletic	42	7	9	5	46	32	14	4	3	48	23	39	76	1-2	2-2
4	Halifax Twn	42	14	6	1	31	11	7	6	8	24	29	15	75	2-2	0-1
5	Morcambe	42	15	4	2	44	17	7	4	10	24	24	27	74	1-0	2-3
6	Stevenage	42	15	3	3	38	15	4	9	8	24	31	16	69	2-0	1-2
7	Exeter City	42	11	3	7	41	22	7	6	8	24	26	17	63	0-0	0-0
8	York City	42	10	5	6	36	26	7	7	7	27	21	16	63	1-2	1-5
9	Burton Albion	42	8	7	6	23	21	8	5	8	27	31	-2	60	1-0	0-1
10	Dagenham	42	8	4	9	31	32	8	6	7	32	27	4	58	0-3	1-1
11	Woking	42	8	7	6	30	20	6	7	8	28	27	11	56	0-3	1-2
12	Cambridge Utd	42	11	6	4	35	24	4	4	13	16	32	-5	55	1-0	2-2
13	Aldershot	42	10	4	7	30	30	6	2	13	31	44	-13	54	4-2	1-2
R	Canvey Island	42	6	8	7	23	27	7	4	10	24	31	-11	51	1-2	1-1
15	Kidderminster	42	8	5	8	21	27	5	6	10	18	28	-16	50	0-0	3-1
16	Ebbsfleet	42	8	4	9	25	25	5	6	10	20	32	-12	49	0-0	0-2
17	Crawley Twn	42	9	4	8	27	22	3	7	11	21	33	-7	47	2-2	0-1
18	Southport	42	7	3	11	24	38	3	7	11	12	30	-32	40	1-2	1-3
19	**FGR**	**42**	**7**	**7**	**7**	**31**	**27**	**1**	**7**	**13**	**18**	**35**	**-13**	**38**		
20	Tamworth	42	4	10	7	17	23	4	4	13	15	40	-31	38	1-3	0-0
R	Scarborough	42	4	7	10	24	30	5	3	13	16	36	-26	37	5-1	0-1
22	Altrincham	42	7	5	9	25	30	3	6	12	15	41	-31	23	5-0	1-2

Altrincham deducted 18 points.

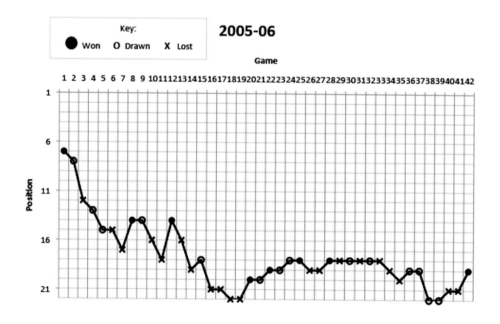

Player	LA	LS	LG	CA	CS	CG	TA	TS	TG
Ryan Clarke	42			4			46		
Alex Meechan	41		5	4		1	45		6
Damon Searle	37			4			41		
Sikani Simpson	31	2		4			35	2	
Paul Wanless	30		10	4		1	34		11
Luke Graham	24	3		4			28	3	
John Richardson	25		2	2			27		2
Abdul Sall	24	2	4	2	1		26	3	4
Julian Alsop	20	3	5	4			24	3	5
Matt Gadsby	20	8		3	1	1	23	9	1
Guy Madjo	18	6	9	3		1	21	6	10
Zema Abbey	18	8	2	1			19	8	2
Adam Garner	16	4		3	1		19	5	
Bruno Teixeira	12	15	5	2	2		14	17	5
Michael Brough	13	1	3				13	1	3
Jon Beswetherick	11	4		1		1	12	4	1
Ben Harding	9		1	2		1	11		2
Mark Beesley	11	5			1		11	6	
Taylor	10						10		
Scott Rendall	8	10	2	1	2		9	12	2
Darren Jones	9	1					9	1	
Lee Howells	6	1		1			7	1	
Scott Rogers	5	5		1	1		6	6	
Jonnie Hayes	4		1	2		1	6		2
Byron Anthony	4						4		
Jamie Gosling	3	6			1		3	7	
Lewis Haldane	3	4					3	4	
Ryan Harley	3						3		
Lee McConnell	2	2					2	2	
Luke Coleman	2	0					2		
Craig Dove	1	4					1	4	
Paul Stonehouse		2		1			1	2	
Ryan Harrison		1		1			1	1	
Gary Owers				1			1		
Michael Whittington		1						1	

2006-07		P	W	D	L	F	A	W	D	L	F	A	GD	Pts	Res H-A	
P	Dagenham	46	16	4	3	40	20	12	7	4	43	28	35	95	0-1	1-1
2.	Oxford Utd	46	11	9	3	33	16	11	6	6	33	17	33	81	1-5	2-0
P	Morcambe	46	11	7	5	29	20	12	5	6	35	26	18	81	1-3	1-1
4.	York City	46	10	6	7	29	22	13	5	5	36	23	20	80	1-1	0-1
5.	Exeter City	46	14	7	2	39	19	8	5	10	28	29	19	78	2-1	0-1
6.	Burton Albion	46	13	3	7	28	21	9	6	8	24	26	5	75	1-0	0-1
7.	Gravesend	46	12	6	5	33	25	9	5	9	29	30	7	74	0-1	1-1
8.	Stevenage	46	12	4	7	46	30	8	6	9	30	36	10	70	4-4	3-3
9.	Aldershot	46	11	7	5	40	31	7	4	12	24	31	2	65	3-0	1-2
10.	Kidderminster	46	7	5	11	19	26	10	7	6	24	24	-7	63	2-1	2-2
11.	Weymouth	46	12	6	5	35	26	6	3	14	21	47	-17	63	3-2	0-1
12.	Rushden & Diamonds	46	10	5	8	34	24	7	6	10	24	30	4	62	0-2	0-2
13.	Northwich Victoria	46	9	2	12	26	33	9	2	12	25	36	-18	58	2-1	0-2
14.	**FGR**	**46**	**10**	**5**	**8**	**34**	**33**	**3**	**13**	**7**	**25**	**31**	**-5**	**57**		
15.	Woking	46	8	8	7	34	26	7	4	12	22	35	-5	57	2-3	3-3
16.	Halifax Twn	46	12	8	3	40	22	3	2	18	15	39	-6	55	2-0	2-2
17.	Cambridge Utd	46	8	4	11	34	33	7	6	10	23	33	-9	55	1-1	1-1
18.	Crawley Twn	46	10	6	7	27	20	7	6	10	24	33	-2	53	1-0	1-3
19.	Grays Athletic	46	8	9	6	29	21	5	4	14	27	34	1	52	0-0	1-1
20.	Stafford Rangers	46	7	4	12	25	33	7	6	10	24	38	-22	52	2-1	1-0
21.	Altrincham	46	9	4	10	28	32	4	8	11	25	35	-14	51	2-2	2-2
R	Tamworth	46	8	6	9	24	27	5	3	15	19	34	-18	48	2-0	1-1
R	Southport	46	7	4	12	29	30	4	10	9	28	37	-10	47	1-2	2-1
R	St. Albans	46	5	5	13	28	49	5	5	13	29	40	-32	40	2-2	0-0

Crawley deducted 10 points.

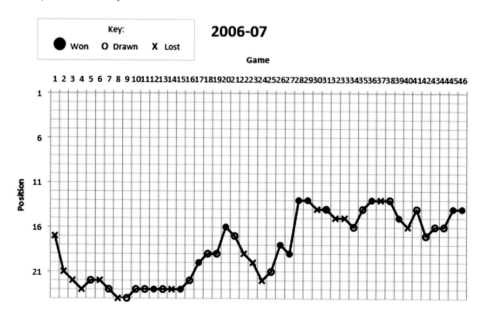

Player	LA	LS	LG	CA	CS	CG	TG	TS	**TG**
L. Afful	25	16	2	3		1	28	16	**3**
M. Beesley	24	7	5	2			26	7	**5**
S. Brough	39	1	2	3		1	42	1	**3**
T. Butler	6	3	2	1			7	3	**2**
Carey-Bertram	14	6	7		1	1	14	7	**8**
S. Clist	44	1	7	3			47	1	**7**
L. Dodgson	4	9	1				4	9	**1**
C. Edwards	9	1					9	1	
C. Giles	22	1	2	2			24	1	**2**
C. Griffin	5	9	1		2		5	11	**1**
J. Hardiker	23		2	1			24		**2**
R. Harrison	2	1		1			3	1	
G. Ipoua	2	5					2	5	
D. Jones	40			3			43		
M. Lamb	1	4					1	4	
A. Lawless	33	5	1	2	1		35	6	**1**
A. Meechan	26	3	2	3			29	3	**2**
K. Nicholson	44		6	2	1	2	46	1	**8**
J. Pitman	23	9	1		1		23	10	**1**
M. Preece	19	11	1	1			20	11	**1**
A. Rigoglioso	9	2	6				9	2	**6**
M. Robinson	11	1	1	1			12	1	**1**
R. Robinson	18			1			19		
A. Russell	15	5	5		1		15	6	**5**
G. Owers									
P. Stonehouse	8	18	2		1		8	19	**2**
P. Wanless	3	5					3	5	
D. Williams	11	6	1	3			14	6	**1**
S. Williams	26			1			27		
A. Zarczynski		3						3	

2007-08		P	W	D	L	F	A	W	D	L	F	A	GD	Pts	Res H-A	
P	Aldershot	46	18	2	3	44	21	13	6	4	38	27	34	101	2-3	1-0
2.	Cambridge Utd	46	14	6	3	36	17	11	5	7	32	24	27	86	3-1	0-2
3.	Torquay Utd	46	15	3	5	39	21	11	5	7	44	36	26	86	2-2	0-1
P	Exeter City	46	13	9	1	44	26	9	8	6	39	32	25	83	1-1	3-3
5.	Burton Albion	46	15	3	5	48	31	8	9	6	31	25	23	81	3-1	1-1
6.	Stevenage	46	13	5	5	47	25	11	2	10	35	30	27	79	4-2	0-0
7.	Histon	46	10	7	6	42	36	10	5	8	34	31	9	72	3-1	2-2
8.	**FGR**	**46**	**11**	**6**	**6**	**45**	**34**	**8**	**8**	**7**	**31**	**25**	**17**	**71**		
9.	Oxford Utd	46	10	8	5	32	21	10	3	10	24	27	8	71	0-0	0-1
10.	Grays Athletic	46	11	6	6	35	23	8	7	8	23	24	11	70	1-2	1-0
11.	Ebbsfleet Utd	46	14	3	6	40	29	5	9	9	25	32	4	69	2-2	2-0
12.	Salisbury City	46	12	7	4	35	22	6	7	10	35	38	10	68	0-3	0-0
13.	Kidderminster	46	12	5	6	38	23	7	5	11	36	34	17	67	2-2	0-1
14.	York City	46	8	5	10	33	34	9	6	8	38	40	-3	62	1-2	2-0
15.	Crawley Twn	46	12	5	6	47	31	7	4	12	26	36	6	60	1-0	0-3
16.	Rushden & Diamonds	46	7	10	6	26	22	8	4	11	29	33	0	59	0-1	2-1
17.	Woking	46	7	9	7	28	27	5	8	10	25	34	-8	53	2-1	1-1
18.	Weymouth	46	7	5	11	24	34	4	8	11	29	39	-20	46	3-2	6-0
19.	Northwich Victoria	46	6	7	10	30	36	5	4	14	22	42	-26	44	4-1	1-1
R	Halifax Town	46	8	10	5	30	29	4	6	13	31	41	-9	42	2-0	1-1
21.	Altringham	46	6	6	11	32	44	3	8	12	24	38	-26	41	3-1	0-1
R	Farsley Celtic	46	6	5	11	27	38	4	4	15	21	48	-38	39	2-2	2-0
R	Stafford Rangers	46	2	4	17	16	48	3	6	14	26	51	-57	25	1-2	3-1
R	Droylsden	46	4	5	14	27	45	1	4	18	19	58	-57	24	3-2	3-5

Crawley deducted 6 points.
Halifax deducted 10 points.

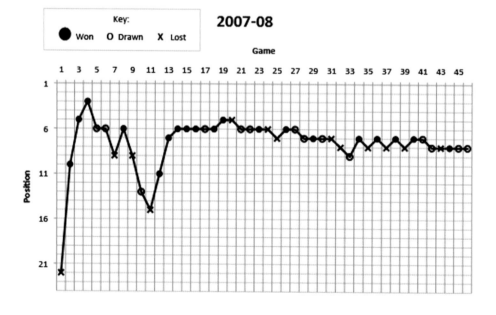

Player	LA	LS	LG	CA	CS	CG	TA	TS	**TG**
Fleetwood	41		27	8	2	9	49	2	**36**
Tonkin	37	1		9			46	1	
Clist	39		3	6		1	45		**4**
Jones	37	2	5	7			44	2	**5**
Lawless	32		2	11		2	43		**4**
Hardiker	31	3		9	1	1	40	4	**1**
R. Robinson	32	1		7			39	1	
Giles	30	2	3	8	1	2	38	3	**5**
Pitman	29	2		6			35	2	
Brough	31	2	1	3			34	2	**1**
Stonehouse	24	11	2	7	2	1	31	13	**3**
Beesley	19	4	11	7		2	26	4	**13**
Preece	17	19	1	7	1		24	20	**1**
Afful	20	22	2	4	6		24	28	**2**
Rigoglioso	18	9	6	5	3		23	12	**6**
Dodgson	16	12	3	5	2	2	21	14	**5**
Burton	14	1		4			18	1	
Carey-Bertram	13	11	7	3	5	2	16	16	**9**
J. Smith	11	14	2	2	7	1	13	21	**3**
Welsh	11	5					11	5	
James	4	3		2			6	3	
Sheehan				1			1		
Ashford									
Davis									
New				1				1	
Shaxton				1				1	

2008-09		P	W	D	L	F	A	W	D	L	F	A	GD	Pts	Res H-A	
P	Burton Albion	46	15	5	3	48	23	12	2	9	33	29	29	88	2-3	2-4
2.	Cambridge Utd	46	14	6	3	34	15	10	8	5	31	24	26	86	2-2	1-0
3.	Histon	46	14	8	1	41	18	9	6	8	37	30	30	83	2-2	1-0
P	Torquay Untd	46	11	7	5	38	23	12	7	4	34	24	25	83	1-2	3-3
5.	Stevenage	46	12	8	3	41	23	11	4	8	32	31	19	81	0-3	1-1
6.	Kidderminster	46	16	2	5	40	18	7	8	8	29	30	21	79	2-2	1-1
7.	Oxford Utd	46	16	3	4	42	20	8	7	8	30	31	21	77	3-3	1-2
8.	Kettering Twn	46	12	5	6	26	19	9	8	6	24	18	13	76	0-2	1-1
9.	Crawley Twn	46	13	5	5	48	26	6	9	8	29	29	22	70	1-0	2-2
10.	Wrexham	46	11	7	5	39	22	7	5	11	25	26	16	66	2-3	1-1
11.	Rushden & Diamonds	46	11	5	7	30	24	5	10	8	31	26	11	63	4-0	2-2
12.	Mansfield Twn	46	14	5	4	35	19	5	4	14	22	36	2	62	1-0	0-3
13.	Eastbourne	46	11	3	9	29	27	7	3	13	29	43	-12	60	1-2	0-1
14.	Ebbsfleet Utd	46	10	9	4	28	19	6	1	16	24	41	-8	58	1-4	1-0
15.	Altrincham	46	9	7	7	30	29	6	4	13	19	37	-17	56	1-3	5-2
16.	Salisbury City	46	8	6	9	29	33	6	7	10	25	31	-10	55	1-2	2-2
17.	York City	46	8	9	6	26	20	3	10	10	21	31	-4	52	1-1	1-2
18.	**FGR**	**46**	**7**	**6**	**10**	**39**	**40**	**5**	**10**	**8**	**31**	**36**	**-6**	**52**		
19.	Grays Athletic	46	12	5	6	31	24	2	5	16	13	40	-20	52	1-1	1-2
20.	Barrow	46	7	10	6	27	26	5	5	13	24	39	-14	51	2-1	1-3
R	Woking	46	6	8	9	21	29	4	6	13	16	31	-23	44	0-2	1-0
R	Northwich Victoria	46	7	5	11	29	26	4	5	14	27	49	-19	43	3-0	0-0
R	Weymouth	46	5	6	12	27	53	6	4	13	18	33	-41	43	4-1	1-1
R	Lewes	46	5	2	16	15	41	1	4	18	13	48	-61	24	4-1	2-3

Key:
● Won   O Drawn   X Lost

2008-09

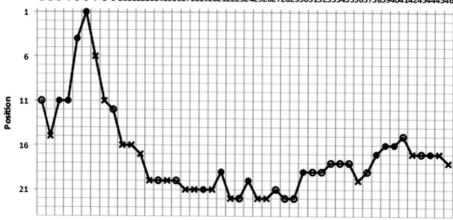

Player	LA	LS	LG	CA	CS	CG	TA	TS	TG
L. Afful	8	16		6	2	2	14	18	**2**
B. Ashford		1		1	1		1	2	
L. Ayres	18	1	2				18	1	**2**
J. Baldwin		1		2				3	
D. Brown	16	2	3				16	2	**3**
T. Burton	24			8			32		
S. Clist	21		1	9		1	30		**2**
J. Else		1						1	
L. Fowler	36	2	1	14		1	50	2	**2**
J. Gill	20			9			29		
J. Hardiker	11		3	3			14		**3**
D. Jones	36		2	8			44		**2**
D. Kempsford	5			5			10		
A. Lawless	30		5	7		1	37		**6**
P. Lloyd	8	5	1		2		8	7	**1**
J. Low	3	1		1		1	4	1	**1**
A. Mangan	35	3	22	11	2	4	46	5	**26**
C. Mcdonald	16	7		3	3	2	19	10	**2**
K. Mohamed	17	11	3	6	4	5	23	15	**8**
L. Molyneaux	2	2		2			4	2	
M. Palmer		2	1					2	**1**
J. Pitman	2						2		
C. Platt	24	12	6	8	3	1	32	15	**7**
M. Preece	29	3	2	9			38	3	**2**
A. Rigoglioso	11	11	4	8	5	3	19	16	**7**
R. Robinson	19	1		6			25	1	
J. Simpson		3			2			5	
J. Smith	31	8	6	14		2	45	8	**8**
P. Stonehouse	37	3		13		1	50	3	**1**
M. Symons	7	10	1	1	7	2	8	17	**3**
C. Thomas	7	2		4	2		11	4	

	2009-10	P	W	D	L	F	A	W	D	L	F	A	GD	Pts	Res H-A	
P	Stevenage	44	16	5	1	44	11	14	4	4	35	13	55	99	0-1	0-2
2.	Luton Twn	44	14	3	5	54	22	12	7	3	30	18	44	88	0-1	1-2
P	Oxford Utd	44	16	4	2	37	10	9	7	6	27	21	33	86	0-1	0-0
4.	Rushden & Diamonds	44	12	6	4	40	21	10	7	5	37	18	38	79	1-0	2-4
5.	York City	44	13	7	2	40	15	9	5	8	22	20	27	78	2-1	0-2
6.	Kettering Twn	44	6	8	8	27	23	12	4	6	24	18	10	66	1-2	2-0
7.	Crawley Twn	44	14	3	5	33	24	5	6	11	17	33	-7	66	1-0	1-3
8.	AFC Wimbledon	44	8	5	9	30	19	10	5	7	31	28	14	64	2-5	0-2
9.	Mansfield Twn	44	9	8	5	34	22	8	3	11	35	38	9	62	1-4	0-1
10.	Cambridge Utd	44	11	4	7	44	24	4	10	8	21	29	12	59	1-1	0-7
11.	Wrexham	44	9	7	6	26	17	6	6	10	19	22	6	58	0-2	1-0
R	Salisbury City	44	11	5	6	33	21	10	0	12	25	42	-5	58	3-1	3-1
13.	Kidderminster	44	11	3	8	31	21	4	9	9	26	31	5	57	1-1	1-2
14.	Altrincham	44	7	7	8	29	25	6	8	8	24	26	2	54	4-3	2-2
15.	Barrow	44	7	9	6	27	29	6	4	12	23	38	-17	52	1-0	1-1
16.	Tamworth	44	7	6	9	26	30	4	10	8	16	22	-10	49	3-4	0-0
17.	Hayes and Yeading U	44	7	7	8	38	38	5	5	12	21	47	-26	48	0-0	3-2
18.	Histon	44	6	9	7	24	28	5	4	13	20	39	-23	46	2-0	2-5
19.	Eastbourne Borough	44	8	7	7	26	29	3	6	13	16	43	-30	46	1-1	0-1
20.	Gateshead	44	10	3	9	24	23	3	4	15	22	46	-23	45	1-0	1-3
21.	**FGR**	**44**	**9**	**5**	**8**	**27**	**29**	**3**	**4**	**15**	**23**	**47**	**-26**	**45**		
R	Ebbsfleet Utd	44	7	4	11	25	36	5	4	13	25	46	-32	44	0-0	3-4
R	Grays Athletic	44	4	5	13	16	41	1	8	13	19	50	-56	26	2-1	1-2

Salisbury deducted 10 points.   Grays deducted 2 points.
Gateshead deducted 1 point.   Chester City results expunged from league.

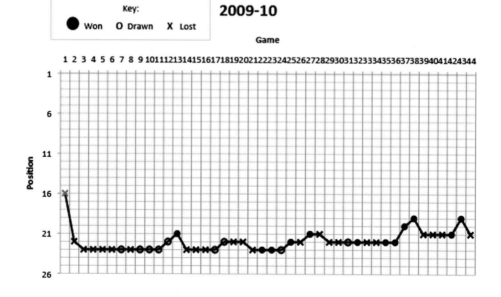

Key: ● Won   O Drawn   X Lost

2009-10

Game

Player	LA	LS	LG	CA	CS	CG	TA	TS	**TG**
S. Adams	7						7		
T. Ameobi	26	2	5	4			30	2	**5**
C. Armstrong	13						13		
L. Ayres	7	2					7	2	
J. Baldwin									
B. Tyrone		2		1				3	
D. Brown	34	8	4	5	1	1	39	9	**5**
T. Burton	26	1		6			32	1	
J. Challinor	7						7		
C. Curran	1	1					1	1	
S. Davies	11	9	1	1	1	1	12	10	**2**
M. Ellis	7						7	0	
J. Else	3	3			1		3	4	
J. Ford		1						1	
M. Fowler		2						2	
C. Henry									
J. Hodgkiss	31		1	6		1	37		**2**
J. Imudia	3						3		
D. Ireland	11						11		
B. Joyce	1	1		1	1		2	2	
D. King	1	3		2			3	3	
P. Lloyd	3	10					3	10	
L. Maxwell		1						1	
C. Mcdonald	14	2		5			19	2	
S. Mensah									
L. Morris	1	8	2				1	8	**2**
J. O'Cearuill	13	1		4			17	1	
M. Palmer		1						1	
T. Pass	1	1					1	1	
C. Platt	35	6	4	4	1	2	39	7	**6**
D. Powell	19	5	6	4	1		23	6	**6**
M. Preece	38	0	2	5	0	1	43	0	**3**
B. Pugh	1	2	0	0	0	0	1	2	**0**
I. Rankin	17	2	3	2	0	1	19	2	**4**
S. Rigg	16	0	6	3	0	0	19	0	**6**
C. Rocastle	14	1	0	1	0	0	15	1	**0**
I. Shaze	0	0	0	0	0	0	0	0	**0**
J. Smith	40	1	8	6	0	1	46	1	**9**
L. Spence	7	0	0	0	0	0	7	0	**0**
R. Stearn	2	5	1	0	0	0	2	5	**1**
P. Stonehouse	41	3	1	6	0	0	47	3	**1**
R. Styche	13	5	5	0	0	0	13	5	**5**
A. Taylor	6	0	0	0	0	0	6	0	**0**
O. Thorne	18	5	1	1	0	0	19	5	**1**
D. Wilkinson	7	0	0	0	0	0	7	0	**0**

	2010-11	P	W	D	L	F	A	W	D	L	F	A	GD	Pts	Res H-A	
P	Crawley Twn	46	18	3	2	57	19	13	9	1	36	11	63	105	0-3	0-1
P	AFC Wimbledon	46	17	3	3	46	15	10	6	7	37	32	36	90	0-0	1-1
3.	Luton Twn	46	14	7	2	57	17	9	8	6	28	20	48	84	0-1	1-6
4.	Wrexham	46	13	7	3	36	24	9	8	6	30	25	17	81	3-0	1-2
5.	Fleetwood Twn	46	12	8	3	35	19	10	4	9	33	23	26	78	1-0	0-2
6.	Kidderminster	46	13	6	4	40	27	7	11	5	34	33	14	72	1-1	0-1
7.	Darlington	46	13	6	4	37	14	5	11	7	24	28	19	71	1-1	0-3
8.	York City	46	14	6	3	31	13	5	8	10	24	37	5	71	2-1	1-2
9.	Newport County AFC	46	11	7	5	44	29	7	8	8	34	31	18	69	0-0	1-3
10.	Bath City	46	10	10	3	38	27	6	5	12	26	41	-4	63	0-0	4-2
11.	Grimsby Twn	46	7	12	4	37	28	8	5	10	35	34	10	62	3-3	1-1
12.	Mansfield Twn	46	9	6	8	40	37	8	4	11	33	38	-2	61	2-1	1-3
R	Rushden & Diamonds	46	10	6	7	37	27	6	8	9	28	35	3	57	2-2	2-2
14.	Gateshead	46	8	9	6	28	28	6	6	11	37	40	-3	57	1-1	1-1
15.	Kettering Twn	46	8	8	7	33	32	7	5	11	31	43	-11	56	0-2	1-2
16.	Hayes And Yeading U	46	10	2	11	34	38	5	4	14	23	43	-24	51	1-0	4-3
17.	Cambridge Utd	46	7	7	9	32	28	4	10	9	21	33	-8	50	1-1	1-1
18.	Barrow	46	9	6	8	31	22	3	8	12	21	45	-15	50	2-3	0-3
19.	Tamworth	46	6	8	9	34	41	6	5	12	28	42	-21	49	4-0	1-2
20.	**FGR**	**46**	**7**	**10**	**6**	**28**	**25**	**3**	**6**	**14**	**25**	**47**	**-19**	**46**		
21.	Southport	46	9	6	8	39	33	2	7	14	17	44	-21	46	0-0	0-4
R	Altrincham	46	6	8	9	29	38	5	3	15	18	49	-40	44	1-0	1-2
R	Eastbourne	46	6	5	12	36	46	4	4	15	26	58	-42	39	3-4	0-0
R	Histon	46	4	3	16	18	45	4	6	13	23	45	-49	28	0-1	3-0

Kidderminster deducted 5 points.   Kettering deducted 2 points.
Rushden and Diamonds deducted 5 points.   Histon deducted 5 points.

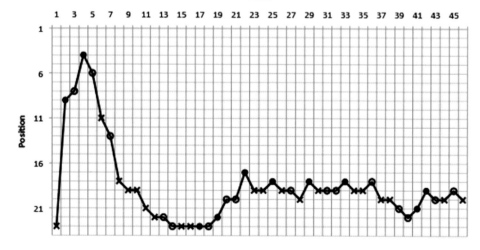

Player	LA	LS	LG	CA	CS	CG	TA	TS	TG
C. Allen	3	2					3	2	
C. Armstrong	24			3			27		
J. Baldwin	1	3			1		1	4	
S. Bartlett	6	4		1			7	4	
J. Bittner	46			2			48		
G. Caines	36	7	3	2			38	7	3
O. Cleaver		1						1	
S. Davies	1	9	1				1	9	1
R. Dyer	26	5	5	2			28	5	5
J. Else	5	12	1		2		5	14	1
L. Enver-Marum	7	11		2			9	11	
C. Flood	5						5		
K. Forbes	23	2	2				23	2	2
L. Fowler	11						11		
M. Fowler	18	2		2			20	2	
B. Gill	2	1					2	1	
B. Gray	4	9					4	9	
J. Grimes	4	1					4	1	
S. Guinan	10	8	5	1			11	8	5
D. Hall	16	1					16	1	
L. Head		4			2			6	
C. Henry		1						1	
I. Herring	10	3	1		1		10	4	1
J. Hodgkiss	21	2		3			24	2	
J. Imudia	2	1					2	1	
L. Jones	45		2	3			48		2
Z. Jones				1			1		
M. Kamara	1	1		1	1		2	2	
Y. Klukowski	30	7	7	3		1	33	7	8
R. Matthews	4	3	1				4	3	1
C. Mcdonald	22	1	4				22	1	4
G. Mills	1	1		1			2	1	
J. Norwood	11		2				11		2
A. Quinn	6		1	2			8		1
M. Somner	14	2	1				14	2	1
C. Stokes	14						14		
R. Styche	41	2	15	2		1	43	2	16
L. Smith	6	4					6	4	
W. Turk	23	2		2	1		25	3	
B. Watson	6	1	1				6	1	1
L. Young	1						1		

	2011-12	P	W	D	L	F	A	W	D	L	F	A	GD	Pts	Res H-A	
P	Fleetwood Twn	46	13	8	2	50	25	18	2	3	52	23	54	103	1-2	0-0
2.	Wrexham	46	16	3	4	48	17	14	5	4	37	16	52	98	1-0	2-1
3.	Mansfield Twn	46	14	6	3	50	25	11	8	4	37	23	39	89	1-1	0-1
P	York City	46	11	6	6	43	24	12	8	3	38	21	36	83	1-1	0-1
5.	Luton Twn	46	15	4	4	48	15	7	11	5	30	27	36	81	3-0	1-1
6.	Kidderminster	46	10	7	6	44	32	12	3	8	38	31	19	76	1-1	0-1
7.	Southport	46	8	8	7	36	39	13	5	5	36	30	3	76	2-3	3-1
8.	Gateshead	46	11	8	4	39	26	10	3	10	30	36	7	74	2-1	0-1
9.	Cambridge Utd	46	11	6	6	31	16	8	8	7	26	25	16	71	2-1	1-1
10.	**FGR**	**46**	**11**	**5**	**7**	**37**	**25**	**8**	**8**	**7**	**29**	**20**	**21**	**70**		
11.	Grimsby Twn	46	12	4	7	51	28	7	9	7	28	32	19	70	0-1	1-2
12.	Braintree Twn	46	11	5	7	39	34	6	6	11	37	46	-4	62	0-2	5-1
13.	Barrow	46	12	6	5	39	25	5	3	15	23	51	-14	60	3-0	1-1
14.	Ebbsfleet Utd	46	7	6	19	34	39	7	6	10	35	45	-15	54	3-1	1-1
15.	Alfreton	46	8	6	9	39	48	7	3	13	23	38	-24	54	4-1	6-1
16.	Stockport County	46	8	7	8	35	28	4	8	11	23	46	-16	51	1-1	1-0
17.	Lincoln City	46	8	6	9	32	24	5	4	14	24	42	-10	49	0-1	1-1
18.	Tamworth	46	7	9	7	30	30	4	6	13	17	40	-23	48	3-1	1-0
19.	Newport County	46	8	6	9	22	22	3	8	12	31	43	-12	47	1-1	0-0
20.	Afc Telford Utd	46	9	6	8	24	26	1	10	12	21	39	-20	46	2-1	0-2
R	Hayes & Yeading	46	5	5	13	26	41	6	3	14	32	49	-32	41	1-3	0-2
R	Darlington	46	8	7	8	24	24	3	6	14	23	49	-26	36	2-0	0-0
R	Bath City	46	5	4	14	27	41	2	6	15	16	48	-46	31	3-0	2-0
R	Kettering	46	5	5	13	25	47	3	4	16	15	53	-60	30	0-1	3-1

Darlington deducted 10 points.   Kettering deducted 3 points.

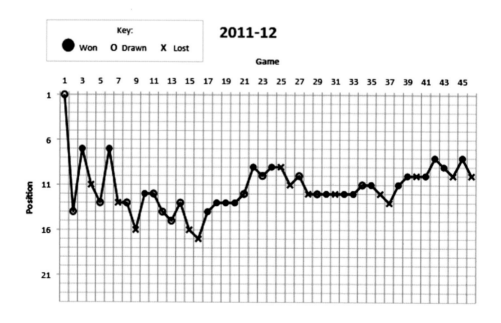

Player	LA	LS	LG	CA	CS	CG	TA	TS	**TG**
C. Allen	10	6					10	6	
A. Bangura	11	1		1			12	1	
S. Bartlett	0								
J. Bittner	19	1		2	1		21	2	
J. Bond	4						4		
M. Bulman	5			1			6		
J. Collins	12		2				12		**2**
K. Forbes	40	1	3	3			43	1	**3**
L. Graham	21	7		1			22	7	
C. Griffin	19	9	7		3		19	12	**7**
L. Henderson	14	8	2				14	8	**2**
C. Henry		1						1	
J. Hodgkiss	46			3		1	49		**1**
J. Imudia	1	1			1		1	2	
Y. Klukowski	38	8	18	3			41	8	**18**
M. Matthews		3						3	
C. Mcdonald	6	5	1				6	5	**1**
J. Norwood	34	4	4		2		34	6	**4**
E. Oshodi	30			2			32	0	
M. Paterson		1						1	
M. Pook		8						8	
J. Rowe	22	6		3			25	6	
S. Russell	18						18		
A. Sandell	3						3		
C. Stokes	45		2	3			48		**2**
R. Styche	9	7	8				9	7	**8**
M. Taylor	27	2	10	3			30	2	**10**
J. Thomson	19	9	1	3			22	9	**1**
C. Todd	2						2		
J. Turley	38	1	2	3			41	1	**2**
W. Turk	2	10			1		2	11	
M. Uwezu	8	17	2	2			10	17	**2**
T. Wright	3	4	2				3	4	**2**

2012-13		P	W	D	L	F	A	W	D	L	F	A	GD	Pts	Res H-A	
P	Mansfield Twn	46	17	3	3	53	17	13	2	8	39	35	40	95	1-2	0-1
2.	Kidderminster	46	15	4	4	49	22	13	5	5	33	18	42	93	0-1	1-0
P	Newport County	46	13	5	5	43	27	12	5	6	42	33	25	85	1-2	5-0
4.	Grimsby Twn	46	13	5	5	42	19	10	9	4	28	19	32	83	0-1	0-1
5.	Wrexham	46	11	9	3	45	24	11	5	7	29	21	29	80	0-0	1-2
6.	Hereford Utd	46	9	6	8	37	33	10	7	6	36	30	10	70	0-1	2-1
7.	Luton Twn	46	10	7	6	43	26	8	6	9	27	36	8	67	1-2	1-1
8.	Dartford FC	46	12	4	7	41	26	7	5	11	26	37	4	66	2-3	1-0
9.	Braintree Twn	46	9	5	9	32	40	10	4	9	31	32	-9	66	4-1	1-3
10.	**FGR**	**46**	**8**	**6**	**9**	**33**	**24**	**10**	**5**	**8**	**30**	**25**	**14**	**65**		
11.	Macclesfield Twn	46	10	6	7	29	28	7	6	10	36	42	-5	63	1-1	2-1
12.	Woking	46	13	3	7	47	34	5	5	13	26	47	-8	62	3-1	0-2
13.	Alfreton	46	9	5	9	41	39	7	7	9	28	35	-5	60	1-1	1-2
14.	Cambridge Utd	46	9	7	7	33	30	6	7	10	35	39	-1	59	1-1	0-0
15.	Nuneaton Twn	46	8	9	6	29	25	6	6	11	26	38	-8	57	1-0	1-1
16.	Lincoln City	46	9	5	9	34	36	6	6	11	32	37	-7	56	3-0	2-1
17.	Gateshead	46	9	9	5	35	22	4	7	12	23	39	-3	55	1-0	1-1
18.	Hyde Fc	46	9	5	9	35	31	7	2	14	28	44	-12	55	3-1	1-0
19.	Tamworth	46	9	4	10	25	27	6	6	11	29	43	-16	55	1-2	1-2
20.	Southport FC	46	7	4	12	32	44	7	8	8	40	42	-14	54	0-1	2-1
R	Stockport County	46	8	2	13	34	39	5	9	9	23	37	-19	50	4-1	1-2
R	Barrow	46	5	7	11	20	35	6	6	10	25	48	-38	46	1-1	2-2
R	Ebbsfleet Utd	46	5	11	7	31	37	3	4	16	24	52	-34	39	4-1	2-0
R	Afc Telford Utd		2	9	12	22	42	4	8	11	30	37	-27	35	0-0	2-1

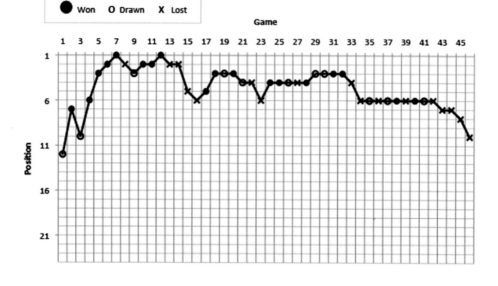

Player	LA	LS	LG	CA	CS	CG	TA	TS	TG
Adjaye E A	22	2		2	1		24	3	
Bangura A	29	4		4			33	4	
Bennett D	5	2					5	2	
Brogan S	7	6	2	2			9	6	2
Brown A									
Brown R									
Bulman M				1			1		
Burns W	5	1	1				5	1	1
Collins J	17	4	1	1			18	4	1
Connolly R	5	2					5	2	
Fowler L	3	2					3	2	
Forbes K	27	6		1	1		28	7	
Green P	20			2			22		
Hodgkiss J	24	2		2			26	2	
Jarvis N	1	1					1	1	
Klukowski Y	35	5	11	4	1	2	39	6	13
Koroma O	5	10		2	1		7	11	
Marsh P	2	3					2	3	
Norwood J	38	3	15	3	2	2	41	5	17
Odubade Y	3	11	1				3	11	1
Oshodi E	39	2	1	4		1	43	2	2
Racine A	24		1	4			28		1
Rowe J	7	7			2		7	9	
Russell S	46			4			50		
Stokes C	35	1	4	4		1	39	1	5
Styche R	8	16	6	3	2	1	11	18	7
Taylor M	33	9	9	3	2	2	36	11	11
Todd C				1			1		
Turley J	35	2	3	4			39	2	3
Viera M	21	13	3	4	1	1	25	14	4
Washbourne G									
Williams S		3						3	
Wright B	10	7	3				10	7	3

	2013-14	P	W	D	L	F	A	W	D	L	F	A	GD	Pts	Res H-A	
P	Luton Town	23	18	3	2	64	16	12	8	3	38	19	67	101	0-0	1-4
P	Cambridge Utd	23	16	4	3	49	14	7	9	7	23	21	37	82	3-2	1-2
3	Gateshead	23	12	7	4	42	24	10	6	7	30	26	22	79	1-0	1-1
4	Grimsby Twn	23	11	7	5	40	26	11	5	7	25	20	19	78	2-1	1-3
5	Halifax Fc	23	16	6	1	55	18	6	5	12	30	39	28	77	2-1	0-1
6	Braintree Twn	23	12	4	7	27	18	9	7	7	30	21	18	74	0-2	1-1
7	Kidderminster	23	15	4	4	45	22	5	8	10	22	38	7	72	1-1	1-4
8	Barnet	23	11	6	6	30	26	8	7	8	29	28	5	70	1-2	1-2
9	Woking	23	11	4	8	32	30	9	4	10	34	39	-3	68	2-2	1-2
10	**FGR**	23	13	6	4	47	22	6	4	13	32	43	14	67		
11	Alfreton	23	13	6	4	45	33	8	1	14	24	41	-5	67	3-1	2-3
R	Salisbury City	23	13	6	4	34	21	6	4	13	24	42	-5	67	4-0	4-1
13	Nuneaton Twn	23	12	4	7	29	25	6	8	9	25	35	-6	66	1-0	1-1
14	Lincoln City	23	10	7	6	30	19	7	7	9	30	40	1	65	4-1	1-2
15	Macclesfield Twn	23	11	5	7	35	27	7	2	14	27	36	-1	61	2-3	2-1
16	Welling Utd	23	10	5	8	31	24	6	7	10	28	37	-2	60	0-0	2-5
17	Wrexham	23	11	5	7	31	21	5	6	12	30	40	0	59	1-1	0-2
18	Southport Fc	23	13	5	5	33	23	1	6	16	20	48	-18	53	3-1	0-2
19	Aldershot Twn	23	11	6	6	48	32	5	7	11	21	30	7	51	3-1	2-2
R	Hereford Ut	23	9	6	8	24	25	4	6	13	20	39	-20	51	1-1	0-1
21	Chester	23	5	12	6	26	30	7	3	13	23	40	-21	51	3-0	2-1
22	Dartford Fc	23	8	3	12	32	35	4	5	14	17	39	-25	44	1-0	1-0
R	Tamworth	23	6	7	10	25	31	4	2	17	18	50	-38	39	1-2	2-1
R	Hyde	23	0	3	20	18	56	1	4	18	20	62	-80	10	8-0	6-2

Alfreton Town deducted 3 points.   Aldershot Town deducted 10 points.

2013-14

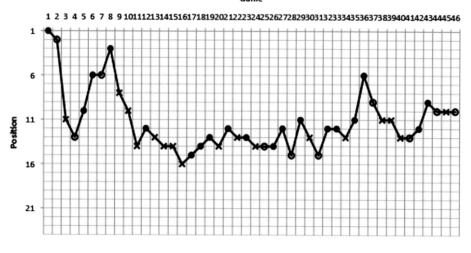

Player	LA	LS	LG	CA	CS	CG	TA	TS	TG
J. Alabi		2		3	1		3	3	
E.A. Adjaye	13	4		5			18	4	
A. Bangura	35	3		2	1		37	4	
M. Barnes-Homer	10	7	5	3	1	1	13	8	6
A. Barry	34	2	3	4	1		38	3	3
D. Bennett	31	1		2			33	1	
J. Binnom-Williams	3						3		
S. Brogan		3			1			4	
M. Bulman									
K. Forbes	3	5		1			4	5	
P. Green	20	3	2	2	1		22	4	2
J. Hodgkiss	33	5	3	4			37	5	3
L. Hughes	18	3	8				18	3	8
B. Jordon	5	1					5	1	
M. Kelly	31	2	9	3			34	2	9
Y. Klukowski	23	13	13	4		1	27	13	14
O. Koroma		5						5	
A. Mangan	3	6					3	6	
N. Martin		1						1	
J. Norwood	40	5	18	4			44	5	18
L. Oliver	11						11		
E. Oshodi	31	3	3	2			33	3	3
G. Pilkington	8						8		
A. Racine	13	2	1		2		13	4	1
L. Rodges	3	7					3	7	
S. Russell	46			5			51		
C. Stokes	20			1			21		
R. Styche	1	5	1		1		1	6	1
M. Taylor	17	8	3		2		17	10	3
J. Turley	19	2	1	5			24	2	1
J. Walker	1	2					1	2	
M. Vieira	3	12	2	1			4	12	2
P. White		1						1	
S. Williams	0	1	0	0	0	0	0	1	0
D. Wright	31	9	8	4	0	0	35	9	8

Bibliography

A Portrait of Nailsworth, Betty Mills, Revised Edition, B.A. Hathaway Printers, Nailsworth.
Centenary History of the Gloucestershire Football Association, Colin Timbrell, T.W. Cole & Sons Ltd, Gloucester.
The Stroud & District Football League 1902–1914, Colin Timbrell, Astral Printing.
Marling School 1887–1987, W. Oliver Wicks, Oxford University Press.
A History of the Gloucestershire County Cricket Club, Canynge Caple, The Worcester Press.
The Stroud News & Gloucestershire County Advertiser.
The Stroud Journal.
Dursley, Berkeley & Sharpness Gazette.
The Official Centenary History of The Southern League, Leigh Edwards, Paper Plane Publishing Ltd.
A View From The Terraces: One Hundred Years of the Western Football League 1892–1992, Sandie and Doug Webb, Addkey Print Ltd.
Forest Green Lily, Lilian Northwood and John Gardiner, J.F. Gardiner.
The Minutes of The Gloucestershire Northern Senior League.
The Minutes of Forest Green Rovers Association Football Club.
Memories of those involved with the club.
The Road To Wembley, Michael Burns, Gibbons Barford Print.
Gloucestershire Northern Senior League: 60 Years of History 1922–1982, Colin Timbrell.
Gloucestershire County League 1968–1989, Les James.

Image Sources

Forest Green Rovers Football Club
Howard Beard
Sylvia Molnar
Marling School
Colin Timbrell
The Stroud News & Journal and *Dursley Gazette*
Bruce Fenn
The Nailsworth Archive
Andy Whiting
Marshall Woodward
Ray Stevens
Andy Bish
Ray Brown
John Porter

Tim Barnard
John Duff
Richard Grant
Peter King
Michael Holland
Tom Vick
Brian Coates
Ann Mackenson
Peter Perch
Colin Timbrell
Jimmy Thomas
Sharpness Football Club
Shane Healey
The Citizen

Visit our website and discover thousands of other History Press books.

www.thehistorypress.co.uk

The History Press